THE LITERATURE OF DEATH AND DYING

This is a volume in the Arno Press collection

THE LITERATURE OF DEATH AND DYING

Advisory Editor
Robert Kastenbaum

Editorial Board
Gordon Geddes
Gerald J. Gruman
Michael Andrew Simpson

*See last pages of this volume
for a complete list of titles*

THE

FEAR OF THE DEAD
IN PRIMITIVE RELIGION

JAMES GEORGE FRAZER

Volumes One,
Two and Three

ARNO PRESS

A New York Times Company

New York / 1977

———●———

Library of Congress Cataloging in Publication Data
Frazer, James George, Sir, 1854-1941.
The fear of the dead in primitive religion.

(The Literature of Death and dying)
Reprint of the ed. published by Macmillan, London,
which was issued as the 1932-1933 Lectures delivered on
the William Wyse Foundation.
Includes bibliographical references.
1. Dead (in religion, folk-lore, etc.)--Addresses,
essays, lectures. 2. Ancester worship--Addresses,
essays, lectures. 3. Religion, Primitive--Addresses,
essays, lectures. I. Title. II. Series. III. Series: Cambridge. University. Trinity College.
William Wyse Foundation. Lectures delivered on the
William Wyse Foundation ; 1932-1933.

BL470.F7 1977   291.2'3   76-19571
ISBN 0-405-09566-X

THE FEAR OF THE DEAD
IN PRIMITIVE RELIGION

MACMILLAN AND CO., LIMITED
LONDON · BOMBAY · CALCUTTA · MADRAS
MELBOURNE

THE MACMILLAN COMPANY
NEW YORK · BOSTON · CHICAGO
DALLAS · ATLANTA · SAN FRANCISCO

THE MACMILLAN COMPANY
OF CANADA, LIMITED
TORONTO

THE
FEAR OF THE DEAD
IN PRIMITIVE RELIGION

LECTURES DELIVERED ON
THE WILLIAM WYSE FOUNDATION
AT TRINITY COLLEGE, CAMBRIDGE
1932–1933

BY

SIR JAMES GEORGE FRAZER
O.M., F.R.S., F.B.A.

FELLOW OF TRINITY COLLEGE, CAMBRIDGE
ASSOCIATE MEMBER OF THE *INSTITUT DE FRANCE*

MACMILLAN AND CO., LIMITED
ST. MARTIN'S STREET, LONDON
1933

COPYRIGHT

PREFACE

THESE lectures were delivered on the William Wyse Foundation at Trinity College, Cambridge, in the Michaelmas Term of 1932 and the May Term of 1933. They are printed almost exactly as they were spoken, except that a few passages, including a long one at the end of the Sixth Lecture, which were omitted for the sake of brevity in oral delivery, are here retained in the text. It was my intention to pursue the subject in subsequent lectures, and ultimately in a systematic treatise which should embrace the substance of all the lectures, together with a good deal of additional matter. But circumstances oblige me to defer for a time, perhaps indefinitely, the execution of this design. Meanwhile, I publish these introductory lectures as an instalment of the larger work in the hope that they may draw the attention of readers to a side of primitive thought which hitherto has hardly attracted the notice it deserves, for there can be little doubt that the fear of the dead has been a prime source of primitive religion.

On the question of how far the almost universal belief in the survival of the human spirit after death, which is implied by the fear of the dead, can be regarded as evidence of the truth of that survival, opinions will doubtless always be divided. From the crudities, inconsistencies and absurdities in which the belief commonly clothes itself, an impartial observer might be tempted to conclude that the spirits of the dead exist only in the imagination of the fond and foolish portion of mankind ; but this conclusion, so little consonant with the natural wishes, and perhaps the instincts, of humanity, is not likely to be ever popular, and it seems probable that the great majority of our species will continue to acquiesce in a belief so flattering to human vanity and so comforting to human sorrow. And it cannot be denied that the champions of eternal life have entrenched themselves in a strong, if not impregnable, position; for if it is impossible to prove the immortality of the soul, it is, in the present state of our knowledge, equally impossible to disprove it. But the batteries of science have an ever longer range, and on this side they may yet make a deep breach in the frowning bastions of faith.

I cannot close this preface without thanking my beloved College of Trinity for the honour it has done me by associating me in these lectures with the memory of my ever dear and honoured friend, William Wyse, who, by his noble Foundation, has not only created an instrument for the advancement of knowledge, but has erected for himself a monument to a life unswervingly devoted to the pursuit of truth and to all that is good and beautiful in humanity. I could wish that my own contribution to the monument were less unworthy of it and of him.

J. G. FRAZER

7th June 1933

CONTENTS

Belief in the Immortality of the Soul almost universal among mankind. Scepticism on the subject rare, but becomes more frequent with the advance of civilization and the progress of thought. Examples of scepticism among primitive (that is, savage or barbarous) peoples. The attitude of primitive peoples to the spirits of the dead very different from that of civilized peoples, being dominated by fear rather than affection. But some primitive peoples seem not to fear the spirits of their own dead, since they bury their bodies in the houses and bring back their souls to the houses when they have died or been buried elsewhere. The motive for house-burial probably connected with the idea of reincarnation, the spirits of the dead being thus supposed to be reborn in the family.

General attitude of primitive peoples to the spirits of the dead is one of fear rather than of affection. Examples from Melanesia, Polynesia, New Guinea, the Indian Archipelago, Asia, Africa and Southern, Eastern and Central Africa.

Fear of the dead in Western and Northern Africa and among the aborigines of America. The spirits of the dead sometimes supposed to help the living in various ways, particularly in hunting, fishing and agriculture. Examples from New Guinea, New Caledonia, the Indian Archipelago, Formosa, India, Africa and America.

Among the benefits which in the opinion of primitive man the spirits of the dead can bestow on their worshippers is that of fertilizing the earth and promoting the growth of the crops. Hence these spirits are conceived to possess proprietary rights over the fruits of the earth, and offerings of first-fruits are made to them at harvest by savages in many parts of the world, as in Melanesia, India and Africa.

Further, the spirits of the dead are thought able to give or withhold rain at their pleasure, hence they are often propitiated in time of drought. Examples from Celebes and Africa.

Further, the spirits of the dead are thought to bestow offspring on women or to render them barren, hence they are propitiated by childless women. Examples from India, Madagascar and Africa.

Further, the spirits of the dead are thought to aid their worshippers

vii

in war by giving them victory over their enemies. Examples from Africa, New Caledonia, Borneo, New Guinea, Sumatra, etc.

Further, the spirits of the dead are supposed to be able to give their worshippers valuable information, hence they are often consulted as oracles, either directly, as in dreams, or indirectly by means of their images or by living mediums, men or women. Examples from Melanesia, Micronesia, New Guinea, etc.

LECTURE I

LECTURE I

MEN commonly believe that their conscious being will not end at death, but that it will be continued for an indefinite time or for ever, long after the frail corporeal envelope which lodged it for a time has mouldered in the dust. This belief in the immortality of the soul, as we call it, is by no means confined to the adherents of those great historical religions which are now professed by the most civilized nations of the world ; it is held with at least equal confidence by most, if not all, of those peoples of lower culture whom we call savages or barbarians, and there is every reason to think that among them the belief is native; in other words, that it originated among them in a stage of savagery at least as low as that which they now occupy, and that it has been handed down among them from generation to generation without being materially modified by contact with races at higher levels of culture. It is therefore a mistake to suppose that the hope of immortality after death was first revealed to mankind by the founders of the great historical religions, Buddhism, Christianity and Islam ; to all appearance, it was cherished by men

3

all over the world thousands of years before Buddha, Jesus Christ and Mohammed were born. Indeed, it is safe to conjecture that these great religious revolutionaries were not in this respect innovators, but that they owed in some measure the rapid success which attended their teaching to the circumstance that they accepted the current and popular belief in immortality and built on it, as on a sure foundation, their towering structures of theology which would topple over and crash to the ground if the belief in immortality were to be proved baseless. No doubt the founders of the historic faiths modified the existing belief in many respects, particularly by giving it an ethical character as the ultimate and supreme sanction of morality. This was a very important innovation ; for in the lower religions, as a rule, the belief in immortality is entirely divested of any ethical significance ; in them the virtuous are not rewarded and the bad are not punished in the life after death ; all goes on in the other world much as in this ; there is no awful judgment to be anticipated by all, no blissful eternity to be hoped for by the good, no eternity of torture to be dreaded by the wicked.

But in these lectures I am not concerned with the belief in immortality as it is taught in the higher religions ; I shall confine myself strictly to that momentous belief as it meets us in what I call primitive religion, by which, roughly speaking, I mean the religion of the backward or uncivilized races ; in other words, savages and barbarians.

When I speak of their religion as primitive I use the word primitive in a relative, not an absolute, sense ; elsewhere I have expressly disclaimed, and I desire here again to disclaim, any knowledge whatever of absolutely primitive man and his religion ; existing savages are doubtless highly developed physically, intellectually and morally, by comparison with their ancestors in the remote past, but by comparison with the civilized nations of the present time they may fairly be described as primitive in a relative sense, and it is in that relative sense alone that I speak of their religion as primitive.

But in treating of the fear of the dead I shall not confine myself strictly to evidence drawn from the customs and beliefs of savages in the ordinary sense of the word ; I shall occasionally, or even frequently, borrow my examples from the beliefs and practices of civilized nations, among whom many primitive practices and ideas concerning the dead exist in the form of survivals, in short, as folklore. For it is one of the most assured results of the study of folklore that the customs and beliefs of the un-educated classes in civilized society often present a surprising analogy to those of savages, and there-fore deserve to be similarly described as primitive by comparison with the customs and beliefs of the educated and cultured members of the community ; in short, under the polished surface of civilized society there exists a deep stratum of savagery, which finds vent in eruptions of crime as well as in the comparatively, or even wholly, harmless and generally picturesque form of folklore.

I have defined the sense in which I employ the term primitive as applied to religion. I wish now to define the sense in which I use the phrase, " the immortality of the soul ". By " the soul " I mean simply the unknown principle of life about which philosophers have disputed from the days of Plato and Aristotle to the present time, and to all appearance are likely to dispute till life on earth is extinguished by some final cosmic catastrophe, unless in the meantime science should crown its long series of victories over nature by discovering the origin of life. And with regard to the word immortality, I employ it somewhat loosely, for the sake of brevity, to include the conception of the prolongation of life after death for a longer or shorter period, or for a wholly indefinite time, not necessarily for ever. Strictly speaking, the term immortality implies the conception of eternity or infinite time, and such a conception is beyond the reach of uncivilized man ; indeed we may perhaps doubt whether even the mind of the most accomplished philosopher and mathematician is capable of grasping it. In any case I shall speak of the immortality of the soul in a much humbler sense as the indefinite persistence of personality after death.

In that sense the belief in immortality has been remarkably widespread and persistent among mankind from the earliest times down to the present. Scepticism on the subject is rare and exceptional ;

it is hardly found among savages but seems to grow commoner with the advance of civilization and the progress of thought. Still, even among savages there have been hardy spirits who doubted or denied the immortality of the soul. The inhabitants of the Tonga Islands in the Pacific thought that the souls of noblemen were immortal, but that the souls of commoners were not.[1] But this aristocratic faith appears to be unique ; at all events I do not remember to have met with any other instance of such a spiritual privilege accorded to nobility. The generality of the Tongan lower orders, I may add, acquiesced in the belief that their souls perished with their bodies, though some of them were presumptuous enough to imagine that they had immortal souls like their betters.[2] Of the primitive tribes inhabiting the southern slopes of Mount Kenya in East Africa it is said, by one who has lived among them and administered them, that they appear to have no idea of a future life and that their general belief seems to be " that a man once dead is completely finished ".[3] The Margi of Northern Nigeria believe in immortality through reincarnation of the souls of the dead in human infants ; but they restrict this privilege to the souls of the good and deny it to the souls of the bad, which, they say, are destroyed by fire.[4] The Roba and northern

[1] W. Mariner, *Account of the Natives of the Tonga Islands* (London, 1818), ii. 99.

[2] W. Mariner, *op. cit.* ii. 128 *sq.*

[3] Major G. St. J. Orde Browne, *The Vanishing Tribes of Kenya* (London, 1925), pp. 205 *sq.*

[4] C. K. Meek, *Tribal Studies in Northern Nigeria* (London, 1931), i. 223.

Yungur of the same region seem to deny immortality impartially to good and bad alike.[1] The Binjhwar, a Dravidian tribe in the Central Provinces of India, are of a different opinion ; they think that only the wicked survive death, becoming malignant ghosts, while the souls of well-behaved people are, to all appearance, simply snuffed out.[2] Thus the beliefs of primitive peoples on the subject of immortality present a considerable variety of choice to any one who might undertake to found a new religion ; he might adopt the democratic doctrine of immortality for everybody ; or the aristocratic doctrine of immortality only for noblemen ; or the moral doctrine of immortality only for the good ; or the immoral doctrine of immortality only for the bad ; or lastly, the blighting doctrine of immortality for nobody. One of these alternatives must surely be right, since taken together they seem to exhaust the possibilities of survival after death ; but which of them is the true solution of this profound problem it is not for the simple-minded anthropologist to decide.

The Assiniboin Indians of North America generally believed that the human soul lives after death, but some of them denied it, holding that death is the end of soul and body alike ; [3] and the same negative belief is said to be held by the Central

---

[1] C. K. Meek, *Tribal Studies in Northern Nigeria*, ii. 462.

[2] R. V. Russell, *Tribes and Castes of the Central Provinces of India* (London, 1916), ii. 334.

[3] E. T. Denig, "The Assiniboin", *Forty-sixth Annual Report of the Bureau of American Ethnology* (Washington, 1930), pp. 498 *sq.*

Caribs of South America.[1] According to the Lakhers, a hill tribe of South-Eastern India, on the borders of Arakan, there is no second life for the dead, but when the dead man's spirit has been for a very long time in Athiki, the underground abode of the departed, the spirit dies again, and after this second death a chief's spirit is turned into a heat mist, and a poor man's spirit becomes a worm ; the heat mist goes up to heaven and vanishes, while the worm is eaten by a chicken, and that is an end of it.[2] Here again we are met by the aristocratic distinction between the fate of nobles and commoners in the after life, and though we are told that for the Lakhers there is no second life for the dead, yet at the same time we learn that the souls of the departed are supposed to exist in Athiki for a very long time, which may be regarded as nearly equivalent to immortality in the loose general sense in which I employ that term. Similarly the eminent Finnish scholar, Professor Karsten, a high authority on the South American Indians, tells us that the Tobas of the Bolivian Gran Chaco " certainly do not believe in the immortality of the soul, an expression often abused especially by Christian missionaries ", but he immediately adds : " On the other hand, the conviction of the continued existence of the soul after death is a positive dogma in their religion ".[3] What Professor Karsten here affirms

[1] W. C. Farabee, *The Central Caribs* (Philadelphia, 1924), p. 82.
[2] N. E. Parry, *The Lakhers* (London, 1932), p. 395.
[3] R. Karsten, *The Toba Indians of the Bolivian Gran Chaco* (Abo, 1923), p. 89.

of the Toba Indians of Bolivia might probably, if we knew all the facts, be affirmed with truth of all primitive races without distinction : they do not believe in the immortality of the soul in the strict sense of the word, for the simple reason that they lack the conception of eternity which that word implies ; but they do most strongly believe in the continued existence of the human spirit after death, and they act on that belief with logical consistency in everyday life by seeking to gain from the spirits of the dead all the benefits, and to avert all the evils, which these ghostly powers are supposed to bestow or to inflict upon mankind. Of this attitude of primitive man towards the dead I shall adduce ample evidence elsewhere in these lectures ; here I will only say a few words as to it by way of introduction to what follows. The general attitude of primitive man—and by primitive man I mean the savage—towards the spirits of the dead is very different from ours in that, on the whole, it is dominated by fear rather than by affection. We think of our beloved dead with sorrow and fond regret, and we can hardly conceive of any greater happiness than that of being reunited to them for ever in a better world beyond the grave. It is far otherwise with the savage. While it would be foolish and vain to deny that he often mourns sincerely the death of his relations and friends, he commonly thinks that their spirits undergo after death a great change, which affects their character and temper on the whole for the worse, rendering them touchy, irritable, irascible, prone to take offence on the slightest pretext and to visit their displeasure on the survivors by inflicting on them troubles of many sorts, including accidents of all kinds, drought, famine, sickness, pestilence and death. For it must always be borne in mind that in primitive religion the spirits of the dead are regularly supposed not only to exist but to exert an active and persistent influence on the life of the survivors by virtue of the very extensive powers which they are believed to possess in their disembodied state. These powers they are thought to put forth either for the good or the ill of their living friends and enemies ; and as they are very jealous of their rights and very revengeful of any neglect or slight on the part of their friends or any injury done them by their enemies, the living have to be constantly on their guard against the dead ; they must do everything in their power to please and nothing to offend these touchy spirits, who are only too ready to pick a quarrel even with the friends whom they loved and cherished in life. This belief in the continued power of the dead to affect the life of the survivors for good or ill is one of the most marked differences between the primitive and the civilized conceptions of life after death. In Protestant religion it has little or nothing to correspond to it, but in Catholicism it has a close analogy in the worship of the saints, those blessed spirits of the dead, who in virtue of their good deeds and their sufferings on earth are believed to possess in heaven the power of aiding and protecting the faithful in this world who submit themselves to their gracious keeping. The saints in glory, therefore, whom the Church commemorates to-day, answer to the spirits of the dead in primitive religion so far as these spirits are conceived in their beneficent aspect as the helpers and patrons of the living.

From what I have said you will have gathered that in the opinion of primitive man the life hereafter is very different from the conception which civilized man frames to himself of that awful subject. The savage in general imagines that life in the next world hardly differs in essentials from life in this world, and that dead men continue to feel the same passions and to experience the same needs which they felt and experienced in life. On this subject the eminent African explorer, Joseph Thomson, observes that by almost all the tribes of Eastern Africa " after death a person was supposed to feel pain, hunger, disease, just the same as before ; he only took a new material existence, which differed from the present in that, like the wind, it could not be seen, though it was known to exist. They had not as yet grasped the idea of a pure spirit." [1] To the same effect a good authority on the Kafir tribes of South Africa tells us that in the opinion of these people the spirits of the dead " are intensely human. . . . The Kafir worships a magnified *very natural man*. The ancestral spirits love the very things they loved before they passed through the flesh ;

[1] Joseph Thomson, in *Proceedings of the Royal Geographical Society* (1882), p. 212.

they cherish the same desires and have the same antipathies. The living cannot add to the number of the wives of ancestral spirits ; but they can kill cattle in their honour and keep their praise and memory alive on earth. Above all things, they can give them beef and beer. And if the living do not give them sufficient of these things, the spirits are supposed to give the people a bad time ; they send drought, and sickness and famine, until people kill cattle in their honour. When men are alive they love to be praised and flattered, fed and attended to ; after death they want the very same things, for death does not change personality." [1] Similarly by the Thonga, a Bantu tribe of South Africa, the life of the other world is regarded as an exact reproduction of this terrestrial existence ; the spirits of the dead are supposed to depart to a great village under the earth, where they till the fields, reap great harvests and live in abundance, and they take of this abundance to give to their descendants on earth ; they have also a great many cattle.[2]

Like most rules, the rule that primitive folk regard the spirits of the dead with more fear than affection appears to be subject to exceptions ; and as I do not wish to prejudge the case in favour of fear by overlooking the contrary instances, I will notice a few exceptions which I have met with before I adduce the mass, or rather a small part of the mass, of the evidence which seems to me con-

[1] Dudley Kidd, *The Essential Kafir* (London, 1904), pp. 88 *sq.*

[2] Henri A. Junod, *The Life of a South African Tribe*, Second Edition (London, 1927), ii. 375 *sq.*

clusively to establish the rule. The first exception I shall cite is that of the Trobriand Islanders, to the east of New Guinea. Speaking of them, Professor Malinowski, who knows them intimately, observes : " The main thing that struck me in connection with their belief in the spirits of the dead, was that they are almost completely devoid. of any fear of ghosts, of any of those uncanny feelings with which we face the idea of a possible return of the dead. All the fears and dreads of the natives are reserved for black magic, flying witches, malevolent disease-bringing beings, but above all for sorcerers and witches. The spirits migrate immediately after death to the island of Tuma, lying in the north-west of Boyowa, and there they exist for another span of time, underground, say some, on the surface of the earth, though invisible, say others. They return to visit their own villages once a year, and take part in the big annual feast, *milamala*, where they receive offerings. Sometimes, at this season, they show themselves to the living, who are, however, not alarmed by it, and in general the spirits do not influence human beings very much, for better or worse. In a number of magical formulae, there is an invocation of ancestral spirits, and they receive offerings in several rites. But there is nothing of the mutual interaction, of the intimate collaboration between man and spirit which are the essence of religious cult." [1]

[1] Bronislaw Malinowski, *Argonauts of the Western Pacific* (London, 1922), pp. 72 *sq.* For full details as to the beliefs of the Trobriand

In this passage, which I have quoted entire, Professor Malinowski does not affirm that the Trobriand Islanders are absolutely devoid of fear of the dead, and as he tells us that the spirits of the dead are sometimes invoked and receive offerings, it is natural to suppose that if these marks of respect were withheld the spirits would be displeased and might find some means of visiting their displeasure on their undutiful relations. In the sequel we shall meet with many examples of such ghostly visitations. However, we may accept it on the high authority of Professor Malinowski that in comparison with many other savage races the Trobriand Islanders are remarkably free from the fear of the dead.

Another people who are reported to enjoy the same happy immunity are the Macheyenga of Eastern Peru, of whom we are told " that they ' have no fear of the dead ', that is, of the ghost or soul of the departed. Nevertheless when one member of the family dies the others desert the home, and build another some distance away. ' They leave the house because they are afraid of the disease that took away the other member of the family, and for no other reason.' "[1] On this statement I would remark that the desertion of a house in which somebody has died is often expressly

Islanders on this subject see Professor Malinowski's article, " Baloma ; the Spirits of the Dead in the Trobriand Islands ", *Journal of the Royal Anthropological Institute*, xlvi. (1917) pp. 353-430.

[1] R. Karsten, *The Civilization of the South American Indians* (London, 1926), p. 479, quoting Farabee, *Indian Tribes of Eastern Peru*, pp. 12, 13, a work which I have not seen.

said to be due to the fear of the ghost of the deceased, and it may be so in the case of the Macheyenga, though the writer who reports the case gives another explanation of the custom. To that custom I shall return elsewhere in these lectures and will illustrate it by examples which seem to put its connexion with the fear of the dead beyond the reach of doubt.

Again, with regard to the natives of some parts of British New Guinea we are told by Dr. W. M. Strong that " it does not seem that there is ever any fear of the ghost of a dead relative. The native has a most intense desire to keep the remains of his dead relative near him. The old custom on the coast, both on the south and on the north coast, was for a dead body to be buried in or under the house or in the village. The government have forcibly compelled the natives to give up this custom. At Maiva, on the south coast, it once became the custom for the natives to openly bury the body in the appointed cemetery, and for them to secretly exhume it afterwards and to bury it in or under the house. In Mekeo it became the custom for the natives to go and live for two or three weeks in the cemetery after a relative had been buried. Special houses were built in the cemetery for this purpose. In the North-Eastern Division I found similar sentiments existing. The native usually places some belongings of the deceased near the grave. The Mekeo natives were anxious that the cemetery shall not be liable to be flooded because ' they do not like their relatives to be in the wet and cold '. I could never find in all this a belief that the ghost would resent any lack of proper treatment, but merely the continuation of the kindly way in which they previously regarded their relatives when living." [1] So far Dr. Strong.

The custom of burying the dead or preserving portions of them, particularly their skulls, in the houses which they inhabited in life has been widespread ; it has prevailed in many parts of Africa, South America and some parts of Micronesia ; and wherever it has prevailed and the survivors have continued to occupy the house containing the relics, we may take it as good evidence that the survivors did not greatly fear the ghost of their dead kinsman, but rather desired to keep him near them. But it is to be observed that many people who bury the dead in the house are in the habit of immediately thereafter abandoning or even destroying the house, which seems a clear indication of a fear of the ghost who may be supposed to haunt it. I shall return to this custom elsewhere ; but here I will only observe that the custom of burying the dead in the house and continuing to inhabit it afterwards appears to have prevailed at an early date in some parts of Italy and Greece. The old writer Servius, whose commentary on Virgil is a gold-mine of folklore, tells us that the ancient Romans were always buried in their houses, and to this custom he traced the worship of the

[1] W. M. Strong, " Some Personal Experiences in British New Guinea ", *Journal of the Royal Anthropological Institute*, xliv. (1919) p. 297.

C

domestic gods, the Lares, which in his opinion were clearly no other than the spirits of the dead.[1]   A later Latin writer, who records the custom in similar terms, informs us that it was afterwards forbidden by law, in order to protect the bodies of the living from the noxious exhalations of the dead,[2] exactly as in our own time the native custom of burying the dead in the house has been forbidden by the British Government, for the same reason, in some parts of Africa [3] and New Guinea.   Modern excavations in various parts of Greece, including Aegina, Attica, Argolis, Melos and Crete, prove that the burial of the dead in the house, particularly in jars interred beneath the floor, was practised by the Greeks, or rather by their predecessors, in Mycenaean, Minoan or earlier times.   Young children especially seem to have been thus buried in jars under the floor of the house.[4]   On this custom Dr. Farnell has justly remarked that " one important reflection is at once suggested : the earlier people, whoever they were, did not fear the contagion of the dead ; believing in the continuance of the soul as we know that they did, they must have regarded the ghost with affection rather than with terror and desired to keep it in or near the family ".[5]

This conclusion can be confirmed by a modern

[1] Servius, on Virgil, *Aen*. v. 64, vi. 151.

[2] Isidore, *Origines*, xv. 11. 1.

[3] A. B. Ellis, *The Tshi-speaking Peoples of the Gold Coast* (London, 1887), p. 239 ; P. Amaury Talbot, *Life in Southern Nigeria* (London, 1923), pp. 142, 146.

[4] See my note on Ovid, *Fasti*, ii. 615 (vol. ii. pp. 467 *sq*.), to which I may refer for fuller details as to house-burial.

[5] L. R. Farnell, *Greek Hero Cults and Ideas of Immortality* (Oxford, 1921), p. 4.

custom of house-burial which was practised till lately by the Gilbert Islanders, a Micronesian people in the Pacific. With them the grave was generally dug in the floor of the house; and a near relative would make a bed of the grave and open it from time to time to look on the beloved remains. The skull was very often removed and kept in a box; and the widow or child of the deceased would sleep and eat beside it, carry it about in all excursions, and frequently anoint it with coconut oil. Rarely the whole skeleton would be dug up from the grave and the bones hung to the ridge-pole of the family meeting-house, from which they were lowered from time to time and anointed for good luck in fishing, war or love.[1] Clearly the Gilbert Islanders did not fear the ghosts of their dead kinsfolk, but desired to keep them at hand in the expectation of receiving help from them in the practical affairs of life. In the sequel we shall see that the spirits of the dead are often supposed to aid their surviving kinsfolk both in peace and war. Similarly the Kingsmill Islanders, another Micronesian people in the Pacific, used sometimes to bury their dead in the house of the nearest relative; sometimes they stowed away the body in the loft of the building, and when the flesh was nearly gone they detached the skull, cleaned it and kept it as an object of worship.[2]

---

[1] A. Grimble, " From Birth to Death in the Gilbert Islands ", *Journal of the Royal Anthropological Institute*, li. (1920) pp. 46 *sq*.

[2] Horatio Hale, *Ethnography and Philology of the United States Exploring Expedition* (Philadelphia, 1846), pp. 99 *sq*.

A different motive for the burial of the dead in the house is suggested by a tradition of the Gonds, the principal Dravidian tribe of India. It is said that formerly they buried the dead " in or near the house in which they died, so that their spirits would thus the more easily be born again in children, but this practice has now ceased ".[1] This Gond tradition, with the motive which it assigns for burying the dead in the house, is confirmed by a practice, still observed in some parts of India, of burying children, especially still-born infants, under the threshold of the house, for which the reason sometimes assigned is that in consequence of the daily passage of the parents across the threshold the child will be born again in the family.[2] The Andaman Islanders bury very young children under the floor of the hut, beneath the hearth, believing that the souls of the dead babies may re-enter their mothers' wombs and be born again.[3] In the light of these customs and beliefs it seems possible that the practice of burying adults in the houses in which they died may sometimes have been prompted by a desire to secure their rebirth in the family. Both the practice of house-burial and the belief in reincarnation are very common in Africa,[4] and the

[1] R. V. Russell, *Tribes and Castes of the Central Provinces of India* (London, 1916), iii. 89.

[2] W. Crooke, *Religion and Folklore of Northern India* (Oxford University Press, 1926), pp. 149 *sq.*, 345 ; further references in my note on Ovid, *Fasti*, ii. 573 (vol. ii. p. 447).

[3] A. R. Brown, *The Andaman Islanders* (Cambridge, 1922), p. 109.

[4] Much evidence of the belief in reincarnation in Africa has been collected by Mr. Theodore Besterman. See his paper, " The Belief in Rebirth among the Natives of Africa (including Madagascar) ", *Folklore*, xli. (1930) pp. 43-94.

coincidence seems to favour the theory that the two things may be vitally connected.

But perhaps nothing proves the absence of the fear of the dead more plainly than the habit which some people have of bringing back the soul of the deceased to the house after they have buried or otherwise disposed of the body elsewhere. The custom seems to be particularly common in India. Thus in some places the Gonds perform on the fifth day after a death the ceremony of bringing back the soul. The relatives go to the river-side and call aloud the name of the dead person, and then enter the river, catch a fish or insect and, taking it home, place it among the sainted dead of the family, believing that the spirit of the dead person has in this manner been brought back to the house. The brother-in-law or son-in-law of the deceased then makes a miniature grass hut in the compound (courtyard) and places the fish or insect inside it. He next sacrifices a pig, which is eaten, and next morning he breaks down the hut and throws away the earthen pots from the house. Further, they spread some flour on the ground and in the morning bring a chicken up to it. If the chicken eats the flour, they say that the soul of the deceased has shown his wish to remain in the house, and he is enshrined there in the shape of a stone or copper coin. If the chicken does not eat the flour, they say that the spirit will not remain in the house. So they take the stone or coin, which represents his spirit, outside the village, sacrifice a chicken to it, and bury it under a heap of stones to prevent the spirit from returning.[1] Thus we see that after the burial the Gonds bring back the soul of the dead to the house and give it the option of remaining there or outside the village. We have also seen that according to tradition the Gonds used to bury their dead in the house in order that their souls might be reborn in the family ; and the same motive may underlie their present practice of bringing back the souls of the dead to the house, for they still believe that the spirits of ancestors are reincarnated in children or in animals. Sometimes they mark a corpse with soot or vermilion, and if afterwards a similar mark is found on any newborn child they think that the dead man's spirit has been reborn in it.[2]

The Ahirs, a caste of cowherds in the Central Provinces of India, similarly bring back the souls of their dead to the house in the form of fish, after they have buried or burnt the bodies elsewhere. The ceremony takes place on the third day after death. The women go with a lamp on a red earthen pot at night to a tank or stream. The fish are attracted by the light, and one of them is caught and put in the pot, which is then filled with water. The pot is brought home and set beside a small heap of flour, and the elders sit round it. The son of the deceased or other near relative anoints himself with turmeric and picks up a stone. The stone

[1] R. V. Russell, *Tribes and Castes of the Central Provinces of India*, iii. 94.

[2] R. V. Russell, *l.c.*

is then washed with water from the pot and placed on the floor, and a cock or a hen is sacrificed to it according as the deceased was a man or a woman. The stone is then enshrined in the house as a family god, and the sacrifice of a fowl is repeated annually. Apparently it is supposed that the dead man's spirit is brought back to the house in the fish and then transferred to the stone by washing it with the water which was in the pot, which held the fish, which contained the soul of the dead.[1]

When a man has been killed by a tiger, the Halbas, a caste of cultivators in the Central Provinces of India, think it absolutely essential to bring back his spirit to the house. The help of a hedge-priest (a Baiga) is invoked to perform the rite. To do this the priest suspends a copper ring on a long thread above a vessel of water and then burns butter and sugar on the fire, muttering incantations, while the people sing songs and call on the spirit of the dead man to return. The thread swings to and fro, and at length the copper ring falls into the pot, and this is taken as a sign that the spirit has come and entered into the vessel. The mouth of the pot is immediately covered and the pot is buried or kept in some secure place. Thus the soul of the dead man is kept in safe custody. The people believe that if the soul were left on the loose to wander at will, it would accompany the tiger which killed the man, and in that bad company it would lure solitary travellers to

[1] R. V. Russell, *Tribes and Castes of the Central Provinces of India*, ii. 28 *sq.*

their doom by calling out their names and offering them a quid of tobacco to smoke, and when the unwary wayfarer put out his hand to take the quid, the tiger would spring on him and gobble him up.[1] Thus we see how the spirit of a perfectly innocent man may, as a victim of circumstances over which he has no control, become a most dangerous ghost, and how necessary it is, in the public interest, to keep his ghost, if I may say so, under lock and key.

The Kharia, a primitive Kolarian tribe of the Central Provinces in India, bury their dead at a distance from the house, but bring back their souls on the tenth day after death. For this purpose they set a lighted wick in a vessel at a cross-road which the man's corpse had passed on its way to the grave, and at which consequently his ghost might naturally be supposed to loiter. There they call on the dead man, and when the flame of the lamp wavers in the wind they break the vessel that holds the lamp, saying that his soul has come back and joined them ; so they go home together.[2] These people also believe that the dead are reborn in children ;[3] hence one of their motives for bringing back the soul of a dead kinsman to the old home may be a hope that he will be born again in the family.

The Khonds, a Dravidian tribe of India, who were formerly notorious for their cruel human sacrifices, also believe that the dead are reborn in children, and like other tribes which cherish that

[1] R. V. Russell, *Tribes and Castes of the Central Provinces of India,* iii. 195 *sq.*

[2] R. V. Russell, *op. cit.* iii. 450.

[3] R. V. Russell. *op cit.* iii. 451.

fond belief they strive to bring back the souls of the departed on the tenth day after the burial or cremation of their bodies. For that purpose outside the village at a cross-road, which is everywhere the favourite haunt of disembodied spirits, they offer rice to a cock, and if the bird eats it they accept it as a sign that the soul has come. So they beg the soul to ride on a bowstick covered with cloth, and mounted on that vehicle the spirit is brought back to the house and installed in a corner with the souls of other dead kinsfolk who are supposed to be awaiting reincarnation.[1]

Similarly the Lohars, a caste of blacksmiths in the Central Provinces of India, believe in the reincarnation of the dead and call their spirits home when they have buried or burnt their bodies. For this purpose rice-flour is spread on the floor of the cooking-room and covered with a brass plate. The women retire and sit in an adjoining room, while the chief mourner, with a few companions, goes outside the village and sprinkles some more rice-flour. They call to the deceased person, saying, "Come! Come!" and then wait patiently till some worm or insect crawls on to the flour. A pinch of dough is then applied to the creature, and, thus caught, the worm or insect is carried home and let loose in the house. The flour under the brass plate is now examined, and it is said that they usually discern the footprints of a person or an animal, indicating the body of the man or beast in which the

---

[1] R. V. Russell, *Tribes and Castes of the Central Provinces of India*, iii. 469.

wandering soul of the deceased has found another place of rest.[1]

The Taonla, a small non-Aryan caste of the Uriya States in India, hold similar beliefs and practise similar customs. They believe in the re-incarnation of the dead, and when a child is born they try to ascertain which ancestor has come back by dropping coloured grains of rice, one by one, in water, and naming an ancestor at every grain ; the first grain that floats gives the desired name. They both bury and burn the dead, and observe a cere-mony for bringing back their souls. Outside the village an earthen pot is placed upside down on four legs as a chair for the soul of the dead to sit on, and on the eleventh day after the death they go to the spot, ringing a bell. Arrived at the place, they spread a cloth before the upturned pot on which the ghost is believed to be sitting, and there they wait till an insect alights on the cloth. The creature is thought to be the soul of the dead, and it is carefully wrapped up in the cloth and carried back to the house. There the cloth is un-folded and the insect allowed to go ; some rice-flour spread on the ground is inspected, and if any mark is found on it they are sure that the dead man's spirit has come home.[2]

Among the Khasis of North-Eastern India, when a man has died in a distant village or district every attempt is made by his family to lead back his spirit,

---

[1] R. V. Russell, *Tribes and Castes of the Central Provinces of India*, iv. 124.

[2] R. V. Russell, *op. cit.* iv. 541.

with or without his calcined bones, to his native place. Emissaries are sent to the village where he died to bring home his mortal remains if possible, but certainly his soul. On their return journey they take great pains to guide the soul on the right road, lest haply it should wander by the way and be lost. They pluck leaves and place them with rice at the wayside as offerings to lure the spirit onward. And when they come to a river, through which the spirit cannot wade, they stretch a cotton thread across it from bank to bank to serve as a bridge for the soul. If the river is broad, they plant notched sticks in its bed and attach the string to their tops, lest the string should droop into the water and the poor soul should fall into it and be drowned or swept away by the current. But if the stream should be very narrow, a stick or even a simple stalk of grass laid across it is deemed a bridge sufficient for the passage of the soul.[1]

A ceremony of bringing back the soul of a dead person after the burial of his body is also practised by the Mailu people of British New Guinea. Three or four days after the burial, eight or ten young men, generally led by the particular comrade (*isigoina*) of the deceased, remain behind at the grave, when the other mourners, who have been engaged in the obsequies at it, have left for the village. They go off into the forest near one of the pieces of

---

[1] H. H. Godwin-Austen, " On the Stone Monuments of the Khasi Hill Tribes ", *Journal of the Anthropological Institute*, i. (1872) pp. 132 *sq.* Compare Capt. T. H. Lewin, *Wild Tribes of South-Eastern India* (London, 1870), pp. 209 *sq.*

land owned by the deceased, there to call back his spirit to the village. While the others hide behind trees or bushes, the special comrade of the deceased calls out to the dead man's spirit, " We are about to sail for sago. Come ! " Meantime all those in hiding put their hands to their ears to catch the reply of the spirit. Again the cry rings out, " We are about to sail to Uri to get pigs. Come, because we are sailing. Oh, companion, we are sailing to Uri to get that pig. Come ! " Sometimes the men in hiding hear an *o* sound which they take to be the voice of some one who died long ago, and not that of their recently departed brother. So they give up that spot and go off to another piece of the deceased's land, where the same calls to his spirit are repeated till they hear a feeble " *oooooo* " in response. Pricking up their ears at that, they cry, " He has come ! " So they run to the path and stand in line on either side of it, while two of them rush off to the village to help the spirit to find his way correctly to his old house. They have to make haste, for the spirit runs fast and leaps as he goes. The other eight men follow at leisure.[1]

The Abchases, a people of the Caucasus, have a remarkable way of recovering the soul of a drowned man after his body has been rescued from the water and buried. Men and women assemble on both banks of the river where the accident took place. A silken thread is stretched across the river, from which a leathern bag is hung so that its lower

---

[1] W. J. V. Saville, *In Unknown New Guinea* (London, 1926), p. 231.

end just touches the surface of the water. The men and women then begin to sing to the accompaniment of lutes. The soul of the drowned man, lingering in the water, is lured by the sweet strains and, emerging from the water, clambers into the bag. No sooner has he done so than one of the company assembled on the bank plunges into the river, ties up the mouth of the bag and carries it, with the captured soul of the drowned man in it, to the grave, where he opens the bag and lets down the soul through a hole in the earth to rejoin its body.[1] In this case the strayed soul is not indeed brought back to the house, but the kindly intention of laying it to rest with its mortal remains is not less conspicuous.

In one way or another the foregoing customs exhibit a tender regard for the spirits of the dead which is very different from that fear and scrupulous avoidance which often, if not generally, characterize the attitude of primitive man to the souls of the departed. This is the brighter aspect of the subject with which we are here concerned. In subsequent lectures I shall have to deal at some length with the darker side of the picture. Here it must suffice to have shown that in primitive religion the fear of the dead is often tempered with affection.

[1] N. v. Seidlitz (Tiflis), " Die Abchasen ", *Globus*, lxvi. (1894) p. 43.

LECTURE II

LECTURE II

AT the close of the last lecture I showed that primitive man sometimes exhibits a respectful regard for his dead kinsfolk by bringing their souls back to the house and installing them there after he has buried or burnt their bodies elsewhere. But this respectful treatment of the ghost is exceptional. The general attitude of primitive man to ghosts, even of his own kinsfolk, is one of fear, and far from attempting to retain them in the dwelling or to facilitate their return, he is at great pains to drive them away, to keep them at a distance, and to bar the house against their unwelcome intrusions. The means to which he resorts for the sake of thus keeping the spirits of the dead at bay are very various and often display an ingenuity and resourcefulness worthy of a better cause. I shall describe some of them presently ; but before I come to details I think it may be well to adduce some evidence as to the general attitude of primitive peoples to the spirits of the dead in order to familiarize you, to some extent, with a mode of thought which is so alien to our own.

For this purpose we may begin with the Melanesians, the dark-skinned, frizzly-haired people who inhabit the long chain of islands stretching along the eastern coasts of New Guinea and Australia, from New Britain on the north to New Caledonia on the south. Speaking of them, the late Rev. Dr. Codrington, one of our highest authorities on the people, observes that " in the Solomon Islands the ghost, being the principal object of worship, occupies . . . a much higher place in the religious world of the natives than it does in the islands which lie to the eastward, and on that account it is desirable, before entering upon details, to draw the distinction between the two classes of ghosts which is generally recognized in the former islands. The distinction is between ghosts of power and ghosts of no account, between those whose help is sought and their wrath deprecated, and those from whom nothing is expected and to whom no observance is due. Among living men there are some who stand out distinguished for capacity in affairs, success in life, valour in fighting, and influence over others ; and these are so, it is believed, because of the supernatural and mysterious powers which they have, and which are derived from communication with those ghosts of the dead gone before them who are full of those same powers. On the death of a distinguished man his ghost retains the powers that belonged to him in life, in greater activity and with stronger force ; his ghost therefore is powerful, and so long as he is remembered the aid of his powers is sought and worship is offered him ; he is the *tindalo* of Florida, the *lio'a* of Sa'a. In every society again, the multitude is composed of insignificant persons, *numerus fruges consumere nati* ; of no particular account for valour, skill or prosperity. The ghosts of such persons continue their insignificance, and are nobodies after death as before ; they are ghosts because all men have souls, and the souls of dead men are ghosts ; they are dreaded because all ghosts are awful, but they get no worship and are soon only thought of as the crowd of the nameless population of the lower world." [1] And again, speaking of San Cristoval ghosts, Dr. Codrington observes : " Here, as elsewhere, a man's ghost has in greater force the power which the man had in his lifetime, when he had it from his communication with the ghosts that went before him ; and those who have lately died have most power, or at least are the most active sources of it. The ghost of the great man lately dead is most regarded ; as the dead are forgotten their ghosts are superseded by later successors to the unseen power." [2]

What Dr. Codrington here says of Melanesian ghosts might probably be said of ghosts everywhere ; they rank in the other world according to the status which the men or women had in this world ; equality exists as little among the dead as among the living ; the power of the ghost is proportioned to the power which the man had in life ; or rather it is at first

[1] R. H. Codrington, D.D., *The Melanesians* (Oxford, 1891), pp. 253 sq.

[2] R. H. Codrington, *The Melanesians*, p. 258.

increased by his transference to the other sphere, though it gradually dwindles with lapse of time, till at last ghost and man are alike forgotten.

Dr. Codrington's testimony as to the essential inequality and transitory nature of Solomon Island ghosts is confirmed by a later observer, Dr. Ivens, who says that " the ghosts of ordinary persons are just mere ghosts, and are doubtless invoked by their own people, but their names do not abide permanently, nor are they invoked generally. At Sa'a, the chiefs of the main branch were all invoked in sacrifice and their names mentioned, but even with them the elder ones of the line gave place to the later." [1]

When from the Melanesians we pass eastward to the Polynesians, the fairer-skinned people who occupy the far-scattered islands of the Central and Eastern Pacific, we find that they also stood in great fear of the spirits of the dead. Thus the Society Islanders believed that these restless souls haunted their old homes and visited the abodes of the living, but seldom on errands of mercy or benevolence. They woke the survivors from sleep by squeaking noises to upbraid them for their past wickedness or to reproach them with the neglect of some ceremonial observance, for which the ghosts had to suffer. Thus the inhabitants of these lovely islands imagined that they lived in a world of disembodied spirits, which, though invisible, sur-

[1] W. G. Ivens, *The Melanesians of the South-East Solomon Islands* (London, 1927), p. 179.

rounded them by night and by day, watching every action of their lives and ready to revenge the smallest slight or the least disobedience to their injunctions, as these were revealed to them by the priests. Convulsions and hysterics, for example, were ascribed to the maleficent action of these spirits, which seized the sufferer, scratched his face, tore his hair and otherwise maltreated him.[1]

In our progress round the world we now pass from the Pacific Ocean to the great island of New Guinea, which forms, as it were, a stepping-stone between the Pacific Ocean and the continent of Asia. Speaking of the natives of British New Guinea in the neighbourhood of Port Moresby, two early missionaries, with one of whom I was personally acquainted before he died a martyr's death, have recorded that " each family has a sacred place, where they carry offerings to the spirits of deceased ancestors, whom they terribly fear. Sickness in the family, death, famine, scarcity of fish, etc.—these terrible spirits are at work and must be propitiated." [2] With reference to the Kiwai Papuans of British New Guinea, the Finnish ethnologist, Professor Landtman, who has made a careful and very complete study of them, tells us that " on the whole the natives stand in great dread of the spirits of the dead, whoever the person may have been in his lifetime. Ghosts are known to carry away the souls of living people and also to cause illness, and

[1] W. Ellis, *Polynesian Researches*, Second Edition (London, 1832–1836), i. 402.

[2] James Chalmers and W. Wyatt Gill, *Work and Adventure in New Guinea* (London, 1885), p. 84.

must therefore be carefully kept away." [1]   A somewhat more favourable opinion of the character of ghosts appears to be held by the Roro-speaking tribes of British New Guinea, for we learn that they are believed to haunt the villages of their people, and if they deserted the village the inhabitants would have no luck at all ; so if they are suspected of having forsaken a village, measures are taken to bring them back. However, it is said that their benevolence is not unconditional ; for if they are annoyed, as for instance by too many quarrels among the women, they will send bad luck in hunting and fishing, and in these circumstances it might even be necessary to drive them out of the village. Moreover, the ghosts make people ill by stealing their souls, and the natives stand in such fear of them that, in order not to encounter a ghost, they will not go out of the village after dark, unless they are accompanied by a friend to keep them in countenance, if it were only for a distance of a few yards. [2] On the whole we seem compelled to admit that the virtues of Roro ghosts are dashed with some serious defects.

The ghosts of Orokaiva people, in the east of British New Guinea, appear to be very little better, or rather a good deal worse. True, every Orokaiva gardener and hunter thinks that the spirits of the dead can send him success in the garden and the chase, but such benevolent conduct on the part of

[1] G. Landtman, *The Kiwai Papuans of British New Guinea* (London, 1927), p. 282.

[2] C. G. Seligman, *The Melanesians of British New Guinea* (Cambridge, 1910), p. 310.

the ghosts is, we are told, " to say the least unusual, and it must be confessed that on the whole the Orokaiva regards his relatives and friends after death as enemies. Any failure of the crops may be attributed to them ; they may baffle the hunter ; they may send the pigs to break through the fences and despoil the gardens." Sickness appears to be attributed by the Orokaiva to the malevolence of ghosts oftener than to any other cause. In short, according to Mr. F. E. Williams, our principal authority on the people, the Orokaiva inherits a body of beliefs regarding the ghosts (*sovai*) which picture them in a variety of horrible and dangerous forms, so that he cannot help regarding them with aversion, and especially with fear.[1] So much for ghosts in New Guinea.

Still moving westward, we come to the Indian Archipelago or Indonesia, which by its long chain of islands links up New Guinea with Asia. The Indonesians, who inhabit the Archipelago, appear to have developed the theory of animism—that is, the doctrine of souls—more fully and with greater logical consistency than any other people on earth ; it is therefore particularly interesting to learn what these people think about the souls of the dead. On this subject the highest living authority, the Dutch missionary, Dr. Albert C. Kruijt, who has laboured for many years in the Archipelago, writes as

---

[1] F. E. Williams, *Orokaiva Society* (Oxford University Press, London, 1930), pp. 283, 284; compare *id.*, p. 285, " It is certain that the Orokaiva goes in real fear of the power of the *sovai* " (ghosts) ; *ib.*, " the genuine fear of the *sovai* which motivates so much of an Orokaiva's conduct ".

follows : " Now and then we meet with instances of the love for the dead one overcoming the fear of his. soul ; this happens especially with dead children. But as a rule the Indonesians feel great fear of the soul of a dead person. They naturally think that the dead person resents leaving this earth, and in his resentment wishes to have his fate shared by others. He therefore tries to carry off the soul-substance of the surviving people into the grave, which will cause them to die." [1]

In these words I believe that Dr. Kruijt has laid his finger on the true cause of the fear, the almost universal fear, of the spirits of the dead. Man fears them because he feels instinctively that they are angels and ministers of death hovering about him in the air and ready to bear away his own soul with them to the unknown world beyond the grave. In the early days of the Crimean war John Bright declared in the House of Commons that the Angel of Death had been abroad throughout the land, you might almost hear the beating of his wings. A like declaration might be made by almost any savage, with this difference, that he imagines himself to be compassed about by a whole host of such gloomy angels, all the spirits of all his dead friends and foes, who lie in wait to clutch him in their cold embrace and to snatch him away from this sweet life on earth. No wonder that he looks on these Harpy spirits with fear and abhorrence.

---

[1] Alb. C. Kruijt, *s.v.* " Indonesi- ans ", in J. Hastings, *Encyclopaedia* *of Religion and Ethics*, vii. (Edin- burgh, 1914) p. 250.

In our progress westward from New Guinea, the first of the great islands which stud these tropic seas is the fantastically shaped island of Celebes. Its centre is inhabited by a race called the Toradyas, who were hardly known in Europe till the Dutch missionaries, Dr. Albert C. Kruijt and N. Adriani, settled among them. As a result of the devoted labours of these two men we now possess a full and exact account of the Toradyas, who accordingly rank among the best known of primitive races, though they are less familiar than they should be out of Holland because the description of them is mostly written in the Dutch language. In regard to the old native religion of the Toradyas, we are informed that their gods fall into two classes : first, gods who have always been gods ; and secondly, the souls of dead men who have only gradually, in the opinion of the Toradyas, attained to the rank of godhead. In the gods of the first class, who have always been gods, may be recognized personifications of natural phenomena or forces. One of these natural deities who is most frequently invoked is the Sun-god, who is said to have come down to earth in human form and instructed mankind in everything that relates to agriculture. The invocations to the Sun-god always begin with an address to him " who is in the east and in the west ". However, we are told that in the life of the Toradyas it is the human gods, the deified spirits of dead men, who play the greatest part. But not all human souls become gods after death. As in daily life a freeman is esteemed above a slave, a chief above an ordinary freeman, so the souls of the dead are conceived to differ in power and standing. The souls of very brave and honoured chiefs are revered as gods; offerings are brought to them, and their help is implored in war as well as in the chase and in the rice-field. And the more generations have elapsed since the death of the brave who have won for themselves a place in popular legend, the greater is the confidence reposed in their godhead. In honour of these human gods a house is built in the village; all these human gods were once men; men need a house, and so do these men-gods. And we can only understand these Toradya men-gods, so Dr. Kruijt tells us, when we know the Toradya himself, for the Toradya imagines his gods to be exactly like himself. The Toradya himself seeks, or rather used to seek, his glory by cutting off the heads of his enemies and bringing back these gory trophies to the village; hence he believes that the gods delight in these proofs of valour, and that they will make him sick if he does not go head-hunting at the proper time. Again, the Toradya is quick to take offence if any one wrongs him in anything; so he thinks that his gods are equally touchy, and that they will manifest their displeasure by blasting the rice, by sending sickness, or by causing mishaps on a journey if a man has done anything contrary to customary law.[1] Elsewhere Dr. Kruijt tells us

[1] A. C. Kruijt, " Het wezen van het heidendom te Posso ", *Mededeelingen van wege het Nederlandsche* *Zendelinggenootschap*, xlvii. (Rotterdam, 1903) pp. 24-26.

that the Toradya conceives life after death to be
exactly like life on earth, for he can imagine no
other. In his opinion the souls of the dead eat and
drink ; they till the fields and keep cattle ; and men
have every motive for treating them well, for on a
good understanding with them depends the success
or failure of the harvest.[1]

Still moving westward from Celebes, we come to
the great island of Borneo. In it the Sea Dyaks
of Sarawak, as we learn from a very good authority—
the Rev. J. Perham—" attribute to the dead a disposition of mixed good and evil towards the living,
and so alternately fear and desire any contact with
them. . . . They do not speak of taking a ' corpse '
to the grave, but an *antu*, a spirit ; as though the
departed had already become a member of that
class of capricious unseen beings which are believed
to be inimical to men. They think the dead can
rush from their secret habitations, and seize in-
visibly on any one passing by the cemetery, which
is, therefore, regarded as an awesome, dreaded
place. But yet this fear does not obliterate affectionate regard, and many a grave is kept clean and tidy
by the loving care of the living ; the fear being
united with the hope of good, as they fancy the
dead may also have the will and the power to help
them." [2] " In times of peril and of need the dead

[1] N. Adriani en Alb. C. Kruijt,
*De Bare-sprekende Toradjas van
Midden-Celebes* (Batavia, 1912), ii.
118.

[2] Rev. J. Perham, " Sea Dyak

Religion ", *Journal of the Straits
Branch of the Royal Asiatic Society*,
No. 14 (December, 1884), p. 300 ;
id., in H. Ling Roth, *Natives of
Sarawak and British North Borneo*
(London, 1896), i. 210 *sq.*

are called upon ; and on the hilltops or in the solitudes of the jungle a man often goes by himself and spends the night in the hope that the spirit of some dead relative may visit him, and in a dream tell him of some charm by means of which he may overcome difficulties and become rich and great." [1]

Passing still westward from Borneo, we come to the last and largest island of the Indian Archipelago, the great island of Sumatra. In it the Bataks, an important people of the interior, are said to share the universal human belief in a life after death. Their ideas about that life, however, are as usual vague, but they seem to think of it as not very different from the present life on earth. From their stories and their custom of invoking the dead it appears that weaving, plaiting, fetching the water, tilling the ground and so forth, are supposed to go on in the other world just as in this one. But they prefer to have nothing to do with the dead, except in so far as the dead can tell them of means to avert or heal sickness. The souls of the dead are believed, indeed, to exercise an influence on the life of the survivors, but on the whole that influence is thought of as unfavourable, and the living endeavour to restrict it and keep it within bounds by the perform-ance of certain ceremonies designed to arm them-selves against the malignity of the dead.[2]

The natives of Nias, an island lying off the

---

[1] E. H. Gomes, *Seventeen Years among the Sea Dyaks of Borneo* (London, 1911), p. 142.

[2] M. Joustra, " Het leven, de zeden en gewoonten der Bataks ", *Mededeelingen van wege het Neder-landsche Zendelinggenootschap*, xlvi. (Rotterdam, 1902) pp. 415, 417.

western coast of Sumatra, are reported to go in fear of the spirits of the dead, which are believed often to make the living sick for the purpose of drawing away their souls with them to the other world. The spirits of dead chiefs are thought to possess this power in a higher than ordinary degree. Hence the natives of Nias do all they can to humour and propitiate the souls of the dead in order that these dreaded spirits may leave the living in peace, and many are the devices to which they resort for this purpose.[1]

Our brief preliminary survey of these ghostly beliefs must now pass from the islands of the Pacific and the Indian Ocean to the continent of Asia. Concerning the Kachins, a tribe of Burma, we are told that the belief in the ancestral spirits has undoubtedly the strongest hold on the popular imagination. Every individual at death becomes a ghost (*tsu*), and at the final obsequies is solemnly dismissed to the region where the ancestral spirits reside. If he stays there, all is well ; the living are left in peace. But if he decides to return, as he may do, to the land of the living, there is apt to be trouble for his surviving relatives. For death is believed by the Kachins to work a radical change for the worse in the spirits of the dead. " The affectionate mother will return from the spirit land and in the shape of a chirping cricket entice the ghost of the still living child to wander away, and death will

---

[1] J. P. Kleiweg de Zwaan, *Die Heilkunde der Niasser* (Haag, 1913), pp. 17 *sq.*

follow in a few months. A departed friend will return and leave his fingermarks on the boiling rice with the result that most of the partakers will sicken and die. An old respected chief, if not properly buried, will cause a drought or deluge, destroying the crops of the whole community. There is apparently no case on record where a departed spirit has improved in company with the shades." [1]

Of the Chukchis, a people of low culture, living under severe natural conditions at the north-eastern extremity of Siberia, we are told that " one of their most prevalent notions is that the dead become wicked spirits, the enemies of mankind. The funeral rites of the Chukchis abound in incantations intended to prevent the return of the dead in the form of wicked spirits. Even the spirit of the nearest relation, returning with the best intentions in the world, cannot but frighten the living and do them harm. A shaman said to me, " The spirit of a (dead) father is no better than the *ivmetoun* (the spirit of epilepsy). He who sees the spirit of his deceased father will suffer from convulsions and die a sudden death." [2]

The Birhors are a primitive jungle tribe of Chota Nagpur in India. Of them it is said by the eminent Indian ethnologist Mr. Sarat Chandra Roy, who has made a special study of the tribe, that so long as he lives the Birhor stands in

---

[1] O. Hanson, *The Kachins* (Rangoon, 1913), pp. 157 *sq.*

[2] W. Bogaraz, " Idées religieuses des Tchouktchis ", *Bulletins et Mémoires de la Société d'Anthropologie de Paris*, Ve Série, vol. v. (Paris, 1904) pp. 351 *sq.*

continuous fear of the spirit-world ; but as soon as he is dead, and until a certain ceremony, called *Umbul-ader*, has been performed, " it is he, or rather his disembodied spirit, that becomes the prime object of fears and concern to his relatives and other people of his settlement. And the observances and ceremonies customary during this period appear to have for their main object the prevention of harm to the *tāndā* (settlement) through his spirit, on the one hand, and, on the other hand, of harm to his spirit through stray, malignant spirits. Even the offering of food laid out for the spirit of the deceased appears to be prompted less by a feeling of affection for him than from a fear of his spirit and a desire to keep it agreeably engaged at a safe distance." [1] And speaking of the Oraons, another tribe of Chota Nagpur, the same high authority similarly observes that some of their funeral ceremonies " would appear to indicate that their original object was to keep the spirits of the dead out of harm's way, to cut off all connection with them so as to avoid all chance of their evil attentions being directed to their living relatives. As a matter of fact, all departed spirits would appear to have been originally conceived of as evil spirits,—all of them, though regarded as ancestral spirits (*Pāch-bā'lār*), were at one time regarded by the Oraons as mischievous spirits or *nāsan bhuts* as well." [2]

The Kunbis, a great agricultural caste of the

---

[1] Sarat Chandra Roy, *The Bir-hors* (Ranchi, 1925), pp. 265 *sq.*
[2] Sarat Chandra Roy, *Oraon Religion and Customs* (Ranchi, 1928), p. 38.

Maratha country in India, are firm believers in the action of ghosts, and never omit the attentions due to the ancestral spirits. On the appointed day the Kunbi calls on the crows, who represent the spirits of ancestors, to come and eat the food which he sets out for them ; and if no crow appears, he is disturbed at the thought of having incurred the displeasure of the dead. So he changes the food and goes on calling till a crow comes and eats the food. From this the Kunbi infers that the first food he offered was not to the taste of his ancestors ; hence, taking the lesson to heart, he continues to offer the other food to the spirits so long as a crow responds to his first invitation to partake of it. The reason why crows are taken to represent the spirits of the dead is probably connected with the widespread notion of the crow's longevity. The Hindoos believe that a crow lives a thousand years, and others think that it never dies except by violence.[1] But while the Kunbi is thus careful to keep on good terms with the spirits of his dead ancestors, he is apparently far from thinking that the action of these spirits is purely beneficent ; for his people have a proverb that Brahmans die of indigestion, goldsmiths (Sunars) die of bile, and Kunbis die of ghosts.[2] In the sequel we shall meet with many examples of the belief that ghosts are often responsible for sickness and death ; it is indeed one of the commonest articles of savage religion, and in the mind of

[1] R. V. Russell, *Tribes and Castes of the Central Provinces of India,* iv. 37.

[2] R. V. Russell, *op. cit.* iv. 40.

primitive man throws a dark shadow on the bright
vision of immortality.

The Kolhatis of Central India believe that the
spirits of dead ancestors enter the bodies of the
living and work evil to them unless they are appeased
with offerings. The Dukar Kolhatis sacrifice a boar
to male ancestors and a sow to female.[1] The
Korkus, a Munda or Kolarian tribe of the Central
Provinces of India, believe that the spirits of their
dead are not finally laid to rest until a ceremony
has been performed which may not take place for
many months or even years after the death. In
the interval the disembodied and unquiet spirits are
thought to possess the power of sending aches and
pains to molest the bodies of their surviving relatives.[2]

With these few notices of Asiatic ghosts we must
content ourselves for the present and pursue our
journey ever westward to Africa, only touching for
a moment at Madagascar on the way. The Sakalavas, a tribe or nation who occupy all the western
portion of that great island, are firm believers in
the existence and almost omnipresence of their
ancestral spirits, to the influence of which they
trace most of the events of life, whether good or
bad, but oftener the bad than the good. In their
opinion, spirits (*lolo*) are everywhere—under the
earth, on the earth, in the water and on the water,
in the river, in the forest, in the air; some trees
and mountains are especially haunted by them, and

[1] R. V. Russell, *Tribes and Castes*   iii. 530.
of the Central Provinces of India.   [2] R. V. Russell, *op. cit.* iii. 565.

almost always the spirit is that of an ancestor. Any unusual event is set down to the action of one of these spirits, who has produced it either to punish some breach of ancestral custom (*fady*) or to attract the attention of the living to himself. All sickness is referred to that cause, and even vice finds an excuse in it. A drunkard has been known to apologize for his drunkenness by laying the blame on the thirsty ghost (*lolo*) who possessed him.[1]

Holding as they do this unfavourable, or at best ambiguous, view of the spirits of the departed, we are not surprised to learn that the Sakalavas " generally like to get rid of their dead at once, and will have nothing to do with corpses unless they are obliged, for they are doubtful as to how their dead relatives will conduct themselves towards those still living ; whether they will act as friends or enemies is not known to anybody. But to secure them as friends, they pour out at least once a year a quantity of rum on the graves of their deceased relatives, and especially on those of their ancestors. This they suppose to be a means of averting the feelings of enmity which they probably might keep up towards some one of the living members of the family ; for, as they were always fond of rum during their lifetime, they also must be so after death." [2] What is here said of Sakalava ghosts might probably be said with equal truth of primitive ghosts in

[1] H. Rusillon, *Un Culte dynastique avec Evocation des Morts chez les Sakalaves de Madagascar* (Paris, 1912), pp. 43 *sq.*

[2] Rev. A. Walen, " The Sakalava ", *The Antananarivo Annual and Madagascar Magazine*, viii. (Antananarivo, 1884) p. 67.

general; they all retain the tastes and passions, the weaknesses and frailties which they had in life; death produces no amelioration, if it does not effect a distinct deterioration, in their moral character.

We now pass to Africa, where the belief in the power of ancestral spirits for good and evil is perhaps more widely spread and more deeply rooted than in any other part of the world. Out of the immense mass of evidence available I can here only pick out, almost at random, a few typical specimens to indicate the depth and diffusion of the belief, which in many tribes takes the form of the worship of ancestors.

We may begin with the Thonga, a Bantu tribe of South-Eastern Africa which has been thoroughly studied by a Swiss missionary, Dr. Henri A. Junod, who has devoted his life to it and given us a masterly account of his dusky flock. Speaking of their religion, he says that in their opinion any man who has departed this earthly life becomes a *shikwemba*, which Dr. Junod does not scruple to translate " a god ",[1] though sometimes he uses the more explicit term " ancestral god ". But the character of these ancestral gods, as it is described by Dr. Junod, hardly squares with our conceptions of divinity; at all events it is of a very mixed sort. He tells us that " the gods can *bless*: if the trees bear plenty of fruit, it is because they have made it grow; if the crops are plentiful, it is because they

[1] Henri A. Junod, *The Life of a South African Tribe*, Second Edition (London, 1927), ii. 372.

forced wizards to increase them, or hindered them from spoiling them ; if you come across a pot of palm wine, it is your god who has sent you that windfall. . . . Often when a man has narrowly escaped drowning, or spraining his ankle on a stump which has caught his foot, he will say : ' The gods have saved me '. But they (the gods) can also *curse*, and bring untold misfortune on their descendants. If the rain fails, it is owing to their anger ; if a tree falls on you, they have directed its fall ; if a crocodile bites you, the gods have sent it ; if your child has fever and is delirious, they are in him, tormenting his soul ; if your wife is sterile, they have prevented her from child-bearing ; perhaps the gods of your mother have done this because you had not given your maternal uncle ' the part of your daughter's marriage price (*lobolo*) ' which he has the right to claim ; in fact any disease, any calamity may come from them." [1]

On the whole Dr. Junod finds that these ancestral spirits of the Thonga have not improved by being raised to the rank of divinities. In fact, he says plainly " they are not better than they were as men. Their *character* is that of suspicious old people, who resent any want of respect, or attention, on the part of their descendants. They wish to be thought of, and presented with offerings. It would seem that they are not actually in need of anything, for they live in abundance, but they exact a punctual observance of the duties of their descendants in

[1] H. A. Junod, *The Life of a South African Tribe*[2], ii. 386.

regard to them. They must eat the first fruits, and have their share of the tobacco leaves. They are jealous, and avenge themselves when forgotten. The only sin which seems to be deserving of punishment is to neglect them." [1] Notwithstanding this very dubious character which Dr. Junod gives to the deified ancestors of the Thonga, he tells us that the people do not stand in perpetual fear of them ; their attitude to these jealous and testy spirits is rather that of indifference ; " natives ask for one thing only : that they may live in peace, and that their gods may interfere with them as little as possible ". [2]

The Bavenda, a Bantu tribe of the Northern Transvaal, recognize a certain mysterious deity named Raluvhimba, who is supposed to live somewhere in the heavens and to be connected with all astronomical and physical phenomena. [3] But he plays only a secondary part in the religious life of the Bavenda. " The direct relationship with their dead ancestors is a much more personal factor in their lives and is the basis of their religious ideas. Their attitude is quite rational ; to them death is a transition between life on this earth and life in the spirit-world, where the dead continue the lives begun on earth, still exerting a powerful influence on their living relatives. The ancestor spirits have themselves experienced ordinary mortal life and so understand the daily trials and difficulties which

[1] H. A. Junod, *The Life of a South African Tribe*[2], ii. 426.
[2] H. A. Junod, *op. cit.* ii. 428.
[3] H. A. Stayt, *The Bavenda* (London, 1931), p. 230.

beset all humanity and their own descendants in particular. The ancestor spirits, *medzimu* (sing. *mudzimi*), have many idiosyncrasies, and if they think that they have been slighted by their descendants, take their revenge by bringing misfortune to them ; they are therefore feared rather than loved. There seems to be a fairly fundamental conception among the Bavenda as to the inherent good of most worldly things, all trouble being associated with the evils of witchcraft or the jealousy and spitefulness of their ancestors." [1] The ancestral spirits which can affect the life of an individual are divided by the Bavenda into two groups—those of the father's lineage and those of the mother's lineage, and curiously enough the ancestral spirits of the mother's lineage are believed to be much more personally and intimately connected with their descendants than those of the father's line ; they cause far more trouble and are consequently more feared and respected than those of the father.[2]

The Bechuana (singular Mochuana) are a great Bantu tribe who inhabit the interior plains of central South Africa, including what used to be called Bechuanaland and parts of the Western Transvaal and the Kalahari desert. Concerning their religion a missionary, who laboured among them for about forty years and has given us a valuable account of their customs and beliefs, writes as follows : " Fear of the dead, whether one's own

---

[1] H. A. Stayt, *The Bavenda*, p. 240.
[2] H. A. Stayt, *op. cit.* pp. 240 *sq.*, 246.

relatives or others, does, however, play an important part in the life of the living Mochuana, who believes that the dead have power over the lives of the living to bless or to curse, to send prosperity or the reverse to their relatives and members of their clan ; especially is this fear potent when the living are conscious of any reason why the deceased should bear ill-will. Many forms of sickness, the onslaught of adversity and ills in general, are laid at the door of the offended spirit, and what may appear to be ancestor worship is simply acts of propitiation, sacrifices of atonement, which are intended to re-concile, and to bring back into harmonious fellow-ship the severed kinship. . . . The attitude of the Mochuana at the grave of his ancestor, immediate or more remote, is one of reverence and awe. Fear fills mind and heart—fear of the unknown powers—fears lest they be inimical. So far as I have been able to gather, it is never love, never thanksgiving, never the desire for communion with the deceased, never even a longing for a renewal of fellowship, that calls forth their offerings and sacrifice, but always the fear that kinship with all it connotes has been severed and must be recovered." [1]

The Ba-ila are a Bantu people of Northern Rhodesia. Like all Bantu tribes, they revere or worship their ancestral spirits as divinities, but their attitude to them is somewhat ambiguous. The spirits are regarded generally as beneficent or

[1] J. Tom Brown, *Among the Bantu Nomads* (London. 1926), pp 98, 99.

neutral, though they may be induced by neglect to make people sick. But some ghosts are incorrigibly bad and do much mischief, either at the bidding of witches and wizards or of their own free will. Not only do these maleficent spirits cause disease by entering the bodies of the living, but they waylay people and strike them dead. Or, without going so far as that, sometimes out of sheer devilry they will play all sorts of pranks, knocking burdens off people's heads, breaking hoes, unhandling axes, upsetting pots of beer and so forth. On the whole Ba-ila ghosts, in putting off the flesh, have not divested themselves of human frailties and weaknesses. As ordinary people in life may at times be jealous, touchy and fickle, so it is with the ghosts ; you can never be quite sure of them ; any omission on your part to do them reverence will be visited by them on your head or on the head of some one dear to you, and when that happens they must be placated by offerings. Hence the attitude of the Ba-ila towards the spirits of their dead resembles their attitude towards their chiefs ; it is a blending of trust and fear ; in a word, it is awe.[1]

The Banyamwezi are a large Bantu tribe of Central Africa, inhabiting the great tableland to the south of Lake Victoria Nyanza. Like all Bantu tribes, they believe that the spirits of their dead ancestors (the *misambwa*) exercise a very great influence on all the events of this mortal life. Hence

[1] Rev. Edwin W. Smith and Captain Andrew Murray Dale, *The Ila-speaking Peoples of Northern* *Rhodesia* (London, 1920), ii. 132, 167 *sq.*

they are prompted to do all they can to keep on good terms with these touchy spirits in order to escape from the troubles which it is in their power to inflict on the living. Thus the whole concern of the native in regard to the dead is to avert the anger of his ancestors and to gain their good graces, and this he does by offering them sacrifice and prayer and thanks. So long as the ancestral spirits are in a good humour, all goes well with the people and there is nothing to fear; but when trouble comes and affairs go ill, it is a sign that the ancestors are displeased, and then it is necessary to propitiate them and to restore friendly relations with their spirits.[1]

The Konde are a Bantu people who inhabit the country about the northern end of Lake Nyasa. Concerning them we are told that the importance of the spirits of the dead in the daily life of the Konde can hardly be exaggerated. From the day when the infant is presented by the head of the family to the spirits of its ancestors until the day of death, when the parting spirit is directed to go in peace to meet his forefathers, the living and the dead are mingled in one stream, they form one community, and are dependent on each other for many of the best things here on earth and in the world below, where the spirits of the dead reside.[2] For though at death the souls of the dying are dismissed to that subterranean region, they are

[1] Fr. Bösch, *Les Banyamwezi* (Münster i. W., 1930), p. 166.

[2] D. R. Mackenzie, *The Spirit-ridden Konde* (London, 1925), p. 190.

usually believed to be able to return to earth and to exert themselves there very energetically ; indeed, the dead are conceived to obtain a great accession of power on passing into the spirit-world, a power both for good and for evil, and to placate them is one of the chief preoccupations of Konde life.[1] As usual, the conditions of life below the earth are thought to be much the same as of life above it. The dead chief is a chief still, and the dead slave is still a slave in the underworld. The rich man is still rich, and the poor man is still poor. The dead wife goes to her dead husband, and the dead children go to their dead parents.[2] The motives which the spirits of the dead have for returning to the land of the living are mainly two.

First, they wish to assure themselves that they still have descendants on earth ; for if the family dies out, it is a dreadful calamity for the ghosts, because in that case they are turned into frogs. Second, the dead desire to make certain that they are not forgotten by the survivors, for the departed spirit who receives no attention from his living kinsfolk becomes of no account in the underworld. Hence the illness or other misfortune which over-takes the survivors is set down by them to the anger of the dead at the slight put upon them.[3] We need not wonder, then, that the spirits of the dead are a matter of anxious concern to the Konde.

The Barundi are another Bantu tribe who in-

[1] D. R. Mackenzie, *The Spirit-ridden Konde* (London, 1925), pp. 191, 192.

[2] D. R. Mackenzie, *op. cit.* p. 193.

[3] D. R. Mackenzie, *op. cit.* p. 195.

habit a district on the western side of Lake Victoria Nyanza. In their belief the dead are always more or less wicked and hostile to the living, even when they had been comparatively good in life. For the dead man has been forced to abandon all that he held dear in life and is therefore filled with envy of the living, who now possess what he has lost. Hence these envious and malicious spirits (*abasimu* or *imisimu*) inflict sickness, dearth, cattle-plague and other evils on the living, who dread them accordingly, and much of the daily life of the Barundi is taken up with the efforts to ward off, restrain, appease and propitiate these dreadful beings. For that purpose the Barundi offer sacrifices to the dead, and these sacrifices, we are told, are merely insurances against the damage that would otherwise be done them by these dangerous spirits ; they are not the expression of disinterested affection for departed kinsfolk. The Marundi sacrifices to the dead only because he fears them.[1]

Of the Basoga, a Bantu people inhabiting a district called Busoga on the northern shore of Lake Victoria Nyanza, Canon Roscoe, our best authority, writes as follows : " In all parts of Busoga worship of the dead forms a most important part of the religion of the people, and the belief in ghosts and the propitiation of them are the chief features of their most constant and regular acts of worship. The gods, with fetishes and amulets, are able to do great things for the living ; but, after all, it is

[1] H. Meyer, *Die Barundi* (Leipzig, 1916), p. 119.

the ghost that is most feared and obtains the most marked attention. In childbirth, in sickness, in prosperity, and in death, ghosts materially help or hinder matters ; hence it behoves the living to keep on good terms with them. It is because of this belief that people frequently make sacrifices of fowls and other animals to the dead and constantly seek their help. First and foremost, it is because of the firm conviction of the presence of ghosts that the elaborate funeral ceremonies are performed. . . . In the beliefs of these primitive people we must relegate the gods to a secondary place after the worship of the dead." [1]

The principal Bantu tribe, or rather nation, of Uganda in Central Africa are the Baganda, who have given their name to the province. Among this interesting and once powerful people my honoured friend, the Rev. Canon Roscoe, laboured for many years and has published the fullest and best account of their customs and beliefs. Speaking of their religion he says, " The last, and possibly most venerated, class of religious objects were the ghosts of departed relatives. The power of ghosts for good or evil was incalculable." [2] " The belief in ghosts, both malevolent and benevolent, was firmly held by all classes, from the highest to the lowest. Existence in another world was a reality to them, and all looked forward to living and moving in the next state. The horrors of mutilation were in-

---

[1] John Roscoe, *The Northern Bantu* (Cambridge, 1915), p. 245.

[2] John Roscoe, *The Baganda* (London, 1911), p. 273.

creased by their ideas of the after-world ; for not only would the maimed person be inconvenienced and made to suffer in this life, but in the next world his ghost would in like manner be maimed. Hence the idea of amputation was so dreaded by men, that a person preferred to die with a limb rather than to live without it, and so lose his chance of possessing full powers in the ghost world. The loss of an eye was not only the sign which marked an adulterer in this life, but the loss would hold good in a future state and mark the man there ; the thief who had been caught and deprived of his hand was for ever maimed, and his ghost bore the stigma of a thief." [1] So exactly, in the opinion of the Baganda, does the ghost resemble the living man, and so unquestioning is their faith in immortality.

[1] John Roscoe, *The Baganda*, pp. 281 *sq.*

LECTURE III

LECTURE III

In the last lecture I adduced some evidence of the fear and worship of the dead in the southern, eastern and central regions of Africa. To complete this portion of our subject, it remains to give some specimens of a similar attitude towards the spirits of the departed in the western and more northern parts of the continent.

Thus, speaking of the natives of the Gaboon district in French West Africa, an experienced missionary observes : " That they had a belief in a future world is evidenced by survivors taking to the graves of their dead . . . boxes of goods, native materials, foreign cloth, food, and formerly even wives and servants, for use in that other life to which they had gone. Whatever may have been supposed about the locality or occupations of that life, the dead were confidently believed to have carried with them all their human passions and feelings, and especially their resentments. Fear of those possible resentments dominated the living in all their attempts at spiritual communication with the dead." [1]

[1] Rev. R. H. Nassau, *Fetichism in West Africa* (London, 1904), p. 237.

In the neighbouring province of Loango the relations of the living to the dead are reported to be friendly up to the time when the ceremony of mourning is performed at the grave, or at all events till the moment when the grave is dug, but after the mourning rites have been duly observed or the body interred, the relations between the living and the dead are said to be decidedly hostile. The mourning rites are the last farewell, the last testimony of affection to the soul of the departed, if indeed he was a person of sufficient importance to merit this token of esteem. Afterwards everybody seeks to keep the spirit of the deceased at arm's length or at a greater distance, and they do not scruple to resort to magical arts to protect themselves against the ghost.[1]

Among the tribes of Northern Nigeria, as we learn from Mr. C. K. Meek, our best authority on the subject, the predominant religious influence is the worship of ancestors, or, in more general terms, the cult of the dead. The tribal god is generally a deified ancestor. As usual, the worship is based on the almost universal belief in the persistence of the human soul after death. In the opinion of these Nigerian people a man who lives to a good old age has a vigorous soul, and when he goes to the next world he takes his spiritual power with him. Hence in his disembodied state he can assist and protect his tribe. He is the intermediary between his

---

[1] E. Pechuel-Loesche, *Die Loango-Expedition*, iii. 2 (Stuttgart, 1907), p. 308.

family and the unknown powers that control the universe. When he leaves the world he must therefore be sent off with due respect and equipped with all that he may need in the far country and on the journey thither. Hence he is commonly provided with a meal on the day of his funeral, and part of his property is buried with him in the grave ; and before the advent of the British Government, if he were a great man or chief, his favourite wife, slave, horse and boy and girl attendants were buried with him ; for one who is great in this world will be great also in the next. The social position which he had on earth must be fully maintained in the life hereafter. To ensure his good-will it is necessary to make periodical offerings at his grave. If these are neglected he will remind his relatives by appearing to them in dreams, and if they were to continue the neglect he would assume a malevolent attitude towards them. For, as usual, the Nigerian dead are said not to divest themselves of their human attributes, nor do they cease to take an interest in mundane affairs. Indeed, their interest is so far kept up that many of them return to earth and are born again in the bodies of their grandchildren.[1] Concerning the Jukun in particular, an important tribe of Northern Nigeria, we are told that their workaday religion is the cult of ancestors. A Jukun regards his dead ancestors as ever present with him ; he never eats food with-

[1] C. K. Meek, *The Northern Tribes of Nigeria* (London, 1925), ii. 12 *sq.*

out making an offering to their spirits, and when things go wrong he is directed by the divining apparatus to some particular ancestor deceased who is in need of sustenance. If he even dreams of an ancestor he will go to his household shrine with an oblation of beer and porridge and address his dead forefather by name, saying, " I have seen you in my sleep. Whether it is good or evil I know not. But I remember you now with these gifts and beseech you to give me and mine health." The ancestral spirits, so thinks the Jukun, can prevent the rain from falling and children from being conceived in the womb ; they can ensure a successful season for the extraction of salt, which is a principal article of commerce ; and when a man finds a dead game animal in the forest, he ascribes the windfall to his ancestors. The ancestors are, indeed, the dominating influence in the life of a Jukun.[1]

This must conclude what I have to say for the present about the fear and worship of the dead in Africa. Brief and fragmentary as is the evidence which I have laid before you, it may suffice to give you some conception of the firm hold which the belief in immortality has on the mind of the native African, and of the deep influence it exercises on his life. Far more than the ordinary civilized man, he is occupied with thoughts of death and the dead ; in the events of daily life, in good and evil fortune he traces the handiwork of these awful beings ; and to them he turns in seasons of distress and danger

[1] C. K. Meek, *A Sudanese Kingdom* (London, 1931), pp. 217 *sq.*

for help and deliverance from the troubles that beset this our mortal life on earth. No wonder that he looks on the spirits of the departed with mingled feelings of hope and fear, of affection and abhorrence. Indeed, it is hardly too much to say that in Africa, so far as it has not been affected by Europe, the living exist in perpetual bondage to the spirits of the dead.

Among the aborigines of America, to whom we must now turn for a few minutes, the fear and worship of the dead have apparently far less importance and extension than among the natives of Africa; yet they have had their place in the religion of the New World as well as of the Old. A few specimens must suffice to complete this rapid and very imperfect survey of ghost worship in primitive religion.

Thus, among the Nootka Indians of British Columbia, there is, or used to be, "great reluctance to explain their funeral usages to strangers; death being regarded by this people with great superstition and dread, not from solicitude for the welfare of the dead, but from a belief in the power of departed spirits to do much harm to the living".[1] Again, concerning the Dacota or Sioux, a great Indian tribe of the United States, we are told that "they have very little notion of punishment for crime hereafter in eternity: indeed, they know very little about whether the Great Spirit has anything to do with their affairs, present or future. All the fear they

[1] H. H. Bancroft, *The Native Races of the Pacific States* (London, 1875–1876), i. 206.

have is of the spirit of the departed. They stand
in great awe of the spirits of the dead, because they
think it is in the power of departed spirits to injure
them in any way they please ; this superstition has,
in some measure, a salutary effect. It operates on
them just as strong (*sic*) as our laws of hanging for
murder. Indeed, fear of punishment from the
departed spirits keeps them in greater awe than the
white people have of being hung." [1]

Again, the Assiniboin, another Indian tribe of
the Upper Missouri, " most sincerely believe in the
theory of ghosts, that departed spirits have the
power to make themselves visible and heard, that
they can assume any shape they wish, of animals
or men, and many will affirm that they have
actually seen these apparitions and heard their
whistlings and moanings. They are much afraid
of these appearances, and under no consideration
will go alone near a burial-place after dark. They
believe these apparitions have the power of striking
the beholder with some disease, and many complaints are attributed to this cause. They therefore
make feasts and prayers to them to remain quiet.
Smaller evils and misfortunes are caused by their
power, and a great many stories are nightly recounted in their lodges of the " different shapes in
which they appear ".[2] Hence the Assiniboin used

[1] Philander Prescott in H. R.
Schoolcraft's *Indian Tribes of the
United States* (Philadelphia, 1853–
1856), ii. 195 *sq.*
[2] E. T. Denig, " Indian Tribes of
the Upper Missouri ", *Forty-sixth
Annual Report of the Bureau of
American Ethnology* (Washington,
1930), p. 494.

to lament the death of their friends for years, perhaps so long as any relatives of the deceased were living ; they instituted feasts in honour of the dead, invoked their spirits, and offered them sacrifices and prayers. And if they neglected thus to pay respect to the souls of their departed kinsfolk, the angry ghosts would visit them in dreams and trouble them with whistling sounds and startling apparitions.[1]

The Tarahumare Indians of Mexico, we are told, " certainly believe in a future life, but they are afraid of the dead, and think that they want to harm the survivors. This fear is caused by the supposition that the dead are lonely, and long for the company of their relatives. The dead also make people ill, that they too may die and join the departed. When a man dies in spite of all efforts of the shamans to save his life, the people say that those who have gone before have called him or carried him off. The deceased are also supposed to retain their love for the good things they left behind in the world, and to be trying every way to get at them. So strong is the feeling that the departed still owns whatever property he once possessed that he is thought to be jealous of his heirs who now enjoy its possession. He may not let them sleep at night, but makes them sit up by the fire and talk." [2]

The attitude of the South American Indians

---

[1] E. T. Denig, *op. cit.* p. 318.
[2] C. Lumholtz, *Unknown Mexico* (London, 1903), i. 380 *sq.*

towards the spirits of the dead has been carefully examined by the eminent Finnish ethnographer, Professor Rafael Karsten, who spent five years in close contact with savages in different parts of the continent and learned their language. Speaking of the subject which here concerns us, Professor Karsten mentions " as an indisputable fact that the dead are feared ",[1] but he would distinguish the fear of the ghost from the fear of the demon who is supposed to have caused the death of a person. However, he tells us that in his belief a careful examination of the two, that is, of the ghost and the demon, would lead to the conclusion that the demons who cause death " have originally been nothing but ghosts of dead men which for one reason or another have assumed a positively evil nature. This, indeed, can in some cases be strictly proved, and it is a well-known fact that certain disembodied souls, especially the souls of wizards, murdered persons, etc., are changed into evil demons who visit other people with sickness and death. The disease- and death-demons, moreover . . . have a tendency to identify themselves with the souls of the departed in a way which, in some cases, makes it practically impossible to distinguish them from each other. The disease-spirit, such seems to be the general belief, having once got possession of the patient and caused his death, will thereafter remain in his body and seize his soul

[1] Rafael Karsten, *The Civilization of the South American Indians* (London, 1926), p. 243.

as well, with the result that he is himself altogether changed into an evil demon independently of what has been his character in life. This belief naturally makes the ideas of the Indians about the spirits of the dead more complicated and also explains why persons who in their lifetime have perhaps been loved and esteemed, after death are feared as malignant and dangerous beings. The change is due to the operation of the strange demon who invaded the deceased. The more power a person had in life, the more dangerous he will become after death, for the obsessing demon lays hold of that power. This is the true reason why old people, and particularly medicine-men, are so greatly feared after death." [1]

Thus, while Professor Karsten distinguishes the soul of a dead person from the demon who has caused his death, he admits that the soul and the demon are sometimes indistinguishable and sometimes actually identical, and he thinks that originally the demon was nothing but the ghost of the dead. Thus on Professor Karsten's theory the ultimate factor in the attitude of the South American Indian to the dead is the fear of their ghosts. The conclusion tallies perfectly with the result of our present inquiry.

That must conclude my brief survey of the general attitude of primitive man to the spirits of the dead in different parts of the world. We must now consider that attitude more in detail and endea-

[1] R. Karsten, *The Civilization of the South American Indians*, pp. 480 *sq.*

vour to understand more fully why primitive man both fears and reverences the spirits of the dead.

From what has preceded you will have gathered that in the opinion of the savage the spirits of the dead not only exist but in their disembodied state retain great powers, by virtue of which they are believed sometimes to benefit, but often to injure, the survivors. That is the root cause of the ambiguous attitude which uncivilized man commonly adopts towards the spirits of the departed. What, then, are the powers for good or evil which he commonly attributes to these potent but dangerous beings? what benefits does he hope for from their favour? what evils does he fear from their ill-will? In what follows I will endeavour to answer these questions; and as I am anxious to do no injustice to the primitive ghost by creating a prejudice against him, I will begin by enumerating some of the benefits he is supposed to confer on the living before I go on to describe some of the troubles and distresses which he is believed to inflict upon them.

In the first place, then, the ghosts are often thought to render a great variety of services to their surviving kinsfolk. Thus, for example, we are told of the Kiwai of British New Guinea that they " are all firm believers in the existence of their ancestors' spirits, that these take an interest in their daily lives, and that they are able to help or mar their undertakings. In all their ceremonies—for fighting, hunting, fishing, gardening—offerings are made and toasts drunk to their ancestors, who are earnestly and solemnly entreated to come to their aid on the projected enterprise. There is never a garden site chosen, a garden fence built, a yam planted or any fishing expedition undertaken without these spirits being called upon to bless and prosper the enterprise." [1]

Thus we see that the spirits of the dead are believed to be able, amongst other things, to aid the living in hunting and fishing, which are industries of capital importance for primitive man, who indeed subsisted mainly by them before he learned to till the ground. It is therefore not surprising to learn that among the benefits which the savage hopes to receive from his ancestral spirits help in hunting and fishing takes a foremost place. Hence at the opening of the turtle-fishing season, when the Kiwai perform a ceremony for the multiplication of turtle, they begin by cleaning up the burial-ground and placing food and pouring coconut milk on the graves for the dead, while they address the spirits, saying, " Give us turtle ; we give you food ". [2] And if a canoe returned unsuccessful from the turtle-fishing, the captain would at once go to his father's grave, clean it up, and pour coconut milk on it, saying, " We have cleaned your grave and given you a drink. Come with us." After that it was thought that next morning he would catch plenty of turtle. [3]

[1] E. Baxter Riley, *Among Papuan Headhunters* (London, 1925), p. 293.

[2] G. Landtman, *The Kiwai Papuans of British New Guinea*, p. 398 ; compare *id.*, p. 296 ; W. N. Beaver, *Unexplored New Guinea* (London, 1920), p. 305.

[3] E. Baxter Riley, *Among Papuan Headhunters*, pp. 125 *sq.*

And before they go out to harpoon dugong, the Kiwai invoke the spirits of their fathers and fore-fathers, saying, " Bring the dugong along for us to-morrow and do not let them return again to the sea ".[1]

In the Trobriand Islands, to the east of New Guinea, a magician who professes to control the fishing will sometimes make an offering of food to the spirits of the dead (*baloma*), saying, " Partake, O spirits, and make my magic thrive " ; or he will dream of an ancestral spirit and say in the morning, " The ancestral spirit has instructed me in the night, that we should go to catch fish ".[2] The natives of the South-East Solomon Islands believe that the ghosts control the bonito fishing, and that they will punish with bodily swellings the fishermen who neglect their worship. To avert this misfortune the fishermen offer coconuts to the ghosts.[3] The Belep, a tribe of New Caledonia, used to make offerings to the skulls of their ancestors and to invoke their spirits before they went out to fish on the reefs.[4]

The Galelarese of Halmahera, an island to the west of New Guinea, revere the souls of their dead ancestors as house-spirits or domestic deities, to whom they make offerings of food. Before a man goes out hunting he prays to these house-spirits, saying, " O spirits of my fathers, pray drive a little

[1] E. Baxter Riley, *Among Papuan Headhunters*, p. 131.

[2] B. Malinowski, *Argonauts of the Western Pacific*, pp. 422 sq.

[3] W. G. Ivens, *The Melanesians of the South-East Solomon Islands*, p. 373 ; compare *id.*, pp. 234, 311.

[4] Father Lambert, " Mœurs et Superstitions de la tribu Bélep ", *Les Missions Catholiques*, xii. (1880) p. 239.

herd or flock together towards us that we may find a little food, and we shall, if need be, at once bring you an offering from it ". But if the hunters come back with an empty bag, they are angry and say, " The house-spirits sit still there and do not drive the least herd together for us ".[1]

The Gonds of Gandla in Central India from time to time organize fishing expeditions in which all the men of a village take part. On such an occasion the women make a mound or platform in front of the house of the leader of the party, and on this platform the fish caught are afterwards laid. The leader thereupon distributes the fish among the people, leaving one fish on the platform. Next morning this fish is taken away and placed on the grave of the leader's ancestor, doubtless as a thank-offering to the dead man's spirit for the fish which he is supposed to have sent to the people. But if no fish are caught for several days, the villagers act very differently. The women go and dig up the platform in front of the leader's house and level it with the ground. Then early next morning all the people go to another village and there dance a certain dance, called the Sela dance, before the tombs of the ancestors of that village. The head-man of that village then levies a contribution on his people and gives the visitors food and drink and a present of money, with which the visitors buy liquor and, going home to their village, offer the liquor in

[1] M. J. van Baarda, " Fabelen, Verhalen en Overleveringen der Galelareezen ", *Bijdragen tot de* *Taal- Land- en Volkenkunde van* *Nederlandsch - Indie*, xlv. (1895) p. 524.

front of the platform which they had demolished. Next morning they go fishing again. Apparently in this elaborate ritual the platform represents the forefathers of the village, whose spirits are supposed to give success in fishing. If the fishers are unsuccessful, they demolish the platform to show their displeasure to the spirits, and then go and dance before the ancestors of another village to intimate the transference of their allegiance from their own ancestors to those of that other village. Their own ancestors will then feel themselves properly snubbed and discarded for their ill-nature in not giving success to the fishing-party. But when they have been in this chastened frame of mind for a few days, the headman of the other village sends them a present of liquor, which suffices to restore their good humour. Thus the spirits of the forefathers receive a salutary lesson, and the people hope that in future the spirits will be more careful of the welfare of their descendants.[1]

Before some of the mountain people of Formosa go out hunting, they invoke the spirits of their ancestors to give them good sport.[2] In Africa, when the Thonga are about to catch a certain fish in water infested by crocodiles, they make an offering to the spirits of their ancestors for protection against the crocodiles. And sometimes they employ a man of an aboriginal tribe to offer a fish to his ancestors, after which the Thonga chief proclaims in a loud

[1] R. V. Russell, *Tribes and Castes of the Central Provinces of India*, iii. 105-107.

[2] Shinji Ishii, " The Life of the Mountain People in Formosa ", *Folk-lore*, xxviii. (1917) p. 125.

voice, " Let the fish abound, and kill them all, but do not bewitch each other ".[1]   When a party of Thonga hunters return to a village after killing a lion, the headman meets them and sacrifices a hen to the ancestral spirits to thank them for having saved the hunters from the maw of the lion.[2]   And when a Thonga hunter has killed a hippopotamus, he prays to the ancestral spirits to give him many more such beasts.[3]

Before the Bakongo, a tribe of the Lower Congo, go out hunting they visit the grave of a great hunter.   There the leader or advocate, as he is called, goes first and kneels with his back to the grave and his face to the hunters. They approach him slowly, and on reaching him as he kneels they spread themselves out and dance round the grave to the rub-a-dub of a drum.   They have brought with them a calabash of palm wine, which they place on the grave.   Then the advocate turns towards the grave, and, shaking his rattle, he prays, saying : " You are blind, but your ears are not deaf. O ears, hear well ! We have come to you, we come kneeling. While you lived in the town, you ate and you drank, now we who are left die of hunger ; give us male and female animals."   Then he takes a cup of the palm wine and pours it out on the grave as an oblation to the famous hunter who sleeps the last sleep there.   The rest of the wine is drunk by the hunters sitting round the

---

[1] Henri A. Junod, *The Life of a South African Tribe*[2], ii. 88.

[2] Henri A. Junod, *op. cit.* ii. 62.

[3] Henri A. Junod, *op. cit.* ii. 71.

grave.[1] When a party of Bakongo hunters have killed an antelope, they catch the blood in a bladder and take it to the advocate, who pours it out on the grave of the great hunter, who is supposed to have heard their prayer and sent them the game.[2] And in this tribe a widow has been known to kneel on her husband's grave and tell him that the people were short of game, apparently in the hope that the ghost would take the hint and send the desired animals to the hunters.[3]

The Jen, a tribe of Northern Nigeria, believe that the spirits of their ancestors return to plague their living relatives who have not given them a proper burial or not kept their graves tidy. So at the beginning of the hunting season a hunter will go to the grave of his father or his paternal uncle, clean away the weeds, and pray to the following effect: " May the ghost (*ijang*) of you, my father, look after me well ; if I did evil in your lifetime I implore your forgiveness ; I have cleaned your grave. I am going on the morrow to the bush to hunt. The bush is not the town ; it is a place of death. Grant that I may have success in my hunting, or, at least, that I may return in safety." [4] And when a Jen hunter has killed a lion, he and his helpers take the lion's body to the graves of famous ancestors and laying it down there engage in a dance, apparently as a token of gratitude to

[1] John H. Weeks, *Among the Primitive Bakongo* (London, 1914), p. 182.
[2] John H. Weeks, *op. cit.* p. 183.
[3] R. P. van Wing, S.J., *Études Bakongo* (Bruxelles, N.D.), p. 282.
[4] C. K. Meek, *Tribal Studies in Northern Nigeria*, ii. 526.

the spirits of the dead for granting them this victory over the king of beasts.[1] Among the Teme, another tribe of Northern Nigeria, before a man goes out hunting he visits the grave of an ancestor and lays some porridge on it with a prayer for success in the chase.[2]

Far away from Africa, on the bleak shores of Bering Strait, the Eskimo believe that the souls of infants who have died at birth can render great services to the hunter in the chase. To secure such a ghostly helper a man will sometimes not hesitate to kill a child. But the murder must be secret, and he must contrive to steal the body so that no one knows of the foul play. Having secured the little corpse, he dries it, puts it in a bag, and wears it on his person, or carries it with him in the canoe when he is at sea. When a hunter carries one of these ghastly relics, it is believed that the ghost of the child, which is very sharp-sighted, will assist him in finding game and direct his spear in its flight so that it shall not miss the animal.[3]

So much for the help which the spirits of the dead are commonly believed by primitive man to give to the hunter and the fisher. They are further supposed, at a more advanced stage of culture, to aid the husbandman by promoting the fertility of the earth, whether in the shape of cereals or of fruit. To this branch of our subject we must now turn our attention for a short time.

[1] C. K. Meek, *Tribal Studies in Northern Nigeria*, ii. 522.
[2] C. K. Meek, *op. cit.* i. 494.
[3] E. W. Nelson, " The Eskimo about Bering Strait ", *Eighteenth Annual Report of the Bureau of American Ethnology*, Part I. (Washington, 1899) p. 429.

G

Thus when the natives of British New Guinea, in the neighbourhood of Port Moresby, begin planting, " they first take a bunch of bananas and sugar-cane, and go to the centre of the plantation, and call over the names of the dead belonging to their family, adding, ' There is your food, your bananas and sugar-cane ; let our food grow well, and let it be plentiful. If it does not grow well and plentiful, you all will be full of shame, and so shall we.' " [1] When the Kiwai of British New Guinea are making a yam-garden in ground which had been cultivated by their people in years gone by, they call on the spirits of their ancestors to help in making the fence and to produce an abundant harvest of yams.[2] And when every man has finished a ceremonial planting of four yams, they all stand erect alongside the garden fence, with bow and arrow in hand, and earnestly implore the assistance of the spirits of all their neighbours from north, south, east and west, concluding their appeal with the mention of their ancestors, who are requested to come and produce a good crop of yams. During this invocation an arrow is placed on every bow-string and held aloft as if the shaft were about to be shot away. Then the weapons are laid down and bull-roarers are whirled with a deafening noise.[3] When the Orokaiva of British New Guinea are burying a member of the tribe, before the body is

[1] J. Chalmers and W. Wyatt Gill, *Work and Adventure in New Guinea*, p. 85.

[2] E. Baxter Riley, *Among Papuan*

Headhunters, p. 93.

[3] E. Baxter Riley, *op. cit.* pp. 95 *sq.*

lowered into the grave, an elderly man addresses the deceased to the following effect : " Go now to a good place, not an evil one ; go to the road of the sunshine, not to the road of the rains ; go where there are neither mosquitoes nor marsh-flies, but where there are pigs in plenty and taro in plenty. Send us pigs and send us taro, and we shall make a feast in your honour." [1]

Similar beliefs and practices prevail in the northern portion of New Guinea which formerly belonged to Germany ; nor is this surprising, for the natives of New Guinea in general are settled people, subsisting by the cultivation of the ground and believing in the pervading influence of ancestral spirits. Thus the Yabim believe that in their field or garden labours they are dependent on the favour of the spirits of the dead (the *balum*). Before they plant taro in the ground which has been freshly cleared from the forest they pray to the spirits of the dead, saying, " Come not so often into the field, remain in the forest. Let the taro of the people who have helped us in clearing the field thrive well. Let the taro of everybody be very great ; and when we now plant our taro in the earth let it all grow luxuriantly." At first they plant only a few shoots of taro, and at the next planting they again invoke the spirits of the dead and seek to win their favour by offering them valuable objects, such as boars' tusks and dogs' teeth, with which the ghosts, like living men, are supposed to ornament themselves.

[1] F. E. Williams, *Orokaiva Society*, p. 214.

And to satisfy their more material wants they offer taro porridge to the spirits. Later in the season they swing bull-roarers in the field, uttering the names of the dead as they do so, in the belief that thereby they ensure especially good crops of all the fruits of the field.[1]

However, in this case there seems to be some ground for thinking that the help of the spirits in cultivating the land is conceived as rather negative than positive ; we have seen that the spirits are invited to stay in the forest and not to come so often into the field, which suggests that they are expected to abstain from injuring, rather than actively to promote, the growth of the crops. This is confirmed by other good evidence concerning the Yabim, from which it appears that their offerings to the ghosts are made for the purpose of inducing them to keep away and refrain from harming the growing crops.[2] The same conclusion is also suggested by the beliefs of the natives near Cape King William in what used to be German New Guinea. These people try to persuade the souls of the dead to avert all injurious influences that might hinder the growth of the yams, which are their staple food ; in particular, the spirits are expected to guard the fields against the incursions of wild boars and the devouring locusts.[3]

The Toradyas of Central Celebes believe that the

[1] H. Zahn, " Die Jabim ", in R. Neuhauss, *Deutsch Neu-Guinea* (Berlin, 1911), iii. 332 *sq.*

[2] See my *Belief in Immortality and the Worship of the Dead*, i.

(London, 1913) pp. 247 *sq.*

[3] Stoltz, " Die Umgebung von Kap König Wilhelm " in R. Neuhauss, *Deutsch Neu-Guinea*, iii. 245.

success or failure of the harvest depends on main-
taining a good understanding with the souls of the
dead ; [1] but here again the help of the spirits would
seem to be conceived as of a negative sort, for we
are told that the offerings of rice, maize, sugar-cane
and so forth which the Toradyas make to the spirits
of the dead at planting their rice-fields are intended
to induce the spirits not to injure the crops.[2]

The mountain tribes of Formosa worship the
spirits of their ancestors both at sowing and at
harvest.[3] Thus in regard to the Atayals or Taiyals,
a notorious tribe of head-hunters, we are told that
" after the rice or millet has been harvested, the
Atayals select a day, during the period of a full
moon, and worship their ancestors. A similar ceremony occurs when seed is sown. The first is to
express their gratitude for a bountiful harvest, which
they attribute to the spirits of their dead ancestors ;
and the second is to beseech a continuance of favour
in respect of the coming harvest. In such case the
ceremony is as follows. Every family makes from
the rice or millet they have harvested, cakes, which
they take during the darkness of night into the thick
wood and, wrapping them in leaves, suspend them
from the branches of trees. The spirits of their
ancestors are expected to partake of their offerings." [4]
Further details concerning the Atayal worship of

[1] N. Adriani en Alb. C. Kruijt,
*De Bare-sprekende Toradjas van
Midden-Celebes*, ii. 118.
[2] N. Adriani en Alb. C. Kruijt,
op. cit. ii. 249.

[3] James W. Davidson, *The Island
of Formosa* (London, 1903), pp.
567, 569, 571, 575, 579.
[4] J. W. Davidson, *op. cit.* p.
567.

ancestors at sowing and harvest have been furnished by a Japanese gentleman, Mr. Shinji Ishii, now deceased, who spent some years in Formosa studying the wild and little-known tribes of the mountains. I was personally acquainted with him during his stay in London, and from the abundant ethnological materials which he had collected in the island he furnished me with a number of legends of a great flood which he had taken down from the lips of the natives.[1] On the subject with which we are here concerned he tells us that among the Taiyals (Atayals) the ceremony of sowing marks the beginning of the new year. It is usually held between February and March of our calendar, when the moon is on the wane; a dark night is selected for the ceremony. When the day, or rather night, has been fixed by the chief, the men go out hunting, and the game they kill is kept for the coming feast, while the women are busy pounding rice and millet and brewing liquor. New fire is kindled by the friction of a drill and must be kept alight till the feast days are over. On the first day of the feast hundreds of small round cakes are baked at the chief's house, and when the night has come, men, one from each family, assemble at the chief's house. Accompanied by one or two of them the chief goes forth. The party carries torches and a basket containing seeds of rice, millet and sorghum, also a piece of boar's flesh and a tub of spirits. The chief himself carries a small hoe. At a short distance

[1] J. G. Frazer, *Folk-lore in the Old Testament*, i. 225 *sqq.*

from the house he digs a hole in the ground in which
he buries the seed and covers it up with earth. Close
beside it he digs another hole and deposits in it some
of the cakes and meat, after which he pours the
liquor on them. The spirits of the ancestors are
then worshipped with the following prayer : " We
now bury seed and meat ; kindly give us good crops
and plenty of game ". The party then return to the
chief's house with the remainder of the liquor and
cakes. When they reach the house, the people who
had remained behind come out to receive them,
while the chief pronounces the words, " A good crop
and plenty of game ". He then gives to each person
a portion of the cakes and liquor.[1]

After the harvest a ceremony is performed by
the Atayals which is called the worship of the
spirits of ancestors, because its intention is to offer
the new crop to them. On the morning of the day
appointed the chief cooks some millet, which is
made into dumplings, and each family sends a man
to the chief's house. Each of these men wraps one
of the dumplings in an oak leaf and ties it to a
branch of a tree which the chief had cut the day
before ; the branch is thus made to look as if it
were bearing a bunch of fruit. Carrying the branch
and followed by all the men, the chief then goes a
little way from the house and there ties the branch
to the bough of a big tree, while he prays to the
spirits of the dead, saying, " O spirits of our an-

[1] Shinji Ishii, " The Life of the   *Folk-lore*, xxviii. (1917) pp. 120-
Mountain People of Formosa ",   122.

cestors, come and help yourselves!"[1] The reason
for performing this ceremony at a big tree is apparently to convey the new millet of the harvest to
the ancestral spirits who live in the tree. Similarly
the Tsous, another mountain tribe of Formosa,
believe that the spirits of their ancestors inhabit a
big tree which grows near the entrance of each of
their villages.[2]

In most Naga tribes of North-East India " the
ancestral souls are regarded as directly responsible
for the crops if indeed they are not immanent in the
grain itself".[3] The Lakhers, another tribe of that
region on the borders of Arakan, perform a sacrifice
in October to the spirits of their ancestors to induce
them to make the crops abundant, the domestic
animals fertile and healthy, and to give good
hunting. At the same time the sacrifice is intended
to please the spirits of the rice and maize and to
prevent them from leaving the village. For this
ceremony the Lakhers make a broad road in front
of the village for the spirits of the dead to come
along, and when it is ready the men of the village
march in procession up and down the road, with
drums and gongs beating, to meet the unseen visitors
and escort them to the house where the sacrifice is
to take place. After this solemn march the Lakhers
of one particular village (Chapi) visit the graves of
all people who have died within the last three years

[1] Shinji Ishii, "The Life of the
Mountain People of Formosa",
Folk-lore, xxviii. (1917) p. 124.
[2] J. W. Davidson, The Island of

Formosa, p. 571.

[3] J. H. Hutton, note in N. E.
Parry, The Lakhers, p. 445.

and place handfuls of every kind of food and flour
on the graves for the spirits of the dead to eat.   The
sacrifice to the dead on this occasion consists of
seeds of every kind of food crop anointed with the
blood of a fowl.   It is deposited at the foot of the
main post at the back of the house.[1]   The Savars,
a primitive tribe of the Central Provinces in India,
" believe that the souls of those who die become
ghosts, and in Bundelkhand they used formerly to
bury the dead near their fields in the belief that the
spirits would watch over and protect the crops ".[2]

The same belief in the power of the spirits of
the dead to promote the fertility of the ground is
common in Africa.   We have seen that, in the opinion
of the Thonga, these potent spirits cause the fruit-
trees to bear fruit and the crops to be plentiful.[3]
An old Portuguese writer has recorded that the
Kafirs of South-East Africa, on the morning after
a burial " proceed to the grave of the deceased,
and pronouncing certain words they throw upon it
millet, beans and rice flour, with which they also
powder one cheek and an eye, and go about without
washing their faces until the flour has entirely disappeared.   By this ceremony they say that they
recommend their crops to the deceased, and they
believe that in this their souls can be of use to them
and grant good harvests." [4]

[1] N. E. Parry, *The Lakhers*
(London, 1932), pp. 445 *sq.*

[2] R. V. Russell, *Tribes and Castes
of the Central Provinces of India*,
iv. 507.

[3] H. A. Junod, *Life of a South
African Tribe*[2], ii. 386.   See above,
p. 51.

[4] J.   Dos   Santos,   " Ethiopia
Oriental ", in G. McCall Theal,
Records of South-Eastern Africa,
vii. (London, 1901) pp. 308 *sq.*

The Bavenda of the Northern Transvaal invoke and propitiate the ancestral spirits before sowing and reaping the corn. In October or November, when the land is ready for sowing, a pot, containing seeds of eleusine, Kafir corn and all the other crops that are to be sown, is carried to the corn-field where the family has assembled. There a priestess, who is usually the father's sister (*makhadzi*) of the head of the family, addresses the ancestral spirits, saying, " Here is food for you, all our spirits ; we give you of every kind of grain, which you may eat. Bring to us also crops in plenty and prosperity in the coming season." [1] And at the harvest-thanksgiving the priestess, in presence of the assembled family, again addresses the ancestral spirits, saying, " I offer you the first grain of the new year that you may eat and be happy ; eat all of you ; I deprive none amongst you. What remains in the ground belongs to me and your little ones. Let them eat and be happy." [2]

The Barea of East Africa celebrate a festival in honour of the dead by way of thanksgiving every year in November after the harvest. Every household brews much beer for the day, and a small pot of the beer is set apart for every dead member of the family and kept for two days, after which the beer is drunk by the living. [3]

The Kam, a tribe of Northern Nigeria, believe that the dead ancestors of their chief are the life

[1] H. A. Stayt, *The Bavenda* (London, 1931), pp. 252 *sq.*
[2] H. A. Stayt, *op. cit.* p. 255.
[3] W. Munzinger, *Ostafrikanische Studien* (Schaffhausen, 1864), p. 473.

and soul of the crops ; hence the chief performs a daily ritual for the purpose of feeding these his royal forefathers, addressing them thus : " You are my forefathers. Once upon a time you did as I now do. If it were not so, then may my offering be of no account before you. But if you did as I now do, then accept this offering, that I and my people may be blessed with corn and health." So saying, he spits into a ladleful of beer and passes it to an official, who pours the beer as a libation into a well in the shrine. It is said that if this ritual were not observed daily the crops would wither.[1] In like manner the Namas, another tribe of Northern Nigeria, believe that the success of agricultural operations depends on the good-will of the royal ancestors, especially of the chief who died last. Hence after sowing, and also in times of drought, it is the Nama custom to perform rites at the graves of former chiefs. The duties are delegated by the chief to a priest in whose family the priesthood is hereditary. The priest goes to the graves and, after a prayer for a successful season and general prosperity, pours a libation on each of the grave-stones.[2]

In some tribes of Northern Nigeria the power of promoting the growth of the crops is not restricted to the ancestors of chiefs ; it is attributed to the ancestral spirits of commoners as well. Thus among the Abo, at the ripening of the Guinea-corn crops,

---

[1] C. K. Meek, *Tribal Studies in Northern Nigeria*, ii. 540 *sq.*
[2] C. K. Meek, *op. cit.* ii. 559.

the head of a household takes some porridge and fish-stew to the family graveyard and attracts the attention of his dead forefathers by smacking a leaf in the hollow of his left hand. Having thus got their ear, he pours a libation of beer, deposits some of the porridge and stew on the ground, and prays the ancestors that the harvest may be bountiful.[1] The Mumuye, another tribe of the same region, preserve the skulls of their dead forefathers in pots, and just before the harvest the head of the household brings out the skulls and pours a libation of chicken's blood and beer on them, praying for a good harvest.[2] Again, among the Yendang, another tribe of this region, when the crops have been gathered, the priest prepares a special brew of beer and goes to the grave of his father, where he pours a libation, saying, " The food which we sought at your hand has been given to us in plenty. We thank you, and we bring you your share." He goes also to the grave of his mother and pours a libation there. All heads of households do likewise.[3] Once more, the Hona, another tribe of Northern Nigeria, make offerings to their ancestors at sowing and harvest ; but if the year has been a bad one the offerings may be withheld. In that case the head of the family enters the shrine of the defaulting ghosts and upbraids them, saying, " This year I will give you nothing, as you have hindered us. We did well by you, but you have done ill by us."[4]

[1] C. K. Meek, *Tribal Studies in Northern Nigeria*, ii. 565 *sq.*

[2] C. K. Meek, *op. cit.* i. 469 *sq.*

[3] C. K. Meek, *op. cit.* i. 486.

[4] C. K. Meek, *op. cit.* ii. 403.

In their worship of ancestors these people clearly go on the principle of payment by results.

A similar faith in the power of the ancestral spirits to make or mar the fruits of the earth prevails widely also among the tribes of the French Sudan, and it finds similar expression in ceremonies of prayer, thanksgiving and worship offered to these spirits at sowing and harvest. The belief and the worship have been recorded by a French administrator, but I will spare you the details, which would be substantially a repetition of the evidence I have adduced from the neighbouring province of Northern Nigeria.[1]

[1] L. Tauxier, *Le Noir du Soudan, pays Mossi et Gourounsi* (Paris, 1912), pp. 70 *sq.*, 104, 189 *sq.*, 191, 237, 270, 322, 323, 356

LECTURE IV

LECTURE IV

In the last lecture I showed that the spirits of the dead are believed by many peoples to promote the fertility of the ground, either positively by the generative virtue they possess, or negatively by guarding the crops against the noxious influences which might otherwise injure or destroy them. Where such beliefs prevail, the spirits of the dead are naturally supposed to possess a proprietary right in the fruits of the earth which entitles them to receive an offering of the first-fruits before the living may partake of the new crop. Elsewhere I have collected some evidence of the custom of offering first-fruits to the dead.[1] I will not repeat it all here but shall content myself with citing a few typical examples.

The South-East Solomon Islanders are among the peoples who strive to keep the souls of the dead beside them in the house. For this purpose, when a death has taken place, they angle for the ghost of the deceased with a sort of little fishing-rod, and, having caught it, they put it, together with some bodily relic of the dead man, such as his

[1] *Spirits of the Corn and of the Wild*, ii. 109 *sqq.*

skull or jawbone or a tooth or a lock of hair, in a case which is deposited in a corner of the dwelling-house. Each householder hangs up offerings of first-fruits beside these cases, which are supposed to contain the souls as well as the bodily relics of his dead kinsfolk.[1] In these islands, when the Canarium nuts were ripe, nobody might eat of them till the first-fruits had been sacrificed to the dead.[2] Similarly when the yams are ripe, the people fetch some of them from the gardens to offer to the ghosts. A man goes to the sacred place and cries with a loud voice to the ghost, "This is yours to eat". So saying, he lays down the yam beside the dead man's skull.[3]

In Viti Levu, the largest of the Fijian Islands, there was a Sacred Place, called the Nanga, where the ancestral spirits were to be found by their worshippers, and whither offerings were taken on all occasions when the aid of the spirits was to be invoked. Thither accordingly the first-fruits of the yam harvest were carried and presented to the ancestors with great ceremony before the bulk of the crop was dug for the people's use, and no man might taste of the new yams until the presentation had been made to the dead. If any one were impious enough to appropriate the yams to his own use before the ancestors had received their proper share, it was thought that he would be smitten with madness.[4]

---

[1] W. G. Ivens, *The Melanesians of the South East Solomon Islands*, p. 178; compare *id.*, pp. 210, 216.

[2] R. H. Codrington, *The Melanesians*, pp. 132 *sq.*

[3] R. H. Codrington, *op. cit.* p. 138.

[4] Lorimer Fison, "The Nanga, or Sacred Stone Enclosure of Wainimala, Fiji", *Journal of the Anthropological Institute*, xiv. (1885) pp. 26 *sq.*

The Oraons of India offer the first-fruits of the
upland rice and of *Panicum miliare* to the ancestral
spirits at their two annual festivals ; these offerings
must be made to the dead before the living may
partake of the new crops.[1] Among the Birhors, a
primitive jungle tribe of India, no man will eat
certain edible flowers and fruits and upland rice till
he has offered the first-fruits of the season to his
ancestral spirits. Similarly he will not sip honey
from certain first flowers of the season till he has
offered a few drops to the souls of his forefathers.[2]

Among the Thonga of South-East Africa the
regular national offering is that of the first-fruits to
the ancestral spirits. The Bantu conception of
hierarchy is clearly illustrated by this custom ;
the ancestral spirits or gods, as M. Junod calls
them, must be the first to enjoy the produce of the
new year, then the chief, the sub-chiefs, the coun-
sellors, the headmen, then the younger brothers in
order of age. There is a stringent taboo directed
against anybody who presumes to precede his
superiors in the enjoyment of the first-fruits. The
law applies to Kafir corn or Kafir plums in certain
clans, and to sorghum, pumpkin leaves, beer and
so forth in others.[3] In offering the first-fruits of the
Kafir corn to his ancestral spirits the chief addresses
these august beings, saying, " Here has the new

[1] Sarat Chandra Roy, *Oraon
Religion and Customs*, p. 33. Com-
pare F. Hahn, " Some Notes on
the Religion and Superstitions of the
Orãos ", *Journal of the Asiatic
Society of Bengal*, lxxii. Part iii.
(Calcutta, 1904) p. 13.

[2] Sarat Chandra Roy, *The Birhors*, pp. 112, 520.

[3] H. A. Junod, *The Life of a
South African Tribe*[2], ii. 403 *sq.*

year come! Precede us, you gods, and eat the first-fruits (*luma*), so that for us also Kafir corn shall help our body, that we may become fat, not thin, that the witches may increase the corn, make it to be plentiful, so that, even if there is only a small field, big baskets may be filled!"[1] And when the first ripe Kafir plums are gathered, the sour liquor obtained from them is poured out on the graves of the dead Thonga chiefs in the sacred wood, and the souls of the chiefs are invoked to bless the new year and the feast which is about to be celebrated.[2]

The Ba-ila of Northern Rhodesia have not, like the Thonga and other Bantu tribes, a tribal or national festival of first-fruits, but before eating of the new maize every man offers some of the fresh cobs privately to his ancestral spirits, placing them above the door and in the rafters of his hut, thereby expressing his gratitude to the spirits, and his hope of similar blessings in the future.[3] But before he makes this domestic offering he takes some new ripe cobs of maize to the grave of an ancestor and kneeling before it says, "So-and-so, here is some of the maize which is ripe first and which I offer to thee".[4]

Among the Yombe of Northern Rhodesia nobody might eat of the first-fruits of the new crops until the chief had sacrificed a bull before the grave of

[1] H. A. Junod, *The Life of a South African Tribe*[2], i. 396.
[2] H. A. Junod, *op. cit.* i. 397.
[3] E. W. Smith and A. M. Dale, *The Ila-speaking Peoples of Northern Rhodesia*, i. 139 *sq.*
[4] E. W. Smith and A. M. Dale, *op. cit.* ii. 179 *sq.*

his grandfather, and had deposited pots of beer and porridge, made from the first-fruits, in front of the shrine. After thanking the ghost of his grandfather for the harvest, and praying him to partake of the first-fruits, the chief and his followers withdrew to feast on the fresh porridge and beer at the village.[1] Among the Konde of Lake Nyasa the first cobs of maize of the new harvest are taken to the chief, who offers them to his ancestors, usually at the place where the trees of the village stand. The heads of families then offer some of the new maize to their own ancestors and, curiously enough, to twins. Not until these offerings have been made to the spirits of the dead may the people eat the new season's crops.[2]

The A-Kamba, a tribe of Kenya, in East Africa, offer the first-fruits of every crop to their ancestral spirits before anybody dare eat of the new crop. Sometimes the offerings are piled on the graves of chiefs ; sometimes they are deposited in a clearing under the sacred wild fig-tree, for the A-Kamba think that the spirits of the dead dwell in wild fig-trees, and they build miniature huts at the foot of the trees for the ghosts to dwell in. The clearing under the fig-tree is called the Place of Prayer. When any crop is ripe, the people assemble, and an old man and woman go to the Place of Prayer, and there calling aloud to the spirits of the dead, ask their permission to eat of the new crop. The people

[1] C. Gouldsbury and H. Sheane, *The Great Plateau of Northern Rhodesia* (London, 1911), pp. 294 *sq.*

[2] D. R. Mackenzie, *The Spirit-ridden Konde*, p. 120.

then dance, and during the dance some woman is sure to be seized with a fit of shaking and to cry out, which is taken to be an answer of the spirits to the people's prayer.[1]

Among the Bura of Northern Nigeria, at the maize harvest, every man who has lost a father or mother chooses three heads of corn, dresses them carefully, and places them on a tray, which he sets by his head at night, and during the night the spirits of the dead father and mother are thought to come and eat the soul of the corn. No man of the tribe will eat fresh corn till he has performed this rite with the first-fruits.[2] The Igbiras, a pagan tribe at the confluence of the Niger and the Benue, bury, or used to bury, their dead in their houses and have great faith in the power of ghosts, to whom they offer the first-fruits of their crops, hanging bunches of the new grain over the burial-places in their huts.[3]

Closely connected with the belief that the spirits of the dead possess the power of fertilizing the earth and promoting the growth of the crops is the belief that these spirits can give or withhold rain at their pleasure ; for everywhere vegetation depends for its very existence on water, and in most countries water is, in the last resort, obtained mainly or exclusively in the form of rain. Hence in dry and

[1] C. W. Hobley, *Ethnology of A-Kamba and other East African Tribes* (Cambridge, 1910), pp. 66, 85 *sq.*

[2] C. K. Meek, *Tribal Studies in Northern Nigeria*, i. 161.

[3] A. F. Mockler-Ferryman, *Up the Niger* (London, 1892), pp. 141 *sq.*

arid regions, where the rainfall is scanty and precarious, and where often not a drop falls for months together, the coming of the rain is a matter of the most anxious concern to the natives, to whom a long drought may bring famine, suffering and death. Accordingly, when they believe that the rain is controlled by the spirits of the dead, we need not wonder that the inhabitants are eager to cultivate the good graces of the departed and appeal to them earnestly for help whenever the expected rain is long delayed.

For example, among the Toradyas of Central Celebes there is a certain village where there is the grave of a famous chief. When the land suffers from unseasonable drought, the people go to the grave, pour water on it, and say, " O grandfather, have pity on us ; if it is your will that this year we should eat, then give rain ". After that they hang a bamboo full of water over the grave ; in the lower end of the bamboo there is a small hole, from which the water drips continually. The bamboo is always refilled with water till rain falls.[1] In this ceremony the religious appeal to the compassion of the dead chief is reinforced by dripping water on his grave, which is essentially a magical rite supposed to produce the desired effect by imitating it.

But it is in Africa, where the belief in the power of ancestral spirits is most deeply felt and most widely acknowledged, that we find these spirits most

[1] A. C. Kruijt, " Regen lokken en regen verdrijving bij de Toradjas van Central Celebes ", *Tijdschrift voor* *Indische Taal- Land- en Volkenkunde*, xliv. (1901) p. 6, citing v. Baarda.

commonly looked to for a due supply of rain. Thus, for example, the Thonga believe that the spirits of the ancestors cause the rain to fall. So, if the spring showers do not come in due time, the first thought of the people will be to offer a sacrifice to their ancestors, especially if the diviner, by means of his divining bones, has announced that the anger of the ancestors is the real cause of the drought. Thereupon men will go to the sacred wood where the ancestors are buried, and there they will chant an ancient mourning song, and some of them will beat the graves with sticks. Also, they will sacrifice a black ram, without any white spot on it, and shed its blood all over the ground. In many of these sacred woods human victims are said to have been formerly offered to the ghosts of chiefs on these occasions.[1]

Among the Bechuanas, when rain is long delayed, it is deemed necessary to sacrifice a sheep or goat or a more costly victim at the grave of a distinguished and still revered or dreaded ancestor. The sacrifice is accompanied by a prayer to the spirit of the dead man, begging him to look on the distress of his children and to come to their aid.[2] Similarly, when a drought had lasted a long time, the Herero of South-West Africa used to go in a body with their cattle to the grave of some eminent man, it might be the father or grandfather of the chief. There they would lay offerings of milk and

[1] H. A. Junod, *The Life of a South African Tribe*[2], ii. 316, 405.

[2] J. Tom Brown, *Among the Bantu Nomads*, p. 131.

flesh on the grave and pray, saying, " Look, O
Father, upon your beloved cattle and children ;
they suffer distress, they are so lean, they are dying
of hunger. Give us rain." But the voice of the
supplicant was almost drowned in the lowing of the
cattle, the bleating of the flocks, the barking of dogs,
the shouts of the herdsmen, and the screams of the
women.[1]

In like manner the Bavenda of the Northern
Transvaal usually trace the failure of rain to the
anger of their ancestors. When the identity of the
particular ancestor who is causing the drought has
been discovered by divination, the people are summoned to dance a certain sacred dance, either in a
village within hearing of the grave of the offended
forefather or in the forest near his tomb. The chief,
accompanied by his kinsfolk, then repairs to the
grave, and after laying the stomach of a sacrificed
ox on it, beseeches the spirit to stay his anger, and
not to let the earth grow hot, and cause his descendants to perish for want of water.[2]

So, again, among the Banyamwezi, when the
rain is unduly delayed and the crops are in danger,
the official rain-maker or diviner will visit the king
and propose to appease the wrath of the royal
ancestors by offering bloody sacrifices on their
tombs. If the king consents, the sacrifice of a bull

<hr />

[1] P. H. Brincker, " Beobachtung-
en über die Deisidämonie der
Eingeborenen Deutsch - Südwest-
Afrikas ", *Globus*, lviii. (1890) p.
323 ; *id.*, in *Mitteilungen des*
Seminars für orientalische Sprachen
zu Berlin, iii. (1900) Dritte Abteilung,
p. 89.
[2] H. A. Stayt, *The Bavenda*, p.
310.

or a he-goat is solemnly performed at the royal graves, which are often under the shadow of great trees.[1] Similarly many tribes of Northern Nigeria ascribe a prolonged drought to the displeasure of the royal ancestors. When that calamity happens in the country of the Zumu, the grave-diggers and custodians of the royal tombs are called on to inspect the graves of former chiefs, and if they find, as they commonly do, that one of the graves has been neglected, the head of the grave-diggers takes immediate steps to repair the neglect. When that has been done, he lays an offering of pumpkins on the grave of the chief who died last, apologizes to him for the neglect, and prays him to send the needed rain.[2]

The Malabu, another tribe of Northern Nigeria, are wont to detach the skull of a dead chief in the spring after the burial, and to preserve it, with the other royal skulls, in a hut set apart for that purpose. When a fresh skull has thus been added to the collection in the royal charnel-house, the head of a certain kindred addresses it, saying, " To-day we have brought you home, so that you may not be left abandoned in the bush. Hinder us not, therefore, from obtaining sufficient rain this season, and send not sickness amongst us." He then pours a libation of beer over the skull, and all hasten home ; for it is believed that on the conclusion of these rites, which coincide with the beginning of the rainy

---

[1] Fr. Bösch, *Les Banyamwezi*, pp. 149 *sqq.*

[2] C. K. Meek, *Tribal Studies in Northern Nigeria*, i. 75.

season, rain will immediately fall. If this does not happen for several days, resort is had to a professional diviner to ascertain the cause. The sage generally declares that the people had offended the late chief on some occasion during his life, and that therefore the angry ghost is holding up the rain. All the seniors, accordingly, accompanied by the new chief, go to the royal skull-hut and tender a formal apology to the ghost, after which rain is sure to follow sooner or later.[1] In the Gola tribe of the same region it is a custom for some senior man, acting on behalf of the community, to offer a prayer for rain before the skull of a man who was reputed to have been a centenarian. The petitioner holds a chicken up to the midday sun and addresses the ghost of the centenarian as follows : " God gave you food so that you lived a hundred years. May we also have food and live to a ripe old age. Behold, our crops are parched for want of rain. We beseech you to ask God to send us rain, so that we and our children may not perish. You cannot speak to us, but you can see us ; so help us, we beseech you." He then kills the chicken and pours the blood over the pot containing the skull.[2]

Thus we see that the spirits of the dead are commonly supposed to possess the power of quickening or blasting the fruits of the earth by giving or withholding rain. Sometimes it is believed that

---

[1] C. K. Meek, *Tribal Studies in Northern Nigeria*, i. 109.
[2] C. K. Meek, *op. cit.* i. 478.

they can also render a woman barren or make her the joyful mother of children. Among the Lakhers of North-Eastern India, when a wife whose parents are dead is childless, the misfortune is ascribed to the displeasure of her deceased father and mother, who are preventing her from having offspring. So to appease their angry spirits a fowl is sacrificed and cooked with rice, and the meat and rice are placed on the graves of the barren woman's parents. And if a wife's father-in-law and mother-in-law are dead, their spirits can also prevent her from having children should they happen to have a grudge at her. In that case it is necessary to propitiate their spirits also with the sacrifice of a fowl.[1] Similarly in Imerina, a province of Madagascar, when a woman does not conceive for a certain time after marriage, she consults a diviner, who, after examining his divining apparatus, informs her which of the ancient inhabitants of the land, or which of her own ancestors is offended with her, and what sacrifice she must offer to appease the angry spirit of the dead in order to obtain a child. For the Merina believe, we are informed, that the commerce of the sexes is by no means essential to the birth of children, which is the work of God and of the ancestors. So after praying and anointing with fat the tomb of an ancestor or of one of the aboriginal inhabitants of the land, the woman who desires to have a child takes a little of the fat from the grave home and rubs it on her belly, believing that in this way the

[1] N. E. Parry, *The Lakhers* (London, 1932), p. 380.

wish of her heart will be granted.[1] The Kwottos of
Northern Nigeria, who believe in the reincarnation
of the dead, think that unless an ancestral spirit
consents to enter a woman's womb she cannot conceive a child. Hence a barren woman consults a
medicine-man and begs him to mediate for her with
the ancestral spirits who are supposed to be responsible for the calamity ; or at least she asks him to
ascertain the cause and prescribe the remedy,
whether that is to be effected by penitence or propitiation.[2] In this tribe the male ancestor who is
believed to be reborn in a woman is usually a deceased grandfather.[3] Holding this view of the
spiritual origin of childbirth, a Kwotto woman will
sometimes make a pilgrimage to a sacred place
known to be haunted by ghosts, in the hope of per-
suading some ghost to enter into her womb and be
born again.[4] Hence, too, before a child is born, the
Kwottos sacrifice fowls and beer to the ancestral
ghosts to induce them to aid the expectant mother
in her hour of need.[5] Similar beliefs as to the
essential part played by ancestral spirits in the birth
of children appear to be held by the Banyamwezi.
Once when a missionary asked a member of the
tribe, " Why do you worship your ancestral spirits
as if they were your gods and you were their
creatures ? " the man replied, " Do you think that

[1] A. Grandidier et G. Grandidier, *Ethnographie de Madagascar*, ii. (Paris, 1914) pp. 245 *sq.*

[2] J. R. Wilson-Haffenden, *The Red Men of Nigeria* (London, 1930), pp. 185 *sq.*

[3] J. R. Wilson-Haffenden, *op. cit.* p. 236.

[4] J. R. Wilson-Haffenden, *op. cit.* p. 237.

[5] J. R. Wilson-Haffenden, *op. cit.* p. 245.

a woman could bear a child if the ancestral spirits did not wish it ? " [1]

Another important service which the spirits of the dead are believed to be able to render to the living is success or victory in war. When war threatened the country of the Thonga, the general of the army used to take a large thorn of a certain kind of tree (*Acacia horrida*) and after sucking it he would spit out, saying, " You, the ancestor-gods, So-and-so, enemies wish to take your country ! Give us valour ! May we stab them with this thorn, with the assegai ! " [2] Speaking of the Bantu tribes of South Africa in general, a good authority says that " the ancestral spirits are interceded with, and begged to help in the war ; indeed many natives seem to think that there is far more real warfare among the ancestral spirits than among the actual warriors. . . . These ancestral spirits are sometimes supposed to be fighting in the air just above the heads of the people, and if only the warriors can be persuaded that their ancestral spirits are with them they will fight with immense bravery and con-fidence." [3] In the old days, when the Awemba of Northern Rhodesia were about to go to war, the king and the elders used to pray daily for victory to the spirits of the dead kings, his predecessors. In the dusk of the evening, on the day before the army set out, the king and the elderly women, who passed for the wives of the dead kings and tended their

[1] Fr. Bösch, *Les Banyamwezi*,
p. 161.
[2] H. A. Junod, *The Life of a*

South African Tribe [2], ii. 405.
[3] Dudley Kidd, *The Essential
Kafir* (London, 1904), p. 307.

shrines, went and prayed at their shrines that the souls of the departed monarchs would keep the warpath free from foes and lead the king in a straight course to the enemy's stockade. These solemn prayers the king led in person, and the women beat their breasts as they joined in the earnest appeal to the dead.[1]

The natives of New Caledonia used to catch the soul of a famous warrior after death and enclose it in a stone which the priest was supposed to carry with him to battle ; but as the stone was heavy the priest contented himself with attaching to his wrist a small round stone which represented the big one that contained the dead warrior's soul. Thus borne to battle by deputy, the spirit of the deceased champion was no doubt supposed to nerve his people to fresh deeds of courage in the fight.[2] Among the Sea Dyaks of Borneo the bodies of mighty warriors were sometimes buried for a time and then exhumed, and their remains kept as sacred relics by their descendants in or near their houses, or it might be on the spur of a neighbouring hill, for the purpose of securing the dead heroes as guardian spirits, whose protection might naturally be looked for above all in time of war.[3] For of the Sea Dyaks in general we are told that " before going forth on an expedition against the enemy, the dead are invoked, and

[1] J. H. West Sheane, " Wemba Warpaths ", *Journal of the African Society*, No. xli. (October 1911) pp. 25 *sq.*

[2] M. Leenhardt, *Notes d'Ethnologie Néo-Calédoniennes* (Paris, 1930), pp. 214 *sq.*

[3] Rev. J. Perham, " Sea Dyak Religion ", *Journal of the Straits Branch of the Royal Asiatic Society*, No. 14 (December 1884), p. 293.

are begged to help their friends on earth, so that they may be successful against their foes ".[1]   In Tobelo, a district in the north of Halmahera, an island to the west of New Guinea, when the people are going to war, the soothsayer prepares a warrior for the combat by supplying him with the soul of a brave ancestor.   In order to do this he throws the man into a sort of swoon, combined with a fit of shivering, and while the patient is in this state, the sage attaches the soul of the deceased warrior to his living descendant.   The soul does not enter into his body nor pass into his blood, but sits astraddle on his neck with its legs hanging down in front on the man's shoulders.   It is not seen or felt by the man himself, and after the battle it flies away, still invisible.   A soldier who is thus reinforced by the soul of a gallant ancestor is sure to kill his adversary in the fight.[2]

But it is not merely to the souls of dead ancestors that the savage resorts for help in war ; he can press the souls of his dead enemies into the same service. The Kiwai of British New Guinea know how to recruit their forces by these unwilling allies.   In the central hall of any one of their club-houses, which are reserved for the use of the men, may be seen two small holes, and in each of the holes is the dried eye of an enemy killed in battle.   Spirits of slain

---

[1] E. H. Gomes, *Seventeen Years among the Sea Dyaks of Borneo* (London, 1911), p. 142.

[2] F. S. A. de Clercq, " Dodads Ma-taoe en Goma Ma-taoe, of Zielenhuisjes in het district Tobélo op Noord-halmahera ", *Internationales Archiv für Ethnographie*, ii. (1889) p. 210; W. Kükenthal, *Forschungsreise in den Molukken und in Borneo* (Frankfurt a. M., 1896), p. 177.

foes are supposed to inhabit the two eyes, and when the builders of the house go forth to war these spirits are thought to possess the power of capturing the souls of the enemy, thus making them weak and impotent, and giving the attacking party an easy victory. In the discharge of this useful office the spirits are supposed to precede the fighting men and to prepare the way for them.[1]

The Bataks, a barbarous people living in the interior of the great island of Sumatra, have, or rather perhaps formerly had, a still stranger and more tragic mode of pressing spiritual recruits into the fighting line. They believed that if anybody made a solemn promise to aid them in battle and died immediately after giving the promise, his disembodied soul would prove a powerful ally in war, striking terror into the breasts of the foe. To procure such an ally they proceeded thus. A lad of some twelve or fifteen years was procured by purchase or violence, and outside the village, generally in the neighbouring forest, he was buried in the ground up to the neck with his arms at his sides. There for four days he was fed with rice strongly seasoned with pepper and salt to make him very thirsty. From time to time his tormentors asked him whether he would bless them and help them in war. At first he naturally refused and threatened rather to curse and injure them. On the fourth day the principal men gathered about him and sought by all sorts of flattering words to wheedle the desired

_____
[1] E. Baxter Riley, *Among Papuan Headhunters*, pp. 88, 90.

I

promise of blessing and help out of him. Meantime a man at the lad's back was busy melting lead. At last, driven to despair by his intolerable sufferings, the victim yielded and said, " My spirit or soul shall guard you ". No sooner were the words uttered than the man behind the boy drew back the victim's head and poured the molten lead into his open mouth. Thus the lad died a sudden death and was prevented from retracting his promise. After dying such a death his soul, it was supposed, would become a mischievous demon, but, bound by his promise not to injure his murderers, he would wreak his vengeance only on their enemies. That he might do so with greater effect, portions of his brain, heart and liver were extracted from his body, and a salve compounded from them was inserted in a magical staff, which was entrusted to a sorcerer. When a war broke out, a sacrifice was offered to the soul of the murdered lad, represented by the magical staff, which was carried to battle at the head of the troop, the soul of the dead lad marching grimly with them against the enemy.[1]

Far less barbarous than this was the custom of the Muyscas, an Indian tribe in the ancient province of Cundinamarca, which now forms part of the State of Colombia in South America. Marching to battle, the Muyscas used to carry, at the head of their regiments, the embalmed bodies of their ancient heroes. This custom, we are told, pre-

[1] J. M. Meerwaldt, " De Bataksche Tooverstaf ", *Bijdragen tot de Taal- Land- en Volkenkunde* *van Nederlandsch-Indie*, liii. (1901) pp. 302-304.

vented them from retreating, for they esteemed it the height of infamy to allow the bodies of their ancestors to fall into the hands of the enemy.[1] We are not told, but may reasonably presume, that the souls of these dead heroes were supposed to accompany their bodies to the fight. The idea that the spirits of the fathers rise from their graves to fight the battles of their children is one that naturally occurs to primitive man : it is not entirely alien to Englishmen of to-day, or at least of yesterday. In the poet's address to the mariners of England he says,

> The spirits of your fathers
> Shall start from every wave—
> For the deck it was their field of fame,
> And Ocean was their grave.

That concludes what I have to say as to the aid which the souls of the dead are thought to give to their descendants in war.

We now pass to a service of a different kind which the spirits of the dead are commonly supposed to render to their surviving kinsfolk by giving them counsel and advice in times of doubt, danger or distress. In short, the spirits of the dead are often consulted as oracles by the living. Elsewhere I have treated this part of our subject at some length.[2] Here it must suffice to cite a few typical cases.

The oracles of the dead are commonly supposed

---

[1] H. Ternaux-Compans, *Essai sur l'ancien Cundinamarca* (Paris, Librairie A. Bertrand, N.D.), pp. 66 *sq.* Compare A. de Herrera, *The General History of the Vast Continent and Islands of America*, translated by Captain Stevens (London, 1725), v. 86.

[2] *Folk-Lore in the Old Testament*, ii. 517 *sqq.*

to be imparted either directly by the ghost or indirectly by a medium, a living person who is
believed to be possessed by the spirit of the dead
and to speak with his voice or at least in his name.
Sometimes the communication is effected by means
of an image of the dead, sometimes by means of one
of his bodily relics, especially the skull, less often a
jawbone.

The oracular function of ghosts may be illustrated
by the beliefs and practices of the Melanesians.
These people believe that the knowledge of future
events is conveyed to them by a spirit or ghost
speaking with the voice of a living man, one of the
wizards, who is himself unconscious while he speaks.
In the island of Florida, for example, men might
be sitting in their canoe-house discussing an expedition, perhaps to attack some unsuspecting village.
One among them, known to have his ghost of
prophecy, would sneeze and begin to shake, a sign
that the ghost had entered into him ; his eyes would
glare, his limbs twist, his whole body be convulsed,
and foam would burst from his lips ; then a voice,
apparently not his own, would be heard from his
throat, approving or disapproving of what was
proposed.   Such a man used no means of bringing
the ghost on him ; it came on him, as he believed,
of its own free will ; its ghostly power overmastered
him, and when it departed it left him quite exhausted.[1]   Again, we are told that, in the belief of
the Melanesians, ghosts make known to men who

[1] R. H. Codrington, *The Melanesians*, p. 209.

use them secret things which the unaided human
intelligence could not find out. In the Solomon
Islands, for instance, when an expedition has started
in a fleet of canoes, there is sometimes a hesitation
whether they shall proceed, or a question in what
direction they shall go. While they are hesitating,
a man who knows the ghosts may say that a ghost
has just stepped on board, for did not the canoe tip
over to one side, weighed down by the invisible
passenger ? So he asks the ghost, " Shall we
proceed ? Shall we go to such and such a place ? "
If the canoe rocks, the answer is yes ; if it lies on
an even keel, the answer is no.[1]

In the Solomon Islands both men and women
can be possessed and inspired by ghosts, and there
are professional mediums whose services are employed when any one wishes to ascertain the cause
of sickness in a particular case. A deputation is
sent to such a person on behalf of the sick, and the
sage straightway falls into a trance, and speaks
with the voice of the ghost that has taken possession
of him or her, saying, " I am So-and-so ", naming
the person whose ghost is supposed to be speaking.
For instance, at Sa'a there was a man named
Soiolo who used to be possessed by the ghost of a
woman called the Twin's Wife. The paroxysms
would come on him quite suddenly, but they were
generally associated with bad health or nervous
prostration. The utterances of the Twin's Wife by
his mouth were all of trouble and confusion and

[1] R. H. Codrington, *The Melanesians*, p. 210.

death. During the time of possession he would swallow hot coals or chew up the cockle-shells used for scraping yams. As a rule, whatever is said by a person thus possessed by a ghost is believed and followed, be it never so foolish, since his utterances are supposed to be inspired by the ghost. The same thing is more or less true of the utterances of a mad person, who is similarly supposed to be possessed and inspired by a ghost. His wild whirling words and the convulsive movements of his body are attributed to the action of the ghost who has entered into him.[1] Indeed, it may be laid down as a general rule that in primitive society there is no sharp distinction between inspiration and insanity. On this point, Dr. Codrington, speaking of the Melanesians, says that " the possession which causes madness cannot be quite distinguished from that which prophesies, and a man may pretend to be mad that he may get the reputation of being a prophet ".[2]

The natives of Ambrym, a Melanesian island in the New Hebrides, carve wooden images of their ancestors, by means of which they communicate with their spirits and consult them oracularly. If a man is in trouble, he blows his whistle at nightfall near the image of his ancestor, and if he hears a noise he thinks that the spirit of the ancestor has approached and entered the image. So he proceeds to tell the image his sorrows and asks the spirit for

[1] W. G. Ivens, *The Melanesians of the South-East Solomon Islands*, pp. 191 *sq.*

[2] R. H. Codrington, *The Melanesians*, p. 219.

help. Occasionally sacrifices are offered to the ancestral images, as is shown by the pigs' jaws which are often found tied to these venerable figures.[1]

The belief in the survival of the soul after death and in the power of the dead to affect the living is deeply rooted in the minds of the Mortlock Islanders, a Micronesian people in the Pacific. Every man believes himself to be surrounded by the souls of his departed forefathers, who hover about him unseen, protect him from danger, and foresee what will befall him. But the spirits cannot speak with everybody, only with the seers or necromancers who have learned the art of communing with the dead. So when a man desires to consult the ancestral spirits, he betakes himself to one of the wizards, acquaints him with his business, and makes him a present. The wizard then sits down on the ground and invokes the spirits. They come and light upon him ; they take possession of him ; he becomes a man inspired. The signs of inspiration are a convulsive twitching of the hands, a violent nodding of the head, and other equally plain tokens of ghostly possession. The spirits now open his mouth and speak through him. Now one spirit announces his presence and now another ; for every spirit can at pleasure give his answer to the seer, though the answer is always couched in a special language, quite different from the speech of daily life. The state of possession or

[1] Felix Speiser, *Two Years with the Natives in the Western Pacific* (London, 1913), p. 206.

inspiration does not last very long, and on awakening from his trance the seer communicates to his hearers the message which he has received from the oracular spirits of the dead.[1]

In New Guinea also the spirits of the dead are frequently supposed to impart oracular information to their surviving kinsfolk. At Mawatta, a village of British New Guinea near the mouth of the Fly River, the skulls of the dead were not uncommonly kept by their relatives. When an important man died, the corpse would be buried up to the neck until the flesh of the head had decayed, leaving the bones bare. The skull was then detached from the body and preserved. The skulls of relatives, thus treasured, are often consulted on the temporal affairs of life. The owner places them by his pillow at night, and in sleep each dead man's spirit comes and communicates with the sleeper in a dream. All sorts of valuable information about gardens or wizards or hunting may thus be imparted by the ghost.[2] The Kiwai, a Papuan people of British New Guinea, believe that they can obtain oracular communications directly from the ghost by questioning the dead man at his grave or by sleeping on the grave, in which case the soul of the departed will visit the sleeper in a dream and give the desired answer. And in order to obtain advice from his

---

[1] Max Girschner, "Die Karolineninsel Namōluk und ihre Bewohner", *Baessler Archiv*, ii. (1912) pp. 193 *sq.* Compare J. G. Frazer, *The Belief in Immortality and the Worship of the Dead*, iii. 120 *sq.*

[2] W. N. Beaver, *Unexplored New Guinea* (London, 1920), p. 63.

dead parents a Kiwai will sometimes dig up their skulls from the grave, wash them clean, rub them with sweet-scented herbs, and sleep close to them, apparently with one skull in each armpit. Sometimes in so doing he will provide himself with a stick and threaten to smash the skulls, if the ghosts of his parents do not appear promptly. In a Kiwai folk-tale the laggard ghosts excuse themselves for being late by pleading that they are old and cannot move fast.[1]

The Mailu, a Papuo-Melanesian people of British New Guinea, keep the skulls of their dead in their houses and believe that the ghosts continue to reside in the skulls. The family accordingly consults the ghosts in the skulls and invokes them in all incantations, as when they are setting up a mark of taboo on coconuts to protect them against thieves.[2]

The Papuans of Geelvink Bay, in the northern part of Dutch New Guinea, believe that the spirits of the dead not only exist but possess superhuman power and exercise great influence over the affairs of life on earth, being able to protect the survivors in danger, to stand by them in war, and to grant success in hunting and fishing. In order to communicate with these powerful beings they make wooden images of their dead, which they keep in their houses and consult from time to time. Every family has at least one such

[1] G. Landtman, *The Kiwai Papuans of British New Guinea*, p. 295.
[2] B. Malinowski, " The Natives of Mailu ", *Transactions of the Royal Society of South Australia*, xxxix. (1915) pp. 583, 653.

ancestral image, which forms the medium whereby the soul of the departed communicates with his or her surviving kinsfolk. These images are not only kept in the houses but carried in canoes on voyages, in order that they may be at hand to help and advise their relatives. At these consultations the inquirer may either take the image in his hands or crouch before it on the ground, on which he places his offerings. The spirit of the dead is thought to be in the image and to pass from it into the inquirer, who thus becomes inspired by the soul of the deceased and so gains supernatural knowledge. The sign of inspiration in the medium is that he shivers and shakes. It is especially in cases of sickness that these oracular images are consulted.[1]

In preparing a body for burial the Betsileo of Madagascar are careful to place a piece of money in the mouth of the corpse for the purpose, as they say, of " opening the lips of the dead " when his ghost comes to visit the family. For the appearance of a ghost who could not speak and give them advice would be a presage of misfortune.[2]

[1] J. G. Frazer, *The Belief in Immortality and the Worship of the Dead*, i. 307-309, where I have cited the authorities.

[2] G. Grandidier, " La Mort et les funérailles à Madagascar ", *L'Anthropologie*, xxiii. (1912) p. 330.

LECTURE V

LECTURE V

In the last lecture I dealt with the oracular function of the ghost, that is, with the belief that the spirits of the dead can communicate with the living and convey to them valuable information which otherwise might not be accessible to the unassisted human intelligence ; and I showed that the communication is often made by a medium, whether a man or woman, who is supposed to be possessed by the ghost and to speak with his voice and in his name. This oracular function of ghosts I illustrated from the beliefs and practices of the Melanesians and other islanders of the Pacific.

In Africa similar beliefs and practices are widespread among the native races, especially the Bantu. Thus with regard to the Ba-ila of Northern Rhodesia we are told that the prophets who claim to be inspired by the ghosts of the dead play a very important part in the life of the people. As the mouthpieces of the worshipful spirits, they are the legislators of the community and, generally speaking, receive a great deal of credit. The word of the prophet is enough to condemn to death for witchcraft a perfectly innocent man or woman. And such is the extraordinary credulity of the people that often they will destroy their grain or kill their cattle at the bidding of a prophet.   The ghost is supposed to enter into the chest of the prophet and to speak from it.   He tells who he is, saying, " I am So-and-so ".   The matter of the prophecy may be very various.   It may be a prediction of famine or drought or a plentiful harvest ;   it may foretell a ravening by a lion or the rebirth of the ghost himself in a woman known to be with child.[1]

But in Africa it is, above all, the ghosts of dead chiefs or kings which are consulted as oracles of the highest authority.   Thus among the Barotse, a Bantu tribe of the Upper Zambesi, the souls of dead kings are inquired of and give responses by the mouth of a priest.   Each royal tomb is, indeed, an oracle of the dead.   It stands within a sacred enclosure which only the priest may enter.   For it is he who acts as intermediary between the royal ghost and the people who come to pray and sacrifice at the shrine.   All over the country these temple-tombs may be seen, each in its shady grove, where the spirits of the dead kings are consulted on matters of public concern as well as by private persons on their own affairs.[2]

Among the Bantu tribes of Northern Rhodesia the spirits of dead chiefs or kings sometimes take possession of the bodies of living men or women and prophesy through their mouths.   When the

[1] E. W. Smith and A. M. Dale, *The Ila-speaking Peoples of Northern Rhodesia*, ii. 140-142.

[2] Eugène Beguin, *Les Marotsé* (Lausanne et Fontaines, 1903), pp. 120-123.

spirit of a dead chief comes over a man, he begins to roar like a lion, whereupon the women gather together and beat the drums, shouting that the chief has come to pay them a visit. The man thus temporarily possessed and inspired may prophesy of future wars or impending attacks by lions. While the inspiration lasts he may eat nothing cooked by fire, but only unfermented dough. However, the spirit of a departed chief takes possession of women oftener than of men. " These women assert that they are possessed by the soul of some dead chief, and when they feel the ' divine afflatus ', whiten their faces to attract attention, and anoint themselves with flour, which has a religious and sanctifying potency. One of their number beats a drum, and the others dance, singing at the same time a weird song, with curious intervals. Finally, when they have arrived at the requisite pitch of religious exaltation, the possessed woman falls to the ground, and bursts forth into a low and almost inarticulate chant, which has a most uncanny effect. All are silent at once, and the *bashing' anga* (medicine-men) gather round to interpret the voice of the spirit." [1]

Among the Basoga of the Central District, in the Uganda Protectorate, the souls of dead chiefs are in like manner consulted as oracles through the medium of women who act as their interpreters or prophetesses. When a chief has been dead and

[1] C. Gouldsbury and H. Sheane, *The Great Plateau of Northern Rhodesia* (London, 1911), p. 83.

buried for some months, his ghost appears to one of his kinsmen and says, " I wish to move ". On learning of the ghost's wish the new chief orders the grave of his predecessor to be opened and the skull removed. When the skull has been cleansed, it is wrapped up in the skins of a cow, a sheep and a gazelle, the eye-sockets having previously been filled in with the beads which the deceased chief wore round his neck in life. The new chief now sends for a woman, who must be a member of the clan to which the nurse of the late chief belonged. To her he commits the duty of guarding the skull, acting as the medium of the ghost, and attending to its wants. A special escort then conducts the woman to a place where a large house is built for her reception. There the skull is deposited in a shrine or temple, which is deemed the house of the ghost, and there the woman becomes possessed by the ghost and reveals his wishes. Thither, too, the new chief sends offerings to the spirit of his father. However, the skull and the ghost remain in this place of honour only during the lifetime of the ghost's successor. When he, too, has gone the way of all flesh, the old skull and the old ghost are forced to vacate the premises and to shift their quarters to a wooded island in the river, where the skulls and ghosts of all former chiefs are permanently lodged. No house there shelters them from the inclemency of the weather. Each skull is simply deposited in the open, with a spear stuck in the ground beside it. The prophetess who waited on it in the temple accompanies it to its long home in the island, and there she may continue to interpret the oracles of the royal ghost to anybody who may care to consult him. But few people think it worth while to ask the advice of the old ghost in the island when they can get the latest information from the new ghost in the temple.[1] *Sic transit gloria mundi.*

Such is, or was till lately, the practice as to oracular ghosts among the Basoga of the Central District. But among the Basoga of the North-Western District the custom is somewhat different, for there it is not the skull but the lower jawbone of a dead chief which is kept to serve as the means of communicating with his spirit. It is cleansed, wrapped in a skin decorated with cowry shells, and sent to a temple in a remote part of the district, where the jawbones of all former chiefs are preserved. The guardian is a priest and medium, who holds converse with the ghost and conveys any message from him to the ruling chief.[2]

Among the Baganda, the powerful neighbours of the Basoga on the west, it was also the jawbone of a dead king rather than his skull which was deemed the vehicle of his ghost and the instrument of his oracular utterances ; for, curiously enough, the Baganda think that the part of their bodies to which the ghost cleaves most constantly is the jawbone. So in the temple which was built for each dead king of Uganda his lower jawbone was rever-

[1] John Roscoe, *The Northern Bantu* (Cambridge, 1915), pp. 227 *sq.*
[2] J. Roscoe, *op. cit.* pp. 226 *sq.*

K

ently preserved. The temple, a large conical hut of the usual pattern, was divided into two chambers, an outer and an inner, and in the inner chamber or holy of holies the precious jawbone was kept for safety in a cell dug in the floor. The prophet or medium, whose business it was to be inspired from time to time by the ghost of the dead king, dedicated himself to his holy office by drinking a draught of beer and a draught of milk out of the royal skull, which thus served as a means of putting him in intimate relations with the spirit of the deceased monarch. When the ghost gave an audience, the jawbone, wrapped in a decorated packet, was brought forth from the inner shrine and set on a throne in the outer chamber, where the people gathered to hear the oracle. On such occasions the prophet stepped up to the throne, and addressing the royal ghost informed him of the business in hand. Then he smoked one or two pipes of home-grown tobacco, and the fumes bringing on the prophetic fit he began to speak in the very voice and with the characteristic turns of speech of the departed monarch. However, his rapid utterances were hard to understand, and a priest was in attendance to interpret them to the inquirer. The living king thus consulted his dead predecessors periodically on affairs of state, visiting first one and then another of the temples in which their sacred relics were preserved with religious care.[1]

[1] John Roscoe, " Notes on the Manners and Customs of the Ba- ganda ", *Journal of the Anthropological Institute*, xxxi. (1901) pp.

Similarly among the Banyoro, another great tribe of Uganda, the ghosts of dead kings used to be consulted as oracles by their living successors. Over the king's grave a mound of earth was raised with a flat top, which was covered with a grass carpet and overlaid with the skins of cows and leopards. This mound was the throne where the king's ghost was said to take its seat at any ceremony. Before the throne offerings were presented to the ghost, and there, too, requests were made when the reigning king wished to consult his deceased father upon matters of state or when sickness appeared in the royal household. The late king was commonly spoken of as being asleep, but never as dead.[1]

So much for the oracular function of ghosts. That concludes what I had to say about the spirits of the dead in their beneficent aspect. I have shown that these spirits are commonly believed by primitive or savage man to help him in many ways, particularly by enabling the hunter to kill game and the fisherman to catch fish ; by making trees to bear fruit and the earth to produce crops of various kinds ; by sending rain to refresh and fertilize the thirsty ground ; by enabling women to bear children ; by granting success and victory in war ; and by imparting precious information and advice on all the

129 sq. ; id., " Further Notes on the Manners and Customs of the Baganda ", Journal of the Anthropological Institute, xxxii. (1902) pp. 44 sqq. ; id., The Baganda (London, 1911), pp. 109-113, 283-285 ; id.,

" Worship of the Dead as practised by some African Tribes ", Harvard African Studies, i. (1917) pp. 39 sq.

[1] John Roscoe, The Northern Bantu, p. 53.

affairs of life to such as apply to them in the proper way either directly or through the appointed intermediaries. These are, indeed, very substantial benefits, since they appear to secure a supply of food, protection against enemies, and the continuation of the species. We need not wonder, therefore, that people who hold these beliefs should revere the spirits of the dead and that they should take all the means in their power to ensure the favour and to avoid the displeasure of these potent beings, on whom they imagine themselves to be dependent not only for the support, the security and the comforts of life, but even for existence itself. Their feelings towards the spirits are naturally, therefore, of a mixed sort ; for while they are grateful for the benefits received, they are uncertain how long these may continue, since they are conceived to be liable at any moment to be forfeited by any neglect or oversight in the marks of attention which the souls of the dead expect to receive from the survivors. Thus the gratitude and affection of the living are strongly tinged with anxiety and fear. For though the spirits of the dead are thought to confer many benefits on the survivors, they are also believed to bring on them evils and calamities of many sorts, including the last evil, death. To this, the gloomy side of the belief in ghosts, we must now turn our attention.

To begin with, ghosts are sometimes thought to disturb the ordinary course of nature in various alarming ways, as by causing earthquakes, thunder-

storms, drought and famine.   Thus, for example, the
Kiwai of British New Guinea attribute earthquakes
to the action of ghosts walking underneath the
ground in a party with their women and children.
They say that just as big strong men drag heavy
burdens through the forest, so do big strong ghosts
push their way through the earth ; and that if you
look at the reflections on the surface of pools you
can see these earthquake spirits passing along.[1]   A
similar belief is entertained by the Orokaiva of
British New Guinea, who further think that an
earthquake presages sickness,[2] which accordingly
they set down to the account of the ghosts.   The
Kai of Northern New Guinea believe that the
entrance to the subterranean world of the dead is
at a certain cave at the mouth of which there stands
a tree.   When a ghost arrives at the cave on his way
to his long home, he perches on the tree for a time,
waiting for a favourable moment to plunge into the
abyss.   So when the Kai feel the earth shaking
under them or hear a rumbling noise down below,
they say that a ghost has just jumped from the tree,
causing the earth to quake.[3]

The natives of Timor, an island in the Indian
Archipelago, think that an earthquake is produced
by the spirits of the dead underground who are
struggling to force their way up to the surface of
the earth.   So when a shock of earthquake is felt,

[1] G. Landtman, *The Kiwai Papuans of British New Guinea*, p. 281.
[2] F. E. Williams, *Orokaiva Society*,
p. 184.

[3] Ch. Keysser, " Aus dem Leben
der Kaileute ", in R. Neuhauss,
Deutsch-Neu-Guinea (Berlin, 1911),
iii. 149.

the Timorese knock on the ground and call out, "We are still here", to let the unquiet spirits of the dead know that there is no room for them on the surface of the earth.[1] The Andaman Islanders in like manner hold that earthquakes are caused by some mischievous male spirits of their deceased ancestors, who, impatient at the delay of the resurrection, combine to shake the palm-tree on which the earth is thought to rest, hoping thus to destroy the cane bridge which stretches between this world and heaven and is the only prop of the sky. However, these impious resurrectionists down below are careful not to play their pranks during the dry season, because, the surface of the earth being then much cracked with heat, they fear that it might collapse and bury them under the ruins instead of toppling over in one solid block and thus, so to say, lifting up the hatches which now batten down the dead. That is why in the Andaman Islands earthquakes only occur in the rainy season. Such is the Andaman theory of earthquakes as reported by Mr. E. H. Man, an excellent authority.[2] A somewhat different version of the theory is reported by another good authority, Professor Radcliffe-Brown. The account which he received from a native was that an earthquake is caused by the spirits of the dead dancing underground at the reception of a newcomer from the upper world. On such an occasion the spirits of the dead hold a ceremony

[1] A. Bastian, *Indonesien*: II. *Timor und umliegende Inseln* (Berlin, 1885), p. 3.

[2] E. H. Man, *On the Aboriginal Inhabitants of the Andaman Islands* (London, N.D.), p. 86.

to welcome or initiate the raw ghost into the mysteries of the new life down below. The ceremony includes a dance at which the rainbow serves as a screen for the dancers, which they shake by their jumps ; and this shaking of the rainbow produces an earthquake.[1]

The Lakhers of North-Eastern India also give more than one explanation of earthquakes. According to one view, the earth is attached to the sky by cords so close together that of all birds only the martin and the swallow can fly between them. But spirits can also fly between them ; and when a chief dies, his soul flies between the cords, and as it passes it cuts one of the cords with a dagger, which causes an earthquake.[2] The Lusheis, another tribe of the same region, say that the people of the lower world shake the upper world in order to know if any one is still alive there. So when an earthquake happens, some Lushei villages resound with shouts of " Alive ! alive ! " to reassure the people down below and so induce them to stop the earthquake.[3]

In Africa the Banyoro think that earthquakes are produced by dead kings moving about underground, which causes the earth to shake.[4] They also attribute earthquakes to the struggles of a dead king named Isaza to escape from Dead-land and return home to the land of the living.[5] The

[1] A. R. Brown, *The Andaman Islanders* (Cambridge, 1922), pp. 147 *sq.*
[2] N. E. Parry, *The Lakhers*, pp. 486 *sq.*
[3] J. Shakespear, *The Lushei Kuki Clans* (London, 1912), p. 184.
[4] J. Roscoe, *The Northern Bantu*, p. 93.
[5] J. Roscoe, *The Bakitara or Banyoro* (Cambridge, 1923), p. 325.

Baluba, a large tribe in the upper valley of the Congo, imagine that earthquakes are produced by the spirits of the dead fighting among themselves underground just as living people fight with each other above ground.[1] In antiquity a precisely similar opinion was attributed to the great philosopher Pythagoras,[2] whose so-called symbols, whoever may have been their author, are little more than a collection of popular superstitions which furnish a rich harvest to reapers in the field of folklore.[3]

Again, storms of thunder and lightning are thought by some savages to be caused by the spirits of the dead. Thus, concerning the Bantu tribes of South Africa we are told that " the Kafirs have strange notions concerning the lightning. They consider that it is governed by the *umshologu*, or ghost, of the greatest and most renowned of their departed chiefs, and who is emphatically styled the *inkosi* ; but they are not at all clear as to which of their ancestors is intended by this designation. Hence they allow of no lamentation being made for a person killed by lightning ; for they say that it would be a sign of disloyalty to lament for one whom the *inkosi* had sent for, and whose services he consequently needed ; and it would cause him to punish them, by making the lightning again to descend and do them another injury."[4] The savage

[1] Le R. P. Colle, *Les Baluba*, ii. (Bruxelles, 1913) p. 428.

[2] Aelian, *Var. Hist.* iv. 17.

[3] J. G. Frazer, *Garnered Sheaves* (London, 1931), pp. 130 *sqq.*; Fr. Boehm, *De symbolis Pythagoreis*, *Dissertatio Inauguralis* (Berlin, 1905).

[4] Mr. Warren's Notes, in Col. Maclean's *Compendium of Kafir Laws and Customs* (Cape Town, 1866), pp. 82 *sq.*

Conibos, of the Ucayali River in Eastern Peru, imagine that thunder is the voice of the dead,[1] and among them when parents who have lost a child within three months hear thunder they go and dance on the grave, howling turn about.[2] Apparently they fancy that in a peal of thunder they hear the voice of their dead child calling to them from the grave.

The Choroti Indians of the Gran Chaco believe that thunder and lightning are caused by a great number of evil spirits rushing through the air and making their onset on the village. Every time that a peal of thunder is heard, these Indians, sitting in their huts, shout and scream loudly to frighten the demons away. These demons appear to be conceived of as the souls of old men of the tribe, who in their lifetime were skilled in the magic art.[3] Thus in the opinion of the Chorotis it is the spirits of the dead who are responsible for thunder and lightning. Similarly the wild Jibaros, an Indian tribe of Ecuador, think that thunder and lightning are caused by a band of dead warriors, who, under cover of the noise, are attacking the Indians. So during a violent thunderstorm the Jibaro men may be seen brandishing their lances against the sky, leaping and shouting defiance at their invisible foes. Hence they call thunder by a name which means, " The

---

[1] W. Smyth and F. Lowe, *Journey from Lima to Para* (London, 1836), p. 240.

[2] De St. Cricq, " Voyage du Pérou au Brésil ", *Bulletin de la Société de Géographie*, IVme Série, vi. (Paris, 1853) p. 294.

[3] R. Karsten, *The Civilization of the South-American Indians*, p. 359.

enemies are fighting ". Lightning they imagine
to be an old Jibaro warrior, one of their ancestors.[1]
That storms of thunder and lightning are the work
of the spirits of the dead is the belief also of the
warlike Araucanians, an Indian tribe of Chili.
Concerning them a Spanish historian of Chili tells
us that not a storm bursts upon the Andes or the
ocean which these Indians do not ascribe to a battle
between the souls of their fellow-countrymen and
the dead Spaniards. In the roar of the wind they
hear the trampling of the spectral horses, in the peal
of the thunder the roll of the ghostly drums, and
in the flashes of lightning the fire of the ghostly
artillery.[2]

Further, the souls of the dead are sometimes
believed to cause drought and famine. This belief
is held by the Chinese, who, though certainly not a
primitive people, retain many primitive superstitions under their ancient civilization ; in particular
they cherish a strong faith in the existence and power
of their ancestral spirits, whose worship, indeed,
forms the main feature of their religion. The
Chinese are convinced that when human bodies or
bones are left unburied and exposed to the air, the
souls of their late owners feel the discomfort of
showers of rain, just as living men would do if they
were exposed without shelter to the inclemency of
the weather. Accordingly these unhappy souls do
all in their power to prevent the rain from falling,

[1] R. Karsten, *The Civilization of the South-American Indians*, p. 360.
[2] J. ¡ I. Molina, *Geographical,*

Natural and Civil History of Chili (London, 1809), ii. 92 *sq.*

and often their efforts, according to the Chinese, are only too successful. Then drought ensues, the most dreaded of all calamities in China, because bad harvests, dearth, and famine follow in its train. Hence it has been a common practice of the Chinese authorities, in time of drought, to order the burial of the dry bones of the unburied dead for the purpose of putting an end to the scourge and conjuring down the rain. For example, in the year A.D. 108, after a long drought, the Governor of Honan caused to be interred the bones of ten thousand strangers which were bleaching outside the walls of the city, whereupon rain fell abundantly and the harvest was very fine that year. Again, in the year A.D. 481 the Emperor issued a decree as follows : " The rains of the season do not trickle down, so that the tender sprouts of spring hang heavily. Wherever human bones lie, orders must be issued by the authorities to have them buried, and none may be left uncovered, in order that the spirits may become aware of these acts and the catastrophe be deprecated." [1]

The Lakhers of North-Eastern India similarly believe in the power of the spirits of the dead to create a famine by blighting the crops. They are in the habit of erecting memorials to their dead, ordinarily in the shape of a flat stone accompanied by a wooden post, but for chiefs and persons of importance pyramids and small stone walls are set up in addition. The erection of such a memorial

---

[1] J. J. M. de Groot, *The Religious System of China*, iii. (Leyden, 1897) pp. 918 *sq.*

marks the final separation of the dead man's spirit from his living kinsfolk. The day after the ceremony the whole village is tabooed ; no one may do any work, and the women may neither spin nor weave. It is thought that, if this taboo were not observed, the dead man's spirit would carry off with it to the other world the spirits of rice and of all other edibles, and that consequently there would be a famine.[1]

Similar beliefs in the power of the dead to cause famine by withholding the rain are held by Bantu tribes in South Africa, for example, by the Pondomisi tribe. In 1891 it happened that there was a time of intense heat and severe drought. So the tribe ascribed the calamity to the wrath of a dead chief, named Gwanya, at the treatment of one of his descendants, who had been arrested and sent before a colonial court for a criminal offence. The departed chief had been buried in a deep pool of a river ; so to appease his angry spirit cattle were slaughtered as a peace-offering on the banks of the pool and the flesh was thrown into the water, together with new dishes full of beer. Apparently the soul of the offended chief was mollified by these attentions and he withdrew his ban on the rain. At all events copious showers fell a few days later, which naturally confirmed the belief of the tribe that they had done the right thing, and that the spirit of the late chief was appeased.[2]

[1] N. E. Parry, *The Lakhers*, pp. 414 *sq.*

[2] G. McCall Theal, *Records of South-Eastern Africa*, vii. (Cape Town, 1901) p. 400.

In these various ways the spirits of the dead are believed by primitive man to trouble and afflict the living. But the standing accusation which he levels against them is that they are the causes, often the most general causes, of sickness and death. This is the great damning blot on their character : this is their one unforgivable sin : their other faults, their frailties and weaknesses, might perhaps be overlooked and excused, or at least palliated, but this one cannot. Not that all savages believe sickness and death to be the work of the spirits of the dead exclusively or mainly ; many tribes think that these dreaded evils are wrought for the most part not by the ghosts but by living sorcerers ; and where this belief prevails its effects on the life of the people are much more disastrous. For while people cannot normally punish a ghost for his offences, since he is beyond their reach, they can punish a living sorcerer, who is well within the reach of tribal law and justice. Hence in tribes who firmly believe that every death is brought about by sorcery, every natural death is commonly followed by the judicial murder of the sorcerer who is supposed to have caused the death by his nefarious arts ; and the murders may easily be multiplied when suspicion falls on several persons, all of whom must clear their character by submitting to a poison ordeal which may prove fatal to many. Thus, while a belief in ghosts has slain its victims by thousands, a belief in sorcery has slain its victims by tens of thousands, or rather by millions ; for this fatal error, or rather obsession, is still rampant in some parts of the world, above all in Africa, where it has prevailed from time immemorial, and where tribes are known to have actually extinguished themselves by their blind faith in sorcery and their infatuated devotion to the poison ordeal as an infallible test of truth. Hence, strange as it may seem, the recognition of ghosts or spirits of the dead, apart from sorcery, as causes of disease and death marks a real and important step in the moral and social, if not in the intellectual, progress of our species, for it has saved countless human lives by preventing countless judicial murders.[1]

The evidence for the belief of primitive man in the spirits of the dead as the causes of disease and death is immense. In these lectures I can only give a small selection from it.

Thus, to begin with the Melanesians, we are told that by them " any sickness that is serious is believed to be brought about by ghosts or spirits ; common complaints such as fever and ague are taken as coming in the course of nature. . . . Generally it is to the ghosts of the dead that sickness is ascribed in the eastern islands as well as in the western ; recourse is had to them for aid in causing and removing sickness ; and ghosts are believed to inflict sickness not only because some offence, such as a trespass, has been committed against them, or because one familiar with them has

---

[1] Compare my book, *The Belief in Immortality and the Worship of the Dead*, i. 31-58.

sought their aid with sacrifice and spells, but because there is a certain malignity in the feeling of
all ghosts towards the living, who offend them by
being alive." [1] Sometimes a man will fancy that
he has offended his dead father, uncle or brother.
In that case he needs no special intercessor ; he or
one of his kinsfolk will sacrifice to the offended ghost
and beg him to take the sickness away ; it is a
family affair. But if he does not know to what ghost
he has given umbrage, he will call in a wizard to
ascertain the truth and prescribe the remedy. This
the sage may do by divination. For example, he
may hang a stone by a string which he holds in his
hand, while he calls over the names of the persons
who died lately. When the stone swings at the
mention of a certain name, that is the name of the
ghost who is causing the sickness. Then it remains
to ask what shall be given to appease the anger of
the ghost—a mash of yams, a fish, a pig or what not.
The answer is given in the same way ; and whatever the ghost may express his preference for is
offered on the dead man's grave, and the sickness
is expected to depart.[2] Sometimes the wizard
ascertains the identity of the offended ghost in a
dream. For example, he may meet the ghost in
his dream, and the ghost may inform him that the
sick man had offended him by trespassing on his
preserves, and that to punish the trespass he, the
ghost, had taken away the man's soul and im-

[1] R. H. Codrington, *The Melanesians*, p. 194.

[2] R. H. Codrington, *op. cit.* pp.
195 *sq.*

pounded it in a magic fence in the garden. The dreaming wizard then begs for the restoration of the lost soul and asks the ghost's pardon on behalf of the sick man, who meant no disrespect. So the mollified ghost accepts the apology, pulls up the fence in which the soul of the sick man was impounded, and lets it out. So the released soul returns to the sick man, who of course recovers.[1] The natives of San Cristoval, one of the Solomon Islands, think that if a man was gentle and killed nobody in his life, he will be cruel and kill many people after his death. Hence all persons who are taken ill in the first months after the death of such a man put down their illness to the account of his ghost; so they quit their houses and flee to the mountains, where they hide, hoping thus to give the slip to the bloodthirsty ghost and so to recover their health.[2]

The Orokaiva of British New Guinea appear to ascribe sickness to the malevolence of ghosts oftener than to any other cause.[3] Of these people we are told that by them no agency is more readily made responsible for human illness than are the ghosts (*sovai*), who are so often regarded as dangerous and spiteful. Strange as it may seem, it is especially the ghosts of near relations who are blamed for sickness, and they are sometimes thought to enter the bodies of their victims at the very funeral when the

[1] R. H. Codrington, *The Melanesians*, p. 208.

[2] L. Verguet, " Arossi ou San-Christoval et ses habitants ", *Revue d'Ethnographie*, iv. (1885) p. 211.

[3] F. E. Williams, *Orokaiva Society*, p. 283.

mourners are embracing the corpse.[1] To induce a
ghost to quit the body of the sufferer the Orokaiva
make offerings to it.[2] The Mailu of British New
Guinea in like manner sometimes attribute sickness
to the ghosts of the sick man's relations who are
trying to draw his soul away. The wizard can see
the ghost at his deadly work ; it may be the ghost
of the patient's father or brother. So the watchers
over the sick or dying man address the spirit, saying,
" Go away ! Don't call him ! Leave him alone ! "[3]

In like manner the Kiwai of British New Guinea
think that, when a child is made sick by ghosts who
are trying to carry off its soul, it is oftenest the ghosts
of the child's dead grandparents who are engaged
in this attempt on its life. But the wily wizard spits
the juice of a certain plant over the ghosts, which
stupefies them and drives them away ; so the sick
child is made whole. Hence among the Kiwai it is
necessary to guard all little children against the
ghosts of their dead relatives, but especially against
the ghosts of their grandparents, who are apt to come
in the night and snatch away the baby's soul,
prompted, we are told, by their solicitude as to how
the little one is cared for.[4] Similarly, again, in
Tumleo, a small island off the north coast of New
Guinea, sickness is sometimes attributed to the
agency of the ghosts of the sick man's grandfather
and father, who have entered into his body. So in

---

[1] F. E. Williams, *Orokaiva Society*,
p. 293.
[2] F. E. Williams, *op. cit.* p. 304.
[3] W. J. V. Saville, *In Unknown*
New Guinea, p. 219.
[4] G. Landtman, *The Kiwai Papu-*
ans of British New Guinea, p.
271.

order to expel the ghostly intruders, two men strike
the body and legs of the patient lightly with certain
plants, inviting the ghosts to come out of the sufferer,
and praying that he may be made whole.[1]

The natives of Nias, an island to the west of
Sumatra, believe that the spirits of the dead often
try to make men sick in order that they too may die
and so bear the ghosts company to the land of the
dead. It is especially the souls of dead chiefs which
are credited with this fatal power.[2] The wild tribes
in the mountains of Formosa attribute disease to
the displeasure of the spirits of the dead, and they
engage a priestess to pray for the favour of these
dangerous beings.[3] The Khmers of Cambodia think
that sickness is caused by a ghost who is hovering
near the sufferer or has entered into his body. And
since a ghost can only be combated by a ghost,
they invoke the aid of the patient's ancestral spirits,
especially the spirit of one particular friend, usually
a doctor, who died long ago and is thought to have
constituted himself the spiritual patron and protector of his former clients in this world. So a
sorceress is called in to exorcise the ghost who has
taken possession of the sick man. This she does
with the help of water, oil and rice-spirit, to the
accompaniment of noisy music. Sometimes the
doctor questions the ghost as to his reason for afflict-

[1] M. J. Erdweg, " Die Bewohner
der Insel Tumleo, Berlinhafen,
Deutsch-Neu-Guinea ", Mittheilun-
gen der anthropologischen Gesellschaft in Wien, xxxi. (1901) pp. 284
sq.

[2] J. P. Kleiweg de Zwaan, Die
Heilkunde der Niasser (The Hague,
1913), p. 17.

[3] J. W. Davidson, The Island of
Formosa, p. 580.

ing the sufferer, and the ghost answers that in his
lifetime he had been injured or insulted by the sick
man, who had dirtied his house, thrown stones into
his yard to frighten his family, or passed him in
the street with an air of disdain. So to appease the
resentment of the ghost the doctor fashions a rude
clay image, which he offers to the ghost as a substitute for his victim. If the ghost graciously accepts
the exchange all is well, and the patient may expect
to recover.[1] Similar theories as to the causes of
disease appear to be held and similar practices to
be observed for the cure of it in Siam and the Shan
States of Burma.[2]

The Birhors, a jungle tribe of India, revere their
ancestral spirits, which each family installs in an
inner tabernacle or shrine of the hut and propitiates
with offerings of food and drink. But if their descendants neglect to make these offerings, the
ancestral spirits may punish them by inciting the
demons (*bhuts*) to cause sickness in the family. It
is said that out of a touch of natural affection the
ancestral spirits do not generally themselves cause
sickness to their surviving relatives, they only
instigate other spirits thus to avenge the neglect
of their undutiful kinsfolk.[3] Among the Korkus,
a Munda or Kolarian tribe of the Central Provinces
in India, when a person is sick his friends attribute
the sickness to the anger of some god or ancestral

[1] J. Moura, *Le Royaume du
Cambodge* (Paris, 1883), i. 175 *sq.*
[2] H. S. Hallett, *A Thousand Miles
on an Elephant in the Shan States*
(Edinburgh and London, 1890),
pp. 105-108, 276.
[3] Sarat Chandra Roy, *The Birhors*, pp. 305 *sq.*

spirit. So they wave a handful of grain over the patient and then carry it to the village priest (*bhumka*). The priest thereupon makes a heap of it on the floor, and, sitting over it, swings a lighted lamp suspended by four strings from his fingers. He then repeats slowly the names of the village deities and the sick man's ancestors, pausing after each name, and the name at which the lamp stops swinging is that of the offended god or ancestral spirit. He next inquires in a similar manner whether the god or ancestor is to be appeased by the sacrifice of a pig, a chicken, a goat, a coconut, or what not.[1]

In Africa also sickness is often traced to the anger of ancestral spirits who are offended with their surviving kinsfolk for some real or imaginary injury and take this mode of punishing them for their undutiful behaviour. The Thonga, for example, think that the ancestral spirits are incarnate in certain little harmless snakes, of a bluish-green colour, which are often seen crawling in the thatch of the roof or along the walls. These the Thonga suppose to be their ancestral spirits paying them a visit; so they will not kill the reptiles, imagining that were they to do so the ancestral spirits would punish them with disease. Hence, when disease has broken out, a soothsayer may declare by means of his divining bones that somebody has hurt one of the sacred snakes, and that the offended spirit must be appeased by a sacrifice.[2] The diviner ascertains by

[1] R. V. Russell, *Tribes and Castes of the Central Provinces of India*, iii. 560 *sq.*

[2] H. A. Junod, *The Life of a South African Tribe*[2], ii. 384.

his divining bones what particular ancestral spirit is causing the sickness, and how he is to be propitiated. The propitiatory sacrifice may consist, for example, of a hen or a bracelet. If it is a fowl, after killing it and addressing the ancestral spirits, the priest takes a feather and a claw of the bird, ties them together, and fastens them to the wrist or ankle of the patient. If the offended ghost is an ancestor on the mother's side of the house, the feather and claw are attached to the sufferer's left wrist or ankle ; but if the angry spirit is an ancestor on the father's side, the feather and claw are attached to the right wrist or ankle. If the offering consists of a bracelet, the priest will pour consecrated beer over it and say his prayers. Then the bracelet will be fastened to the patient's foot, and he may not remove it or exchange it for anything ; it belongs to the ancestral spirits.[1] The Bavenda similarly believe that sickness may be caused by the spirit of a dead ancestor either on the father's or the mother's side of the house, but they think that it is oftener a ghost on the mother's side than on the father's that is causing the trouble. As usual, the diviner ascertains the particular ghost who is causing the illness, and having done so he prescribes the appropriate offering ; in some cases a black goat has to be sacrificed at the grave of the angry ancestor.[2]

The Ba-ila ascribe many sicknesses and deaths to the direct action of the ancestral spirits who are

---

[1] H. A. Junod, *The Life of a South African Tribe*[2], ii. 395-397.

[2] H. A. Stayt, *The Bavenda*, pp. 247 *sq.*, 251 *sq.*

offended by neglect. Delirium is supposed to be caused by ghosts speaking from within the sufferer; and if the patient dies, they say that the ghosts have taken him away.[1] In this tribe, when a man wastes away without any visible cause he is thought to have a malevolent ghost within him which is devouring the food he takes. So his friends put him in a hut, where young girls under puberty make a new fire in order that the smoke may drive out the intruding ghost.[2] Should a child fall sick, the parents will go to a diviner, who may pronounce that the sickness is caused by ancestral spirits either on the father's or on the mother's side of the house. If he lays the blame on the mother's ancestors, the father will wax exceeding wroth, roundly declaring that they have no right to sicken his child.[3] When a man is thought to be possessed by a particularly troublesome and dangerous ghost, his friends will sometimes attempt to heal him by holding his head forcibly over a potsherd full of burning coals and medicinal herbs in order that the pungent fumes may drive away the ghost that is obsessing him; and should the patient break away from his captors, they follow him with the potsherd till he falls down. Then they throw away the potsherd, and he gets up and goes home, free from the tormenting ghost.[4]

Similar beliefs and practices concerning ghosts

[1] E. W. Smith and A. M. Dale, *The Ila-speaking Peoples of Northern Rhodesia*, i. 245.

[2] E. W. Smith and A. M. Dale, *op. cit.* i. 235.

[3] E. W. Smith and A. M. Dale, *op. cit.* ii. 166.

[4] E. W. Smith and A. M. Dale, *op. cit.* ii. 168 *sq.*

as the causes of disease prevail among the Nyanja-speaking tribes of Nyasaland. Thus a diviner may ascribe a child's illness to the anger of the ghost of the child's grandmother, who thinks that she is not duly kept in mind by her grandchild, and demands a fowl to soothe her ruffled feelings. So the father of the child will offer a fowl to the grandmother's ghost, saying, " Grandmother, there is the fowl for which you are causing a person to be ill ; you harden your heart all for the sake of a fowl ; go, let your little child alone, that he also shall walk about as his companions do ; you must not see fit to take a man, only for the sake of a fowl ". With these words he kills the fowl, and, having cooked the flesh, offers some of it to the grandmother's ghost, saying, " Here is the fowl we have killed for you. Eat of it."[1]

[1] R. Sutherland Rattray, *Some Folk-lore Stories and Songs in Chinyanja* (London, 1907), pp. 120 sq.

LECTURE VI

LECTURE VI

In the last lecture I dealt with the belief of primitive man that sickness and death are often caused by the spirits of the dead, and I illustrated the belief and the practices to which it gives rise by examples drawn from savage races in various parts of the world. Towards the end of the lecture I dealt with the belief and the practices as they are found among the Bantu tribes in the more southerly parts of Africa. I now resume the subject at the point where I broke off.

The theory that sickness is often caused by the spirits of the dead is widely held by the Bantu tribes of the Uganda Protectorate, and in order to effect a cure these tribes sometimes exorcise the ghost instead of propitiating him by sacrifice, the treatment varying with the nature of the particular ghost who is supposed to be doing the mischief.

Thus, to begin with the Bambwa, who were a wild and turbulent mountain tribe living on the western slopes of the great Ruwenzori range, these savages, like so many others, attributed illness to the action of ghosts. When a medicine-man, on being consulted, declared that a particular case of sickness was caused by an angry ghost of a member of the sick man's own family, the ghost had to be appeased by the offering of a goat, which was killed by having its throat cut near a shrine built at the spot where the ghost was supposed to reside. The blood was allowed to run on the ground by the shrine, and prayers were put up to the ghost that in return for the sacrifice he would refrain from causing further trouble.[1] If, however, the ghost that was inflicting the sickness was judged to belong to a hostile clan, he met with a very different reception. The medicine-man began by killing a fowl and letting the blood flow over various medicines which he had brought with him and spread out in front of the patient. He then proceeded to make incisions in the flesh of the sick man's chest, arms, legs and back, and, after powdering some of the medicines, which had an irritating effect, in the palm of his hand, he spat on his thumb, dipped it into the powder, and rubbed the powder into the incisions in the patient's body. As if this was not enough to expel the ghost, a small hut was built near-by and the sufferer was laid in it, after which the hut was set on fire. A strong man was deputed to stand by, and as soon as the sick man was in danger of burning alive he was snatched from the flames by his stalwart friend. By this time the ghost was thought to have found the place too hot for him and to have fairly taken to his heels, leaving

---

[1] J. Roscoe, *The Bagesu and other Tribes of the Uganda Protectorate* (Cambridge, 1924), pp. 153 *sq.*

the sick man to recover. To complete the cure the medicine-man then took the fowl which he had killed, and, having cooked the flesh, offered it to the ghost, praying him not to harm the man again.[1]

The Banyankole, a pastoral tribe inhabiting the south-western district of the Uganda Protectorate, think that the spirits who cause sickness are either the ghosts of people belonging to other clans, or else the ghosts of relatives, but never the ghost of a father, who is deemed too tender-hearted to molest his surviving progeny. But a widower may be troubled by the jealous ghost of his late spouse, who resents his taking a second wife and may kill her rival if she is not appeased by offerings. If the ghost of the late wife obstinately refused to accept an atonement, the new wife might not remain in the house of her husband but had to go back to her parents.[2]

In this tribe, when a ghost proved unusually obstreperous, it was sometimes necessary to eject him from the patient's body by cunning or force. In that case the diviner told the relatives what medicine-man to send for and what preparations to make. A goat of a particular colour, always either black or black and white, was tied to the head of the patient's bed during the night, so that the ghost might pass from the sufferer into the animal. In the morning the medicine-man came dancing and singing and passed a bunch of sticks and herbs all

---

[1] J. Roscoe, *The Bagesu*, p. 154.
[2] J. Roscoe, *The Banyankole* (Cambridge, 1923), p. 138.

round the house by way of sweeping together all the evil influences into one place. Next he killed the goat which had been tied to the bed, and which was now supposed to contain the troublesome ghost. After that, a fowl was brought and passed round the goat, and when the ghost had incautiously vacated the goat and passed into the fowl, the bird was buried alive in the gateway through which the cows entered the kraal, thus preventing the ghost from returning to make fresh trouble.[1] Sometimes, in order to expel the ghost, the medicine-man rubbed the patient down with his hands, pressing the ghost from his head out at his feet and the tips of his fingers, and when the ghost sought to escape it was caught in a pot and burned or drowned.[2]

Among the Banyoro or Bakitara, a great tribe of Uganda to the north of the Banyankole, the treatment of sick people supposed to be infested by ghosts was similar, though with some differences. With them, also, the treatment varied according to whether the ghost was hostile and determined to destroy the patient, or whether it was the ghost of some member of the sufferer's own clan.   In the latter case, as among the Banyankole, a goat was tied up near the patient's bed, and the medicine-man besought the ghost to pass from the sick person into the animal ; but when the ghost was supposed to have complied with the request and entered into the goat, the animal was not killed ; on the contrary it became sacred and lived near the bed ever after-

[1] J. Roscoe, *The Banyankole*, p. 139.   [2] J. Roscoe, *op. cit.* p. 141.

wards. It might not be killed, and nobody might strike or ill-use it. Should it die, the owner must replace it with another at once. If it had kids, the man had to ask the ghost's leave before he might use any of the young animals, and one of them had always to be left for the ghost. But when the ghost would not accept an animal as the price of quitting the sick person, a girl or woman-slave was offered him instead. She took the place of an animal, slept all night near the patient's bed, and was said to receive the ghost, after which she became a favoured member of the family. She might not be sold or sent away, nor dared the family ill-treat her, because of her connexion with the ghost. These family-ghosts seem invariably to have attacked women ; Canon Roscoe, who is our authority for these customs of the Banyoro, never heard of a case of a man's illness being treated in this way.[1]

But when the ghost who was causing the sickness was of another clan and hostile, a very different treatment was meted out to him. The medicine-man took a black goat, which he kept with him all night, and early in the morning he made his preparations to capture and destroy the ghost. The patient, wearing a black bark-cloth, lay on a bed near the door, and the medicine-man prepared a heap of herbs near the bed. The black goat was thrown on the heap and killed, and pieces of the flesh were roasted on spits over a fire which was kindled for the purpose near the bed. When a little

[1] J. Roscoe, *The Bakitara or Banyoro* (Cambridge, 1923), pp. 285 *sq.*

of the flesh was cooked it was put into a pot near the bed, and some blades of grass were arranged over the mouth of the pot in such a way that the least disturbance of the air set them in motion. Some of the patient's friends were now set to watch this pot with instructions to inform the medicine-man if the grass moved. The reason for these preparations was that ghosts were thought to be shy creatures, shunning the light of day in the presence of spectators. A place of retreat in the pot was therefore prepared for the ghost who was afflicting the patient. The medicine-man sat on the other side of the fire, shaking his rattle and chanting incantations to persuade the ghost to come out of the patient and eat the meat. Smelling the savoury odour of the roast flesh, the ghost did come out, and, peering about for some place where it could eat unseen, it descried the pot and entered it. But in doing so it disturbed the blades of grass on the mouth of the pot, causing them to wave. The movement did not escape the watchers, and they at once reported it to the medicine-man. Quick as thought he seized a skin which he had ready to hand, clapped it on the mouth of the pot and tied it down, thus securing the ghost inside the pot in durance vile. Sometimes the ghost would call out from the pot, but his remonstrances were vain. The medicine-man was adamant. To make assurance doubly sure he smeared clay over the skin and carried away the pot with the imprisoned ghost in it to waste land, where he burned pot and ghost together, or he threw them into running water. But the attempt to drown the ghost was thought dangerous, because the pot might break in the water, and the ghost, thus rescued from a watery death, might return and renew his attack on the patient.[1]

In this tribe another mode of dealing with a hostile ghost was to smoke him out of the patient's body. The sick man, wearing fetishes, was laid on his bed, and a pot full of hot embers was put on the floor beside him. Sheep's wool or cock's tail-feathers, together with certain herbs, were thrown on the embers, causing the place to reek with foul smoke. Sometimes a bark-cloth was spread over the patient, and the pot with the smouldering embers was put under it. When the sufferer, sweating freely and more dead than alive, was at last uncovered, the ghost was supposed to have left him, driven out by the stinking fumes. But the medicine-man saw it lurking somewhere in the room, and he gave chase, making frantic efforts to catch it and holding a pot in which he sought to entrap it. But sometimes the ghost escaped from the house, and the medicine-man pursued it, screeching and hitting about in the air and trying to drive it back. The struggle might last some time, but in the end the medicine-man was sure to be successful in catching the ghost and covering up the pot with the struggling ghost inside of it. Then he carried the pot to waste land, where he burned it and the ghost. That was the end of the ghost ; so the sick man and his clan were rid of him.[1]

[1] J. Roscoe, *The Bakitara or Banyoro*, pp. 286 *sq.*

M

Among the Bagesu, a cannibal tribe living on the slopes of the lofty Mount Elgon in Kenya, a medicine-man sometimes attributes sickness to ghostly possession and declares that it must be cured by propitiating the ghost. He may say that the ghost is that of some relative which has been offended by his living kinsman and takes this mode of wreaking his revenge. Should the patient be a rich man, a hut is built as a shrine for the ghost with a long pole projecting through the apex of the thatched roof. The patient gives the medicine-man a goat or an ox to offer to the ghost ; the animal is killed near the shrine, the blood is caught in a vessel and put into the shrine with a portion of the meat. The people assemble in numbers to take part in the ceremony. After making the offering of blood, the medicine-man climbs the roof of the hut, and spikes a large piece of meat on the pole. Then he cuts it into small morsels which he throws among the crowd, who scramble for them and eat them. The sickness is supposed to be widely scattered by this ceremony and thus rendered harmless, while the patient quickly regains his usual health.[2]

The Nilotic Kavirondo in Kenya are quite different racially from the Bantu tribes who occupy most of the Uganda Protectorate, in which till lately Kavirondo was included. But their theory of disease caused by ghostly possession does not differ essentially from that of their Bantu neighbours. It is

[1] J. Roscoe, *The Bakitara or Ban-yoro*, pp. 287 *sq.*

[2] J. Roscoe, *The Northern Bantu*, p. 177.

true that they seem to trace sickness oftener to black magic than to ghosts, but when they see the hand of a ghost in a case of illness, their treatment of it conforms to what we may call the orthodox pattern. As usual, a medicine-man is consulted, and his ordinary verdict is that the ghosts of grandparents are afflicting their grandchildren because their father failed to perform the duties of a son to his father in his old age. The sage will now order a shrine to be built at the grave of the grandparent concerned, and the sick person's father offers a sheep or a goat at the grave, pouring out the blood as a libation on the ground and then eating the meat on the spot with a few relatives. The medicine-man can afterwards treat the sufferer with reasonable hope of restoring him to health, because the offended ghost has now been pacified and will allow the sick man to benefit by the treatment.[1]

Among the Bantu tribes in the valley of the Congo similar views are current as to sickness and disease caused by the spirits of the dead, and similar methods of cure are adopted. Thus, for example, among the Baluba, a large tribe in the Belgian Congo, the sickness of a child is sometimes thought to be due to the displeasure of his dead mother, because she thinks that her child has not received his proper share of the goods which she bequeathed at her death. When this has been revealed to the father by the medicine-man, he hastens to place in his child's hand a lance-head or a hoe, according as

1 J. Roscoe, *The Northern Bantu*, pp. 285 *sq.*

the child is a boy or a girl, enjoining the little one to hold it tight. Then he takes a white fowl or a small she-goat and gives it as a present to the sick child. Next morning he goes out into the forest and addressing the spirit of his dead wife, the mother of the sick child, he cries, " O thou who wast my wife, leave my child, torment him no more ! Go, return to thine abode in the underworld ! " The dead mother hears the father's cries, and content that her child has now received something she leaves him in peace. So the sick child recovers.[1]

So among the Baholoholo, another Bantu tribe of the Belgian Congo, when a man falls sick, the medicine-man may tell him that the sickness is due to the anger of his dead paternal grandmother. When he learns this melancholy truth, the sick man cries aloud to his grandmother's ghost, beseeching her not to let him die, and next morning he sends his sons to his grandmother's grave. They go and erect a little hut on the grave, and bury a fowl at the foot of the hut, and pour out a libation of beer. Mollified by these attentions the grandmother's ghost leaves her grandson alone, and he naturally recovers.[2]

But sometimes in this tribe the medicine-man declares that it is not the grandmother's ghost but the ghost of the patient's own father that is making him ill and calling him away to the spirit-land. This

---

[1] Le R. P. Colle, *Les Baluba*, ii. (Bruxelles, 1913) pp. 786 *sq.*

[2] R. Schmitz, *Les Baholoholo* (Bruxelles, 1912), p. 214.

case is much more serious than the other, because it is much more difficult to appease the ghost of a father than the ghost of a grandmother. So in the evening the medicine-man, accompanied by the brothers or sons of the patient, goes to the father's grave and digs up the body or the mouldering bones. Of these relics he burns a part, keeping only the skull and a few bones for his own future use. If the body has entirely disappeared, the medicine-man catches a rat, a lizard or any other little animal he may have found in digging up the grave. Whatever the animal may be, the sage declares that the soul of the sick man's father has entered into it; so he burns the creature solemnly, which is thought to render the father's ghost impotent, and the patient accordingly recovers.[1]

Among the Ewe-speaking peoples of the Slave Coast, in West Africa, sickness is often thought to be caused by some ancestral ghost, who requires the services of his descendant in Dead-land, and so is hastening his departure from the land of the living. In such a case the sick man sends for a priest, pays him a fee, and begs him to dispatch his soul to Dead-land to stop the importunities of the family ghost. The priest professes to send his soul on this mission by falling into a trance, and on coming to himself again he informs the patient that he has been to Dead-land and has seen the ghost who is causing the trouble. If he thinks that the patient is not very ill and in no risk of his life, he comforts

[1] R. Schmitz, *Les Baholoholo*, p. 215.

him with the assurance that the unquiet ghost has been pacified ; but if he judges the case to be serious and the issue doubtful, he confines himself to cautious ambiguities.[1]

Among the Yungur-speaking peoples of Northern Nigeria, if a person falls sick, he consults a diviner, who may declare that the sickness is due to an ancestral spirit. In that case the sick man has a small representation of the dead ancestor made for him in pottery, it may be either a figurine or simply a pot. Having obtained his figurine or pot, the owner kills a chicken and sprinkles the blood over the symbol with a prayer that, if it is indeed the ancestral spirit who is causing his illness, he will graciously accept the sacrifice and leave his descendant alone. The chicken is then cooked and eaten by the patient in the company of his relatives. If the sickness continues, the patient may again consult the diviner, who may this time prescribe the sacrifice of a goat. As most people have at various times been attacked by sickness, most possess pots or figurines for the abode of the spirits of dead grandfathers, fathers or even brothers. These pots are placed close to the owner's head at night, and when beer is brewed for any festival, libations are poured on the pots.[2]

That concludes what I have to say as to the belief that the spirits of the dead are often the causes of sickness and death. The evidence which I have

[1] A. B. Ellis, *The Ewe-speaking Peoples of the Slave Coast of West Africa* (London, 1890), pp. 109 *sq.*

[2] C. K. Meek, *Tribal Studies in Northern Nigeria*, ii. 460.

thus far adduced may suffice to prove that in the opinion of primitive or savage man the spirits of the dead are the sources of many of the ills which beset this our mortal life on earth ; in particular that he sees their handiwork in earthquakes, thunderstorms, drought, famine, disease and death. No wonder that he regards the supposed authors of such evils with awe and fear, and seeks to guard himself against them by all the means at his command. These means are various, and the devices to which he resorts in self-defence are manifold. Their general aim is, first, to send the spirits away, and next, to keep them at a distance; for so long as he believes them to be hovering near him the savage can never feel himself safe from their attacks ; in short, he desires, as far as possible, to rid himself of their dangerous neighbourhood. That this is his real wish and intention will appear, I think, from the many shifts and expedients which he adopts in order to banish the ghost from his old home and to prevent him from returning to it. These shifts and expedients are exceedingly various, some of them are very extraordinary, and taken altogether they exhibit in primitive man, as I have observed before, a resourcefulness and ingenuity worthy of a better cause. Regarded from the point of view of their intention, these expedients fall into two classes, according as they are meant to send the ghost away, or to keep him away and prevent him from returning. Regarded from the point of view of the means adopted to effect these purposes, the expedients fall into two general classes according as they are either fair or foul, in other words, according as they tend to propitiate or to compel the ghost. For, roughly speaking, the means employed to guard against ghosts are either persuasion, fraud or force, of which persuasion may be said to be fair, and fraud and force to be foul. All these means of guarding the living against ghosts I propose to illustrate by examples in what follows, and as I desire to place the character of ghosts and of primitive man in the best light possible, I will begin with what I have called the fair means of dealing with ghosts before I pass on to the foul, which must be reserved for subsequent lectures.

In the first place, then, when a death has taken place, primitive man often asks the ghost to go away and not to come back. This is the method of persuasion ; an appeal is made to what we may call the better feelings of the ghost.

Thus, for example, in the Kakadu tribe of Northern Australia, when a woman was buried, the women and children, led by an elderly female, marched round the grave in single file singing words to the following effect, which were supposed to be addressed to the spirit of the deceased : " You lie down quietly, do not come back, lie down all right —if the children see your spirit, later on they will be sick ".[1] At the conclusion of mourning the natives of New Caledonia, who make images of

[1] Baldwin Spencer, *Native Tribes of the Northern Territory of Aus-* *tralia* (London, 1914), pp. 240 sq.

their dead as memorials, accost the spirit of the deceased, saying, " Return now to your maternal kinsfolk in the forest.   Leave us.   We have loved you and made your portrait." [1]   The Kiwai of British New Guinea think that the ghost is apt to haunt the neighbourhood of his old home for some days after his decease ; so for a few nights after a death all the doors of the houses are kept carefully barred, and no one ventures out in the dark.   If the people in the house fancy that they hear the prowling ghost whistling outside or tapping at the barred door, they throw out food for the importunate spirit and beg him to go away, saying, " You go back, do not come.   You belong to the dead ; there is no use of your coming." [2]   Among the natives of the Purari Delta, in British New Guinea, when the detached heads of the departed kinsfolk are finally buried, the master of the ceremonies is said to address their spirits somewhat as follows: " Depart now for good and all.   Never return to our village. All these bodies of pigs and dogs are for you; so, too, all these coconuts and garden stuff (*talo*).   Now I bury you under the ground.   You are done with for ever." [3]

Among the Toradyas of Central Celebes, when a married person is buried, a rattan is placed on the coffin and cut in two, with these words : " Your marriage is cut off, your relation to your children

[1] M. Leenhardt, *Notes d'Ethnologie Néo-Calédoniennes* (Paris,1930), p. 9.
[2] G. Landtman, *The Kiwai Papuans of British New Guinea* (London, 1927), pp. 281 *sq.*

[3] F. E. Williams, *The Natives of the Purari Delta* (Port Moresby, 1924), pp. 222 *sq.*

is cut off. Go away and look no more after them."[1] And among the same people, when the deceased was the last of a group of brothers and sisters, they throw a handful of rice after the corpse, when it is being carried out of the house, and say, "Come not back. You have no longer any brothers or sisters here, and we do not yet wish to follow you." If the funeral procession passes other houses, the people in the houses call out to the dead man, "Go away. Look no more round at us ", and they throw out ashes to blind the ghost and prevent him from seeing his way back. And at the grave, when the body is being lowered into it, they cry out to the dead person, saying, "Go straight on. Call us not, for we are still well off here. Go to your fathers and mothers and your kinsfolk (who are dead) and plant bananas and sugar-cane for us."[2] Among the Alfoors of Minahassa in Northern Celebes, when a wife has died before her husband, the widower is led by a woman, with his head muffled, from the house to the place where his marriage was celebrated, there to take a last farewell from his departed spouse. The children and nearest relations follow, lamenting. Arrived at the place, the woman beseeches the spirit of the dead wife to go away and not to come and trouble the widower and children and make them ashamed.[3] In the Tumbuluh tribe

---

[1] N. Adriani en Alb. C. Kruijt, *De Bare-sprekende Toradjas van Midden-Celebes*, ii. 95.

[2] N. Adriani en Alb. C. Kruijt, *op. cit.* ii. 98.

[3] " De godsdienst en godsdienst plegtigheden der Alfoeren in de Menahassa op het eiland Celebes ", *Tijdschrift voor Nederlandsch Indië*, December 1849 (Groningen, 1849), p. 400.

of Minahassa, when a man has died, his spirit is solemnly invited to set out on the journey to the spirit-land and not to look back, for the way is now open. And some time afterwards the relatives go to the garden of the deceased, where a bamboo platform has been set up, laden with specimens of all the fruits which the dead man had cultivated. They all gather round the platform, while one of the eldest calls out in a loud voice, " O So-and-so, take something of all this produce for your journey. We also are going away." [1] Among the Southern Amis, a tribe of Formosa, at a burial it is customary for one of the family to throw a handful of earth on the grave and, addressing the deceased, to say, " You shall not return ".[2] In the Nicobar Islands, when a corpse is being carried out to burial, a medicine-man (*menluana*) commands the disembodied spirit to go quietly to the grave and remain there till the memorial feast takes place, when it will be required to proceed to the land of the dead. The spirit is further exhorted not to wander about in the meantime and frighten the living with its ghostly presence.[3]

The Kachins of Burma think that after a burial the spirit of the dead seeks to re-enter the house, but being foiled in the attempt, he finds the entrance to the pig-pen under the floor open, so he passes in

[1] J. G. F. Riedel, "Alte Gebräuche bei Heirathen, Geburt und Sterbefällen bei dem Toumbuluh-Stamm in der Minahassa (Nord-Selebes)", *Internationales Archiv für Ethnographie*, viii. (1895) pp. 108, 109.

[2] J. W. Davidson, *The Island of Formosa* (London, 1903), p. 579.

[3] E. H. Man, "Notes on the Nicobarese", *The Indian Antiquary*, xxviii. (1899) p. 258; *id.*, *The Nicobar Islands and their Inhabitants* (Guildford, N.D.), p. 137.

by it and takes up his abode for a time there on the ground. At the final obsequies the priest takes a spear in his hand, gives a terrific yell and, thrusting the spear into the floor, orders the ghost, who is lurking under it, to quit the house through the door of the pig-pen by which it had entered.[1] The Karens of Burma stand in great fear of the apparitions of the dead, so to appease the ghosts and prevent them from returning to haunt the living, the people go to the forest and there deposit a little basket of coloured rice, saying, " Ghosts of those who died by falling from a tree, ghosts of those who died of hunger or thirst, ghosts of those who died by a tiger's tooth or a serpent's fang, ghosts of those who perished of small-pox or cholera, ghosts of those who died of leprosy, do not molest us, do not catch us, do not do us any harm. Stay here in this wood. We will take care of you ; we will bring you red, yellow and white rice for your subsistence." [2] The Karieng are the aboriginal inhabitants of Siam, who, when the Siamese or Thai invaded the country from the north, retreated to the mountains on the east and west, where they still remain.[3] They burn their dead, after which they detach a bone from the skull and hang it on a tree, together with the clothes, ornaments and weapons of the deceased. After performing dances and pantomimes accompanied by

[1] W. J. S. Carrapiett, *The Kachin Tribes of Burma* (Rangoon, 1929), pp. 40, 44.

[2] Bringaud, " Les Karins de la Birmanie ", *Les Missions Catho-* *liques*, xx. (1888) p. 208.

[3] Mgr. Pallegoix, *Description du royaume Thai ou Siam* (Paris, 1854), i. 54.

mournful songs, some of the elders carry away the bone and the belongings of the departed and bury them secretly at the foot of a distant mountain, begging the ghost not to return and torment his family, since everything that he owned has been buried with him.[1]

Under the surface of their ancient civilization the Chinese have retained many primitive beliefs and customs concerning the dead. In some places on the eve of a burial tables covered with viands are placed before the tablet in the house which represents the deceased, and a priest addresses the spirit of the departed as follows : " We are now about to move your remains to the tomb ; and as you must of necessity accompany them to the tomb, and there remain with them in perpetuity, we have prepared for you a parting feast. Partake of it, we pray you." [2] And when the body has been lowered into the grave, the geomancer or the priest again addresses a few words to the soul of the deceased, telling it to remain with the corpse.[3] The Goldi are a primitive people of Eastern Asia, on the banks of the Amoor River. A Russian traveller has described one of their funerals, which he witnessed. The corpse was buried in a grave outside the village. Though the distance was short, the funeral procession halted thrice on the way, brandy was poured on the coffin, and the mourners called out to the dead, " Drink ! A happy journey to the land of souls ! Come not

---

[1] Mgr. Pallegoix, *Description du royaume Thai ou Siam* (Paris, 1854), i. 57 *sq.*

[2] J. H. Gray, *China* (London, 1878), i. 299 *sq.*

[3] J. H. Gray, *op. cit.* i. 304.

back, and take none of thy children with thee ! "
After the body was interred, a little hut was erected
at the grave, and the women called out to the dead
man, " We have built you a beautiful house. Farewell ! Take not thy wife and children to thee when
they come to pay thee a visit." [1]

The primitive Birhors of India bury with a dead
man a miniature hunting-net, an axe and two small
sticks used to support a net, and accosting his spirit
one of the elders says, " Go thou and hunt that
way. Do not come this way again." But if the
deceased was a woman, they bury with her a bundle
of fibres and say to her, " Do thou work with these.
Do not come back to us." [2] Among the Oraons of
India, when a corpse has been carried to the cremation-ground to be burnt, women put rice in the dead
man's mouth, saying, " Take, eat. Now you have
given us up. Now you have seen your way. Go,
taking with you all your sicknesses and sins." [3]
The Limbus, a tribe of Bengal, who are probably
of Mongolian descent, sometimes burn, but oftener
bury, their dead. A shaman or medicine-man (*phed-
angma*) attends at the funeral and delivers a brief
address to the departed spirit, concluding with a command to go whither his fathers have gone before and
not to come back to trouble the living with dreams. [4]

---

[1] " Schimkjewitschs Reisen bei
den Amurvölkern ", *Globus*, lxxiv.
(1898) p. 272.

[2] Sarat Chandra Roy, *The Birhors* (Ranchi, 1925), p. 270.

[3] Sarat Chandra Roy, *Oraon Religion and Customs* (Ranchi, 1928),

pp. 173 *sq.*

[4] (Sir) H. H. Risley, *Tribes and
Castes of Bengal, Ethnographic
Glossary* (Calcutta, 1891–1892), ii.
19 ; W. Crooke, *Popular Religion
and Folk-lore of Northern India*
(Westminster, 1896), ii. 57 *sq.*

When the Bana, a negro tribe of the Cameroons in West Africa, have buried one of their members, the men brandish their clubs threateningly at the soul (*lauona*) of the deceased, saying, " Soul, remain in the grave. Come not out of it. Every man must die. Give us no trouble." [1] The Kpelle, a negro tribe of Liberia, dislike the notion of the return of the ghost and think that only a bad ghost takes that liberty. After a death they always beg the spirit of the departed not to visit the living.[2] When the Verre, a tribe of Northern Nigeria, have laid a dead body in the grave, a priest addresses the deceased, saying, " You have lived long. Go now to the Sun and declare that you are the last of living men, and that it is useless to send for any more of us. And do you bear us no malice—return not to earth to interfere with our crops or prevent our women bearing children." [3]

At the burial of a North American Indian it used to be customary to address a few words to his departed spirit, asking him to remain in his own place and not to disturb his surviving friends and relatives.[4] Among the Tarahumare Indians of Mexico, when a man dies his weeping widow tells him that, " now that he has gone and does not want to stay with her any longer, he must not come back to frighten her or his sons or daughters or any one else.

---

[1] G. von Hagen, " Die Bana ", *Baessler-Archiv*, ii. (Leipzig and Berlin, 1912) pp. 108 *sq.*

[2] D. Westermann, *Die Kpelle* (Göttingen and Leipzig, 1921), p. 179.

[3] C. K. Meek, *Tribal Studies in Northern Nigeria*, i. 435.

[4] H. R. Schoolcraft, *Indian Tribes of the United States*, iv. 65.

She implores him not to carry any of them off, or do any mischief, but to leave them all alone. A mother says to her dead infant, ' Now go away! Don't come back any more, now that you are dead. Don't come at night to nurse at my breast. Go away, and do not come back ! ' And the father says to the dead child, ' Don't come back to ask me to hold your hand, or to do things for you. I shall not know you any more. Don't come walking around here, but stay away.' " [1]

But not content with requesting or commanding the souls of the dead to go away and not to come back, primitive man is often at pains to facilitate their departure and to speed them on their long journey to the spirit-land. Thus, for example, the Garos of Assam believe that the journey to the spirit-land, which they call Mangru-Mangram, " is a long one and the spirit is provided with a guide, the necessary eatables for the journey, and money for his requirements, exactly as if he were about to set out on a long journey on earth. These requirements are provided by the sacrifice of the necessary animals, and the offering of food and liquor at the shrines which form the last resting-place of the deceased." [2] The provisions thus made for securing a safe passage of the soul to the other world may no doubt be sometimes dictated by an affectionate regard for the spirit of the deceased, but taken along with the often repeated requests or commands to the

---

[1] C. Lumholtz, *Unknown Mexico* (London, 1903), i. 382.

[2] A. Playfair, *The Garos* (London, 1909), p. 103.

spirit to go away and stay away, they are probably prompted rather by fear of the ghost and a desire to get rid of him once and for all. Whatever their motive, the measures taken by the survivors for speeding the ghost on his way are varied in kind and shed an interesting light on the conceptions which primitive man forms of the life after death. It is therefore worth while to consider them in some detail.

In the first place, then, the savage sometimes furnishes the soul of the deceased with elaborate instructions as to the route he is to follow to the other world. Thus, for example, among the Kachins of Burma, at the final obsequies a priest, holding a spear before him and stepping on a sword, exhorts the spirit of the dead to leave its place in the house and to follow the central post up to the house-ridge and then depart by the front gable. Thence over grass, brush and trees, hills and mountains, brooks and rivers, the road is shown, until finally the White River is reached, which is the boundary between the land of the living and the land of the dead. The priest conducts the soul of the deceased across the rueful stream, exhorting it not to fear the wild boars on either bank, but, disguising itself by putting on the mask or forehead of a monkey, to pass nine cross-roads and at the tenth to turn off to the realm of the ancestral spirits. This is only a brief summary of the directions with which, as with a vade-mecum, the soul of a dead Kachin is provided to guide him to his long home.

N

We are told that to rehearse the formula at full length would occupy a whole night.[1] However, the route of Kachin souls to Dead-land varies with the particular tribe and clan to which the deceased belonged. On one of the routes the soul encounters a formidable caterpillar which seems to bar the road, raising and lowering its long body alternately. The priest instructs the dead man to wait till the body of the caterpillar is at its lowest point, and then to jump over it and pursue his way to where the spirits of his forefathers are waiting for him in the sacred grove (*numshang*) of the Happy Land.[2]

When the Kayans, a tribe in the interior of Borneo, are conveying a corpse in a coffin to its final place of rest, whether in a tree or on a pole, they repeatedly caution the dead man not to lose his way, but to be sure to take the middle road of three, avoiding the right-hand road, which leads to Borneo, and the left-hand road, which leads to the sea.[3]

But primitive man does not confine himself to telling the ghost the way he should go; he helps to open the path for him. Thus, for example, it is conceivable that after death the soul may be lingering in the skull, unable to find its way out; so among the Kurmis, a caste of cultivators in the Central Provinces of India, a son will sometimes strike his dead father's skull seven times with a log on the

[1] Rev. O. Hanson, *The Kachins* (Rangoon, 1913), p. 207.
[2] J. S. Carrapiett, *The Kachin Tribes of Burma* (Rangoon, 1929), p. 44 *sq.*
[3] James Brooke, *Journals*, i. 265.

funeral pyre, in order to crack his crown and so let out his soul.[1]   The Kirars, another caste of cultivators in the same province, content themselves with touching the head of a corpse with a bamboo before it is laid on the funeral pyre, " by way of breaking it and allowing the soul to escape if it has not already done so ".[2]

When a Birhor is dying, all persons present in the chamber of death stand aside or walk out of the hut, leaving the door open so that the parting soul may meet with no obstacle in setting out on its last journey.[3]   To clear the way for the soul of a dying man the Karens of Burma will sometimes make a hole in the thatched roof of the house, leaving it to the discretion of the soul to take its departure by the hole, by the door, by a window or by any other aperture it may prefer.[4]   Similarly among the Basutos of South Africa, when a native died within a hut, it used to be the practice to make a hole in the thatch of the roof to let his soul go out by it, since the Basutos think that the spirits of the dead cannot pass through any openings that are used by living people.[5]   In many parts of Germany it is said to be still customary after a death to open doors and windows in order to let the soul fly away ; in some places people even wave cloths to hasten its

[1] R. V. Russell, *Tribes and Castes of the Central Provinces of India*, iv. 75.

[2] R. V. Russell, *op. cit.* iii. 491.

[3] Sarat Chandra Roy, *The Birhors*, p. 261.

[4] J. B. Bringaud, " Un chapitre de l'ethnographie des Birmans Karins ", *Les Missions Catholiques*, xxviii. (Lyons, 1896) p. 521.

[5] T. Lindsay Fairclough, " Notes on the Basuto ", *Journal of the African Society*, iv. (1904–1905) p. 204.

departure.[1] In some parts of the Highlands of Scotland, when a person is dying, the door of the room is left slightly ajar to let his soul escape, but not wide enough to permit foul fiends to enter ; [2] from which we seem bound to infer that, in the opinion of these Highlanders, a fiend is more corpulent than a ghost. In the north-east of Scotland, " in the very moment of death all the doors and windows that were capable of being opened were thrown wide open, to give the departing spirit full and free egress, lest the evil spirits might intercept it in its heavenward flight ".[3] In some parts of England, at a death every bolt and lock in the house is unfastened, that the soul of the dying man or woman may fly freely away.[4]

When the body of a king of Michoacan, in Central America, was borne at midnight to the funeral pyre, it used to be preceded by torch-bearers and by men who swept the road, crying, " Lord, here thou hast to pass. See that thou dost not miss the way." [5] In Kan-Sou, a province of China, they place chairs at intervals along the road where a funeral procession passes, and the soul of the deceased is popularly believed to sit and rest on them

[1] R. Wuttke, *Sächsische Volkskunde* [2] (Dresden, 1901), p. 319. See further my essay, " On certain Burial Customs as illustrative of the Primitive Theory of the Soul ", *Garnered Sheaves* (London, 1931), p. 9. The references given there could easily be multiplied.

[2] Ch. Rogers, *Social Life in Scotland* (Edinburgh, 1884–1886), iii. 234.

[3] Rev. Walter Gregor, *Folk-lore of the North-East of Scotland* (London, 1881), p. 207.

[4] T. F. Thiselton Dyer, *English Folk-lore* (London, 1884), p. 230 ; J. Brand, *Popular Antiquities of Great Britain* (London, 1882–1883), ii. 231.

[5] H. H. Bancroft, *Native Races of the Pacific States* (London, 1875–1876), ii. 620 *sq.*

before pursuing his weary way to the grave.[1] In
Europe similar attentions to the comfort of the poor
ghost on his last journey are not unknown. Thus
in Masuria people think that the soul of a deceased
person always follows his body to the grave ; so if
the corpse is to be buried in another village, when
the funeral procession comes to the boundary a
handful of straw is thrown out from the hearse that
the ghost may sit on it and rest.[2]

A ghost notoriously experiences a difficulty about
crossing water ; hence some people considerately
provide a bridge for his use when he has to pass a
stream on his way to his last resting-place. Thus,
among the Khasis of Assam, when a funeral procession is conveying the calcined bones of a deceased
person to a cairn, where they are to repose, a man
walks in front strewing leaves of a certain sort to
guide the soul of the dead to the cairn, and if a
stream has to be crossed, a rough bridge of branches
and grass is thrown over it for the passage of the
ghost.[3] A similar custom is observed by the Chins
of Burma. They burn their dead and inter the
bones in the ancestral burial-ground, which is
generally situated in the depths of the jungle. When
they convey the bones to the cemetery they take with
them some cotton-yarn, and " whenever they come
to any stream or other water, they stretch a thread
across, whereby the spirit of the deceased, who

[1] J. Dols, " La vie chinoise dans
la province de Kan-sou ", *Anthropos*, x.-xi. (1915–1916) p. 744.
[2] M. Toeppen, *Aberglauben aus*
Masuren (Danzig, 1867), p. 109.

[3] P. R. T. Gurdon, *The Khasis*
(London, 1914), p. 134.

accompanies them, may get across it too. When
they have duly deposited the bones and food for the
spirit in the cemetery they return home, after bidding
the spirit to remain there, and not to follow them
back to the village." [1] For some time after a death
the Karens of Burma stretch threads beside the
footbridges in order to enable the spirit of the dead
to pass by them without meeting the living folk who
cross the bridges.[2] When the Trung Cha, a tribe
in the mountains of Tonquin, are conveying a dead
body to the place of burial and have to cross a
stream, they fasten a band or ribbon of white cloth
from bank to bank to serve as a bridge for the soul
of the deceased, lest it should fall into the water and
be swept away by the current.[3] The Chinese believe that the souls of the dead, on their way to the
other world, have to cross a certain river by a bridge,
but that the souls of the wicked fall from the bridge
into the stream, where they are tormented by
serpents and crocodiles. However, the Buddhist
monks have a way of guarding against these painful
accidents. They set up a miniature bridge of paper
or cloth, and while some of them are mumbling
prayers, one of them passes the memorial tablet of
the deceased across the bridge, thus securing for
the poor sinner a safe passage over the sombre
stream to the other world.[4]

[1] Rev. G. Whitehead, " Notes on
the Chins of Burma ", *The Indian
Antiquary*, xxxvi. (1907) pp. 214 *sq.*
[2] Max and Bertha Ferrers, *Burma*
(London, 1900), p. 153.

[3] E. Diguet, *Les Montagnards du
Tonquin* (Paris, 1908), pp. 102 *sq.*
[4] J. Dols, " La vie chinoise dans
la province de Kan-sou ", *Anthropos*,
x.-xi. (1915-1916) p. 742.

Savages who dwell beside the sea sometimes provide their dead with canoes in which their souls may sail away to their final place of rest. Thus in Mille, one of the Marshall Islands in the Pacific, it used to be customary to wrap the dead in mats and bury them ; after which a little canoe, fitted with a sail and laden with pieces of coconuts or other food, was taken down to the shore and sent off with a fair wind " to bear far away from the island the spirit of the deceased, that it may not afterwards disturb the living ".[1] In Nukahiva, one of the Marquesas Islands in the Pacific, the American seaman, Captain David Porter, who spent some months in the island in 1813, was told by the natives that they believed the abode of the dead " to be an island, somewhere in the sky, abounding with everything desirable ; that those killed in war and carried off by their friends, go there, provided they are furnished with a canoe and provisions ; but that those who are carried off by the enemy, never reach it, unless a sufficient number of the enemy can be obtained to paddle his canoe there ".[2] Near a grave in a sacred grove of the island Captain Porter saw four fine war canoes, provided with outriggers and decorated with human hair and streamers. In the stern of each of them was the effigy of a man holding a paddle as if in the act of steering. On inquiry of the natives Captain Porter learned that the dignified figure

---

[1] H. Hale, *Ethnography and Philology of the United States Exploring Expedition* (Philadelphia, 1846), p. 89.

[2] Captain David Porter, *Journal of a Cruise to the Pacific Ocean* (New York, 1822), ii. 113.

seated in the stern of the most magnificent canoe
represented a priest who had been killed not long
before by their enemies, the Happahs. In the
bottom of the priest's canoe were the putrefying
bodies of two natives (Typees) whom the Americans
had recently killed in battle, and lying about the
canoe were many other corpses of men with the flesh
still on them. The three other canoes, Captain
Porter was informed, belonged to different other
warriors who had been killed or had died not long
before. " I asked them ", continues Captain Porter,
" why they had placed their effigies in the canoes,
and also why they had put the bodies of the dead
Typees in that of the priest ? They told me (as
Wilson interpreted) that they were going to heaven,
and that it was impossible to get there without
canoes. The canoe of the priest, being large, he was
unable to manage it himself, nor was it right that
he should, he being now a god. They had therefore
placed in it the bodies of the Happahs and Typees,
which had been killed since his death, to paddle him
to the place of his destination ; but he had not been
able yet to start, for the want of a full crew, as it
would require ten to paddle her, and as yet they had
only procured eight. They told me also that the
taboo, laid in consequence of his death, would continue until they had killed two more of their enemies,
and by this means completed the crew. I inquired
if he took any sea stock with him. They told me
he did, and pointing to some red hogs in an enclosure,
said that they were intended for him, as well as a

quantity of bread-fruit, coconuts, etc., which would be collected from the trees in the grove. I inquired if he had to go far; they replied, no; and pointing to a small square stone enclosure, informed me that was their heaven, that he was to go there. This place was tabooed, they told me, for every one except their priests." [1]

The Kiwai of British New Guinea are accustomed to leave a canoe, or at all events a piece of one, beside a grave, to enable the soul of the dead to voyage to Adiri, the land of departed spirits.[2] The Melanaus of Borneo " build picturesque boats, decorated with flags and other embellishments, which are dedicated to the use of departed spirits, who are supposed to travel in them on marine migrations. These crafts are placed near their graves." Sometimes these boats, laden with a supply of clothes and food for the use of the dead, were sent floating out to sea on a strong ebb tide to waft the spirit to its long home. In former times a slave-woman was often chained to the boat to serve her dead master on his last voyage.[3]

Sometimes the canoe which conveys the spirit of the dead to the other world, is like the spirit itself, invisible. It was so in the funeral ceremony which the Nakelo tribe of Fiji used to perform for their dead chiefs. While the body of the chief was lying

[1] Captain David Porter, *Journal of a Cruise to the Pacific Ocean* (New York, 1882), ii. 109-111. Compare J. G. Frazer, *The Belief in Immortality and the Fear of the Dead*, ii. 364-366.

[2] G. Landtman, *The Kiwai Papuans of British New Guinea*, p. 264; E. Baxter Riley, *Among Papuan Headhunters*, p. 166.

[3] Charles Brooke, *Ten Years in Sarawak* (London, 1866), i. 78 *sq.*

in state in his house, surrounded by a silent multitude of his subjects, three old men of a certain clan approached, holding fans in their hands. One of them entered the house, while the other two waited in the doorway. He flourished his fan over the dead man's face and called him, saying, " Rise, sir, the chief, and let us be going. Broad day has come over the land." And the soul of the dead man was believed to rise up at the call. Holding his fan horizontally a little above the floor, and walking backwards, the old man led the spirit from the house. The other two old men joined him at the doorway, holding their fans in like manner about two feet above the ground as a shelter for the spirit, who was clearly supposed to be of short stature. Thus they went along the path, followed in reverential silence by a multitude of men, no women being allowed to join the procession. When they came to the bank of the river, one of the three old men who were escorting the chief's spirit climbed a tree and cried in a loud voice, " Themba, bring over the canoe ! " This call he repeated thrice, whereupon the people fled in all directions and hid themselves. For Themba was the Nakelo Charon who ferried departed souls across the river. After summoning the ghostly ferryman the three old men waited by the riverside until they saw a wave rolling in towards the shore, which they believed to be the surge of the approaching canoe. They said that a blast of wind accompanied it, and that the wave dashed the spray over the bank. At that sign they averted their faces, pointed their fans suddenly to the river, and cried aloud, " Go on board, sir ! " After that they ran for their lives, for no eye of living man might look on the embarkation of the dead chief's soul.[1]

Some people who bury their dead obligingly furnish them with ladders on which to climb up to heaven, or to wherever the place of bliss may be. Thus when the Mangars, one of the fighting tribes of Nepaul, have buried one of their number, two bits of wood, about three feet long, are set up on either side of the grave, and in one of them are cut nine steps or notches forming a ladder for the spirit of the dead to ascend to heaven. The maternal uncle officiates as priest at the burial, and as he steps out of the grave he bids a solemn farewell to the dead and calls upon him to ascend to heaven by the ladder which stands ready for him.[2] It is a popular belief in Russia that the soul of a dead person has to rise from the grave ; hence to assist him in rising it is, or used to be, customary with the peasants to bury certain utensils with him in the grave, such as little ladders and plaited thongs. Even at the present day, when many of them have forgotten the origin of the custom, the peasants of some districts make little ladders of dough and have them baked for the benefit of the dead. " In the

---

[1] Rev. Lorimer Fison, " Notes on Fijian Burial Customs ", *Journal of the Anthropological Institute*, x. (1881) pp. 147 *sq.*

[2] Sir H. H. Risley, *Tribes and Castes of Bengal, Ethnographic Glossary*, ii. 75 ; W. Crooke, *Popular Religion and Folk-lore of Northern India*, ii. 60 *sq.*

Government of Voroneja a ladder of this sort, about three feet high, is set up at the time when a coffin is being carried to the grave ; in some other places similar pieces of dough are baked in behalf of departed relatives on the fortieth day after their death, or long pies marked cross-wise with bars are taken to church on Ascension Day and divided between the priest and the poor. In some villages these pies, which are known as *Lyesenki* or 'Ladderlings ', have seven bars or rungs, in reference to the ' Seven Heavens '." [1] Clearly nothing could be more appropriate than that the souls of the dead should ascend to the Seventh Heaven on Ascension Day by swarming up a long pie as a ladder marked with seven rungs. But the custom need not be, and probably is not, of Christian origin. In many graves of ancient Egypt, belonging to the later period, ladders have been found, and it is a reasonable conjecture of Professor Adolf Erman that they were intended to help the souls of the dead to clamber out of the sepulchral shafts.[2] The Shans of Burma, though they do not provide the dead man with a ladder, sometimes supply its place with a rope, which hangs down into the grave until the coffin has been finally lowered into it. Then the rope is pulled out in the direction of the north, " to help the spirit of the dead person to begin his journey to Mount Meru, the great spirit moun-

---

[1] W. R. S. Ralston, *The Songs of the Russian People* [2] (London, 1872), pp. 110 *sq.* Compare J. N. Smirnov, *Les Populations finnoises des bassins de la Volga et de la Kamma* (Paris, 1898), p. 141.

[2] Adolf Erman, *Die ägyptische Religion* [2] (Berlin, 1909), pp. 210 *sq.*

tain, which lies, it is believed, north of our
world ".[1]

Some people think that the soul of a dead person
needs an animal or bird to guide or carry him to the
spirit-land, and they obligingly provide him with
the necessary creature. A dog is often employed
as the guide of the soul. Thus among the Greenlanders, " when little children die and are buried,
they put the head of a dog near the grave, fancying
that children having no understanding, they cannot
by themselves find the way, but the dog must guide
them to the land of souls ".[2] Similarly the Catios
Indians of Colombia, in South America, think that
a dead man needs a dog to conduct him to the spirit-
land, and apparently (though this is not expressly
stated) they furnish him with a canine guide.[3]
Some of the Garos of Assam believe that the souls
of the dead could never find their way unaided to
the spirit-land ; so at the cremation-ground they
kill a dog and burn it with the corpse to guide the
dead man's soul to Chikmang, the land of souls.[4]
Among the Lakhers, when a child dies who has not
yet learned to talk, a dog must be killed in order
that the child's soul may hold on to the dog's tail
and so find its way to Athiki, the land of the dead.[5]
The Meo, a tribe of mountaineers in Tonquin, dress

[1] Mrs. Leslie Milne, *Shans at
Home* (London, 1910), p. 95.
[2] Hans Egede, *Description of
Greenland* (London, 1818), p. 153.
[3] Fr. Severino de Santa Teresa,
" Religion und soziale Verhältnisse
der Catios-Indianer in Kolumbien ",

Archiv für Religionswissenschaft,
xxiii. (1925) p. 296.
[4] W. W. Hunter, *Statistical Account of Assam* (London, 1879), ii.
154; A. Playfair, *The Garos* (London, 1909), p. 109.
[5] N. E. Parry, *The Lakhers*, p. 388.

a dead man in his best clothes, taking care to undo all the fastenings in them in order to let his soul fly freely away ; and to the right hand of the corpse they tether a dog, which is to guide the departed spirit to the other world.[1] According to one account, the dog in question is made of lacquer,[2] but no doubt in that case he serves the purpose quite as well as the living animal.

Some people prefer a pig to a dog as the guide of the departed soul to its long home. Thus among the Lolos, a primitive aboriginal people of Southern China, as soon as a death has taken place, a pig is led to a fountain, where it is killed. They think that in the other world the soul of the deceased person, being a newcomer, will not know where to find water to slake his thirst, but that the soul of the dead pig, fresh from its slaughter at the fountain, will be sure to guide its master's spirit to some spring or stream.[3] On the day after a death the Khyeng of Arakan tie a dead fowl to the big toe of the deceased, and a priest addresses the dead man as follows: "O spirit, thou hast a long and wearisome journey before thee, so a hog has been killed upon whose spirit thou mayest ride, and the spirit of the dead fowl will so terrify the worm guarding the portals of paradise that thou wilt find an easy entrance ".[4]

---

[1] E. Diguet, *Les Montagnards du Tonquin* (Paris, 1908), pp. 143 *sq.*

[2] H. Baudesson, *Au pays des superstitions et des rites* (Paris, 1932), p. 129 ; *id.*, *Indo-China and its Primitive People* (London, N.D.), p. 174.

[3] A. Liétard, *Au Yun-nan. Les Lo-lop'o* (Münster i.W., 1913), p. 171.

[4] Major G. E. Fryer, " On the Khyeng People of the Sandoway District, Arakan ", *Journal of the Asiatic Society of Bengal*, xliv. (1875) p. 43.

The Bhils, a primitive people of Central India, appear to choose the horse, if it be only a clay horse, as the best vehicle for wafting the human soul to heaven. On the tops of high hills they are said to erect images of horses made of burnt clay and arranged in rows on platforms. An English surgeon, who inquired the meaning of the custom, received the following explanation : " Heaven is supposed to be but a short distance from earth, but the souls of the dead have to reach it by a very painful and weary journey, which can be avoided to some extent during life by ascending high hills, and there depositing images of the horse, which in addition to reminding the gods of the work already accomplished, shall serve as chargers upon which the soul may ride a stage to bliss ". The surgeon adds that " the more modest (of the Bhils) make a hollow clay image, with an opening in the rear, into which the spirit may creep. An active Bhil may, in this fashion, materially shorten the journey after death. Both men and women follow the custom." [1]

In India the favourite animal for the conveyance of the soul to heaven is the sacred cow. Hence, when a Brahman dies, a calf is allowed to wander in the name of the deceased, in order that, by grasping its tail, the dead man may cross the dreaded river Virja nadi, which divides the land of the dead from the land of the living.[2] But it is

[1] T. H. Hendley, Surgeon, " An Account of the Maiwar Bhils ", *Journal of the Asiatic Society of* *Bengal*, xliv. (1875) pp. 347 *sq.*

[2] J. Abbott, *The Keys of Power* (London, 1932), p. 397.

not Brahmans alone who find salvation in this quaint fashion. When a Kir, member of a caste of cultivators in the Central Provinces of India, is about to die, he makes a present of a cow to a Brahman in order that, by catching hold of the animal's tail, he may cross in safety the horrible River of Death.[1] A similar custom is observed by the Kurmis, another caste of cultivators in the same province.[2]

Some people choose a bird as the vehicle to waft the soul of the dead to the realms of bliss. On the evening of a burial the Iroquois used to release a bird over the grave " to bear away the spirit to its heavenly rest ".[3] Among the Yorubas of West Africa, after a death the deceased is called thrice by name and adjured to depart and no longer to haunt the dwellings of the living; and to facilitate his departure a fowl is sacrificed, " which, besides a right-of-way for his soul, is supposed also to guide it ".[4] At a death the Khasis of Assam sacrifice a cock, which is called " The cock that scratches the way ", because it is thought to scratch a path for the spirit of the dead to the next world.[5] The Karens of Burma cremate their dead and deposit the calcined bones in a shrine consisting of a miniature hut, on which there is always the rude carving of a bird. This bird represents a certain mythical creature which is supposed to convey the spirit of

[1] R. V. Russell, *Castes and Tribes of the Central Provinces of India,* iii. 483.

[2] R. V. Russell, *op. cit.* iv. 74.

[3] Lewis H. Morgan, *League of the Iroquois* (Rochester, 1851), p. 174.

[4] A. B. Ellis, *The Yoruba-speaking Peoples of the Slave Coast of West Africa* (London, 1894), p. 160.

[5] R. T. Gurdon, *The Khasis* [2] (London, 1914), p. 132.

the deceased on its wanderings over rivers and chasms.[1] The Tho of Tonquin fasten duck's feathers to the clothes of a dead person in order to enable his spirit to fly over the streams that may cross his path in the other world.[2] Many peoples have been in the habit of supplying their dead with money or its equivalent to enable them to defray the expenses of the journey to the other world. Elsewhere I have given many examples of the custom,[3] which might easily be multiplied ; here I must content myself with citing a few typical specimens. Thus the Khasis of Assam place money in the coffin beside the corpse, " so that the spirit of the deceased may possess the wherewithal to buy food on its journey ".[4] The Lolos insert money and rice in the mouth of the corpse, thus providing him both with food and travelling expenses for his last journey.[5] Among the Mosquito Indians of Central America every child soon after birth has a bag of seeds tied round its neck " in order to pay the price of being ferried across a certain river that separates this from the next world, should it die young ".[6] The Kakhyens of Burma put a piece of silver in

[1] Max and Bertha Ferrers, *Burma* (London, 1900), p. 153.

[2] Baudesson, *Au pays des superstitions et des rites* (Paris, 1932), pp. 128 *sq*. In the English translation of this book the bird is incorrectly described as a goose. The French word is *canard*. See H. Baudesson, *Indo-China and its Primitive People* (London, N.D.), p. 172.

[3] J. G. Frazer, " On certain Burial Customs as illustrative of the Primitive Theory of the Soul ", *Journal of the Anthropological Institute*, xv. (1886) pp. 77-79 ; *id.*, *Garnered Sheaves* (London, 1931), pp. 19 *sq*.

[4] P. R. T. Gurdon, *The Khasis* [2] (London, 1914), p. 133.

[5] A. Liétard, *Au Yun-nan. Les Lo-lop'o* (Münster i.W., 1913), p. 172.

[6] Chas. N. Bell, " The Mosquito Territory ", *Journal of the Royal Geographical Society*, xxxii. (1862) p. 254 ; H. H. Bancroft, *Native Races of the Pacific States*, iii. 543.

O

the mouth of a corpse " to pay ferry dues over the streams the spirit may have to cross ",[1] and a similar custom is observed by the Burmese generally ; between the teeth of the dead they insert a piece of gold or silver called *kado akah*, that is, " ferry toll ", to pay for the passage of the mystic river which is known to 'exist, but concerning which it is difficult to extract any definite information from the Burmese.[2] The coin which the ancient Greeks inserted in the mouth of the dead to pay Charon for ferrying them across the Styx [3] is the most familiar case of a ferry-toll provided by survivors for the comfort and convenience of the ghosts.[4] But it is not so commonly known that in antiquity at the city of Hermion there was a short cut to hell down through a chasm, which avoided the necessity of going round by the Styx ; so the thrifty people of Hermion put no money in the mouths of their dead to pay for their passage across the river, which would have been a perfectly needless expense. According to the local legend, it was through this chasm that Hercules dragged up Cerberus, the hound of hell,[5] so that he had no ferry-toll to pay to Charon either for himself or for the dog. The pawky hero might almost have been a Scotchman.

[1] J. Anderson, *Mandalay to Momien* (London, 1876), p. 143.

[2] C. J. F. S. Forbes, *British Burma* (London, 1878), p. 93; Shway Yoe (Sir J. G. Scott), *The Burman* (London, 1882), ii. 338.

[3] Lucian, *De luctu*, 10.

[4] Strabo, viii. 6. 12, p. 373.

[5] Pausanias, ii. 35. 10.

INDEX

Abasimu, malicious spirits, 59

Abchases, the, try to recover the soul of the dead, 28-9

Abo, the, their propitiation of the dead, 92

Acacia horrida, 110

Adiri, the land of departed spirits, 185

Adriani, N., on the Indonesians, 41

Aegina, house-burial in, 18

Africa, house-burial in, 17, 18; the belief in reincarnation in, 20 *n.*[4]; the fear of the dead in, 49-69; the propitiation of the dead in, 78-81, 89-93; the offering of the first-fruits to the dead in, 99-102; drought produced by the dead in, 103-7, 140; the dead invoked in warfare in, 110-11; consulted as oracles in, 125-31; earthquakes attributed to the dead in, 135-6; illness attributed to the dead in, 148-66; driving away the dead in, 175; speeding the dead on their way in, 179; the dead provided with guides in, 192

Afterworld, the primitive notion of the, 12-13, 43, 44, 50-51

Agriculture influenced by the dead, 39, 43, 46, 51-2, 74-5, 81-102, 138-40, 175; taught by the Sun-god, 41

Ahirs, the, bring back the soul of the dead to the house, 22-3

A-Kamba, the, offer their first-fruits to the dead, 101-2

Alfoors, the, drive away the dead, 170

Ambrym, the natives of, consult the dead as oracles, 118-19

America, North, the fear of the dead in, 69-71; driving away the dead in, 175; the dead provided with animals as guides in, 189, 192

——, South, burial in the house in, 17; the fear of the dead in, 71-3; the use of the dead in warfare in, 114-15; the dead regarded as the cause of storms in, 137-8; the dead provided with guides in, 189

Amis, the Southern, drive away the dead, 171

Amputation, aversion to, 60-61

Ancestral spirits, the belief in, 45 *sqq.* and *passim*

Andaman Islanders, the, their practice of house-burial, 20; attribute earthquakes to the action of the dead, 134-5

Animals, the dead provided with, as guides, 189-93

Animism, the elaborate, of Indonesia, 39; in Madagascar, 49-50

Antelope-blood offered to the dead, 80

Antu, a spirit, 43

Arakan, the dead provided with guides in, 190

Araucanians, the, attribute storms to the action of the dead, 138

Argolis, house-burial in, 18

Aristotle, 6

Assam, speeding the dead on their way in, 176, 181, 193; the dead provided with guides in, 189, 192

Boats provided for the dead, 183-5

Bonito fishing controlled by the dead, 76

Borneo, the fear of the dead in, 43-4; the invocation of the dead in, 111-112; speeding the dead on their way in, 178, 185

Brahmans die of indigestion, 48; provided with calves as guides on death, 191

Bright, John, 40

Bull-roarers, 82, 84

Bundelkhand, 89

Bura, the, offer their first-fruits to the dead, 102

Burial in the house, 17-21

Burma, the fear of the dead in, 45-6; illness attributed to the dead in, 147; driving away the dead in, 171-2; speeding the dead on their way in, 177-8, 179, 181-2, 188-9; the dead provided with guides in, 192-3; the dead provided with money in, 193-4

Calf, a, provided for the dead as a guide, 191

Cambodia, illness attributed to the dead in, 146

Canoes provided for the dead, 183-5

Cape King William, the natives near, their invocation of the dead, 84

Caribs, the Central, their denial of survival, 8-9

Catios Indians, the, provide the dead with dogs as guides, 189

Celebes, the fear of the dead in, 41-3, 84-5, 103, 169-71

Cerberus, 194

Chapi, 88

Charms given by the dead, 44

Charon, 194

Chiefs deified after death, 42; feared after death, 36, 45, 90-91, 140; their spirits consulted as oracles, 126-31

Chikmang, the land of souls, 189

Childbirth influenced by the dead, 108-10, 175

Children buried in the house, 20; reincarnation into, 20, 22, 24, 26, 126; help given by the souls of, 81

Chinese, the, attribute drought to the action of the dead, 138-9; drive away the dead, 173; speed the dead on their way, 180-81, 182; provide the dead with pigs as guides, 190

Chins, the, speed the dead on their way, 181-2

Choroti Indians, the, attribute storms to the action of the dead, 137

Chota Nagpur, the fear of the dead in, 46-7

Chukchis, the, view the dead as wicked, 46

Cocks, the dead provided with, as guides, 192

Codrington, Dr. R. H., on the Melanesians, 34, 35, 36, 118

Conibos, the, regard thunder as the voice of the dead, 137

Convulsions ascribed to the action of the dead, 37, 46

Corn, the help of the dead invoked in the growing of, 90, 91-2

Cows, the dead provided with, as guides, 191-2

Crete, house-burial in, 18

Cricket, manifestation of the dead in the form of a, 45

Crocodiles, the dead invoked against, 78-9

Crops influenced by the dead, 39, 43, 46, 51-2, 74-5, 81-102, 138-40, 175

Crows as representatives of the dead, 48; their longevity, 48

Dacota, the, their awe of the dead, 69-70

Dead, the, almost universally feared, 5-6, 10-11; their influence on the living, 11-12; their life similar to that on earth, 12-13, 43, 44, 50-51; exceptions to the fear of, 13-29; their skulls preserved, 17, 19, 76, 92, 98, 106-7; buried in the house, 17-21, 102; their spirits brought back to the house, 21-9, 97-8; driven away by the living, 33 sqq.,

THE FEAR OF THE DEAD
IN PRIMITIVE RELIGION
VOL. II

MACMILLAN AND CO., LIMITED
LONDON · BOMBAY · CALCUTTA · MADRAS
MELBOURNE

THE MACMILLAN COMPANY
NEW YORK · BOSTON · CHICAGO
DALLAS · ATLANTA · SAN FRANCISCO

THE MACMILLAN COMPANY
OF CANADA, LIMITED
TORONTO

THE
FEAR OF THE DEAD
IN PRIMITIVE RELIGION

LECTURES DELIVERED ON
THE WILLIAM WYSE FOUNDATION
AT TRINITY COLLEGE, CAMBRIDGE

BY

SIR JAMES GEORGE FRAZER
O.M., F.R.S., F.B.A.

FELLOW OF TRINITY COLLEGE, CAMBRIDGE
ASSOCIATE MEMBER OF THE *INSTITUT DE FRANCE*

VOL. II

MACMILLAN AND CO., LIMITED
ST. MARTIN'S STREET, LONDON

1934

PRINTED IN GREAT BRITAIN
BY R. & R. CLARK, LIMITED, EDINBURGH

PREFACE

In this second course of lectures on the " Fear of the Dead in Primitive Religion " I resume the subject at the point at which I left off at the end of the first course. I said there that primitive man attempts to get rid of the dangerous spirits of the dead by one or other of two methods, either the method of persuasion and conciliation or the method of force and fraud. In the first course I illustrated the former method, that of persuasion and conciliation, by a variety of examples. I now take up the second method, that of force and fraud, or deception. For primitive man imagines that the spirits of the dead are not only amenable to physical force, but that they can be deceived or cheated into doing his will. In the present course I have dealt mainly with the method of force, showing how primitive man attempts to drive away the spirits of the dead by sheer physical force, and to keep them at a distance by interposing physical obstacles between him and them. The method of fraud or deception practised on the spirits of the dead has been incidentally illustrated ; but this curious aspect of primitive religion must be reserved for fuller treatment in a subsequent work, in which I shall hope to discuss many other important sides of the subject, which the limitations of time have compelled me to pass over at present. Meanwhile this volume concludes the second course of my lectures on the William Wyse Foundation at Trinity College.

J. G. FRAZER

April 1934

CONTENTS

LECTURE I

LECTURE I

In my former lectures on the fear of the dead in primitive religion, I reached or anticipated certain general conclusions which it may be well to recapitulate before I proceed to develop the subject in further detail. We saw that the belief in immortality, or to speak more correctly, the belief in the survival of human personality for an indefinite time after death, has been widespread if not universal among mankind, being shared by the races of lower culture, whom we call savages or barbarians, as well as by the civilized nations who now cherish the belief as a fundamental article of their religious creed. But among the races of lower culture, who may be called primitive in a relative sense by comparison with the civilized nations, the spirits of the dead appear to be predominantly feared rather than loved, for they are believed to be the sources of many evils which afflict humanity, including the last evils, sickness and death. Hence, primitive man is often at great pains to send these dangerous spirits away and to keep them at a safe distance from him. At the same time, I pointed out in my lectures, and I desire now to repeat, that this fear of the dead appears to be by no means characteristic in the same degree of all the races of men, even those of lower culture, for many of them observe customs which appear to be inconsistent with such a fear, and to indicate rather respect and affection for the souls of the departed. Thus, for example, many peoples have been accustomed to welcome home the spirits of the dead and entertain them at a great festival once a year, of which the rites of All Souls' Day in Europe have furnished a conspicuous instance down to modern times.[1] Again, many peoples have been in the habit of burying their dead in their houses ; a practice which is hardly consistent with a deep-seated fear of the dead and a dread of close contact with them. Other peoples, again, though they do not bury the dead in the house, attempt to bring back their spirits to the house and to install them there, which incontestably proves that they expect to reap some benefit from the presence of the spirits in the dwelling. For it is commonly supposed that the spirits of the dead can confer many benefits on the living, if only they are duly propitiated, and kept in good humour, though they are quick to resent any fancied slight or neglect on the part of the survivors. Among the benefits so anticipated appears to be the hope that the spirits will ultimately be reborn in the infants of the family. Once more, the practice of embalming the bodies of the dead, as has been well pointed out by Mr. Warren Dawson,[2]

---

[1] I have collected many examples of such festivals in *The Golden Bough*, Part IV. *Adonis, Attis, Osiris*, ii. pp. 51 *sqq.*

[2] Warren R. Dawson in *Folk-Lore*, xliv. (December 1933) p. 416.

undoubtedly aims at preserving the bodies of the dead, and presumably, therefore, their spirits, for an indefinite time after death, which would certainly not be done if the living did not expect to receive some benefit from the continued existence of the dead. The classic land of embalming was ancient Egypt, and in its extant literature, as I am informed by our eminent English Egyptologist, Mr. Alan H. Gardiner, there is very little trace of a fear of the dead. To sum up : the attitude of primitive man to the spirits of the dead is complex ; it is a compound of hope and fear, of affection and aversion, of attraction and repulsion, and in any attempt to analyse it, full account should be taken of all these conflicting emotions and tendencies. But in investigating our complex subject it is legitimate, I trust, to single out some one particular element of the compound for special examination. That must be my justification for here concentrating attention on the element of fear in the attitude of primitive man towards the spirits of the dead.

In my last lecture, I dealt with the means which primitive man adopts for banishing the dangerous spirits of the dead and keeping them at a distance. I said that these means fall into two classes, which may be distinguished respectively as fair or foul, according as they are based on either persuasion and conciliation, or on force and fraud. When the method of persuasion and conciliation is adopted, the ghost is invited or entreated to go quietly away to the spirit-land and to stay there, not returning to torment the living with his unwelcome attentions. He is provided with directions for the journey to the spirit-land and with a guide to conduct him thither : he receives food to eat and money to defray his expenses on the road ; and he is furnished with a bridge or a boat to enable him to cross any rivers or seas which he may encounter on his passage to the far country. But in the opinion of many primitive peoples, there are obdurate and obstreperous spirits who, turning a deaf ear to blandishments and a blind eye to the accommodations obligingly offered them for the journey, obstinately persist in haunting their old home, and persecuting their surviving kinsfolk in a great variety of ways. In the case of such incorrigible spirits nothing remains but to drive them away by sheer force, and to force in such circumstances primitive man does not hesitate to have recourse. This introduces us to the foul treatment of the spirits of the dead to which we must now turn our attention.

Thus, for example, at a burial in Melville Island, North Australia, all the men present have been seen to charge at the invisible spirit of the dead man, throwing sticks and spears at it in order to drive it into the grave.[1] The Arunta of Central Australia believe that after his death a man's ghost is free to walk the earth for a period of twelve or eighteen months, but that after that time it is necessary to confine his restless spirit within narrower bounds.

[1] Baldwin Spencer, *Native Tribes of the Northern Territory of Australia* (London, 1914), p. 233.

The favourite haunt of the ghost is believed to be the burnt and deserted camp where he died. Here accordingly, on a certain day, a band of men and women, the men armed with shields and spear-throwers, assemble and begin dancing round the charred and blackened remains of the camp, shouting and beating the air with their weapons and hands in order to drive away the lingering spirit from the spot he loves too well. When the dance is over the whole party proceeds at a run to the grave, chasing the ghost before them. In vain the poor ghost makes a last bid for freedom and doubles back towards the camp ; the leader of the party, making a long circuit, cuts off the retreat of the fugitive. Finally, having run the ghost to earth they trample him down into the grave, dancing and stamping on the heaped-up soil, while with downward thrusts through the air they beat and force him underground.[1] After a series of deaths a band of the Kamilaroi tribe in New South Wales used to scour the country, dancing and beating the air with branches to drive away the dangerous spirits of the dead, while a chorus of women and girls helped them by their songs.[2] The natives of the Banks' Islands believe that after a death the spirit of the deceased does not at once depart, but continues to haunt the neighbourhood for five or ten days ; but as they

[1] Baldwin Spencer and F. J. Gillen, *The Native Tribes of Central Australia* (London, 1899), pp. 498-508.
[2] Rev. Wm. Ridley, *Kamilaroi, and other Australian Languages* (Sydney, 1875), p. 149 ; *id.* " Report on the Australian Language and Traditions ", *Journal of the Anthropological Institute*, ii. (1873) p. 269.

think it undesirable that the ghost should linger for more than five days they drive it away with shouts and blowing of conches, and sometimes with the booming sound of bull-roarers.[1] At Ureparapara in these islands, the ceremony of ghost-driving is peculiar and remarkable. " Bags of small stones and short pieces of bamboo are provided for the people of the village, and are charmed by those who have the knowledge of the magic chaunt appropriate for the purpose. Two men, each with two white stones in his hands, sit in the dead man's house, one on either side. These men begin to clink the stones one against the other, the women begin to wail, the neighbours—who have all assembled at one end of the village—begin to march through it in a body to the other end, throwing the stones into the houses and all about, and beating the bamboos together. So they pass through till they come to the bush beyond, when they throw down the bamboos and bags. They have now driven out the ghost, who up to this time has been about the house, in which the widow has for these five days never left the dead man's bed except upon necessity ; and even then she leaves a coconut to represent her till she returns. At Motlav the ghost is not driven away unless the man who has died was badly afflicted with ulcers and sores, either a *gov* covered with sores, or a *mamnagita* with a single large ulcer or more. When such a one is dying the people of his village send word in time to the next village westwards, as the

[1] R. H. Codrington, *The Melanesians* (Oxford, 1891), p. 267.

ghost will go out following the sun, to warn them to be prepared. When the *gov* is dead they bury him, and then, with shell-trumpets blowing and the stalks of coconut fronds stripped of some of the leaflets beating the ground, they chase the ghost to the next village. The people of that village take up the chase, and hunt the ghost further westward ; and so on till the sea is reached. Then the frond stalks are thrown away and the people return, sure that the ghost has left the island, and will not strike another man with the disease."[1]

In San Cristoval, one of the Solomon Islands, when a burial is taking place, a man goes to the hut of the deceased, and, standing at the door, fishes for the soul of the dead man with a fishing-rod baited with betel nut ; and when he has caught it, puts the ghost with the bait into a little bag. Later on the bag will be put with the skull of the dead man wherever it is kept. After the soul of the deceased has thus been caught and deposited in the bag, other men come to the door of the hut and fish for the ghosts who may have come to the hut to prey on the flesh of the corpse. The bait in this case is a dracaena leaf. The other men come, some with torches, some with sticks, and entering the hut dash their torches and sticks against the walls to drive out the lingering and dangerous ghosts.[2] In this custom it will be observed that though the ghost of the dead man is carefully removed from the hut

[1] R. H. Codrington, *The Mela-nesians*, pp. 270-271.

[2] C. E. Fox, *The Threshold of the Pacific* (London, 1924), p. 212.

which he inhabited, it is not driven away to a distance, but is deposited with the skull wherever that may be kept, obviously in order that the spirit of the deceased may abide with his mortal remains. So far, therefore, the custom does not conform to the general type of driving away ghosts to the bourne from which no traveller returns.

Among the Sulka of New Britain, after a death has taken place, a deep hole is dug in the hut of the deceased and the corpse is placed over it, and kept there for some time. Then follows the ceremony of driving out the ghost from the hut. The time for performing the ceremony is communicated secretly to the men who are appointed to carry it out, lest the ghost should overhear and prepare to resist. The time is always in the early morning when the first cry of a certain bird is heard. At that moment the natives raise a great shout, and the ghost-drivers, entering the hut, beat and shake the walls, and set fire to coconut leaves with which they dance wildly about, thus expelling the ghost of the deceased. When they have done their work, they throw away the burning leaves on the path. Thereby the ghost is believed to be frightened and to be driven finally away.[1]

In Fiji the old custom of driving away the spirit of the dead has been described as follows by Captain Erskine, who witnessed it about the middle of the nineteenth century. " As soon as this feast was

[1] M. S. C. Rascher, " Die Sulka, ein Beitrag zur Ethnographie Neu-Pommern ", *Archiv für Anthropo-* *logie*, xxxiv. (1904) p. 214; R. Parkinson, *Dreissig Jahre in der Südsee* (Stuttgart, 1907), p. 185.

over (it was then dark) began the dance and uproar which are always carried on either at natural or violent deaths. All classes then give themselves up to excess, especially at unnatural deaths of this sort, and create all manner of uproar by means of large bamboos, trumpet-shells, etc., which will contribute to the general noise which is considered requisite to drive away the spirit and to deter him from desiring to dwell or even to hover about his late residence. The uproar is always held in the late habitation of the deceased, the reason being that as no one knows for a certainty what reception he will receive in the invisible world, if it is not according to his expectations, he will most likely repent of his bargain and wish to come back. For that reason they make a great noise to frighten him away, and dismantle his former habitation of everything that is attractive, and clothe it with everything that to their ideas seems repulsive." [1]

In the Marquesas Islands of the Pacific, after a death, the ghost was believed not to abandon the corpse definitely for the first two nights. On the third night, a priest, stepping out on the terrace in front of the house, implored the wandering soul of the deceased to depart ; and by way of enforcing the request, a band of men, armed with spears and other lethal weapons, went about in the outer darkness, beating the bushes and stabbing the thatched roofs of the houses in order to drive the lingering

[1] J. E. Erskine, *Journal of a Cruise among the Islands of the Western Pacific* (London, 1853), pp. 475-477.

ghost away. If, roused by the clamour, the dogs began to bark, the priest would say, " The soul is departing ".[1]

In the Gilbert Islands of the Pacific " on the three nights following a death the ceremony of *bo-maki* was performed. All the people irrespective of their kinship to the deceased, gathered together in the darkness, with sticks of pandanus wood and the butt ends of coconut leaves in their hands, at the southern extremity of the village, and forming a line abreast from east to west, slowly advanced northwards, beating the ground and trees before them with their staves. Not a word was uttered. When the line had swept through the settlement from south to north it stopped, and the participants disbanded in silence. All pedestrians who happened upon the party while it was at work would seize a staff without a word, join in and when it was finished pass on their way. The object of the ceremony was to encourage the soul to leave the neighbourhood of the body and also to drive away any evil spirits that might wish to possess it. Immediately life was extinct the family began a great wailing and yelling which was kept up by relays for three days without intermission, except when the ceremony of *bo-maki* was being performed ; to have sustained it during that rite would have been to encourage the soul of the dead to linger about the body and haunt the living."[2] In these same islands it was customary at

[1] M. Radiguet, *Les Derniers Sauvages* (Paris, 1882), pp. 284 *sqq.*

[2] Arthur Grimble, " From Birth to Death in the Gilbert Islands ", *Journal of the Royal Anthropological Institute*, ii. (1921) p. 44.

a burial to place two coconuts in the hands of the corpse, as an additional precaution to prevent the ghost from returning to haunt his kinsfolk. " The body was kept for three or nine days, being buried on the fourth or tenth, as the case might be. Those who kept it for the shorter period were of the opinion that, as the soul had finally been driven away from its neighbourhood on the third repetition of the *bo-maki* ceremony, it might safely be laid to rest on the fourth day. But many families, and particularly those of Tarawa and Butaritari, believed that the soul might reinhabit the body at any time during the nine days after death, and so, though they took the greatest pains to prevent it, still kept its fleshly tenement available until the last moment."[1]

The Kiwai of British New Guinea believe that the spirits of the dead normally depart to Adiri, the far-off spirit-land, in the west ; but some of them are thought to linger behind, and to haunt the villages intent on mischief. So it becomes necessary to drive away these malignant spirits with blasts of the conch shell.[2]

The Kiwai are also accustomed to burn the platform on which a corpse has been exposed and gifts which have been deposited on the grave. Moreover, they chew ginger in order to drive away the lingering spirit of the dead.[3]

In the Purari delta of British New Guinea, at a death some of the natives wave branches of the

[1] A. Grimble, *op. cit.* p. 45.
[2] W. N. Beaver, *Unexplored New Guinea* (London, 1920), p. 177.
[3] G. Landtman, *The Kiwai Papuans of British New Guinea* (London, 1927), p. 259.

coconut palm over the corpse in the house to waft the spirit of the deceased to spirit-land, before they carry out the corpse to burial.[1]

The natives about Hood Bay and Port Moresby in British New Guinea " believe, too, in the death-lessness of the soul, but their ideas as to its abode or condition are very vague and indefinite. A death in the village is the occasion of bringing plenty of ghosts to escort their new companion and perhaps fetch some one else. All night the friends of the deceased sit up and keep the drums going to drive away the spirits. When I was sleeping one night at Hood Bay a party of young men and boys came round with sticks, striking the fences and posts of houses all through the village. This I found was always done when any one died, to drive back the spirits to their own quarters on the adjacent moun-tain tops."[2]

Among the Roro-speaking peoples of British New Guinea when a corpse has been laid in the grave a near relative takes a branch of a tree and strokes the body from foot to head, in order to drive away the spirit. In Yule Island similarly two men stroke the corpse from head to foot with a certain herb to drive away the spirit. After the spirit has been thus swept from the corpse the same two men, shouting and brandishing sticks and torches, chase the spirit beyond the bounds of the village into the bush,

[1] J. H. Holmes, *In Primitive New Guinea* (London, 1924), pp. 218, 219.

[2] The Rev. W. G. Lawes, " Notes on New Guinea and its Inhabitants ", *Proceedings of the Royal Geographical Society*, ii. (1880) p. 615.

where, with a last curse, they hurl at it the sticks or torches they have in their hands.[1]

After a death or a series of deaths, the Orokaiva of British New Guinea celebrate a drama, a dance and a feast in honour of the recently deceased. At the conclusion of the ceremonies, the paraphernalia of the dancers are placed on a raft, and the spirit or the spirits of the dead are supposed to embark along with them and to float down the river to its mouth : meanwhile, the chief man of the village calls out the names of all the deceased and bids them go right down to the sea and there to turn into crocodiles, sharks and snakes.[2]

Among the Papuans of Geelvink Bay in Dutch New Guinea after the burial, you may hear about sunset a great uproar in all the houses of the village : the people are yelling and throwing sticks about with the object of driving away the dreaded ghost. They have given him all that he can expect to get : to wit, a grave, a banquet and funeral ornaments ; and now they beseech him not to intrude upon the survivors, and not to kill them or fetch them away, as the Papuans put it.[3]

In some of the Turki tribes of Siberia it is believed that after a death the soul of the deceased is free to roam about for forty days, after which, if

[1] C. G. Seligman, *The Melanesians of British New Guinea* (Cambridge, 1910), p. 275.

[2] F. E. Williams, *Orokaiva Society* (Oxford, 1930), pp. 253 *sqq.*, pp. 279 *sq.*

[3] J. L. van Hasselt, " Die Papuastämme an der Geelvinkbai (Neu-Guinea) ", *Mitteilungen der Geographische Gesellschaft zu Jena*, ix. (1891) p. 101 ; cf. J. B. van Hasselt, " Die Noeforezen ", *Zeitschrift für Ethnologie*, viii. (1876) p. 196.

it is still hanging about, the *shaman* drives it out and drums it down to hell. To secure a favourable reception for the dead man in his new abode, the *shaman* is said, after conducting the soul personally thither, to serve out brandy to the devils all round.[1]

Among the Western Bhotias of Thibet there is performed on the last day of the obsequies a final ceremony for getting rid of the soul of the deceased. A venerable sage gives his last instructions to the departing spirit. The clothes of the deceased are taken and placed upon an animal which represents the dead man. A man then leads forth the animal to a spot far from the village, while all the villagers beat the poor creature to drive it away and prevent its return. In Chaudans the animal is allowed to go free, but elsewhere low-caste Bhotias, or Thibetans, speedily dispatch it and eat its flesh. So glad are the villagers that the spirit has departed, that they return singing and dancing, and after this, the men and women shave, cut their hair, wash their heads and wear rings on their ears and hands.[2]

Among the Kunbis, a great agricultural caste of the Central Provinces of India, after all the other funeral rites have been performed, the chief mourner goes to the door of the house and, breaking an areca-nut on the threshold and placing it in his mouth, spits it out of the door, signifying the final ejectment of the spirit of the deceased from the

[1] W. Radloff, *Aus Siberien* (Leipsig, 1884), ii. p. 52.
[2] Charles A. Sherring, *Western Tibet and the British Borderland* (London, 1906), pp. 129, 130.

dwelling.[1] Among the Savara, a hill tribe of Southern India, as soon as a death has taken place in a house, a gun is fired at the door in order to drive away the spirit of the deceased.[2]

Among the Kachins of Burma, after a death in a house a priest attempts to lure the soul of the deceased out of the dwelling by means of a bait attached to the end of a string, of which he, sitting in the house, holds one end, while a man seated at the door holds the other and baited end of the string. If the soul is judged not to take the bait, as a further inducement to the soul to depart, the priest throws a spear at it, and tells it that the house is full of caterpillars, serpents and wild boars, which will bite the poor soul if it does not at once make off. When the priest feels sure that the ghost has really departed from the house, he takes his spear in his hand, and harangues the spirit as follows : " We have made solemn funeral rites for you ; we have offered you fowls and pigs and buffaloes, and we give you now these two images of birds to sell on the road ; take all these objects, these provisions for the journey and especially all evil omens, and go to your great-grandfather, by way of your tomb and those of your father and grandfather ".[3]

It is believed by the Malagasy that the spirits of

[1] R. V. Russell, *The Tribes and Castes of the Central Provinces of India* (London, 1916), iv. p. 36.

[2] E. Thurston, *Castes and Tribes of Southern India* (Madras, 1909), vi. p. 324 ; Fred. Fawcett, " On the Soaras (or Savaras), an aboriginal Hill People of the Eastern Ghats of the Madras Presidency ", *Journal of the Anthropological Society of Bombay*, i. (1886) p. 248.

[3] P. Ch. Gilhodes, " Mort et funérailles chez les Katchins (Birmanie) ", *Anthropos*, xiii. (1917–1918) pp. 264, 265

the dead hover about the towns and even revisit their former homes, " and it is customary in great floods or downpours of rain for the people to beat the sides of their houses with great violence to drive away, as they say, the *angatra* or spirits who may be seeking to re-enter and shelter themselves beneath the ancestral roof ".[1]

After a death the Bari of the Nilotic Sudan carry burning grass round the house to drive away the soul of the deceased, which otherwise would worry the survivors.[2]   Among the Bakarewe, who inhabit an island of the Victoria Nyanza, on the fifth day after a burial, a relative of the deceased enters the house and turns everything upside down in the chamber where the dead man breathed his last. This he does in order to expel the ghost lest he should return to haunt and molest the survivors. The service which the kinsman thus renders to the family is a dangerous one, and no sooner has he performed it than he demands his reward, which is at once given him in the shape of a hoe, or a goat. Having got it, the ghost-driver departs quickly to his own house.[3]

Speaking of the natives of the Gabun district of West Africa, a very experienced American missionary tells us that " the feelings in the hearts of the mourners are very mixed.   The outcry of affection, pleading with the dead to return to life, is sincere, the

[1] Henry W. Little, *Madagascar* (Edinburgh and London, 1854), p. 84.
[2] C. G. Seligman and Brenda Z. Seligman, *Pagan Tribes of the Nilotic Sudan* (London, 1932), p. 291.
[3] P. Eugène Hurel, " Religion et vie domestique des Bakarewe ", *Anthropos*, vi. (1911) p. 299.

survivor desiring the return to life to be complete ;
but almost simultaneously with that cry comes a fear
that the dead may indeed return, not as the accustomed embodied spirit, helpful and companionable,
but as a disembodied spirit, invisible, estranged,
perhaps inimical, and surrounded by an atmosphere
of dread imparted by the unknown and unseen.
The many then ask, not that the departed may
return, but that, if it be hovering near, it will go
away entirely. Few were those who during the life
of the departed had not on occasion had some quarrel
with him, or had done him some injustice or other
wrong, and their thought is, ' His spirit will come
back to avenge itself! ' So guns are fired to frighten
away the spirit and to cause it to go far off to the far
world of spirits, and not take up residence in or near
the town to haunt and injure the living."[1]

Among the Ewe-speaking people of Togoland in
West Africa, when the relatives of a dead man visit his
fields for the first time after his death, they are careful
to drive away his spirit by shouts and gun shots.[2]

In Loango, when many spirits of the dead are
believed to be haunting and troubling a village, the
inhabitants resort to strong measures for expelling
them. Fires are kindled everywhere ; houses are
swept and cleaned out ; the people rush about shouting and screaming, and men fire guns and brandish
chopping knives to drive away the spirits.[3]

[1] R. H. Nassau, *Fetichism in West Africa* (London, 1904), pp. 223-224.
[2] J. Spieth, *Die Ewe-Stämme* (Berlin, 1906), p. 121.
[3] E. Pechuel Loesche, *Die Loango-Expedition*, iii. 2 (Stuttgart, 1907), p. 309.

In aboriginal America, also, the custom of expelling the spirit of the deceased has often been observed and recorded. Thus, for example, among the Eskimo of Bering Strait, the ceremony has been described by an eye-witness as follows. On the evening of the second day after the death, the men in every house in the village took their domestic buckets and, turning them bottom upwards, went about thrusting the bottom of the vessel into every corner and into the smoke-hole and the doorway. This, it was said, was done to drive out the shade or ghost if it should be in the house, and from this custom the second day is called *a-hun-ig-ut*, or " the bottom day ". After this was done, and the people were ready to retire for the night, every man took a long grass stem and, bending it, stuck both ends into the ground in a conspicuous place in the middle of the doorway. They said that this would frighten the spirit off, for should it come about and try to enter the house, it would see this bent grass, and believing it to be a snare, would go away, fearing to be caught. On the lower Yukon, below Ikogmut, " the housemates of the deceased must remain in their accustomed places in the house during the four days following the death, while the shade is believed to be still about. During this time all of them must keep fur hoods drawn over their heads to prevent the influence of the shade from entering their heads and killing them. At once, after the body is taken from the house, his sleeping-place must be swept clean and piled full of bags and other things, so as not to leave any room for the shade to return and reoccupy it. At the same time, the two persons who slept with him upon each side must not, upon any account, leave their places. If they were to do so the shade might return and, by occupying the vacant place, bring sickness or death to its original owner, or to the inmates of the house. For this reason none of the dead person's housemates are permitted to go outside during the four days following the death. The deceased person's nearest relatives cut their hair short along the forehead in sign of mourning. During the four days that the shade is thought to remain with the body, none of the relatives are permitted to use any sharp-edged or pointed instrument for fear of injuring the shade and causing it to be angry and to bring misfortune upon them. One old man said that should the relatives cut anything with a sharp instrument during this time, it would be as though he cut his own shade and would die."[1]

Among the Shuswap of British Columbia, often after a death the *shaman* is called in by the relatives of the deceased. It is believed that the ghost of the dead person is eager to take one of his nearest relatives with him to the spirit-land. The *shaman* is called in to drive away the ghost. He sees the ghost and orders all the members of the mourning family to stay in the house, which the ghost cannot enter. Then he addresses the ghost, telling him that he

[1] E. W. Nelson, " The Eskimo of Bering Strait ", *18th Annual Report* *of the Bureau of American Ethnology* (1899), pp. 314, 315.

cannot have the person he wants. Thus he induces the ghost to go away and not to trouble the family any more.[1] Some of the Canadian Indians, whom the Jesuits called the Mountaineers, believed that when a man died in a hut his soul passed out of it by the smoke-hole in the roof, and they beat the walls of the hut with sticks to hasten its departure.[2] Among the Ojebway Indians, on the evening after a burial when it began to grow dark, the men used to fire their guns through the smoke-hole in the roof, while the women beat the walls of the hut with sticks in order to drive away the lingering ghost. As a further precaution against the return of the ghost, they cut thin strips of birch bark and hung them inside the walls of the hut, as scarecrows to frighten away the poor soul if nevertheless it should come back to disturb their slumbers.[3]

Among the Cora Indians of Mexico after a death wizards were engaged to hunt out and drive away the soul of the deceased. This they did by smoking their pipes and poking branches into all the corners of the house, until they pretended to find the lurking ghost, whom thereupon they summarily ejected.[4]

Thus we have seen that, in many parts of the world, primitive man has been in the habit of driving

---

[1] *Sixth Report on the North-Western Tribes of Canada* (*Report of the British Association for 1890*, separate reprint); Second General Report on the Indians of British Columbia, by Dr. Fr. Boas, p. 85.

[2] *Relations des Jésuites* (Canadian reprint) (Quebec, 1858), i. Année 1634, p. 23; cf. *id.*, 1633, p. 11; *id.*, 1639, p. 44.

[3] Peter Jones, *History of the Ojebway Indians* (London, 1861), pp. 99-100.

[4] H. H. Bancroft, *The Native Races of the Pacific States of North America* (London, 1875–1876), i. p. 744.

forcibly away the dangerous ghosts of the dead. In civilized Europe similar usages have not been unknown. Thus, the Germans sometimes wave towels about or sweep the ghost out with a besom,[1] just as in old Rome the heir solemnly swept out the ghost of his predecessor with a broom specially made for the purpose.[2] So like is human nature in all latitudes and under all varieties of culture.

[1] A. Wuttke, *Der deutsche Volksaberglaube*, Second Edition (Berlin, 1869), §§ 725, 737 ; F. Schmidt, *Sitten und Gebräuche bei Hochzeit, Taufen und Begräbnissen in Thüringen*, p. 85 ; J. A. E. Kohler, *Volksbrauch, Aberglauben, Sagen und andre alte Überlieferungen im Voigtlande* (Leipsic, 1867), p. 254.

[2] Festus, *s.v. everriator*, p. 68, ed. W. M. Lindsay : " Everriator vocatur, qui iure accepta hereditate iusta facere defuncto debet ; qui si non fecerit, seu quid in ea re turbaverit, suo capite luat. Id nomen ductum a verrendo. Nam exverriae purgatio quaedam domus, ex qua mortuus ad sepulturam ferendus est, quae fit per everriatorem certo genere scoparum adhibito, ab extra verrendo dictarum." In this passage the ghost is not expressly mentioned, but on the analogy of the customs described above he may be inferred with a high degree of probability.

LECTURE II

LECTURE II

In the last lecture we saw that in many parts of the world, after deaths have taken place, primitive man has been in the habit of driving away the spirits of the departed because he believes that the continued presence of these spirits in their old haunts might bring many calamities on the living. But once he succeeded to his satisfaction in banishing these dangerous spirits to a distance, his anxiety is by no means over ; for he thinks that the spirits can return and persecute the survivors ; especially by carrying off their souls with them to dead land. Hence, having banished the spirits of the dead to what he conceives to be a safe distance, he nevertheless adopts a great many precautions to prevent their return. To these precautions, which are very varied and often very curious, we must now direct our attention.

Thus, to begin with, failing to distinguish the immaterial and spiritual from the material and corporeal, he imagines that the spirits of the dead can be arrested by physical obstacles, and accordingly he proceeds to erect such obstacles in the way of the returning spirits, in the hope that the spirits will be unable to surmount them and to reach him and his fellows ; in short, he attempts to barricade the road against them.

Thus, for example, some of the Tungus are said to make a barrier of snow and trees.[1]

Amongst the Mangars, one of the fighting tribes of Nepal, when the mourners are returning from the grave, " one of their party goes ahead and makes a barricade of thorn bushes across the road, midway between the grave and the house of the deceased. On the top of the thorns he puts a big stone on which he takes his stand, holding a pot of burning incense in his left hand and some woollen thread in his right. One by one the mourners step on the stone and pass through the smoke of the incense to the other side of the barrier. As they pass, each takes a piece of thread from the man who holds the incense, and ties it round his neck. The object of this curious cere-mony is to prevent the spirit of the dead from coming home with the mourners and establishing itself in its old haunts. Conceived of as a miniature man, it is believed to be unable to make its way on foot through the thorns, while the smell of the incense, to which all spirits are highly sensitive, prevents it from surmounting this obstacle on the shoulders of one of the mourners." [2] The Chins of Burma burn their dead and collect their bones in an earthen pot. Afterwards, at a convenient

[1] T. de Pauly, *Description ethno-graphique des peuples de la Russie* (St. Petersburg, 1862), Peuples ouralo-altaïques, p. 71.

[2] H. H. Risley, *Tribes and Castes of Bengal, Ethnographic Glossary*, ii. (Calcutta, 1891) pp. 95-96.

season, they carry away the pot containing the bones to the ancestral burial place. "When the people convey the pot of bones to the cemetery, they take with them some cotton-yarn, and whenever they come to any stream or other water, they stretch a thread across, whereby the spirit of the deceased, who accompanies them, may get across it too. When they have duly deposited the bones and food for the spirit in the cemetery they return home, after bidding the spirit to remain there and not to follow them back to the village. At the same time they block the way by which they return by putting a bamboo across the path." [1] Thus the mourners make the way to the grave as easy as possible for the ghost, but obstruct the way by which he might return from it.

Among the Kachins, another tribe of Burma, when the mourners are returning from the grave precautions have to be taken against any onslaughts by the spirit of the dead. A long bamboo is procured and split in half for about half-way or more up its length. One half is fixed in the ground, the other lying loose. Between the two halves a wedge is inserted about three or four inches off the ground, thus forming a triangle with the wedge as base. All those who have attended the funeral pass through the triangle, the priest and the butcher bringing up the rear. Either of these two knocks away the wedge after having passed over it and the two halves

---

[1] Rev. G. Whitehead, "Notes on the Chins of Burma", *Indian Antiquary*, xxxvi. (1907) pp. 214 *sqq.*

of the bamboo close with a snap. Those who have guns fire as many shots as they can into the bamboo to frighten away the dangerous spirit of the deceased. In this custom the split bamboo is the obstacle interposed between the mourners and the pursuing ghost ; while the two pieces of the bamboo are held apart the gateway is open to let the mourners pass through ; but when the two pieces are allowed to come together with a snap the gate is closed in the face of the baffled ghost and the mourners feel themselves to be safe from his pursuit.[1]

Among the Moïs, a primitive tribe of Tonkin, when the mourners are returning from a burial, they make their way through a narrow passage constructed of reeds on trees, hoping thus to rid themselves of the ghost who will be brushed off by contact with the reeds or trees.[2]

Among the Lakhers, a tribe of Assam, when a death has taken place in a village all the people are very much afraid lest the spirit of the dead should enter their houses during the night and do them harm. To prevent this each householder places his paddy pestle across the doorway. When the dead person's spirit arrives at the door it sees the pestle, and, mistaking it for a huge serpent, retreats in terror. More intelligent spirits are said to recognize the pestle, but, fearing that it might fall and crush them if they attempt to enter, return whence they came. In Tisi, a village of the Lakhers, to prevent

[1] W. J. S. Carrapiett, *The Kachin Tribes of Burma* (Rangoon, 1929), p. 47.

[2] H. Baudesson, *Au pays des superstitions et des rites* (Paris, 1932), p. 130.

the ghost of the deceased from re-entering his house on the night of the funeral, they take a hen, and standing on the ladder leading to the house, cut off its feathers, allowing them to fall on each side of the ladder. These feathers are supposed to form a barrier which the ghost cannot cross. The cutting of the feathers is meant to intimate to the ghost that if he ventures to return to the house they will cut him up just as they cut off the feathers.[1]

Among the Dhobas, a primitive tribe of the Central Province of India, on the ninth, eleventh or thirteenth day after a death, when the ceremonial impurity ends, the male members of the sept are shaved on the banks of a river and their hair is left lying there. When they start home they spread some thorns and two stones across the path. Then, as the first man steps over the thorns, he takes up one of the stones in his hand and passes it behind him to the second, and each man successively passes it back as he steps over the thorns, the last man throwing the stone behind the thorns. Thus the dead man's spirit in the shape of the stone is separated from the living and prevented from accompanying them home.[2] In this custom the ghost is apparently supposed to adhere to the hair of the mourners, till the hair has been shorn off and left on the bank of the river ; and though the ghost attempts to pursue the mourners home, he is stopped on his way by the barrier of thorns.

[1] N. E. Parry, *The Lakhers* (London, 1932), p. 403.
[2] R. V. Russell, *The Tribes and Castes of the Central Provinces of India*, ii. (London, 1916) pp. 516, 517.

Again, when the Aheriyas of the North-Western Provinces of India burn the corpse they fling pebbles in the direction of the pyre to prevent the spirit accompanying them. In the Himalayas when a man is returning from the cremation ground, after the burning of a corpse, he places a thorny bush on the road wherever it is crossed by another path, and the nearest male relative of the deceased on seeing this, puts a stone on it, and pressing it down with his feet, prays the spirit of the dead man not to trouble him.[1] Here again the thorns serve as a barrier against the pursuing spirit. In India the custom of erecting barriers against the return of the ghost appears to be by no means confined to the wild tribes of the present day, but to go back to a remote antiquity. It was the ancient rule that when the mourners left the cremation ground the officiating priest raised a barrier of stones between the dead and the living.[2] In the *Satapatha-Brâhmana*, an ancient Indian book of religious ritual, it is said that the officiating priest, having fetched a clod from the boundary, deposits it midway between the grave and the village, saying : " This I put up as a bulwark for the living, lest another of them should go unto that thing ; may they live for a hundred plentiful harvests, and shut out death from themselves by a mountain ". The priest is said thus to make a

---

[1] W. Crooke, *The Popular Religion and Folklore of Northern India*, ii. (London, 1896) p. 57.

[2] W. Crooke, *Religion and Folklore of Northern India* (edited by R. E. Enthoven) (London, 1926), p. 237, referring to *Rajendralala Mitra*, ii. 123, 136 ; E. J. Atkinson, *The Himalayan Districts of the North-Western Provinces of India*, ii. (Allahabad, 1884) p. 832.

boundary between the dead forefathers and their living descendants.[1] The great Marātha leader Śivaji is said to have crawled through a perforated stone, to escape from the ghost of the Mogul General he had killed.[2]

Among the Sea Dyaks of Borneo the mourners who are the last to leave the grave plant sharpened stakes in the ground, so that the spirit of the dead may not follow them to the house, the stakes planted in the ground being supposed to prevent its return.[3] Similarly the Kiwai of British New Guinea put up sticks on the path which the ghost is supposed to have taken, in order to block the road against its return.[4]

Among the Kpelle, a negro tribe of Liberia, ropes are stretched round the base of a house or the walls of a town to ward off evil spirits, among whom mischievous ghosts are no doubt included. Between one of the villages and a graveyard two posts used to be planted in the ground with wattle - work stretched between them, in order to prevent the ghosts from coming from the graveyard to molest the villagers.[5]

In Loango, similarly, a cord protected by an

[1] *Satapatha - Brāhmana*, translated by J. E. Egeling (Oxford, 1900), Part V. p. 440 ; *Sacred Books of the East*, vol. xliv.

[2] J. Abbott, *The Keys of Power* (London, 1932), p. 504.

[3] E. H. Gomes, *Seventeen Years among the Sea Dyaks of Borneo* (London, 1911), p. 138 ; cf. J. Perham, " Sea Dyak Religion ", *Journal of the Straits Branch of the Royal Asiatic Society*, No. 14 (1884), p. 291.

[4] G. Landtman, *The Kiwai Papuans of British New Guinea* (London, 1927), p. 282.

[5] D. Westermann, *Die Kpelle ; ein Negerstamm in Liberia* (Leipsic, 1921), pp. 203-204.

appropriate charm is stretched and a furrow is traced all round a village. Further, a sacrificial victim, generally a goat, is carried round the whole circumference and is afterwards sacrificed. If these precautions fail to keep out the ghosts the inhabitants are at their wits' end, and think of abandoning the site altogether.[1]

Like the inhabitants of the Old World, the aborigines of America have sometimes been wont to erect barriers as a protection against the intrusion of unwelcome ghosts. Thus among the Shuswap of British Columbia mourners use thorn-bushes for pillow and bed in order to keep away the ghost of the deceased. They also lay thorn-bushes all round their beds for the same purpose.[2] So among the Bella Coola Indians, another tribe of British Columbia, the bed of a mourner must be protected against the ghost of the deceased. The relatives of the dead stick a thorn-bush at each corner of their bed. After four days these bushes are thrown into the water. Mourners must rise early and go into the woods, where they stick four thorn-bushes into the ground, at the corners of a square, in which they must cleanse themselves by rubbing their bodies with cedar branches. They also swim in ponds. After swimming they cleave four small trees and creep through the clefts, following the course of the

[1] E. Pechuel-Loesche, *Die Loango-Expedition*, iii. 2. (Stuttgart, 1907) p. 310.

[2] Fr. Boas, Second General Report on the Indians of British Columbia, *Sixth Report on the North-Western Tribes of Canada* (*Report of the British Association for 1890*), separate reprint, p. 91.

sun. This they do on four subsequent mornings, cleaving new trees every day.[1]   In this latter custom the passage of the mourner through cleft trees is another mode of evading the pursuit of the ghost, just as we have seen that Kachin mourners returning from the grave creep through a split bamboo for a similar purpose.   Among the Thompson Indians, another tribe of British Columbia, after a death, a string of deer-hoofs with a short line attached was hung across the inside of the winter house, to prevent the ghost from entering.   During four successive nights an old woman pulled at the string frequently to make the hoofs rattle.   Branches of juniper were also placed at the door of the house, or were burned in the fire for the same purpose.[2]   Some of the Algonkin Indians of Canada used to stretch nets round their huts in the meshes of which they sought to catch any spirits of the dead who might attempt to enter from the wigwams of their neighbours.[3] Among the Huichol Indians of Mexico no strong liquor is drunk at burial feasts.   Instead, a cross, made from a kind of *salvia*, is hung up in the house to prevent the soul of the deceased from re-entering the house and to keep him from getting into the

[1] *Seventh Report on the North-Western Tribes of Canada* (*Report of the British Association for 1891*, separately paged extract), Third Report on the Indians of British Columbia, by Dr. Fr. Boas, p. 13. On the custom of creeping through cleft trees or other narrow openings to escape from a ghost, see *The Golden Bough*, Part VII. *Balder the Beautiful*, ii. pp. 174 *sqq.*

[2] James Teit, " The Thompson Indians of British Columbia " (*Memoirs of the American Museum of Natural History*, ii. Anthropology I.; *The Jessup North Pacific Expedition*, iv. (April, 1900) p. 331.

[3] *Relations des Jésuites* 1639, vol. i. (Quebec, 1858) p. 44.

distillery and spoiling the wine. For the same purpose branches are put upon the paths leading to the distillery and the jars of liquor are covered.[1]

As usual, savage custom has its counterpart in civilized Europe. In Savoy there is a curious belief attached to the custom of closing all doors and windows when a funeral is about to pass. The peasants say that if this were not done the soul of the dead might escape into a house through some open door or window.[2] This belief probably gives the clue to the common European custom of lowering the blinds of all windows in a house of mourning.

Among the barriers which primitive man attempts to interpose between himself and the dreaded spirits of the dead, a prominent place is taken by water and fire. Thus, to begin with water, after burying a body the Ngarigo of South-east Australia were wont to cross a river in order to prevent the ghost from pursuing them.[3] Obviously they shared the common opinion that ghosts for some reason are unable to cross water.

The natives of Nias, an island to the west of Sumatra, attribute contagious diseases to the ill-will of the spirits of the dead : hence, the bodies of persons who die of such diseases do not receive regular obsequies, but are either thrown away in the forest or are buried in an island, to prevent the return of their dangerous ghosts.[4]

[1] C. Lumholz, *Unknown Mexico*, ii. (London, 1903) pp. 243-244.

[2] Estella Canziani, *Costumes, Traditions and Songs of Savoy* (London, 1911), p. 136.

[3] A. W. Howitt, *Native Tribes of South-east Australia* (London, 1904), p. 461.

[4] Elio Modigliani, *L' Isola delle Donne* (Milan, 1895), p. 198.

The use of water as a barrier against a ghost may be illustrated from a practice of the Ainu of Japan, as it is described from personal experience by the Rev. John Batchelor, our principal authority on these primitive people. He had visited the grave of an old woman, in the company of the woman's son. The son would by no means approach within fifty yards of the grave for fear of his mother's ghost. " Upon returning to the hut, the man, together with the women, brought a bowl of water to the door, and requested me to wash my face and hands. Whilst at my ablutions the women commenced to beat me and brush me down with *inao* (sacred whittled sticks). Upon inquiring into the ideas which moved the people to act in this manner, I discovered that the washing was to purify me from all uncleanness contracted at the grave through contact with the ghost of the deceased, and that the beating and brushing with *inao* was to drive away all evil influences and diseases she may have aimed at me. The water and *inao* were the antidote against, and the corrective for, the evil intentions the spirit is supposed to have directed towards me out of her wicked spite for trespassing on her domain." [1]

Among the Taungthu of Upper Burma, when the corpse is carried outside the house, the chief mourner, widow or widower, son or daughter, pours water over the body and says : "As a stream divides

---

[1] Rev. John Batchelor, *The Ainu and their Folk-lore* (London, 1901), pp. 549, 550.

countries so may the water poured now divide us ".[1]

In the *Satapatha-Brâhmana* it is prescribed that seven furrows should be dug on the north side of the grave and filled with water, for sin not to pass beyond, for indeed sin cannot pass beyond seven rivers. The mourners returning from the grave throw three stones each into these northern furrows and pass over them, saying : " Here floweth the stony one ; hold on to each other, rise and cross over, ye friends : here will we leave behind what unkind spirits there be, and will cross over to auspicious nourishments ". On this custom a commentator observes : " These seven furrows are straight, running from west to east ; thus separating the grave from the north, the world of men ". In the text just quoted the seven furrows are represented as a barrier which sin cannot cross, but this moral explanation of the custom is probably a priestly interpretation. We may suspect that the water of the seven furrows was originally intended to prevent the ghost from following the mourners on their return from the grave.[2]

In Africa, among the Bangala of the Upper Congo, the Rev. John H. Weeks witnessed a good example of the use of water as a barrier to divide the dead from the living. He says : " Walking one day in Monsembe I saw an incident that re-

[1] G. W. Scott and J. P. Hardiman, *Gazetteer of Upper Burma and the Shan States*, Part I. vol. i. (Rangoon, 1900) p. 554.

[2] *Satapatha-Brâhmana*, translated by Julius Egeling, Part V. (Oxford, 1900) pp. 437 *sqq.*

called Burns' ' Tam o' Shanter ' to my mind. There had been a death in a family and the relatives had just performed all the necessary rites and ceremonies and were returning to their homes. A small trench some twenty feet long was dug with a hoe. The relatives took up their position on the side of the trench nearest to the grave, the medicine-man stood on the other side, and his assistant was placed at the end of the trench with a large calabash of water. At a signal the water was poured into the trench, and while it was running the medicine-man took each person by the hand, and mumbling an incantation pulled him or her over the running water. When all had been pulled over, one by one, the water was allowed to run until the calabash was empty. I asked the reason of the ceremony, and they told me that it was to keep the spirit of their deceased, and buried, relative from following them. It was very evident from the rites observed that they thought the spirits could not cross running water." [1]

With regard to the natives of the Gabun district we are told by the Rev. Robert Nassau that " when they have finished the work of burial, they are in great fear, and are to run rapidly to their village, or to the nearest body of water, river or lake or sea. If in their running one should trip and fall it is a sign that he will soon die. They plunge into the

[1] John H. Weeks, *Among Congo Cannibals* (London, 1913), pp. 102-103 ; cf. *id.*, " Anthropological Notes on the Bangala of the Upper Congo River ", *Journal of the Royal Anthropological Institute*, xxxix. (1909) p. 454.

water, as a means of ' purification ' from possible
defilement. The object of this purification is not
simply to cleanse the body, but to remove the
presence or contact of the spirit of the dead man or
of any other spirit of possible evil influence, lest
they should have ill-luck in their fishing, hunting
and other work." [1]

A much attenuated form of the water barrier
against ghosts is observed amongst the Basutos ;
a man with holy water follows the funeral, sprinkling
with the holy water the footprints of the men who
carry the corpse.[2]

Widows and widowers are often supposed to be
peculiarly liable to be haunted by the ghosts of their
deceased spouses, and special precautions are accordingly taken to protect them from these importunate
spirits. The Bakongo of the Lower Congo River
resort to the water barrier as the means of guarding
both widows and widowers in these melancholy circumstances. In the case of the widow, " if it is the
woman's first husband who has died, she must take
his bed, and one or two articles he commonly used,
to a running stream. The bed is put in the middle
of the stream and the articles placed on it. The
woman washes herself well in the stream and afterwards sits on the bed. The medicine-man goes to
her and dips her three times in the water and dresses
her. Then the bed and articles are broken and the
pieces thrown down-stream to float away. She is

[1] Rev. Robert H. Nassau, *Fetichism in West Africa* (London, 1904),
pp. 218-219.

[2] *Verhandlungen der Berliner
Gesellschaft für Anthropologie*
(1877), p. 84.

now led out of the stream, and a raw egg is broken
and given to her to swallow. A toad is killed and
some of its blood is rubbed on her lips, and a fowl is
killed and hung by the roadside. These sacrifices
having been made to the spirit of the departed one,
she is free to return to her town." [1] Clearly, the
Bakongo suppose that by placing the widow in her
bed in the middle of a river they oppose an insuper-
able obstacle to the attentions of her husband's
ghost; but to make assurance doubly sure, they
afterwards seek to pacify the ghost by a sacrifice.
The treatment of a widower among the Bakongo is
somewhat similar, if the woman was his first wife.
He must stay in his house for six days, but on the
morning of the seventh day the male relatives of his
deceased wife come to escort him to a running
stream. On arrival at the stream one of the kinsmen
takes the bed and throws it into the water. Then
he scrapes the widower's tongue, shaves him, pares
his nails, makes three cuts in his arm, and finally
immerses him three times in the river, to " wash
away the death ", or rather, as we may suppose,
his wife's ghost.[2]

With this African application of the water barrier
to protect the widow we may compare a somewhat
similar custom observed by the Papuans of Geelvink
Bay in Dutch New Guinea. A widow must not
leave her dwelling for several months, for the spirit
of her dead husband is still associated with her, and

[1] J. H. Weeks, *Among the Primi-*   172, 173.
tive Bakongo (London, 1914), pp.   [2] J. H. Weeks, *op. cit.* p. 173.

if she went about the men who met her might be taken ill or die. Her hair is shorn in sign of mourning. After her hair is shorn, she is bathed, and in order that she may not meet any one in taking her bath, a canoe is brought under the house, a hole is made in the floor and she descends into the boat.[1] Thus these Papuan widows, like their African sisters, are surrounded by water as a barrier against their husbands' ghosts.

Among peoples of the lower culture, it is a common custom for mourners after a burial or a funeral to plunge completely into water. The custom is usually interpreted as a mode of cleansing the mourner from the impurity which he has contracted by contact with the dead. But in all such cases it is safe to conjecture that the original motive was fear of the ghost, and a wish to interpose a barrier of water between the living and the dead. And even when the custom has degenerated into a simple ablution of some part of the mourner's person, or into a still slighter contact with water, it seems probable that the underlying motive has been a desire to wash off the clinging ghost, or otherwise to get rid of him by the interposition of water. With regard to the Hindoos, we are told that they regard themselves as defiled by simple presence at a funeral, and immediately after contracting this defilement they go and plunge into water, and no

---

[1] J. L. van Hasselt, " Eenig Aanteekeningen arngaande de bewoners der Nord-Westkust van Nieu Guinea, meer bepaaldeligk de Stam der Noefoorezen ", *Tijdschrift voor Indische Taal- Land- en Volkenkunde,* xxxii. (1889) p. 591

one dare enter his house before he has thus purified himself.[1]

Among the people of Ambaca in Angola, the surviving relative, whether husband or wife, is carried from the grave on the back of a person of the same sex and thrown into the river for ablution or purification. On returning to his house, the person so purified is secluded ; he may not converse with any person of the opposite sex, nor eat anything that has been boiled, nor wash himself[2] for eight days.

In some parts of the Cameroons all present at a burial throw handfuls of earth on the grave and then run away lest they should die the same death as the deceased. Those who live near the coast afterwards throw themselves into the sea, but the inland people in the like circumstances plunge into a river.[3]

A traveller in the Cameroons tells us how, after witnessing the execution of a man accused of witchcraft, the whole population of the village, men, women and children, ran to the shore, and stripping themselves of their clothes, bathed in the sea to wash off, as he says, the witchcraft, but probably rather the dangerous spirit of the sorcerer just set free from its earthly tenement.[4]

Among the Kaffirs of South Africa all persons who touched a corpse or any of the dead man's

[1] J. A. Dubois, *Mœurs, institutions et cérémonies des peuples de l'Inde* (Paris, 1825), i. p. 244.
[2] F. T. Valdez, *Six Years of a Traveller's Life in Western Africa* (London, 1861), p. 296 *sq.*

[3] C. Cunym, " De Libreville au Cameroun ", *Bulletin de la Société de Géographie*, xvii. (1896) pp. 340-341.
[4] R. Buchholz, *Reisen in West-Afrika* (Leipsic, 1880), p. 143.

effects were obliged to go through certain ceremonies and then to bathe in running water before they might associate with their companions.[1]

Among the Ba-Ila-speaking tribes of Northern Rhodesia, when the grave has been filled up and before the diggers have stepped off from it, water is brought and all who have handled the corpse wash their hands over the grave. This they do, it is said, to cleanse them from the defilement they have contracted.[2]

Among the Fangs of West Africa, after the death of a chief, his wives are shut up in a hut, where they have to stay five days mourning for him. On the evening of the fifth day they lie down on the felled trunks of banana trees laid side by side, and all the people of the village, from the youngest to the oldest, pour water over them. The women have to lie there all night without stirring, and next morning their heads are carefully shaved with bits of broken glass. Afterwards the villagers form a double line, men on one side, women on the other, armed with swords and other weapons, and the women have to run the gauntlet between these two rows, being well belaboured in their passage.[3] In this custom the beating of the widows is doubtless a secondary precaution to rid them of their husband's ghost, lest

---

[1] G. McCall Theal, *Ethnography and Condition of South Africa* (London, 1919), p. 222; Dos Santos, in *Records of South-Eastern Africa*, edited by G. McCall Theal, vii. (1901) p. 401.

[2] E. W. Smith and A. M. Dale, *The Ila-Speaking Peoples of Northern Rhodesia*, ii. (London, 1920) p. 106.

[3] P. Trilles, " Chez les Fangs : leurs mœurs, leur langue, leur religion ", *Missions Catholiques*, xxx. (1898) pp. 521, 522.

he should be clinging to their persons, despite the sousing of their bodies with water.

Among the Nyanja-speaking peoples of the Nyasaland Protectorate, when a grave has been filled in the mourners go to a river and bathe in it, the men up-stream and the women down-stream.[1] When the Damara or Herero of South-West Africa have buried a body they pour bowls of water on the grave before retiring from it.[2]

In North Guinea, after a corpse has been buried, the bearers rush to the water and wash themselves thoroughly before they return to the town.[3] Among the Bare-speaking Toradjas of Central Celebes the mourners in returning from a burial step in vessels of water, doubtless in order to escape from the ghost.[4] In New Zealand, among the Maoris, all who had attended a funeral used to betake themselves to the nearest stream and plunge several times head under in the water.[5] In Tahiti all who had assisted at a burial fled precipitately and plunged into the sea, casting also in the sea the garments they had worn.[6] Among the Singhalese of Ceylon the funeral party bathe before returning to the house, and are

[1] R. Sutherland Rattray, Some Folk-Lore, Stories and Songs in Chinyanja (London, 1907), p. 94.
[2] C. J. Andersson, Lake Ngami (London, 1856), p. 467.
[3] J. Leighton Wilson, Western Africa (London, 1856), ch. 17.
[4] N. Adriani in A. C. Kruijt, De Bare'e-sprekende Toradjas van Midden Celebes, ii. pp. 98, 99.

[5] W. Yate, An Account of New Zealand (London, 1835), p. 137; R. Taylor, Te Ika A Maui, or New Zealand and its Inhabitants, Second Edition (London, 1870), p. 224; Annales de la Propagation de la Foi, xv. (1843) pp. 23-24.
[6] Rev. William Ellis, Polynesian Researches, Second Edition (London, 1832–1836), i. p. 403.

supplied by the washerwoman with newly washed clothes ; during their absence the house is well cleansed and purified by the sprinkling of water mixed with cow-dung.[1] The Oraons of Bengal after attending a burial always bathe before they return to the village.[2] In the Shan States of Burma, it is said that similarly all persons who have handled a corpse are obliged to bathe before they return to the village.[3]

Among the Kiwai of British New Guinea, mourners returning from a burial swim in the sea. Those who have carried the dead body spit ginger over their hands and afterwards rub them with a sweet-smelling herb. Until they have done so, nobody will touch his own body with his hands. After washing they smear face and body with clay, which is renewed from time to time.[4] In this custom the water, the ginger and the clay are probably alike regarded as protectives against the ghost. Similarly the natives of Rook, an island off the north-east coast of New Guinea, go and purify themselves in the sea immediately after a burial.[5]

Among the aborigines of America the use of water as a barrier against the dead appears to be familiar. Thus of the Songish Indians of Van-

[1] A. Perera, " Glimpses of Singhalese Social Life ", *Indian Antiquary*, xxi. p. 382.

[2] E. T. Dalton, *Descriptive Ethnology of Bengal* (Calcutta, 1872), p. 262 ; Sarat Chandra Roy, *Oraon Religion and Customs* (Ranchi, 1928), p. 175.

[3] " Notes on the Manners, Customs, Religion and Superstitions of the Tribes inhabiting the Shan States ", *Indian Antiquary*, xxi. p. 119.

[4] G. Landtman, *The Kiwai Papuans of British New Guinea* (London, 1927), p. 265.

[5] P. Ambrosoli, " Extrait d'une notice sur l'Ile de Rook ", *Annales de la Propagation de la Foi*, xxvii. (1855) p. 363.

couver Island we are told that after a burial the whole tribe used to go down to the sea and bathe, wash their heads and cut their hair.[1] Among the Tarahumare Indians of Mexico on the occasion of a death by suicide all the women, after bidding farewell to the dead body, ran quickly into a deep waterhole, splashing into it, clothes and all, that nothing from the dead might attach itself to them.[2] In ancient Mexico all those who had helped to bury a king of Michoacan bathed afterwards.[3] Amongst the Mosquito Indians all persons returning from a funeral undergo a lustration in the river.[4] Among some of the Indians of Peru ten days after a death, the relatives of the deceased used to assemble and conduct the next of kin to a river or its springs where they thoroughly washed and scrubbed him to rid him, no doubt, of the contagion of death, or rather, as we may surmise, of the ghost of the deceased, who might be adhering to him.[5]

In civilized Europe also the barrier of water has sometimes been resorted to as a protection against the spirits of the dead. Thus, for example, in some parts of Transylvania " it is usual for the procession returning from a funeral to take its way through a river or stream of running water, sometimes going

---

[1] *Sixth Report of the North-Western Tribes of Canada* (*Report of the British Association for 1890*), Second General Report on the Indians of British Columbia, by Dr. Fr. Boas, p. 23.

[2] C. Lumholtz, *Unknown Mexico* (London, 1903), p. 389.

[3] H. H. Bancroft, *Native Races of the Pacific States*, ii. p. 621 ; Brasseut de Bourbourg, *Histoire des nations civilisées de Mexique et de l'Amérique Centrale* (Paris, 1857–1859), iii. p. 85.

[4] H. H. Bancroft, *op. cit.* i. p. 744.

[5] Padre Pablo de Arriaga, *Extirpación de la Idolatria del Peru* (Lima, 1621), p. 33.

a mile or two out of their way to avoid all bridges, thus making sure that the vagrant soul of the beloved deceased will not follow them back to the house".[1] The Wends of Geislitz make a point of passing through running water after a burial; in winter, if the river is frozen, they break the ice in order to wade through the water.[2] In modern Mytilini and Crete if a man will not rest in his grave they dig up the body, ferry it across to a little island, and bury it there.[3] The Kythniotes of the Archipelago have a similar custom, except that they do not take the trouble to bury the body a second time, but simply tumble the bones out of a bag and leave them to bleach on the rocks, trusting to the "silver streak" of sea to imprison the ghost.[4] In many parts of Germany, in modern Greece and in Cyprus, water is poured out behind the corpse as it is being carried from the house, in the belief that, if the ghost returns, he will not be able to cross it.[5] Sometimes,

[1] E. Gerard, *The Land beyond the Forest* (Edinburgh and London, 1888), p. 316.

[2] K. Haupt, *Sagenbuch der Lausitz* (Leipsic, 1862–1863), i. p. 254.

[3] B. Schmidt, *Das Volkleben der Neugriechen* (Leipsic, 1871), p. 168.

[4] J. T. Bent, *The Cyclades* (London, 1885), p. 441 sq.

[5] A. Kuhn, *Märkische Sagen und Märchen* (Berlin, 1843), p. 368; J. D. H. Temme, *Die Volkssagen in Altmark* (Berlin, 1839), p. 77; F. Nork, *Sitten und Gebräuche der Deutschen und ihrer Nachbarvölker*, p. 479; A. Wuttke, *Der deutsche Volksaberglaube* (Berlin, 1869), p. 737; C. M. Rochholz, *Deutscher Glaube und Brauch* (Berlin, 1867), i. p. 177; G. Lammert, *Volksmedizin und medizinischer Aberglauber aus Bayern* (Wurzburg, 1869), p. 105; M. Toppen, *Aberglauben aus Masuren* (Danzig, 1867), p. 108; A. Witschel, *Sagen, Sitten und Gebräuche aus Thüringen* (Vienna, 1878), ii. p. 258; Panzer, *Beiträge zur deutschen Mythologie* (Munich, 1848–1855), i. p. 257; *Folk-Lore Journal*, ii. p. 170; C. Wachsmuth, *Das alte Griechenland im neuen* (Bonn, 1864), p. 119; Tettau und Temme, *Die Volkssagen Ostpreussens, Litauens und Westpreussens* (Berlin, 1837), p. 286; A. Kuhn, *Sagen, Gebräuche und Märchen aus Westphalen* (Leipsic, 1848), ii. p. 49.

by night, the Germans pour holy water before the door ; the ghost is thought to stand and whimper on the further side.[1] In some parts of the North-East of Scotland after a death the neighbours did not yoke their horses unless there was a stream of running water between them and the house in which the dead body lay.[2]

In ancient Greece the relations washed themselves after the funerals.[3] So long as a corpse was in the house a vessel of water stood before the street door, that all who left the house might sprinkle themselves with it.[4] Sometimes after a death the house of mourning was sprinkled with salt water.[5] In old Rome the barrier of water after a death survived in a much attenuated form : it sufficed to carry water three times round the persons who had been engaged in the funeral and to sprinkle them with the water.[6] The ancient Scythians in mourning washed themselves and took a vapour bath.[7] A very peculiar case of our water barrier is recorded by Plutarch ; he says that when a man had died of dropsy or consumption his children had to sit with their feet in water till the corpse had decayed.[8] Apparently,

[1] Wuttke, op. cit. § 748 ; Rochholz, op. cit. i. p. 186.
[2] Rev. Walter Gregor, Notes on the Folk-Lore of the North-east of Scotland (London, 1881), p. 207.
[3] Scholia on Aristophanes, Clouds, 838.
[4] Pollux, viii. 65 ; Hesychius and Suidas, s.v. ἀρδάνιον ; cf. Wachsmuth, op. cit. p. 109.
[5] H. Roehl, Inscriptiones Graecae Antiquissimae (Berlin, 1883), No. 395 ; G. Dittenberger, Sylloge In-scriptionum Graecarum, No. 468 ; P. Cauer, Delectus Inscriptionum Graecarum propter dialectum memorabilium, 2 (Leipsic, 1883), No. 530.
[6] Virgil, Aeneid, vi. 228. Servius on this passage speaks of carrying fire round similarly. We shall return presently to the barrier of fire.
[7] Herodotus, iv. 73, 75.
[8] Plutarch, De sera numinis vindicta, c. 14.

although Plutarch does not say so, this was a precaution to prevent the ghost of a man who had died
of dropsy from attacking his surviving children and
afflicting them with the malady which had proved
fatal to him. We have seen that among the Toradjas of Celebes mourners on returning from a funeral
planted their feet in vessels of water, apparently to
evade the pursuit of the ghost. For a similar purpose apparently, when a man has died of dropsy
among the natives of Rajamahall in India, they do
not bury the body but throw it into a river and then
bathe themselves in another part of the river.[1] Thus
they adopt in a double form the barrier of water
against the ghost of a man who has died of dropsy ;
first they throw his body into a river and then they
bathe themselves in another part of the same river,
so making assurance doubly sure. Alike in the
Greek and the Indian custom the notion seems to be
that on homoeopathic principles water is the best
preservative against death by dropsy. So similar
is the rut in which error has flowed in ancient Greece
and in modern India.

---

[1] Th. Shaw, " On the Inhabitants near Rajamahall ", *Asiatic Researches*,
iv. (Calcutta, 1795).

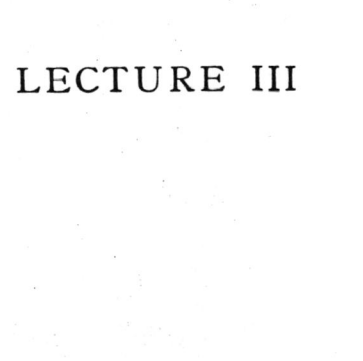

LECTURE III

LECTURE III

In the last lecture I dealt with some of the barriers which primitive man erects to prevent the spirits of the dead from returning to haunt and trouble the living ; in particular I described the barrier of water which he sometimes adopts for that purpose. Often with the same object he has recourse to a barrier of fire.[1]

Thus, for example, among some of the Tartars it used to be customary for all persons returning from a burial to leap over a fire made for the purpose, " in order that the dead man might not follow them ; for apparently in their opinion he would be afraid of the fire ".[2]

In the like circumstances some Tartars instead of leaping over a fire used to pass between two fires, but the object of the passage was no doubt the same.[3]

Among the Yakut no one but the gravediggers accompanies a corpse to the grave, and even they hasten to complete their work and return home ; on

[1] On the barrier of fire against the spirits of the dead, cf. *The Golden Bough*, Part IV. *Balder the Beautiful*, ii. pp. 17-19.

[2] J. G. Gmelin, *Reise durch Si-berien* (Göttingen, 1751 – 1752), i. 333.

[3] Johannes de Plano de Carpini, *Historia Mongolorum* (d'Avezac edition) (Paris, 1838), c. iv.

their way back they do not stop or look behind, and when they enter the gate of the village, they and the animals which drew the coffin to the grave must pass through a fire made of the straw on which the dead man lay and the wood left from the making of the coffin. Other things which have been in contact with the dead, such as the shovel, are also broken and burnt.[1] According to another authority, " the Yakut bury their dead as a rule on the day of the death, and in order not to take the demon of death home with them, they kindle fires on the way back from the burial and jump over them in the belief that the demon of death, who dreads fire, will not follow them, and that in this way they will be freed from the persecutions of the hated demon of death ".[2] In this passage the demon of death is probably a mistake of the writer for the ghost of the deceased ; the conception of a demon of death is by no means primitive. In Sikkim, when members of the Khambu caste have buried a corpse, all persons present at the burial " adjourn to a stream for a bath of purification, and, on re-entering the house, have to tread on a bit of burning cloth, to prevent the evil spirits who attend at funerals from following them in ".[3] Here again, the barrier of fire is probably directed not so much against evil spirits in general as against the spirit of the dead. It will be observed

---

[1] M. A. Czaplicka, *Aboriginal Siberia* (Oxford, 1914), p. 160.

[2] W. L. Priklonski, " Über das Schamanthum bei den Jakuten " in A. Bastian's *Allerlei aus Volks- und Menschenkunde* (Berlin, 1888), i. 319 ; cf. V. Priklonski, " Todtengebräuche der Jakuten ", *Globus*, lix. (1891) p. 85.

[3] J. A. H. Louis, *The Gates of Thibet* (Calcutta, 1894), p. 116.

that these people seek to protect themselves against the spiritual danger by a barrier of water as well as by a barrier of fire.

In China, after a corpse has been interred fires are kindled at the four corners of the cemetery to prevent the soul of the deceased from wandering away from the grave.[1] And when the funeral party returns to the house a fire of straw is kindled at the door, and all the members of the family pass over it and through the flames, after which they believe themselves to be safe from the pursuit of the ghost.[2] But sometimes as an additional precaution on entering the house, they wash their eyes with water in which the leaves of the pomeloe tree have been boiled.[3] Thus they reinforce the barrier of fire by a barrier of water. Again in China, when a coroner has been holding an inquest on a dead body, the mandarins who have attended the inquest step over a small fire before they enter their palanquins to be carried home, and the ceremony is repeated at the door of their house.[4]

Among the Oraons of Bengal on the return of a funeral party to the house a fire of chaff is kindled in the courtyard and oil poured on it to create a smoke. Over this smoke every one of the party places the palms of his or her hands by way of ceremonial purification.[5] Among the Birhors, a

[1] P. J. Dols, "La Vie chinoise dans la province de Kan-sou (Chine)", *Anthropos* x.-xi. (1915–1916) p. 756.

[2] Dols, *op. cit.* p. 741.

[3] J. H. Gray, *China* (London, 1878), i. p. 305; cf. *id.* p. 287.

[4] J. J. M. de Groot, *The Religious System of China* (Leyden, 1892), p. 137; cf. *id.* p. 32.

[5] Sarat Chandra Roy, *Oraon Religion and Customs* (Ranchi, 1928), p. 175.

primitive tribe of Chota Nagpur in India, after a body has been buried, standing at the grave the son or grandson of the deceased takes up a lighted torch in his right hand and some one stands beside him pressing his left eye with one hand. With his left eye thus closed, he walks round the grave three times, and then puts the torch over the corpse's mouth.[1] Thus the heir appears to place a barrier of fire between himself and the dead. And among the same people, when the funeral party has returned from the grave they bathe and have to undergo a further ceremony of purification by fire. In their absence a fire of charcoal has been prepared by the women, and on the approach of the funeral party a quantity of aromatic resin of the *sal* tree is sprinkled on the fire to produce a strong-smelling smoke. Arriving there each one of the party touches the fire with his left great toe and waves his left hand over the fire.[2] Thus, once more a barrier of fire reinforces a barrier of water. Among the Lakhers of Assam, when a dead man has been buried in another village, before leaving the lands of the village in which the funeral has taken place, a fire is kindled, and the visitors step over the fire. A disease-bearing spirit cannot pass over a fire and so is unable to follow the visitors home.[3] Among the Lhota Nagas, another tribe of Assam, when a death by accident has taken place, the friends of the dead man build a little shed and put some clothes and

[1] Sarat Chandra Roy, *The Bir-hors* (Ranchi, 1925), pp. 270, 271.
[2] Sarat Chandra Roy, *op. cit.*
[1] p. 272.
[3] N. E. Parry, *The Lakhers* (London, 1932), p. 405.

food in it.   On the day after the death, an old man lights a fire in front of the house and sacrifices a cock.   All the members of the family come out of the house stark naked and, after stepping over the fire, enter the shed, where they remain six days without speaking to any one, their food being provided by friends.[1]   As we shall see later on, the ghosts of all persons who die by accident or violence are particularly dreaded, and special precautions have to be taken against them.   The example of the Lhota Nagas is a case in point.   Among these same Lhota Nagas, when a man has been drowned on a fishing expedition the accident is announced in the village before the return of the fishers.   An old man thereupon comes forth from the village and lights a fire on the path by which the fishers are returning ; and every one of the fishers must step over the fire before he returns to the village.[2]   Among the lower castes of Upper India, when the mourners return from a funeral they touch a stone, cow-dung, iron, fire and water, which have been placed outside the house in readiness when the corpse was removed, and after a cremation the officiating Brahman touches fire in order to purify himself and to bar the return of the ghost.[3]   In these latter cases the mere touching of fire is probably a later substitute for an older custom of stepping over it.   In the Nicobar

[1] W. Crooke, *Religion and Folk-lore of Northern India*, edited by R. E. Enthoven (London, 1926), p. 239 *sq.*

[2] J. P. Mills, *The Lhota Nagas* (London, 1922), p. 162.

[3] W. Crooke, *The Popular Religion and Folklore of Northern India* (London, 1896), ii. p. 59.

Islands, while a dead body is lying in a house, a fire is kindled and maintained at the foot of the house ladder. The intention of the fire is said to be partly to keep the disembodied spirit far off, partly to apprise friends at a distance of the sad occurrence. The fire is either kindled directly by the friction of sticks or is obtained from another fire, which is known to have been so ignited.[1] From this account it appears that the soul of the deceased is supposed to have quitted the house before the burial, and the object of the fire is to prevent it from re-entering the dwelling.

In Africa also the barrier of fire against the spirits of the dead meets us in a variety of forms. Thus we read of a Bushman who, fearing to be haunted by the ghost of his dead wife, first dashed the head of the corpse to pieces, and after burying the body, lighted a fire upon the grave, as an additional precaution to prevent the return of her spirit.[2] Among the Tumbuka of Nyasaland, when a burial party is returning from the grave, they are met by a medicine-man who has kindled a great fire on the path into which he has thrown some roots ; each member of the party must pass through the flames before he returns to the village.[3] Among the Atonga of what used to be called British Central Africa, mourners returning from the grave bathe in water. Then the chief undertaker fetches a torch of grass pulled from the

[1] E. H. Man, *The Nicobar Islands and their People* (London, n.d.), p. 133.
[2] Henry Lichtenstein, *Travels in Southern Africa* (London, 1815), ii. p. 61.
[3] D. Fraser, *Winning a Primitive People* (London, 1914), p. 159.

roof of the dead man's hut, lights it at the fire in the same hut, jumps over it himself, and then holds it a few inches from the ground for the whole party to jump over, one by one. After being rubbed with certain roots on back and front by a woman they are deemed to be sufficiently purified to return home.[1] Among the Boloki of the Upper Congo, a good instance of the barrier by fire was witnessed by Mr. Weeks ; he says : " One day I saw an old woman whom I knew very well sitting in the centre of a ring of fire, and upon inquiry I found that she had had much to do with preparing a corpse for burial, and at the close of the ceremony she had to be purified. A ring of fire made of small sticks encircled her ; she took a leaf, dried it, crunched it in her fist, and sprinkled it on the fire, moving her hands, palms downwards, over the fire ring. When the fire had died out a witch-doctor took hold of the little finger of her left hand with the little finger of his right hand, and, lifting her arm, he drew her out of the fire circle purified. She was now supposed to be cleansed from all contamination with the dead."[2] Among the Fangs of West Africa, after a month of mourning, the widows of the deceased are obliged to step across a fire in the middle of the village ; and while some leaves are still burning under their feet, they sit down and their heads are shaved. From this moment they are purified from mourning, or, as the writer who reports it suggests, delivered from the

[1] A. Werner, *The Natives of British Central Africa* (London, 1906), pp. 162-163.

[2] J. H. Weeks, *Among Congo Cannibals* (London, 1913), p. 102.

ghost of their husband and they now can be passed on to his heirs.[1]

Among the Ewe-speaking people of the Slave Coast, " in Agweh a widow is supposed to remain shut up for six months in the room in which her husband is buried, during which time she may not wash or change her clothes. Food is carried to her by the family. According to report, in bygone days widows underwent a kind of fumigation in these burial chambers, a fire being lighted on the floor and strewn with red peppers, till they were nearly suffocated by the fumes. At the end of the period of mourning the widows wash, shave the head, pare the nails, and put on clean cloths ; the old cloths, the hair and the nail-parings being burned. At Agweh men who have lost their head wives do this also, after having remained shut up in a room of the house for eight days."[2] The purification of widows by fire and water on the Gold Coast has been described as follows by Miss Mary Kingsley. " To the surf and its spirits the sea-board dwelling Tschwis bring women who have had children and widows, both after a period of eight days from the birth of the child, or the death of the husband. A widow remains in the house until this period has elapsed, neglecting her person, eating little food, and sitting on the bare floor in the attitude of mourning. On the Gold Coast they bury very quickly, as they are

[1] E. Allegret, " Les Idées religieuses des Fañs (Afrique Occidentale) ", Revue de l'Histoire des Religions, i. (1904) p. 220.

[2] A. B. Ellis, The Ewe-Speaking Peoples of the Slave Coast of West Africa (London, 1890), p. 160.

always telling you, usually on the day after death, rarely later than the third day, even among the natives, and the spirit, or *srah*, of the dead man is supposed to hang about his wives and his house until the ceremony of purification is carried out. This is done, needless to say, with uproar. The relatives of each wife go to her house with musical instruments —I mean tom-toms and that sort of thing—and they take a quantity of mint, which grows wild in this country, with them. This mint they burn, some of it in the house, the rest they place upon pans of live coals and carry round the widow as she goes in their midst down to the surf, her relatives singing aloud to the *srah* of the departed husband, telling him that now he is dead and has done with the lady, he must leave her. This singing serves to warn all the women who are not relations to get out of the way, which of course they always carefully do, because if they were to see the widow their own husbands would die within the year." Arrived at the surf, they strip every rag off the widow and throw it into the surf ; and the widow is arrayed in a suit of dark blue baft in which she returns home.[1]

The Goajire Indians of Colombia keep up great fires at night in the village to ward off the ghosts of their dead enemies, who are apt to come and attack them with knives in the darkness ; but protected by this barrier of fire they feel themselves quite safe from their invisible foes.[2]   And in the same tribe

---

[1] Mary H. Kingsley, *Travels in West Africa* (London, 1897), p. 515.   [2] H. Candelier, *Rio Hacha et les Indiens Goajires* (Paris, 1893), p. 171.

when a man has been buried custom requires that his nearest relatives should keep up a great fire near the grave for nine days after the burial, to protect their deceased kinsman from the ghosts of their dead enemies, who would otherwise come to molest him ; for according to their belief life is not really extinct until nine days after death.[1] In this case it will be observed that the barrier of fire is directed not against the ghost of a dead friend, but against the ghosts of dead enemies, who might come by night to injure him.

In Europe also the barrier of fire against ghosts has not been unknown. In Mecklenburg, if fire and water are thrown after the corpse as it is being carried out the ghost will not afterwards appear in the house.[2] In ancient Rome, no doubt for a similar purpose, mourners returning from a funeral used to step over fire.[3] Some South Slavonians returning from a funeral are met by an old woman carrying a vessel of live coals. On these they pour water, or else take a live coal from the hearth and fling it over their heads.[4] In Ruthenia the barrier of fire against a ghost is still more attenuated ; mourners merely look steadfastly on the stove or place their hands upon it.[5]

So much for the barriers which primitive man erects to protect himself against the return of the spirit of the dead, but even when he has driven away

[1] Op. cit. p. 220.
[2] Bartschl, Sagen, Märchen und Gebräuche aus Mecklenburg (Vienna, 1879–1880), ii. p. 96.
[3] Festus, s.v. aqua et igne.
[4] W. R. Ralston, Songs of the Russian People (London, 1872), p. 320.
[5] W. R. Ralston, loc. cit.

these dangerous spirits and placed obstacles in the way of their return, he is still far from feeling easy, he still fears that they may break through the obstacles and return to haunt and torment the living. He is not, however, at the end of his resources, he has still many devices by which he hopes to bar the return of the ghosts, or at all events to render them impotent for mischief. Thus, for instance, failing as usual to distinguish the spiritual from the corporeal, he imagines that by tying up or mutilating and maiming a corpse he simultaneously ties up or mutilates and maims the dead person's ghost in exactly the same manner. To take instances : the Dieri of Central Australia used to tie the great toes and the thumbs of a corpse together to prevent the ghost from walking. The ceremony was witnessed by a constable, who describes it as follows : " Some of the younger men went off to dig a grave, and the elder ones proceeded to tie the great toes of the body together very securely, with strong, stout string, and then tied both the thumbs together behind the back, the body being turned face downwards whilst the latter operation was going on. From the manner in which the strings were tightened and the care taken over that part of the business, one would think that even a strong, healthy living man could not break or rise from such bonds. In reply to me they said that the tying was to prevent him from ' walking '." [1] Among the natives of the Herbert River in South-

---

[1] R. Brough Smyth, *The Aborigines of Victoria* (London, 1878), i. p. 119.

East Australia a near relative of the deceased used to beat the corpse with a mallet so violently as often to break the bones. Incisions were also generally made in the stomach, on the shoulder and in the lungs and filled with stones. The legs were generally broken for the express purpose of preventing the dead man from walking at night. The beating of the body, we are told, was for the sake of so frightening the ghost as to prevent it from haunting the camp, and the stones were put in the body to prevent it going too far afield.[1] Speaking of the natives of Queensland the Swedish traveller Lumholtz says : " The fact that the natives bestow any care on the bodies of the dead is doubtless owing to their fear of the spirits of the departed. In some places I have seen the legs drawn up and tied fast to the bodies, in order to hinder the spirits of the dead, as it were, from getting out to frighten the living. Women and children, whose spirits are not feared, receive less attention and care after death." [2] And speaking of the Australian aborigines in general another authority observes : " When a man dies, it is a very widely-spread custom for the relations to tie up the limbs of the corpse securely, so as to prevent his coming out of the grave in the shape of a ghost ".[3] The same writer describes as follows the usual mode of burial among the Australian aborigines : " Shortly after death, the body, in the

[1] A. W. Howitt, *The Native Tribes of South-Eastern Australia* (London, 1904), p. 474.
[2] C. Lumholtz, *Among Cannibals* (London, 1889), pp. 277-278.
[3] E. M. Curr, *The Australian Race* (Melbourne and London, 1886), i. p. 44.

case of a man, is reduced as nearly as possible to the
shape of a ball. To effect this the knees are forced
up to the neck and firmly tied to it ; the heels are
then pressed against the hams, the arms lie flat along
the sides, and are secured in each instance in these
positions by cords. Some tribes tie the thumbs together ; others burn the thumb nails besides. . . .
The object sought in tying up the remains of the
dead is to prevent the deceased from escaping from
the tomb and frightening or injuring the survivors.
The more nearly related and more influential in life,
the more the deceased is feared."[1] To take some
particular examples, concerning the natives near
Newcastle in Western Australia, we are told that,
" in burying the dead, besides taking off the finger
nails, the thumb and forefinger of each hand are tied
tightly together, with the object of preventing the
corpse from escaping from the tomb and frightening
the survivors. The more nearly an individual is
related to the deceased the greater is his fear of the
ghost."[2] Again, about the natives near Perth in
Western Australia it is recorded that : " The limbs
of the corpse are securely tied together with bands of
rushes or bark, so as, if possible, to hinder it from
getting out of the grave and wandering about in the
shape of a ghost, of which the Australian Black in
all parts is perpetually apprehensive ".[3] Again,
concerning the Whajook tribe in Western Australia,
we read that : " Before interment the hair is cut off

[1] E. M. Curr, *op. cit.* i. p. 87.   *Australian Race*, i. p. 324.
[2] G. Whitfield in E. Curr's *The*   [3] E. M. Curr, *op. cit.* i. p. 330.

and the nails burnt. This, and the binding of the corpse into the shape of a ball, are to prevent its escape from the grave."[1] Once more, concerning the natives in the neighbourhood of King George's Sound we are informed that at burial " the knees of the corpse are doubled up and tied ; the forefinger and thumb of the right hand are tied together, the thumb nail is burnt off, to prevent, as they say, the deceased digging his way out and using his spears ".[2]

It is reported that, in most parts of Central Borneo, when a death has taken place the corpse is brought out from the chamber into the common room of the house and there securely fastened down to the floor by bandages, tightened by pegs, which are passed round the arms and legs, the neck, the chest, and the trunk, constricting the body in such a way that even a strong living man would not be able to get up. The object of this constriction is said to be to prevent the ghost from returning to the body and doing harm to the living.[3] Among the Taungthu, a widely spread race of Upper Burma, when a man dies the thumbs and great toes of the corpse are tied together, and this is said by some to be intended to hinder the dead man from walking.[4] With a similar object we are told the ancient Indians used to put fetters on the feet of their dead, in order to prevent their ghosts from returning to the land of

[1] E. M. Curr, *op. cit.* i. p. 339.

[2] E. M. Curr, *op. cit.* i. p. 348.

[3] Oscar von Kessel, " Über die Volksstämme Borneos ", *Zeitschrift für allgemeine Erdkunde*, N.F. iii. (1857) pp. 377-410.

[4] J. G. Scott and J. P. Hardiman, *Gazetteer of Upper Burma*, Part I. i. (Rangoon, 1900) p. 554.

the living and molesting the survivors.[1] Among the Chuvash of Russia, when a very ugly man has died, they fasten his corpse down into the grave with iron, lest his ghost should come back to scare living folk by his ungainly appearance.[2] And whenever a wicked and quarrelsome man dies they think that his ghost will certainly return to wreak its spite upon the living. In order to obviate this danger they take strong measures to hinder the man, or rather his ghost, from escaping from the coffin ; they drive nails through the heart and soles of the feet of the corpse ; they nail the coffin securely down, and to make assurance still surer they constrict it with iron hoops.[3] Similarly, among the Cheremiss, a neighbouring tribe of Russia, when a bad man dies they drive nails through his heart and the soles of his feet to prevent his ghost from coming back and harming the survivors.[4] Among the Barundi of Central Africa when a person has died the men tie the limbs of the corpse tightly together on purpose, it is said, to prevent the return of the ghost, which they greatly fear.[5]

In America among the Tupinambas of Brazil the custom at burial is said to have been as follows : "The corpse had all its limbs tied fast, that it might

[1] H. Zimmer, *Altindisches Leben* (Berlin, 1879), p. 402.

[2] H. Vambéry, *Das Türkenvolk* (Leipsig, 1885), p. 462.

[3] A. Erman, " Briefliche Nachrichten über die Tschuwaschen und die Tscheremisen des Gouvernments Kaspan ", *Archiv für wissenschaftliche Kunde von Russland*, i. (1841) p. 376.

[4] A. F. von Haxthausen, *Studien über die innern Zustände, das Volksleben und inbesondere die ländlichen Einrichtungen Russlands* (Hannover, 1847), i. p. 449m.

[5] Hans Meyer, *Die Barundi* (Leipsic, 1916), p. 113.

not be able to get up and infest its friends with its visits ".[1]   A custom curiously different from the foregoing is reported of some of the Eskimo at Bering Strait.   The corpse is tied up in a bundle with cord, the head being forced down between the knees, and in this state it is drawn up through the smoke hole in the roof and carried to the graveyard till the coffin is ready for it.   Just before the body is placed in the coffin the cords that bind it are cut, in order, they say, that the ghost may return and occupy the body and move about if necessary.[2]   In this case the cords which bind the body are clearly supposed to bind the ghost also, but the custom of untying them before placing the body in the coffin indicates that these Eskimo do not greatly dread a possible return of the ghost to its mortal remains in the grave.

So much for the custom of tying up the corpse in order to prevent the ghost from roving and doing a mischief to the survivors, but for the same purpose primitive man sometimes resorts to still stronger measures.   He breaks the bones of the dead body, or otherwise mutilates it in such a fashion as would disable a living man, thinking thus to disable the ghost in a precisely similar manner.   We have seen that some of the Australian aborigines break the legs of the dead to hinder their ghosts from walking.

A tribe of the Cameroons in West Africa adopted still more forcible measures for accomplishing the

[1] Robert Southey, *History of Brazil*, i. (1817) (London, 1817) p. 258.
[2] E. W. Nelson, " The Eskimo about Bering Strait ", *18th Annual Report of the Bureau of American Ethnology* (1896–1897), Part I. (1899) p. 314.

same purpose ; as described by Dr. Nassau, an excellent authority, the custom was as follows. " Of one tribe in the upper course of the Ogowe, I was told, who, in their intense fear of ghosts, and their dread of the possible evil influence of the spirits of their own dead relatives, sometimes adopt a horrible plan for preventing their return. With a very material idea of a spirit, they seek to disable it by beating the corpse until every bone is broken. The mangled mass is hung in a bag at the foot of a tree in the forest. Thus mutilated the spirit is supposed to be unable to return to the village, to entice into its fellowship of death any of the survivors." [1] Among the Afars, a Danakil tribe on the southern borders of Abyssinia, all the bones of a corpse are broken before it is buried.[2] The motive for doing so is not mentioned by our authority, but we may conjecture that the object is thereby to render the ghost helpless. Among the Herero or Damara of South-West Africa, the backbone of a corpse is broken immediately after death. " The Herero say that in the spinal cord lives a small worm (maggot) which becomes after death the ghost of the deceased. This can be killed by fracturing the backbone : hence the proceeding here mentioned." [3] Thus it would appear that the Herero adopt the radical expedient of not merely

[1] Rev. R. H. Nassau, *Fetichism in West Africa* (London, 1904), p. 234.

[2] Ph. Paulitsche, *Ethnographie Nordost Afrikas. Die materielle Cultur der Danâkil, Galla und Somâl* (Berlin, 1893), p. 205.

[3] The Rev. G. Viehe, " Some Customs of the Ovaherero ", *South African Folk-Lore Journal*, i. Part III. (May 1879) p. 55 ; cf. C. J. Anderson, *Lake Ngami* (London, 1856), p. 226 ; P. H. Brincker, " Beobachtungen über die Deisidämonie der Eingeborenen Deutsch-Südwest-Afrikas ", *Globus*, lviii. (1890) p. 322.

disabling but killing the ghost. To this practice of killing the ghost we shall return later on.

Among the Kissi on the borders of Liberia the souls of dead witches and wizards are greatly dreaded. And when one of these folk dies the people smash his or her skull with heavy blows of a stone, believing that if this precaution is not adopted the ghost would issue from the grave on the third day after death and returning to the houses would beat the inhabitants and carry off their goods.[1] Of the Indians of the Californian Peninsula in North America we are told that formerly they had broken the spine of the deceased before burying them, and had thrown them into the ditch rolled up like a ball, believing that they would rise up again if not treated in this manner.[2]

But the breaking of the bones of the corpse is not the only mutilation of the body to which primitive man resorts for the purpose of disabling the ghost. He sometimes maims or mangles the body in other ways at least as radical. Thus with regard to the Kwearriburra tribe of Queensland in Australia we are told " that unless strong preventive measures are taken, the spirits of departed members of the tribe rise from their graves and continually haunt and otherwise annoy those who are still in the flesh. Accordingly, elaborate precautions are adopted, to keep the unfortunate ghosts confined in the grave

[1] H. Néel, " Note sur deux peuplades de la frontière Libérienne, les Kissi et les Toma ", L'Anthropologie, xxiv. (1913) p. 462.

[2] Account of the Aboriginal Inhabitants of the Californian Peninsula, etc. Report of the Smithsonian Institution for 1864, p. 387.

which holds their mortal clay. The *modus operandi* is as follows : On the death of a member of the tribe, his or her head is cut off and the trunk placed in a grave in the usual squatting position, and covered up. A fire is then lighted on the top, in which the head is roasted ; when it is thoroughly charred it is broken up into little bits amongst the hot coals, and the fire is then left to die gradually out. The theory is that the spirit rising from the grave to follow the tribe misses its head, and goes groping about to find it ; but being bereft of its head, it is of course blind, and therefore, not being able to see the fire, gets burnt. This frightens it so terribly that it retires into the grave again with all expedition, and never again presumes to attempt a renewal of social intercourse with the human denizens of this world." [1] Among the natives of Australia others cut off the thumbs of their dead enemies in order that their ghosts may not be able to throw spears. [2]

For a similar purpose apparently when the Tupi Indians of Brazil killed and ate a prisoner they cut off his thumb because of its use in archery, but they did not eat it with the rest of the body. [3] Other Australian aborigines put hot coals in the ears of a corpse to keep the soul in the body and prevent it from following them till they have got a good start away from him. As a further precaution they bark the

[1] F. C. Urquhart, " Legends of the Australian Aborigines ", *Journal of the Anthropological Institute*, xiv. (1885) p. 88.

[2] A. Oldfield, " On the Aborigines of Australia ", *Transactions of the Ethnological Society of London*, N.S. iii. (1865) p. 287.

[3] R. Southey, *History of Brazil*, vol. i. Second Edition (London, 1822), p. 231.

trees in a circle round the spot, so that when the ghost succeeds in extricating himself from the body and setting off in pursuit of his friends, he may wander round and round in a circle and never overtake them.[1]

The Toradjas of Central Celebes believe that men can become werewolves. When a man has been found guilty of this horrible crime they take him to a lonely spot and hack him to pieces, but they fear that if they were bespattered with his blood they would themselves be turned into werewolves. Further, they place the severed head of the werewolf beside his hinder-quarters, with the avowed intention of hindering his soul from coming to life again and pursuing his depredations.[2]

The Birhors of Bengal believe that the ghost of a woman who dies within a short time of childbirth is very dangerous, and to prevent her ghost from issuing from the grave they prick the soles of her feet with thorns.[3] Similarly the Sântals, another primitive people of Bengal, believe that the ghosts of a certain class of women are very dangerous. They are supposed to lick their victims to death, filing off their flesh with their rough tongues. When any of these women die, the survivors slide thorns into the soles of their feet, thus rendering them lame and powerless to pursue their victims.[4]

[1] A. W. Howitt, *Native Tribes of South-East Australia* (London, 1904), p. 473.

[2] A. C. Kruijt " De weerwolf bij de Toradja's van Midden-Celebes ", *Tijdschrift voor Indische Taal-*, *Land- en Volkenkunde*, Deel xli. (1899) p. 559.

[3] S. Chandra Roy, *The Birhors* (Ranchi, 1925), p. 267.

[4] Rev. F. T. Cole, " Sântâl Ideas of the Future Life ", *Indian Antiquary*, vii. (1878) p. 274.

LECTURE IV

LECTURE IV

In the last lecture I dealt with some of the devices to which primitive man resorts for preventing the dangerous spirits of the dead from returning to attack the living. I illustrated the barrier of fire which he seeks to interpose between himself and the ghosts. Further I described some of the other very different ways in which he attempts to achieve the same object by tying up or mutilating the corpse, in the belief that by so doing he disables the ghost from doing any harm to the survivors. I propose now to illustrate this custom further by examples drawn from Africa, America and Europe.

In Africa, among the natives of the Gabun district of West Africa, " people who while they were living were supposed to have witch power are believed to be able to rise in altered form from their graves. To prevent one who is thus suspected from making trouble, survivors open the grave, cut off the head, and throw it into the sea,—or in the interior, where there is no great body of water it is burned ; then a decoction of the bolondo bark is put into the grave. (The bolondo is a poison ; even a little of it may be fatal.) " [1] Thus these natives appear to

[1] R. H. Nassau, *Fetichism in West Africa* (London, 1904), p. 220.

think that if decapitation should fail to disable the ghost poison will have the desired effect. An old writer of the eighteenth century has described these West African practices in more detail. He tells us that when a case of sickness was ascribed to the action of the malignant ghost of a man who had lately died, they used to dig up the body and cut off the head, from which they asserted that blood flowed : this blood they collected and made out of it plasters which they applied to the body of the sick man and mixed with his food, and drink, assuring him of a speedy recovery, since the dead man, having had his head cut off, had no longer strength to come and disturb him. But the case was deemed much more difficult when the man whose spirit was tormenting the patient had not been buried, because he had been killed and eaten by his enemies or by wild beasts. In that case the medicine-man spread nets round the house of the sick man and even into the forest, in order that the soul of the dead man might be caught in the net when he came to annoy the sufferer. When a bird, rat, lizard, ape or other animal was caught in the net it was taken to be the incarnation of the dead man's soul. The medicine-man took it to the sick man and said : " Rejoice ; we've got him ; he shan't escape ". But before he killed the animal he demanded another fee. When this was agreed to he killed the animal, to the sick man's joy. But to prevent the soul returning the animal must be ground to powder and swallowed by the sick man. When the man had swallowed it,

digested it and voided it they thought that he was
finally rid of the tormenting ghost.[1] The Mossi of
the Western Sudan have a great respect for their
chiefs during their life but treat their bodies with
something less than respect after their death. As
soon as a chief has died they pierce his hands and
feet with large thorns to prevent his ghost from
returning to catch and carry off one of his relatives,
for they think that if he attempted to seize somebody
the thorns would hurt him so grievously that he
would at once relinquish his intended prey. The
corpse is then thrown into a ditch.[2] The Ba-
Ila-speaking people of Northern Rhodesia regard
with great contempt any man who dies childless.
When such a one dies " they cut off his little finger
and little toe, and enclose a piece of charcoal in his
fist, before burying him. Their reason for doing
this is obscure. They suppose that it will either
prevent his being reborn, or if it fails to that extent,
at least they will be able to recognize him by the
absence of those members should he return to earth."[3]
Among the Wawanga of the Mount Elgon district
in Kenya, when a case of illness is attributed to the
action of a malignant ghost, they will sometimes dig
up the body of the suspected man and burn the bones
over a nest of red ants, and the ashes are swept into
a basket and thrown into a river. But sometimes
instead of digging up the body the relatives of the

[1] J. B. Labat, *Relation historique de l'Éthiopie Occidentale*
(Paris, 1732), ii. pp. 209-212.
[2] P. E. Mangin, " Les Mossi ",
Anthropos, ix. (1914) p. 732.
[3] E. W. Smith and A. M. Dale,
*The Ila-Speaking Peoples of North-
ern Rhodesia*, ii. (London, 1920) p. 1.

sick man drive a stake into the head of the grave, and, to make assurance doubly sure, pour boiling water down after it.[1] This is no doubt thought to give a final quietus to the ghost who is causing the illness. Among the Ovambo of South-West Africa, the souls of dead magicians are especially dreaded. Hence, when a magician dies it is customary to dismember the body and to cut the tongue out of the mouth. They think that if these precautions are adopted the soul of the dead man cannot become a dangerous ghost ; the mutilation of the body has practically disarmed his spirit.[2]

The custom of decapitating a corpse in order to disable the dangerous ghost which we have seen practised in Australia and Africa, is observed also by the Armenians. They not only cut off the head but smash it or stick a needle into it or into the dead man's heart.[3]

In America, among the Eskimo about Bering Strait, when a man of evil reputation died they used to cut the sinews of his arms and legs to prevent his ghost from returning to the body and causing it to walk about at night as a ghoul.[4] The Rev. J. Owen Dorsey, our highest authority on the Omahas, was told by these Indians that " when a man was killed by lightning, he ought to be buried face downwards and the soles of his feet had to be slit. When this

[1] Hon. K. R. Dundas, " The Wawanga and Other Tribes of the Elgon District of British East Africa ", *Journal of the Royal Anthropological Institute*, xliii. (1913) p. 38.

[2] Herman Tönjes, *Ovamboland, Land, Leute, Mission* (Berlin, 1911), pp. 193-197.

[3] M. Abeghian, *Der armenische Volksglaube* (Leipsic, 1899), p. 11.

[4] E. W. Nelson, " The Eskimo about Bering Strait ", *18th Annual Report of the Bureau of American Ethnology*, 1896-97 (1899), p. 423.

was done, the spirit went at once to the spirit land, without giving further trouble to the living.   In one case (that of a Wejinecte' man, Jadegi, according to George Miller and Frank La Fléche) this was not done, so it was said that the ghost *walked*, and he did not rest in peace till another person (his brother) was slain by lightning and laid beside him."[1]

The Lengua Indians of the Paraguaian Chaco inflict on the bodies of the dead or dying certain strange mutilations, the exact object of which is not clear, though some of them appear certainly to be directed not so much against the ghost of the deceased as against the sorcerer who is suspected of having caused the death.   These mutilations are described as follows by the Rev. W. Grubb, our best authority on these Indians.   " In some cases the only peculiar rite is the placing of hot embers beneath the feet of the corpse and on the head.   If, however, the seat of trouble has been in the head, after the body has been placed in the grave they batter the skull with clubs ; if in the region of the heart, arrows are shot into it, and sometimes a stake is driven through the shoulder and slanting out below the ribs, thus pinning the body to the side of the grave.   In the case of dropsy, the body is shot at, and a bunch of herbs is held by the man conducting the burial.   This is afterwards burnt, and each of the party swallows some of the smoke.   The meaning of these and many more rites which are

---

[1] J. O. Dorsey, " A Study of   *of the Bureau of American Ethno-* Siouan Cults ", *11th Annual Report   logy*, 1889–90 (1894), p. 420.

used I do not fully understand, and I have had opportunities of witnessing only some of them. A very common rite, however, is the cutting open of the side, and the insertion into the wound thus made of heated stones, an armadillo's claw, some dog's bones, and occasionally red ants. The wound is then closed. In cases where haste is necessary, as it always is if the funeral takes place towards sunset, the sick person is not always dead when this operation is performed. In any case, to be efficacious, it must be performed, if not before actual death, certainly immediately afterwards, and before the spirit is supposed to have left the vicinity of the body. The stones are thought to have knowledge communicated by the soul of the dying or dead person, who, being freed from the limitations of the body, is able to recognize more clearly the originator of the trouble. They are supposed to ascend to the Milky Way, and there remain until they find an opportunity to descend on the author of the evil in the form of shooting stars. Consequently the Indians are very frightened when they see a falling star. They have all been guilty in their time, or are supposed to have been guilty, of causing some evil to others, and they are never sure when vengeance in this form may be wreaked on them from some distant quarter." [1]

On these mutilations it may be observed that they are clearly intended to effect the soul of the dead or

---

[1] W. B. Grubb, *An Unknown People in an Unknown Land* (London, 1911), pp. 162, 163.

dying man since they must be inflicted on his body before the soul has quitted it. Apparently they are intended to enable the ghost to avenge himself upon the supposed author of his death rather than to prevent him from injuring other people. So far therefore they differ from most of the other mutilations which we have passed in review, but in them as in the other preceding cases is involved the fundamental fallacy of imagining that you can influence a disembodied spirit by inflicting certain injuries on its mortal remains. It is the old, the ever recurring confusion of body and spirit.

In civilized Europe itself the custom of mangling a dead body for the purpose of maiming and disabling the dangerous ghost of the deceased has not been unknown. Ancient Greek murderers used to cut off the extremities, such as the ears and noses, of their victims, fasten them on a string, and tie the string round the necks and under the armpits of the murdered man. One motive assigned for this custom, and probably the original one, was the wish to weaken him so that he, or rather his ghost, could not take vengeance on his murderer. According to one account (a Scholiast on Sophocles, *Electra*, 445) the murderer fastened the extremities of his victim about his own person, but the better attested and more probable account is that he tied them about the mutilated body of his victim.[1] The practice is

---

[1] Scholiast on Sophocles, *Electra*, 445; Suidas, *s.v* μασχαλισθῆναι. Hesychius and Photius, *Lexicon, s.v.* μασχαλίσματα; Scholiast on Apollonius Rhodius, *Argon.* iv. 477; cf. E. Rohde, *Psyche*, i. 322-326. R. C. Jebb, on Sophocles, *Electra*, 445, with the Appendix, pp. 211 *sqq.*

perhaps illustrated by an original drawing in the
Ambrosian manuscript of the *Iliad*, which represents
the Homeric episode of Dolon ;[1] in the drawing the
corpse of the slain Dolon is depicted shorn of its feet
and hands, which lie beside it, while Ulysses holds
Dolon's severed head in his hand.[2]

" ' The greatest marvel that I know ', says
Walter Map, concerned a Welsh malefactor and un-
believer. He died in the house of William Laudun,
a brave soldier, who told the Bishop of Hereford
how the Welshman returned night by night, and
summoned his fellow-lodgers by name, when they
became ill and died in three days. Now only a few
survived. The Bishop thought that God might
have given permission to the evil angel of the man
to make his dead body restless. He advised Laudun
to dig up the corpse, cut the neck, sprinkle the body
and grave with holy water, and rebury it. In spite
of this being done, the survivors were still assailed,
and finally Laudun himself was summoned. He
drew his sword and pursued the malefactor to the
grave and clave its head to the neck. The trouble
now ceased, and Laudun did not die as a result of
the summons." [3]

The medieval Danish historian Saxo Grammaticus has recorded how, when a pestilence was
raging, the misfortune was attributed to the angry

---

[1] *Iliad*, x. 314.

[2] *Annali dell' Instituto di Corres-
pondeza Archeologica* (Rome, 1875),
tav. d' agg. R. ; A. Baumeister,
Denkmäler des klassichen Alter-

tums, i. 460 *sq.*, Fig. 506.

[3] J. A. MacCulloch, *Medieval
Faith and Fable* (London, 1932),
p. 90, referring to Walter Map,
ii. 27.

ghost of a man who had been killed in a popular tumult shortly before. To remedy the evil they dug up his body, cut off the head and ran a sharp stake through the breast of the corpse. The remedy proved effectual, for the plague ceased.[1] In 1710 when a great pestilence was raging in East Prussia the authorities gave orders that the graves should be opened and the bodies dug up in order to detect the malefactor whose ghost was causing the mischief. Suspicion at last fell upon one, who seems to have inflicted some wounds upon himself, so the corpse was decapitated and the headless body thrown back into the grave with a live dog to keep it company. But strange to say, even after these strong measures had been taken, the plague still continued.[2]

In Eastern Europe from Prussia on the north to Macedonia and Greece on the south, the belief in vampires has been and still is rampant. Vampires are malicious ghosts who issue from their graves to suck the blood of the living, and stringent measures are deemed necessary to hinder or arrest this horrible proceeding. In East Prussia when a person is believed to be suffering from the attacks of a vampire and suspicion falls on the ghost of somebody who died lately, the only remedy is thought to be for the family of the deceased to go to his grave, dig up his body, behead it and place the head between the legs of the corpse. If blood flows from the severed head the man was certainly a vampire,

---

[1] Saxo Grammaticus, *Historia Danica*, lib. I. ed. P. E. Müller (Havniae, 1836), i. p. 43.

[2] M. Toeppen, *Aberglauben aus Masuren* (Danzig, 1867), p. 114.

and the family must drink of the flowing blood, thus recovering the blood which had been sucked from their living bodies by the vampire.[1] Thus the vampire is paid out in kind.

In Serbia and Bulgaria, to prevent a man from becoming a vampire they stick a whitethorn into the navel of his corpse, and burn off all the hair on his body except on the head. Further, they slit the soles of his feet and drive a nail into the back of his head to prevent the skin from being blown up by the devil.[2] These measures are preventive, but to put an end to a vampire his corpse is staked and burned. The stake with which his body is pierced should be of hawthorn. If a butterfly escapes from the grave while the corpse is being stabbed the people run after it, catch it and throw it on a fire. That is the end of the vampire. But if the butterfly escape, woe to the village, for the vampire will avenge himself on the inhabitants till his seven years are up. Some say the vampire should be stabbed with a knife that has never been used to cut bread. Some say the stab should be given through the dried hide of a young bull, for they believe that whoever is sprinkled with the blood of a vampire will himself become a vampire and will soon die. In the Drina district of Bosnia, on the borders of Bosnia, the priest goes at the head of the peasantry to the graveyard ; they open the grave,

---

[1] W. J. U. Tettau und J. D. H. Temme, *Die Volkssagen Ostpreussens, Litauens und Westpreussens* (Berlin, 1835), p. 275.

[2] F. S. Krauss, " Vampyre in südslawischen Volksglauben ", *Globus*, lxi. (1892) p. 326.

fill it with straw ; stab the corpse through the straw with a stake of hawthorn, and set fire to the straw. The fire is kept up till the vampire is reduced to ashes. That prevents his return to plague people.[1] In Wallachia to prevent a man from becoming a vampire they run a long nail through the skull of the corpse, and lay a thorny rose bush on his body, in the hope that should he struggle to emerge from the grave the thorns will so entangle him in his shroud that he will not be able to extricate himself from it and so will remain quietly in the grave.[2] Among the Roumanians of Transylvania the custom and belief concerning vampires are similar. They think that there are two sorts of vampires, either living or dead. The living vampire is generally the illegitimate offspring of two illegitimate persons ; but even a flawless pedigree will not ensure any one against the intrusion of a vampire into the family vault, since every one killed by a vampire becomes likewise a vampire after death, and will continue to suck the blood of other innocent persons until the ghost has been exorcised by opening the grave and either driving a stake through the corpse or else firing a pistol shot into the coffin. To walk smoking round the grave on each anniversary of the death, is also supposed to be effective in confining the vampire ; this is clearly a mild form of the barrier by fire. In very obstinate cases of vampirism it is recommended to cut off the head and replace it in

[1] F. S. Krauss, " Südslavische Schutzmittel gegen Vampyre ", Globus, lxii. (1892) p. 203 sq.

[2] Arthur und Albert Schott, Wallachische Mährchen (Stuttgart, 1845), p. 298.

the coffin with the mouth filled with garlic; or to extract the heart and burn it, strewing the ashes over the grave. Every Roumanian village has some old woman versed in the modes of laying vampires. Sometimes she drives a nail through the forehead of the deceased, or she rubs the body with the fat of a pig which has been killed on the Feast of Ignatius, five days before Christmas. It is also very usual to place the thorny branch of a wild-rose bush across the body to prevent it leaving the coffin.[1]

The belief in the blood-sucking ghost which we call vampires is also widely spread amongst the modern Greeks, who may possibly have borrowed it from their northern neighbours the Slavs. To put an end to the depredations of a vampire they dig up the body of the suspected person, cut out the heart and burn it over the corpse, or as an alternative they burn it with the whole body.[2] " The accordance between the Greek and Slavonic conceptions of the vampire ", says Mr. G. F. Abbott, " is nowhere more apparent than in Macedonia, a province which for many centuries past has been the meeting-point of Slav and Hellene. It is believed that a dead person turns into a vampire ($\beta\rho\nu\kappa o\lambda a\kappa\iota\acute{a}\zeta\epsilon\iota$), first, if at the unearthing of the body the latter is found undecayed and turned face downwards. In such an emergency the relatives of the deceased have re-course to a ceremony which fills the beholder with sickening horror. I was credibly informed of a

[1] E. Gerard, *The Land beyond the Forest* (Edinburgh and London, 1888), i. p. 13.

[2] B. Schmidt, *Das Volksleben der Neugriechen* (Leipzig, 1871), p. 167.

case of this description occurring not long ago at Alistrati, one of the principal villages between Serres and Drama. Someone was suspected of having turned into a vampire. The corpse was taken out of the grave, scalded with boiling oil, and was pierced through the navel with a long nail. Then the tomb was covered in, and millet was scattered over it, that, if the vampire came out again, he might waste his time in picking up the grains of millet and be thus overtaken by dawn. For the usual period of their wanderings is from about two hours before midnight till the first crowing of the morning cock."[1]

In some of the foregoing cases the treatment of the body of a vampire appears to be intended not merely to disable but to destroy the blood-sucking ghost. There is other evidence pointing to the conclusion that primitive man has clearly conceived the possibility of actually killing a dangerous ghost and so putting an end to it once and for all. From his point of view this mode of dealing with the spirit is clearly the most satisfactory of all ; for the ghost once dead can give no more trouble.

To take examples, the Mori-oris, the inhabitants of the Chatham Islands off New Zealand, believed that "after death, the spirit of the departed had power to return to earth and haunt the living, and that a person visited by the *kiko-kiko* (or evil spirit of the dead), and touched on the head by it, would die very soon after such visitation. To prevent the

[1] G. F. Abbott, *Macedonian Folklore* (Cambridge, 1903), pp. 218, 219.

dead from troubling them, they had a curious custom. As soon as breath had left the body, they would all assemble at midnight in some secluded spot, and proceed to kill the *kiko-kiko*. First, kindling a large fire, they would sit round in a circle, each person holding a long rod in his hand ; to the end of each rod a tuft of spear grass was tied ; they would then sway their bodies to and fro, waving the rods over the fire in every direction, jabbering strange and unintelligible incantations." By this means they appear to have imagined that they killed the dangerous ghost.[1]

In the island of Mangaia, in the Central Pacific, the ceremony of killing the ghosts used to be carried out with great pomp in a series of mock battles which have been described as follows by a missionary long resident in the island. The ceremony, he tells us, was called *Ta i te mauri*, or Ghost-Killing. "Upon the decease of an individual, a messenger (' bird ', so called from his swiftness) was sent round the island. Upon reaching the boundary line of each district, he paused to give the war-shout peculiar to these people, adding ' So-and-so is dead '. Near relatives would start off at once for the house of the deceased, each carrying a present of native cloth. Most of the athletic young men of the entire island on the day following united in a series of mimic battles desig-nated '*ta i te mauri*', or slaying the ghosts. The district where the corpse lay represented the ' mauri '

[1] W. T. L. Travers, " Notes of the Traditions and Manners and Cus-toms of the Mori-oris ", *Trans-* *actions and Proceedings of the New Zealand Institute*, ix. (1876) p. 26.

or ghosts. The young men belonging to it early in the morning arrayed themselves as if for battle, and well armed, started off for the adjoining district, where the young men were drawn up in battle array under the name of ' aka-oa ', or friends. The war-dance performed, the two parties rush together, clashing their spears and wooden swords together in right earnest. The sufferers in this bloodless conflict were supposed to be malignant spirits, who would thus be deterred from doing further mischief to mortals. The combatants now coalesce, and are collectively called ' mauri ', or ghosts, and pass on to the third district. Throughout the day their leader carries the sacred ' iku kikau ', or cocoa-nut leaf, at the pit of his stomach like the dead. Arrived at this third village, they find the young men ready for the friendly conflict, and bearing the name of ' aka-oa '. ' The battle of the ghosts ' is again fought, and now with swelling numbers they pass on to the fourth, fifth and sixth districts. In every case it was supposed that the ghosts were well thrashed. Returning with a really imposing force to the place where the corpse was laid out in state, a feast was given to the brave ghost-killers, and all save near relatives return to their various homes ere nightfall. So similar was this to actual warfare, that it was appropriately named ' e teina no te puruki ', *i.e.* ' a younger brother of war '."[1]

In Fiji it was believed to be possible to kill a

---

[1] W. W. Gill, *Myths and Songs from the South Pacific* (London, 1876), pp. 268, 269.

troublesome ghost. Once it happened that many chiefs feasted in the house of Tanoa, King of Ambau. In the course of the evening one of them related how he had slain a neighbouring chief. That very night, having occasion to leave the house, he saw, as he believed, the ghost of his victim, hurled his club at him, and killed him stone dead. On his return to the house he roused the king and the rest of the inmates from their slumbers and recounted his exploit. The matter was deemed of high importance, and they all sat on it in solemn conclave. Next morning a search was made for the club on the scene of the murder ; it was found and carried with great pomp and parade to the nearest temple, where it was laid up for a perpetual memorial. Everybody was firmly persuaded that by this swashing blow the ghost had been not only killed but annihilated.[1]

In Africa, as we have seen, the Herero believe that they can kill a person's ghost by breaking his backbone after death.[2] The Bura and Pabir tribes of Northern Nigeria regard with great fear the ghost of a man who has been killed by lightning and they think that they can kill it. The ceremony of killing it must be performed by the members of a certain clan, the Lasama. Seven days after the burial the men of the clan assemble at the dead man's haunts and there dance and toss up in the air a goat which, as it falls, is caught on the sacred staves. Suddenly one of the men espies the wicked soul, and catching it

---

[1] Charles Wilkes, *Narrative of the United States Exploring Expedition,* New Edition (New York, 1851), iii. 85.
[2] See above, p. 69.

wraps it in grass and deposits it in the dead man's grave. A fee is paid to the men of the clan for rendering this dangerous service by destroying the dangerous ghost.[1] Among the Banyankole of Uganda sickness was sometimes attributed to the action of a malignant ghost. In order to drive out the obsessing ghost who had taken possession of the sufferer's body, a medicine-man made scratches on the patient's body and rubbed some pungent powder into them, till the patient writhed with pain. Smarting from the pain the ghost was now ready to quit the sufferer, and to hasten his departure the medicine-man rubbed the sick man's body down with his hands, pressing the ghost from his head out at his feet and the tips of his fingers. When the ghost sought to escape it was caught in a pot which was placed ready to receive it, and the pot was thrown either into fire or into water, thus either burning or drowning the ghost. In either case there was an end of the ghost.[2] Similarly among the Banyoro of Uganda, when a case of sickness was ascribed to the influence of a ghost who had taken possession of a patient's body, a medicine-man used to lure the ghost out of the body of the sufferer into a pot which he had baited with savoury meat. When the ghost thus tempted entered into the pot, the medicine-man shut it up and carried it to waste land, where he either burned it or threw it into running water, thus

[1] C. K. Meek, *Tribal Studies in Northern Nigeria* (London, 1931), i. p. 169.
[2] J. Roscoe, *The Banyankole* (Cambridge, 1923), p. 141 ; compare J. G. Frazer, *The Fear of the Dead in Primitive Religion* (London, 1933), pp. 157-158.

burning or drowning the ghost.[1] Again, amongst the Baganda the " evil-disposed ghost which attacks people of its own accord, uninfluenced by some living person, is usually thought to be the ghost of the aunt on the male side. These ghosts are sometimes most troublesome, causing the man's wife or his children constant sickness, and nothing will appease them. In such a case the *Mandwa* (priest) has to capture the ghost and destroy it ; he comes to the house bringing either a cow or buffalo horn into which he puts a cowrie or snail shell with a seed of the wild plantain ; this he places on the end of a long stick and passes up the central post of the hut until he reaches the top near the roof. The spirits always take up their abode in the highest part of the conical-shaped huts on the central pole. During the process of capturing the spirit the house is kept in darkness and only two or three people are permitted to be present. When the *Mandwa* (priest) has got the horn to the top of the pole he works it about until the shells and seed make a squeaking noise ; this he pronounces to be the voice of the ghost which has entered the horn ; he then rapidly lowers the horn, covers it with a bit of bark cloth and plunges it into a pot of water ; the ghost thus secured is carried off in triumph to the nearest river and plunged into it ; if there is no river near the priest secures the mouth of the pot, and carries it off into a place where there is some unreclaimed land where he deposits it, and

[1] J. Roscoe, *The Bakitara or Banyoro* (Cambridge, 1923), pp. 286 *sq.* ; compare J. G. Frazer, *The Fear of the Dead in Primitive Religion*, pp. 159-161.

leaves it to be destroyed by the next grass fire."[1] Thus if the ghost escapes death by drowning he is sure to perish in the end by fire. Among the Bavenda of the Northern Transvaal a diviner will sometimes declare that the death of a member of a tribe has been caused by the wicked ghost of an ancestral spirit who must therefore be destroyed in order to protect his descendants against his further attacks. In order to effect this destruction the spear of the wicked spirit is tied round the neck of a black goat ; a heavy stone is attached to it, and the goat with the spear and the stone is thrown into a deep pool. With the goat the ancestral spirit is believed to be thrown into the water and drowned, thus ridding his descendants of any danger from him for ever.[2] Speaking of West African negroes in general, Miss Mary Kingsley observes : " Destroying the body by breaking up or cutting up is a widely diffused custom in West Africa in the case of dangerous souls, and is universally followed with those that have contained wanderer-souls, *i.e.* those souls which keep on turning up in the successive infants of a family. A child dies, then another child comes to the same father or mother and that dies, after giving the usual trouble and expense. A third arrives, and if that dies, the worm—I mean the father—turns, and if he is still desirous of more children he just breaks one of the legs of the body before throwing it in the bush. This

[1] J. Roscoe, " Further Notes on the Manners and Customs of the Baganda ", *Journal of the Royal Anthropological Institute*, xxxii. (1902) p. 43.

[2] H. A. Stayt, *The Bavenda* (Oxford, 1931), p. 252.

he thinks will act as a warning to the wanderer-soul and give it to understand that if it will persist in coming into his family, it must settle down there and give up its flighty ways. If a fourth child arrives in the family, and if it dies, the justly irritated parent cuts its body up carefully into very small pieces, and scatters them, doing away with the soul altogether."[1] Thus the total destruction of a child's body is believed to involve the total destruction of its soul.

[1] Mary H. Kingsley, *Travels in West Africa* (London, 1897), p. 480.

LECTURE V

LECTURE V

In the last lecture I dealt with some of the means which primitive man employs to prevent the spirits of the dead from coming back to trouble and plague the living. In particular I described some of the mutilations which he inflicts on a corpse in the belief that he thereby maims and disables the ghost in like manner. Later, I showed that going still further he imagines that he can not only disable the ghost but kill it and annihilate it. But apart from these strong measures he resorts to a great variety of less severe devices to effect the same object. I propose now to illustrate some of these devices by a series of miscellaneous examples. They display on the part of primitive man an ingenuity and resourcefulness which might, perhaps, have been turned to better account in a better cause; at least they serve to set in a strong light that obsessing fear of the spirits of the dead which has played an enormous part in the history of humanity.

Thus, for example, among the natives of Halmahera or Gilolo, a large island to the west of New Guinea, when any one dies, the members of his

household must change their names ; else the dead
man knows their names and calls them, to keep him
company in the grave ; so that they die. When
any one dies and his eyes remain wide open, they
say that he is looking round for a companion ;
hence, some one else will die soon. So they are
always careful to weight the eyelids of a corpse,
generally with a rijksdollar, in order to keep them
shut. When a corpse is buried, the stem of a banana-
tree must be buried with it to keep it company, in
order that the dead person may not seek a companion among the living. Hence, when the coffin
is lowered into the ground, one of the bystanders
steps up and throws a young banana-tree into the
grave saying : " Friend, you must miss your companions of this earth ; here, take this as a comrade ".
When any one dies and his coffin is made, they must
take the measure of the corpse and make the coffin
fit it exactly ; otherwise, they say (if there is room
and to spare in the coffin) some one else will soon
die. For the same reason the grave must fit the
coffin exactly. A grave must not be dug in a place
all by itself, else the dead person buried in it will
seek to have a companion. (Graves are dug behind
the house, and generally there are old graves there
already.) When a mother has a child that dies
young she must wear the *slendang*, or cloth in which
the child is carried, continually for more than a
month ; otherwise she will have another loss. When
a man who was a werewolf dies, it is necessary to
strew lime on his eyes and to cover his head with a

pan ; for then, they say, his eyes are dim and he cannot see to come and visit the survivors with sickness or death. When some woman dies and they say that she was a *pontianak* (evil spirit), they stick needles under all her nails, and under her armpits they place two hen's eggs : this, they say, is a plaything for her child and therefore she will not spread out her arms to fly about else she would lose the eggs ; and the reason for sticking needles under her nails is that she may not go about as a *pontianak*, for her nails will be sore and thus she will not be able to seize with them.[1]

In the Island of Nias, to the west of Sumatra, at a burial " when they have come to the grave, whither they have proceeded with loud lamentations, the nearest relatives, and not least the women, behave as if they were frantic. When the coffin is lowered into the grave, they make as if they would leap into the grave, stab themselves, and so forth, customs which have their ground in the fear of the ghost of the deceased ; for by so doing they make it clear to him that his death is mourned, in order that his spirit may not, out of revenge, bring misfortune on the surviving relatives. For these reasons, before they go to the grave, the dead man's golden ornaments are shown to him in order that he may take the shadow of them with him to the land of souls ; and from the same consideration some gold is placed

---

[1] M. J. van Baarda, " Fabelen, Verhalen en Overleveringen der Gabelareezen ", collected by H. van Dijken, published and translated by M. J. van Baarda, *Bijdragen tot de Taal- Land- en Volkenkunde van Nederlandsch-Indie*, xlv. (1895) pp. 538-541.

in the mouth of the corpse.[1] In South Nias the corpse is coffined outside of the village, in order that the spirit of the dead may not find the way back to the village to fetch somebody there. For this reason there is, also in North Nias, no regular path to the cemeteries, but on each occasion of a burial a path is cleared to the cemetery.[2] Clearly these people count upon the inability of the ghost to find his way back to the house by a new and unfamiliar path through the forest.

Among the Papuans of Geelvink Bay in Dutch New Guinea, it is a rule that while a burial is proceeding no noise may be made and no work done in the village, for any noise would excite the anger of the ghost, and he would take his revenge on the survivors who show so little regard for his feelings. And after the burial is completed they fasten leaves and branches to the houses and trees as scarecrows to frighten away the ghost, if he should venture to return.[3] The Kiwai of British New Guinea always carry a dead body to the grave head foremost, because they believe that if they carried it in the reverse position the ghost would return to the village.[4] A contrary rule was observed in the neighbouring island of Mabuiag to the south of New Guinea, for there the corpse was always carried out to burial feet foremost, else it was believed that the ghost would

[1] Th. C. Rappard, " Het eiland Nias en zijne bewoners ", *Bijdragen tot de Taal- Land- en Volkenkunde van Nederlandsch-Indie*, lxii. (1909) p. 571.

[2] Th. C. Rappard, *op. cit.* p. 573.

[3] J. B. van Hasselt, " Die Noeforezen ", *Zeitschrift für Ethnologie*, viii. (1876) pp. 188-189.

[4] G. Landtman, *The Kiwai Papuans of British New Guinea* (London, 1927), p. 257.

return and trouble the survivors. As a further precaution to prevent his wandering the thumbs and great toes of the corpse were tied together.[1] The same rule of carrying out a corpse feet foremost to prevent the return of the ghost has been observed by other peoples, as we shall see presently. In the Society Islands of the Pacific, after an elaborate ceremony for the burial of the sins of the deceased, a priest used to step up to the side of the corpse, and taking some small slips of plantain leaf-stalk he fixed two or three of them under each arm, placed a few on the breast, and then, addressing the dead body, said : " There are your family, there is your child, there is your wife, there is your father, and there is your mother. Be satisfied yonder (that is, in the world of spirits). Look not towards those who are left in this world." This concluding ceremony was designed to impart contentment to the deceased, and to prevent his spirit from repairing to the places of his former resort, and so distressing the survivors.[2] Among the Subanos of Mindanao, when men return home after a burial they thrust their chopping knives deeply into the rungs of the house ladder, doubtless to prevent the ghost from returning and climbing up the ladder into the house.[3]

[1] A. C. Haddon, " Funeral Ceremonies ", *Reports of the Cambridge Anthropological Expedition to the Torres Straits*, v. (Cambridge, 1904) p. 248 ; *id.*, " The Secular and Ceremonial Dances of Torres Straits ", *Internationales Archiv für Ethnographie*, vi. (1893) p. 152.

[2] W. Ellis, *Polynesian Researches* (London, 1836), Second Edition, i. pp. 401-403.

[3] F. Blumentritt, " Neue Nachrichten über die Subanon (Insel Mindanao) (nach P. Francisco Sanchez) ", *Zeitschrift der Gesellschaft für Erdkunde zu Berlin*, xxxi. (1896) p. 371.

The dwarf tribes of the Malay Peninsula, the Semang, the Orang Utan and the Kenta, shift their camp immediately after a death, often removing to a great distance, because they fear that the ghost might attack and kill them. They are careful to place a river between them and the old camp, believing apparently that the ghost cannot cross water.[1] This is obviously a case of the water barrier with which we are already familiar.

In Siam a corpse is sometimes placed in the coffin face downwards, in order that the ghost may not find its way back to the house; and for the purpose of rendering his return to the old home still more difficult, the coffin is carried out of the house not by the door but through an opening specially made in the wall. As if this were not enough to baffle the ghost the coffin is carried by the bearers at a run several times round the house, till the ghost may be presumed to be giddy and quite unable to retrace his steps to the familiar dwelling.[2] A similar mode of baffling the ghost and preventing his return to the house is practised by the Shans of Burma. They greatly dread the ghost of a woman who has died in child-bed and take great pains to prevent it from returning, in the form of a malignant spirit, to attack her husband, and torment him. Hence, when the bodies of the dead mother and child are being removed from the house part of the

[1] Paul Schebesta, *Among the Forest Dwarfs of Malaya* (London, n.d.), pp. 106, 143, 236.

[2] E. Young, *The Kingdom of the Yellow Robe* (Westminster, 1898), p. 246; Mgr. Pallegoix, *Description du royaume Thai ou Siam* (Paris, 1854), p. 245.

mat wall in the side of the house is taken down, and
the dead woman and her baby are lowered to the
ground through the aperture. The hole through
which the bodies have passed is immediately filled
with new mats, so that the ghost may not know how
to return.[1] The Palaungs, another tribe of Burma,
entertain a similar dread of the ghost of the woman
dying in childbirth and adopt a similar precaution
to prevent her spirit from returning. The body is
lowered through a hole in the floor of the room in
which she died, then the floor is washed and the hole
is closed with new boards. This, they hope, will
prevent the return of the spirits of the unfortunate
mother and child, to Palaungs, the most terrifying
of unhappy spirits.[2] This mode of preventing a
ghost from returning to the house by carrying out his
corpse through a special opening which is afterwards
immediately closed, is by no means peculiar to
Burma and Siam ; it has been practised by many
other peoples in many other parts of the world.
Elsewhere I have collected the evidence for its
diffusion, but I cannot linger over it now.[3] Among
the Kakhyen of Upper Burma, mourners returning
from the grave strew ground rice along the path and
cleanse their legs and arms with fresh leaves.
Before re-entering the house they are purified with
water by the medicine-man with a sprinkler of grass,

[1] Mrs. Leslie Milne, *Shans at Home* (London, 1910), p. 96.

[2] Mrs. Leslie Milne, *The Home of an Eastern Clan* (Oxford, 1924), pp. 304, 305.

[3] J. G. Frazer, *Garnered Sheaves* (London, 1931), p. 10 *sqq.*; J. G. Frazer, *Belief in Immortality* (London, 1913), i. pp. 452 *sqq.*

and step over a bundle of grass sprinkled with the blood of a fowl sacrificed during their absence to the spirit of the dead. A few days later the ghost of the deceased, who is supposed to be still lingering about his old home, is finally expelled from the house by a great dance.[1]

Among the tribes in the Aracan Mountains in Burma, if a woman who has had children gives birth to a still-born infant a piece of iron is placed in the cradle-coffin, a relation saying : " Return not into the womb of thy mother until this iron is soft as cotton ".[2]

Among the Karens of Burma, when a funeral party is returning from the grave, " each person provides himself with little hooks made of branches of trees, and calling his spirit to follow him, at short intervals, as he returns, he makes a motion as if hooking it, and then thrusts the hook into the ground. This is done to prevent the spirit of the living from staying behind with the spirit of the dead." [3]

In Chittagong, a district of North-Eastern India, when a funeral is taking place a man follows the body, pouring out water behind it all the way from the house to the boundaries ; this is clearly another case of the water barrier. Formerly, when the corpse had been carried out of the house, they used to drive a nail into the threshold to prevent the ghost from returning and entering the dwelling.[4]

[1] J. A. Anderson, *Mandalay to Momien* (London, 1876), p. 144 ; cf. p. 77.

[2] *The British Burma Gazetteer*, i. (Rangoon, 1879–1880) p. 387.

[3] F. Mason, " Physical Char- acters, etc., of the Karens ", *Journal of the Asiatic Society of Bengal*, Part II. No. 1 (1866), p. 28.

[4] Th. Bérangier, " Les funérailles à Chittagong ", *Les Missions Catholiques*, xiii. (1881) pp. 503, 504.

Primitive man fears the spirits of the dead not only while he is awake but while he is asleep, for in sleep he may dream of a ghost, and to his thinking a dream is as real as a waking reality. Hence he deems it very dangerous to dream of the ghost of a dead man on the night after his burial ; for he fancies that the ghost has come in person to disturb him and perhaps to carry off another soul from the house. To avoid these dangers the Lakhers of Assam take elaborate precautions. After a burial when the dead man's relations return home and are about to enter the house, they step on to a sieve containing a little rice, which has been placed ready for the purpose, and go on into the house. This is to show that the soul of the dead has gone to *Athikhi*, the spirit-land, and that his relations are again clean, rice being an emblem of purity. That evening the mother's brother's wife brings a fowl and some *sahmahei* (fermented rice), and sacrifices the fowl to console the souls of the surviving members of the deceased's family, and anoints the big toe of each with the fowl's blood ; she then gives each of them a little fermented rice and returns home. This is an important sacrifice, for it is essential that the souls of the deceased's family should be at peace ; because if any member of it sees any one in his dreams on the night of the funeral, the person dreamed of will soon die also. The belief is that on the night of the funeral the spirit of the deceased comes to visit his family, and if they are dreaming of any one, the deceased's spirit meets the spirit of the person

dreamed of and seizes it and carries it off with him
to *Athikhi*. On the morning after the funeral one
of the neighbours always asks the deceased's relatives
whether they had any dreams during the night or
not ; if the answer is " No ", all is well, but if one
of the family dreamt of any one that night he must
say so, as it is very unlucky for the person dreamed
of. If the dream was that the dead man appeared
again alive in the house, it means that another
member of the family will die. A further precaution
is often taken to prevent the deceased's relations or
other villagers from dreaming on the night of the
funeral. Each householder, before going to sleep,
puts a little cooked rice in a pot, and each member
of the household says, " May my spirit not wander
about to-night, let it remain within this pot " ;
having said this, each person puts his hand inside
the pot and touches the rice. By this means the
spirits are kept imprisoned inside the pots, and as
they cannot wander about and meet other people's
spirits, the owners of the imprisoned spirits do not
dream of any one that night, and so cause no one
any harm. Another way of preventing the soul
from escaping from its owner's house is to place a
paddy pestle across the door, as the soul will fear to
go under it, lest the pestle should fall on it.[1] We
have already seen that these people sometimes place
a paddy pestle at the door of a house to prevent the
ghost from entering ; we now see that they also
place a paddy pestle at the door to prevent their

[1] N. E. Parry, *The Lakhers* (London, 1932), pp. 402, 403.

own souls from going out. Clearly the pestle is regarded as an effectual barrier against the passage of a spirit in either direction.

Among the Kawar, a primitive tribe of the Central Provinces in India, after the funeral the mourners bathe and return home walking one behind the other in Indian file. When they come to a cross-road the foremost man picks up a pebble with his left foot, and it is passed from hand to hand down the line of men until the hindmost throws it away. This is thought to sever their connexion with the spirit of the deceased and prevent it from following them home.[1] Among the Korku, a Munda people of the Central Provinces of India, " in order to lay to rest the spirit of a dead person, who it is feared may trouble the living, five pieces of bamboo are taken as representing the bones of the dead man, and these with five crab's legs, five grains of rice and other articles, are put into a basket and thrust into a crab's hole under water. The occasion is made an excuse for much feasting and drinking, and the son or other representative who lays the spirit works himself up into a state of drunken excitement before he enters the water to search for a suitable hole."[2] Among the Pabia, a small caste in the Bilaspur District of India, " when any one dies in a family, all the members, as soon as the breath leaves his body, go into another room of the house ; and across the door they lay a net opened into the room

[1] R. V. Russell, *The Tribes and Castes of the Central Provinces of* *India* (London, 1916), iii. p. 397.
[2] R. V. Russell, *op. cit.* iii. p. 564.

where the corpse lies. They think that the spirit of the dead man will follow them, and will be caught in the net. Then the net is carried away and burnt or buried with the corpse, and thus they think that the spirit is removed and prevented from remaining about the house and troubling the survivors." [1] In the Punjab the ghosts of sweepers are thought to be malevolent and are much dreaded ; and their bodies are therefore always buried or burnt face downwards to prevent their spirits from escaping. Riots have taken place, and the magistrates have been appealed to, in order to prevent a sweeper being buried face upwards.[2]

The Koryak, a primitive people in the extreme north-eastern corner of Asia, appear to regard the spirits of the dead as hostile to the living from the moment that their bodies have been removed from the house. They burn their dead. At the crema-tion of the body of a girl, her grandfather " took a pole and thrusting it into the body said, ' Of yonder magpie pricked ' . . . or, in a free translation, ' This is the magpie of the underworld which pricked '. He imitated the actions of the magpie of the world of the dead, in order to inform the deceased that she was passing to another world, and must not return to the house. The further actions of the dead girl's grandfather had the same end in view. When the flames of the pyre were dying away, he broke

[1] R. V. Russell, *op. cit.* i. p. 395.
[2] R. V. Russell, *op. cit.* iv. p. 221 ; W. Crooke, *The Popular Religion and Folk-Lore of Northern India* (Westminster, 1896), i. p. 269, re-ferring to Ibbetson, *Punjab Ethno-graphy*, p. 117.

some twigs from the alder and willow bushes that were growing near-by, and strewed them around the pyre. These twigs represented a dense forest that was supposed to surround the burning-place. We left the place while the pyre was still burning. Before leaving the grandfather went round the pyre, first from right to left and then from left to right, in order to so obscure his tracks that the deceased would not be able to follow him. Then stepping away from the pyre toward the houses, he drew a line with his stick on the snow, jumped across it and shook himself. The others followed his example. The line was supposed to represent a river which separated the village from the burning-place." [1] The line on the snow was clearly regarded as representing a water barrier which divided the living from the dead.

In the Bari tribe of the Nilotic Sudan " the body of the rain-maker is submitted to special treatment as soon after death as possible, all the orifices of the body being plugged, lest his spirit should escape by one of these and bring sickness or, becoming a lion or leopard, constitute a danger to the people. The corpse is then ruddled with the usual ochre mixture. As a comment on this, Mr. Whitehead sends the following very interesting account, which further indicates the importance of the process as enabling the new rain-maker to control the spirits of his rain-making ancestors : ' When the rain-maker is

[1] *The Jesup North Pacific Expedition* (*Memoir of the American Museum of Natural History*, New York), vi. *The Koryak, Religion and Myths*, by W. Jochelson (Leyden and New York, 1905), p. 112.

dead, he is plugged, his ears are plugged, his nose is plugged, his eye is plugged, his mouth is plugged, he is plugged, his fingers are plugged. And then he is buried. It is done so that . . . the spirits may not go out, so that the son may manage the father so that he obeys (him), so that the spirits obey the son.' "[1] In the Bachama and Mbula tribes of Northern Nigeria, a new king undergoes a period of seclusion for fifteen days ; he then takes possession of the palace by stepping over a cow killed at the threshold. Two explanations of this rite are given : (1) that in crossing over the body of the cow he left behind him all conduct of a kind which would be inconsistent with his new position ; and (2) that the sacrifice of the cow at the threshold secured the palace against invasion by the late chief's ghost.[2] Of these alternative explanations we cannot doubt that the second is the true one ; the first is too vague and sentimental to be primitive. Among the Wajagga of Mount Kilimanjaro, in East Africa, when the body of a man is carried out to burial, the son of the deceased places a bean in the left ear of the corpse in order that the ghost may take no further part in earthly life and may not come back to plague the house. By way of further precaution, a leaden ornament such as women wear in their ears is attached to the ear of the corpse, as a symbol of the peace which is henceforth to reign between the

[1] C. G. Seligman and Brenda Z. Seligman, *Pagan Tribes of the Nilotic Sudan* (London, 1932), p. 292.

[2] C. K. Meek, *Tribal Studies in Northern Nigeria* (London, 1931), i. p. 4.

living and the dead.[1] In the Tumbuka tribe of Nyasaland a corpse was carried out of the hut not by the door but by a special opening made in the wall. All the dishes, pots, clothes and articles of personal use belonging to the deceased were buried with him. But no metal goods were buried, whether hoes, or arrows, or brass ornaments, because it was feared that these would give the ghost opportunity to return with anger to hurt the friends. The nearest relatives then threw pounded cinders into the grave, that they might not chatter in their sleep or death come to them.[2] The Bana of the Cameroons of West Africa believe that the ghost even of a good man is malignant; hence they take many precautions to prevent it from issuing from the grave, and returning to cause sickness or death in the family. The body is tied up, the eyes are bandaged and it is carried out of the hut feet foremost, because otherwise the ghost might know its way back to the house. In the grave heavy logs are placed on the body to keep it down, and the men brandish their clubs threateningly at the ghost, disclaiming any responsibility for the death.[3] In the Niger Delta, when a woman has died in giving birth to a child, it used to be customary to kill the infant and bury it with the dead mother; but if they decided to keep the child alive they performed a ceremony to prevent

[1] B. Gutmann (Madschame), "Trauer und Begräbnissitten der Wadschagga", *Globus*, lxxxix. (1906) p. 197; *id.*, *Dichten und Denken der Dschagganeger* (Leipsig, 1909), p. 133.

[2] D. Fraser, *Winning a Primitive People* (London, 1914), p. 158.

[3] G. van Hagen, "Die Bana", *Baessler-Archiv*, ii. (1912) p. 109.

the mother's ghost from returning to fetch away her child. A piece of a plantain stem (that portion which has the fruit clustered round it) was procured and forced into the womb of the dead mother. This according to native ideas prevents her spirit coming back to fetch the child, and the mother thinks she has the child with her. This account has been confirmed by an English lady who was present on two occasions when this ceremony was being performed.[1]

In Southern Nigeria, where the belief in the rebirth of the dead is prevalent, dead children are usually buried lying on their side as in sleep. But if for any reason it is deemed undesirable that its soul should be born again the little body is buried face downward, to prevent the return of its soul. Grown men, on the other hand, are buried face upwards in order that they may see straight before them and find their way back again to earth.[2]   In the Ho tribe of Togoland in West Africa, on the fourth day after the burial of a woman or the fifth day after the burial of a man, a relative goes to the grave and sprinkles water on it for the purpose of quietening the spirit of the dead and preventing it from returning to cause another death.[3]

Among the Eskimo of Alaska, near St. Michael, when a *shaman* died no one did any work for three

[1] Le Comte C. N. de Cardi, "Ju-Ju Laws and Customs in the Niger Delta", *Journal of the Anthropological Institute*, xxix. (1899) p. 58.

[2] P. Amaury Talbot, *Life in Southern Nigeria* (London, 1923), pp. 144-145.
[3] J. Spieth, *Die Ewe Stämme* (Berlin, 1906), p. 704.

days afterwards. The following night, when the people prepared to retire, each man in the village took his urine-tub and poured a little of its contents before the door, saying, " This water is our water ; drink "—believing that should the ghost return during the night and try to enter, it would taste this water, and, finding it bad, would go away.[1] Among the Skuñgen Indians of Vancouver Island, as soon as a death has taken place the body is immediately taken out of the house by an opening in the wall from which the boards have been removed, because it is believed that the ghost would kill every one if the body were to stay in the house. The implements of the deceased are deposited close to the body, else his ghost would come and get them. Sometimes even his house is broken down.[2] The Déné-Dindjie Indians of North-West America surround the tombs of the dead with long poles to which ribands of different colours are fastened. The intention is to amuse the soul of the deceased and thus keep it beside the corpse.[3]

Among the Araucanians of Chili when a corpse is being carried out to a place of burial a woman walks behind it, strewing ashes on the path to prevent the spirit of the dead from returning to its late abode.[4]

[1] E. W. Nelson, "The Eskimo about Bering Strait", *18th Annual Report of the Bureau of American Ethnology* (1896–97) (1899), p. 312.
[2] *Sixth Report on the North-Western Tribes of Canada* (*Report of the British Association for 1890*, separate reprint), Second General Report on the Indians of British Columbia, by Dr. Fr. Boas.
[3] E. Petitot, *Monographie des Déné-Dindjies* (Paris, 1876), p. 47.
[4] J. Ignatius Molina, *The Geographical, Natural and Civil History of Chili*, translated from the original Italian (London, 1809), ii. p. 91.

With regard to the Pehhuenches, an Indian tribe of Chili, speaking an Araucanian dialect, we are told that they greatly fear the spirits of the dead, and the nearer the relation of the survivor to the deceased the greater is his fear of the ghost. To prevent a ghost from returning they carry the corpse out of the tent feet foremost, for if they carried it out in any other posture they believe that the ghost will return. Further, when they are shifting camp, abandoning a site where they have tarried for some time and where several of their number have died and been buried, they take elaborate precautions to obscure their tracks by crossing them in various directions for the purpose of baffling the pursuit of the ghosts who might be following their comrades to their new home.[1] Among the Lengua Indians of the Para-guaian Chaco a witch-doctor had been persuaded by the missionary to build a superior hut with a small opening for a door. But after an old man had died and been buried the witch-doctor's wife and family made very considerable alterations in the hut; in particular they blocked up the little door of the new hut, making it appear like a part of the wall, and opened a small gap on the opposite side instead. The reason for this alteration was explained to the missionary by the wizard himself. He said that this was done on purpose to puzzle the ghost. He, while in the body, knew the house well, but the alterations were so considerable that it was supposed his ghost

---

[1] E. Poeppig, *Reise in Chile, Peru und auf dem Amazonen-* *strome während der Jahre 1827–1832* (Leipsig, 1835–1836), i. p. 393.

would not recognize it and would be particularly nonplussed when it made for the entrance to find it a solid wall.[1] The Indians of Brazil, in the neighbourhood of Rio de Janeiro, used greatly to fear lest the spirit of the dead should return and do them harm. To prevent the return of a dead man's ghost they rolled up his body and tied it tightly ; but lest he, or rather his ghost, should undo the fastenings and come back to haunt them they adopted the further precaution of confining the corpse in a great earthenware jar, battened down with an earthenware lid.[2]

In civilized Europe itself, if, in spite of all precautions, the ghost should make his way back from the grave, steps were taken to barricade the house against him. Thus, in some parts of Russia and East Prussia an axe or a lock is laid on the threshold, or a knife is hung over the door,[3] and in Germany as soon as the coffin is carried out of the house all the doors and windows are shut, whereas so long as the body is still in the house, or at least immediately after the death, the windows (and sometimes the doors) are left open for the soul to escape.[4] In the

---

[1] W. B. Grubb, *An Unknown People in an Unknown Land* (London, 1911), pp. 165, 166.

[2] A. Thevet, *La Cosmographie Universelle* (Paris, 1575), ii. p. 959.

[3] W. Ralston, *Songs of the Russian People* (London, 1872), p. 318 ; A. Wuttke, *Der deutsche Volksaberglaube* (Berlin, 1869), §§ 736, 766 ; M. Töppen, *Aberglauben aus Masuren* (Danzig, 1867), p. 108.

[4] C. L. Rochholz, *Deutsche Glaube und Brauch* (Berlin, 1867), i. p. 171 ; A. Schleicher, *Volkstümliches aus*

Sonnenberg (Weimar, 1858), p. 152 ; W. Sonntag, *Tödtenbestattung*, p. 169 (Halle, 1878) ; A. Wuttke, *op. cit.* §§ 725, 737 ; A. Gubernatis, *Storia comparata degli usi funebri in Italia e pressi gli altri popoli Indo-Europei*, p. 47 ; G. Lammert, *Volksmedizin und medizinischer Aberglaube aus Bayern* (Würzburg, 1869), pp. 103, 105, 106 ; F. Schmidt, *Sitten und Gebräuche*, pp. 85, 92 ; L. Strackerjan, *Aberglaube und Sagen aus dem Herzogthum Oldenburg* (Oldenburg, 1867), ii. p. 129 ;

Hebridean Islands of Mull and Tiree the barricade against the ghost assumes an easy and gentle form; a sprig of pearlwort fastened over the lintel of a door from which a corpse has been carried is thought sufficient to deter the poor ghost from passing the threshold and re-entering his old home.[1]

W. Tettau und J. D. H. Temme, *Die Volkssagen Ostpreussens, Litauens und Westpreussens* (Berlin, 1837), p. 285; A. Kuhn, *Märkische Sagen und Mährchen* (Berlin, 1843), p. 367; F. Nork, *Die Sitten und Gebräuche der Deutschen und ihrer Nachbarvölker* (1845), pp. 479, 482; J. A. E. Köhler, *Volksbrauch, Aberglauben, Sagen und andere alte Über-* *lieferungen in Voigtlande* (Leipsig, 1867), pp. 251, 254; F. Panzer, *Beiträge zur deutschen Mythologie* (Munich, 1848–1855), i. 263; A. Kuhn und W. Schwartz, *Norddeutsche Sagen, Märchen und Gebräuche* (Leipsig, 1848), p. 435.

[1] J. G. Campbell, *Superstitions of the Highlands and Islands of Scotland* (Glasgow, 1900), p. 241.

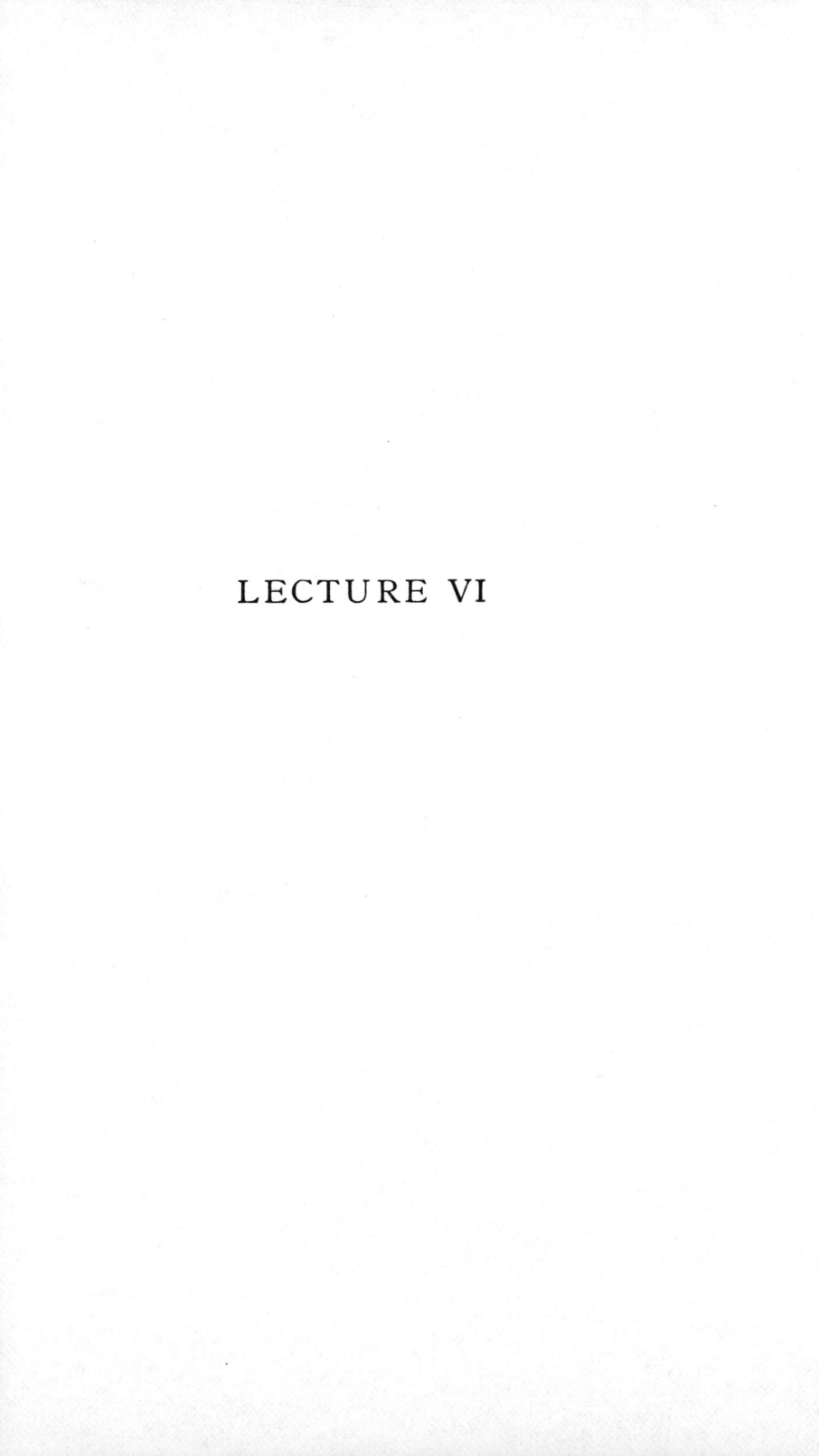

LECTURE VI

LECTURE VI

In the last lecture I gave some miscellaneous examples of the devices which primitive man adopts to prevent the spirits of the dead from returning to molest the living. To-day we turn to a device of another kind, which has had different and very important consequences. With many primitive peoples it has been customary to destroy all a dead man's property in order to prevent his ghost from returning to claim and enjoy it. Wherever this custom has been rigorously observed it has proved a fatal bar to economic progress, by preventing that accumulation and transmission of property which is essential to the advance of industry, and indeed to the very life of civilized society. Hence the tribes which have practised the custom have remained in a state of poverty and savagery from which they can never emerge so long as they adhere to this wasteful and ruinous practice.

Thus, for example, speaking of the natives of Melville and Bathurst Islands to the north of Australia, Baldwin Spencer observes : " The paper bark in which the body had been wrapped and all the dead woman's belongings were burnt in the fire, and afterwards the ashes were completely and carefully covered over. In the case of a man his weapons are broken up and then burnt in the same way. In most tribes all the belongings of a dead person are the property of some special individual,, such as a mother's brother, but here they are all destroyed." [1] From this statement we may infer that most Australian tribes preserve the belongings of the dead and pass them on to their next of kin ; they are therefore in a more hopeful condition for economic progress than the natives of Melville and Bathurst Islands, who systematically destroy all the property of the dead.

Among the Wonkonguru of the Lake Eyre district of Central Australia, as soon as a man dies his body is brought out of the hut by the men. It is then tightly bound up with hair or fibre rope until it is a stiff package, when it is deposited in a grave about three feet deep. All the personal belongings of the dead person are broken at the grave of a man so that his spirit will not come back and use them. Women's belongings are not broken. The covering of his hut and the sticks to make it are also put on the grave, and then wood is piled on top. The wood is provided so that when the dead person " jumps up "—that is, rises from the grave—he will have a supply of firewood handy, and the sticks and hut covering are put there so that, in case it is cold when the dead man comes back, he can build a shelter. [2]

[1] Baldwin Spencer, *Native Tribes of the Northern Territory of Australia* (London, 1914), p. 243.

[2] G. Horne and G. Aiston, *Savage Life in Central Australia* (London, 1924), pp. 162-163.

Thus the attitude of these people towards the spirit of a dead man exhibits a mixture of fear and tender regard. They break his personal belongings because they fear that the ghost will come back and use them, but they provide the ghost with the means of obtaining warmth and shelter on cold nights at the grave.

Among the natives of San Cristoval, one of the Solomon Islands, after a man's death his property is destroyed ; his trees are cut down, his nuts and yams strewn about the ground, his bowl broken. The broken property is placed on the grave. A favourite dog or pig is also buried in a grave and their belongings are also broken ; in the case of a pig the bowl from which it fed will be broken, and in the case of a dog its owner's pig-hunting spear will be stuck up on the grave and never used again.[1] In some of the Solomon Islands a chief's fruit trees are cut down after his death.[2] Among the Sulka of New Britain, when a man died his plantations were laid waste, his fruit trees were cut down, the fruits themselves hacked in pieces, his pigs were killed and cut up and his weapons were broken. In the case of a wealthy or distinguished man his wives would also be killed after his death.[3] The motive for all this destruction is not assigned by our authority, but we may conjecture that it was a fear lest the ghost of the dead man should return and attempt to enjoy his property and his wives.

[1] C. E. Fox, *The Threshold of the Pacific* (London, 1924), p. 211.

[2] W. G. Ivens, *Melanesians of the South-east Solomon Islands* (London, 1927), p. 215.

[3] R. Parkinson, *Dreissig Jahre in der Südsee* (Studgart, 1907), p. 185.

The natives of Niue, or Savage Island, in the Pacific disposed of the dead by setting their bodies adrift in canoes, or by laying the body on a pile of stones in the bush and covering it over with coconut leaves. After a time the bones were gathered and deposited in family caves or vaults. All the plantations, coconut trees, and other fruit trees of a person who died, were destroyed and thrown into the sea that they might go with him to the world of spirits.[1] Among the Kiwai Papuans of British New Guinea, after a burial some of the most valuable ornaments of the deceased are usually, but not always, kept by the heir, while the rest are destroyed or given away to people outside his or her group, sometimes to other villages. The near relatives do not want to keep the things of everyday use which have belonged to the dead person, lest they should themselves die, no doubt at the hands of the ghost, coming back to reclaim his property from the new owner. Even the harpoon-shaft of a man is often broken to pieces, out of which the people manufacture harpoon-heads or daggers. The people say that a harpoon-shaft is sometimes broken in two, and the butt end kept, to which a new shaft of bamboo is attached, so that the weapon can be used again.[2] Apparently they think that the ghost will not recognize his harpoon when once it has been broken or cut in pieces. At the same time they show a dawning sense of the permanent value of property by occasionally allow-

[1] G. Turner, *Samoa* (London, 1884), p. 306.

[2] G. Landtman, *The Kiwai Papuans of British New Guinea* (London, 1927), p. 263.

ing some of the most valuable ornaments of the deceased to be kept by his heir.

In the Nicobar Islands after a death, if the stores of food belonging to the deceased or other occupants of his hut were not removed prior to the death they are at once carried away to another hut for issue after the burial. Some of the coconut-shell water-vessels are taken with their contents to the entrance of the hut, where an uneven number (generally 3, 5 or 7 pairs) are violently dashed against a post so as to crack the shells. In like manner all of the bulk of the portable property of the deceased, such as (in the case of a man) his spears, pots, baskets, paddles, plates and a great variety of other articles, are broken or otherwise rendered unserviceable ; and then the whole are conveyed to the cemetery in order to be deposited at the proper time on the grave or at the head-post, this being one of the essential sacrifices prescribed by time-honoured custom. The motive for depositing the broken property on the grave or at the head-posts is variously explained by the natives. Some say that it is done in order that all may see how sincere the mourners are in their intention of denying themselves the use or benefit of any of the property, notwithstanding its undoubted value in their eyes. " Another reason given for this wholesale destruction of property is that strangers who have no respect for the sacredness of tabued or sacrificed articles might appropriate uninjured and serviceable objects regardless of the displeasure of the disembodied spirit, who would unquestionably resent any such token of indifference and disrespect by wreaking vengeance probably on those through whose remissness such misconduct had been rendered possible." [1] However, we may surmise that here as elsewhere the true original motive for destroying a dead man's property was to prevent his ghost from returning to make use of it.

The Banar in Tonquin are said to burn all objects used by the deceased in order that he may not return and trouble the living by asking for his property.[2]

The Koryaks of North-Eastern Asia cremate their dead and burn with the body the weapons and household furniture of the deceased, such as spears, quivers and arrows, knives, hatchets and kettles ; and they kill the deer which drew the corpse to the cremation ground and throw the fragments into the fire.[3]

The Savara of Southern India burn their dead, and with the body they burn everything that the dead man had : his bows and arrows, his dagger, his necklaces, his reaping-hook for cutting paddy, his axe, some paddy and rice, and so forth. Mr. Fawcett was told that all a man's money was burnt with him, but he thought that the statement was doubtful, though perhaps a little of the money might be so destroyed. When he asked the reason why a man's property is thus destroyed with his body he

[1] E. H. Man, *The Nicobar Islands and their People* (London, n.d.), pp. 131, 132, 138.

[2] E. Reclus, *Nouvelle Géographie Universelle*, viii. p. 869.

[3] S. Krasheninnikov, *The History of Kamtschatka and the Kurilski Islands*, translated into English by James Grieve, M.D. (Gloucester, 1764), p. 233.

was told that, if they did not destroy it, the man's spirit would come back and demand it of them, and trouble them.[1]

In Africa among the Yoruba-speaking peoples of the Slave Coast, on the day after a burial, all the articles which the deceased had in daily use, such as his pipe, his mat, his calabashes, and other things of small value, are carried out into the bush and burnt. Up to this point the soul of the deceased is supposed to be lingering near his old home, and the destruction of his property is to signify that there is no longer anything belonging to him. In former times the destruction of property was carried much further. Usually the room in which the deceased is buried is closed and never used again ; sometimes the roof is removed. Rich families even abandon the house altogether. The deceased is then called thrice by name and adjured to depart and no longer to haunt the dwellings of the living. After this a fowl is sacrificed, which, besides securing a right-of-way for the soul, is supposed also to guide it. The feathers of the fowl are scattered round the house, and the bird itself carried out to a cross-roads, where it is cooked and eaten.[2] In a former lecture I gave other examples of a bird or an animal employed to conduct the souls of the dead to the spirit-land.[3]

[1] E. Thurston, *Castes and Tribes of Southern India*, vi. (Madras, 1909) p. 325 ; Fred. Fawcett, "Notes on the Soaras (or Savaras), an Aboriginal Hill People of the Eastern Ghats of the Madras Presidency", *Journal of the Anthropological Society of Bombay*, i. (1886) p. 249.

[2] A. B. Ellis, *The Yoruba-Speaking Peoples of the Slave Coast of West Africa* (London, 1894), p. 159.

[3] J. G. Frazer, *The Fear of the Dead in Primitive Religion* (London, 1933), pp. 189 *sqq.*

In the African kingdom of Gingiro the old
custom of destroying the property of the dead has
been reported as follows by Jesuit travellers of the
seventeenth or eighteenth century. After describing
the death of a king and the installation of his
successor, they proceed : " The new king calls all the
dead one's favourites and orders them to be killed to
bear the dead king company in the other world.
Then they burn the house the old king lived in, with
all his moveables, goods and furniture, not sparing
anything, though never so valuable ; and even
when any private man dies, they burn not only his
house, but the very trees and plants that are about
it, and being asked why they do so, they answer, to
the end, that the dead man, who was us'd to those
places, do not return to them, invited by his former
habitation, and delight in walking among those
trees." [1] Among the Bogos of Central Africa, as
reported by the French traveller, R. Caillié, when
the head of a family dies it is common to burn everything that is in the house. At the foot of his bed
the corpse is buried ; a fire is kindled over his head
every night, and the relations come and talk to him.
The family of the deceased who are ruined by this
act of superstition are supported till the next harvest
by the village, for even their rice is not saved from
the flames.[2]

With regard to the Kaffirs of South-East Africa,
an old Portuguese writer says that after the death

[1] F. B. Tellez, S.J., *The Travels of
the Jesuits in Ethiopia* (London,
1710), p. 199.

[2] R. Caillié, *Travels through
Central Africa to Timbuctoo* (London, 1830), p. 164.

and burial of a man " they burn the thatched house in which he resided with all it contains, so that no one may possess anything that the deceased made use of during his lifetime, or may even touch it, and if it so happens that some one touches anything belonging to the deceased he does not enter his house until he has washed in the river. The ashes of the burnt house with any pieces of wood not quite consumed they put on the top of the grave."[1] Summing up the evidence of earlier writers on this subject, the historian of South Africa, Dr. McCall Theal, says that : " There was an idea that something connected with death attached to the personal effects of the deceased, on which account whatever had belonged to him that could not be placed in the grave, his clothing, mats, head-rest, etc., was destroyed by fire. The hut in which he had lived was also burned, and no other was allowed to be built on the spot. If he had been the chief, the whole kraal was removed to another site. Those who touched the corpse or any of the dead man's effects were obliged to go through certain ceremonies, and then to bathe in running water before associating again with their companions."[2] Speaking of the Kaffirs of Natal, that is the Zulus, a good authority says that "the deceased's personal articles are buried with him, the assegais being broken or bent, lest the ghost, during some

---

[1] Fr. J. dos Santos, *Eastern Ethiopia*, in G. McCall Theal, *Records of South-Eastern Africa*, vol. vii. (London, 1901) Book II. p. 307.

[2] G. McCall Theal, *Ethnography and Condition of South Africa before* A.D. *1505* (London, 1919), i. 221-222.

midnight return to air, should do injury with them ".[1]

Among the aborigines of America also the custom of destroying a dead man's property, or at all events of refusing to make use of it, from a fear of his ghost has been widely diffused, especially in South America. Thus, among the Ahts of Vancouver Island after a death, the whole of a dead man's personal effects that had not been given away before his death were deposited with him—except his best canoes, his house-planks, and fishing and hunting instruments, which, with any slaves he may have had, were inherited by his eldest son. But if his friends were very superstitious they burnt the dead man's house with all its contents, or they removed the materials, and built the house in another place.[2] Thus, with regard to the Ahts it would appear that while the people as a whole had advanced to the stage of inheriting a dead man's most valuable property, the more superstitious members of the community adhered to the ancient custom of destroying it utterly by fire. Among the Knisteneaux Indians, if a dead man's property was not buried with him his ghost was supposed to return and sit on a tree near the house, armed with a gun, ready to shoot the frugal relatives who had thus deprived him of the use of his goods.[3] The Digger Indians of California burn all the property of the deceased, so

---

[1] J. Shooter, *The Kafirs of Natal and the Zulu* (London, 1857), p. 240.
[2] G. M. Sproat, *Scenes and Studies of Savage Life* (London, 1868), pp. 159, 160.
[3] A. Mackenzie, *Voyages through the Continent of North America*, p. cvi.

that the spirit of the dead man may have all that he needs in the other world, and not return to look for it among his surviving friends.[1] Similarly, the Kutchan Indians of the Colorado regarded the property of a dead man as fraught with danger, and accordingly they burned it with fire together with the hut in which he had died.[2] With regard to the Maidu of California who systematically burned the property of the dead, Professor Roland B. Dixon observes that "owing to the general custom of burning most, if not all, of the property of a man at his death, there was little that could be inherited. Such things as were not destroyed seem to have generally been regarded as the property of the eldest son, although other children and relatives often shared with him."[3]

Thus, while the Maidu destroyed the great bulk of the dead man's property, they seem to have had a faint beginning of a custom of allowing some of it to pass by inheritance to his surviving kinsfolk, especially to his eldest son. In that tribe the custom of burning the property of the dead was a solemn annual ceremony carried out by the whole body of the people collectively on a special burning ground set apart for the purpose. The property to be destroyed was first attached to tall poles or collected at their foot; after being thus exposed to public view for a time it was thrown on the fire, until the flames were almost choked by the weight of the

[1] M. Macfie, *Vancouver Island and British Columbia*, p. 449.
[2] *Zeitschrift für Ethnologie*, ix. p. 348.
[3] R. B. Dixon, "The Northern Maidu", *Bulletin of the American Museum of Natural History*, xvii. (1902) p. 226.

superincumbent property. At the burning held at Mooretown in 1900 there were about a hundred and fifty poles filled with objects, so the amount of property sacrificed was not small. " The purpose of the whole ceremony is to supply the ghosts of the dead with clothing, property and food in the other world. Each family gives to its dead what it can afford ; and the whole ceremony is distinctly individual, in that there is no general offering for the dead as a body, but each family offers directly to its own relatives only . . . there is considerable property placed with the body in the grave, and sometimes some is burnt at the time of burial. The main reliance is, however, placed on the supplies offered at the annual burning. After sacrificing thus for three or four years it seems to be felt that enough has been done ; and, as a rule, the family does not continue to offer property for a relative at the burnings for more than four or five years." [1]

The practice of the Mosquito Indians as regards the property of the dead appears to be inconsistent. " When a death takes place, they generally bury a bow and arrows, a gourd calabash, and knife, and sundry other articles with the body, and carefully keep in repair a small hut built over the grave, in which they deposit from time to time such little offerings as a yard or two of cloth, a bunch of plantains, a bottle of rum, etc. They have also the custom of destroying everything belonging to a dead

[1] R. B. Dixon, *op. cit.* pp. 241 *sqq.*, 254. (The quotation is from pp. 253, 254.)

person, burning his clothes, splitting his canoes, and, worst of all, cutting down his fruit trees." [1]

Similarly, at a man's death the Indians of Nicaragua destroy all the property that he had earned or otherwise acquired in his lifetime ; they destroy also his trees and all his banana plantations. The writer who records the custom adds that in consequence these Indians never prosper. [2]

The Catio Indians of Colombia in South America carry a corpse out of the hut not by the usual door but by another opening, in order that the ghost may not be able to find his way back to his old dwelling. And they bury the dead man's property with him in the grave, because they fear that otherwise his ghost would come back to reclaim it, but apparently they do not break or destroy the articles which they deposit with the dead. [3]

Speaking of the Indian tribes in the valley of the Orinoco the great German traveller Humboldt says : " Some tribes, for instance the Tamanacs, are accustomed to lay waste the fields of a deceased relative, and cut down the trees which he has planted. They say ' that the sight of objects which belonged to their relation makes them melancholy '. They like better to efface than to preserve remembrances. These effects of Indian sensibility are very detri-

[1] C. N. Bell, " The Mosquito Territory, its Climate, People, Productions, etc.", *Journal of the Royal Geographical Society*, xxxii. (1862) p. 254.

[2] Dr. Bruno Mierisch, " Eine Reise nach den Goldgebieten im Osten von Nicaragua ", *Petermann's Mitteilungen*, xxxix. (1893) p. 31.

[3] Joseph und Maria Schilling, " Religion und soziale Verhältnisse der Catios-Indianer in Kolumbien ", *Archiv für Religionswissenschaft*, xxiii. (1925) p. 296.

mental to agriculture, and the monks oppose with energy these superstitious practices, to which the natives converted to Christianity still adhere in the missions." [1] While we can accept Humboldt's statement as to the destruction of the property of the dead among these Indians, we may doubt the truth of the motive which he puts in the mouth of the people. They seem to have been converted to Christianity, and were probably unwilling to reveal to a traveller that fear of the spirits of the dead which we can hardly doubt was the true original motive of the practice.

Among the Kobeua Indians of North-West Brazil on the borders of Colombia the dead are buried in the communal house. On the closed grave are burned the bow and arrows, the fish-traps and other implements of a man or the baskets and sieve of a woman, and her pots are smashed and the fragments thrown away in the forest, in order that nothing of the goods of the dead may remain behind, and that the soul be not compelled to return to claim the property and to punish the survivors for their negligence or avarice.[2]

The Macusi Indians of British Guiana burn the property of the dead.[3]

After a death the Conibos Indians of the Ucayale River in North-Eastern Peru break everything in the

---

[1] F. H. A. von Humboldt, *Personal Narrative of Travels to the Equinoctial Regions of America*, English translation (London, 1852), ii. p. 487.

[2] T. Koch-Grünberg, *Zwei Jahre unter den Indianern* (Berlin, 1909–1910), ii. p. 150.

[3] R. Schomburgk, *Reisen in Britisch - Guiana* (Leipsic, 1847–1848), p. 422.

house and then set it on fire ; afterwards they cover the whole site of the burnt hut with a thick layer of ashes to receive the tracks of the ghost if he should come to revisit his old dwelling.[1] The Yaguas on the upper waters of the Amazon destroy everything that a dead man possessed or even touched ; they kill his domestic animals and they lay waste his gardens.[2]

In the Bororo tribe of Central Brazil it is the rule that all the things which a dead man had made use of should be either burnt or thrown into a river or deposited in the basket which contains his bones, in order to give his ghost no inducements to return and fetch or enjoy his property. Professor von den Steinen witnessed the destruction of the property which had belonged to a dead woman ; indeed the property of all the members of her family who had lived in the same hut with her was destroyed. A man decked with green leaves represented the dead woman, who lay buried under a covering of green leaves. This leaf-decked representative of the dead took part in a dance. A man with two rattles led the dance, behind him followed the leaf-decked man, and next came four others. After dancing and singing in chorus they ran away into the wood. The representative of the dead woman then blew a flute to summon two persons who had long been dead and buried. It was deemed necessary that their ghosts should be present at the ceremony of

[1] F. de Castelnau, *Expédition dans les parties centrales de l'Amérique du Sud*, iv. (1851) p. 384.

[2] F. de Castelnau, *op. cit.* v. (Paris, 1851) p. 19.

making over the property to the dead woman, in order that they should welcome their new comrade in the spirit-land and convince her that nothing that belonged to her had been withheld, so that she should have no excuse for coming back as a ghost to reclaim the missing articles. These two dead persons were represented by two men covered with mud, who came out of the wood carried on the bodies of two others. They jumped about, while bull-roarers were swung. A fire was kindled and the property of the deceased and her family was collected and burned, while the men danced round the fire. The leaf-decked man was held down by the two mud-covered men. Afterwards he was released and danced about with another man in a feather head-dress, throwing the things about and stepping into the flames.[1]

Yuracares are a tribe of Indians inhabiting the Cordilleras of Santa Cruz de la Sierra to the north east of Cochobamba. They bury with the dead his clothes, his bow and arrows, and presents for dead relatives in the other world, and they inter with him all the movable property which he had used and not given away in his lifetime. They break his wife's kitchen utensils on the grave. The writer who reports the custom adds that " they burn everything that he has not given away, for fear of his soul returning to the house to look for it and to terrify the survivors or touch them with the stick which a

---

[1] K. von den Steinen, *Unter den Naturvölkern Zentral-Brasiliens* (Berlin, 1894), pp. 502, 506 *sqq.*

ghost is supposed to carry and the touch of which brings death ".[1]

The Araucanians of the Pampas and the Puelches and the Patagonians burn all a dead man's possessions on his grave and slaughter his domestic animals, his horses and dogs, that they may accompany him to the other world.[2] Among the Lengua Indians of the Paraguaian Chaco " the personal belongings and animals of the deceased are destroyed at his death, evidently with the idea that they may prove useful to him in the after-life. The reason given by the Indian for doing this is that the ghost would otherwise haunt the relatives."[3] For the same reason they not only abandon but destroy by fire the village in which a death has taken place, believing that the site is haunted by the hovering spirit of the deceased for about a month, after which they suppose that the spirit will depart and no longer trouble them.[4] In like manner at the southern extremity of the continent the Onas of Tierra del Fuego destroy all a dead man's property at his death except his dogs, and they shun the place of his death and burial, making a long detour to avoid it, whenever their nomadic life has brought them once more into the neighbourhood.[5]

The disastrous economic and moral effects of this systematic destruction of the property of the dead

[1] A. d'Orbigny, *Voyage dans l'Amérique Méridionale* (Paris, 1835), iii. Iʳᵉ Partie, 209.

[2] A. d'Orbigny, *L'Homme américain* (Paris, 1839), i. pp. 196, 238.

[3] W. B. Grubb, *An Unknown People in an Unknown Land* (London, 1911), p. 122.

[4] W. B. Grubb, *op. cit.* pp. 122, 160 *sqq.*

[5] C. R. Gallardo, *Los Onas* (Buenos Aires, 1910), pp. 321 *sqq.*

which has prevailed so widely among the Indians of South America have been well pointed out by the French traveller, Alcide d'Orbigny, who witnessed and has described the practice of the custom in several tribes of that continent.

Speaking of the Patagonians who practise the custom, this discerning traveller observes : " They have no laws, no punishments inflicted on the guilty. Each lives as he pleases, and the greatest thief is the most highly esteemed, because he is the most dexterous. A motive which will always prevent them from abandoning the practice of theft, and at the same time will always present an obstacle to their ever forming fixed settlements, is the religious prejudice which, on the death of one of their number, obliges them to destroy his property. A Patagonian who has amassed during the whole of his life an estate by thieving from the whites or exchanging the products of the chase with neighbouring tribes, has done nothing for his heirs ; all his savings are destroyed with him, and his children are obliged to rebuild their fortunes afresh—a custom which, I may observe in passing, is found also among the Tamanaques of the Orinoco who ravage the field of the deceased and cut down the trees which he has planted ;[1] and among the Yuracares, who abandon and shut up the house of the dead, regarding it as a profanation to gather a single fruit from the trees of his field. It is easy to see that with such customs they can nourish no real ambition since their needs

[1] F. H. A. von Humboldt, *Voyage aux régions équinoxiales*, viii. 273.

are limited to themselves ; it is one of the causes of their natural indolence, and it is a motive which, so long as it exists, will always impede the progress of their civilization. Why should they trouble themselves about the future when they have nothing to hope from it ? The present is all in all in their eyes, and their only interest is individual ; the son will take no care of his father's herd, since it will never come into his possession ; he busies himself only with his own affairs and soon turns his thoughts to looking after himself and getting a livelihood. This custom has certainly something to commend it from the moral point of view in so far as it destroys all the motives for that covetousness in heirs which is too often to be seen in our cities. The desire or the hope of a speedy death of their parents cannot exist, since the parents leave absolutely nothing to their children ; but on the other hand if the Patagonians had preserved hereditary properties, they would without doubt have been to-day in possession of numerous herds, and would necessarily have been more formidable to the whites, since their power in that case would have been more than doubled, whereas their present habits will infallibly leave them in a stationary state, from which nothing but a radical change will be able to deliver them." [1]

Here, for the present, I must bring these lectures to a close, but I am far from having exhausted the subject ; there remain large and important aspects

[1] Alcide d'Orbigny, *Voyage dans l'Amérique Méridionale*, ii. (Paris and Strasburg, 1839–1843) pp. 99 sq. ; compare *id., L'Homme américain* (Paris, 1839), ii. p. 74.

of it on which I have hitherto said little or nothing. In future I shall hope to supply some at least of these omissions. Meantime, perhaps, even in these short lectures I have said enough to give you an idea, however imperfect, of the extent and depth of that fear of the spirits of the dead which, for good or evil, has played a great part in the development of religion.

INDEX

Abbott, Mr. G. F., on the Greek and Slavonic conceptions of the vampire, 86

Aborigines, American, destroy property of the dead, 128 ; Australian, tie up corpse to prevent return of ghost, 64 ; mutilate dead to prevent ghosts from walking, 68 ; their precautions to prevent return of ghost, 71, 72

Abyssinia, bones of corpse broken before burial in, 69

Adiri, the land of departed spirits, 13

Afars, the, of Abyssinia, break bones of corpse before burial, 69

Africa, the fear of the dead in, 18, 19 ; driving away the dead in, 19 ; water used as barrier against dead in, 38, 39 ; use of water barrier against ghosts in, 40, 41, 44, 45 ; use of water for purification in, 43, 44 ; use of water after funerals in, 45 ; barrier of fire against dead in, 58, 59 ; corpse tied up to prevent return of ghost in, 67 ; corpse mutilated to prevent return of ghost in, 68, 69 ; dead mutilated to kill ghost in, 69 ; mutilation of dead in, 75 ; poison used to prevent return of ghost in, 75, 76 ; animal killed and eaten to prevent return of ghost in, 76 ; sickness attributed to the dead in, 76 ; magician's body mutilated in, 78 ; killing the ghost in, 90-94 ; destruction of soul by cutting up child's body in, 93, 94 ; precautions taken to prevent return of ghost in, 110, 111 ; water sprinkled on grave to prevent return of spirit in, 112 ; property of the dead destroyed in, 125, 126

African negroes, West, cut up child's body to destroy soul, 93, 94

Agweh, barrier of fire against dead in, 60

Aheriyas, the, obstruct return of dead, 32

Ahts, the, of Vancouver Island, destroy property of the dead, 128, inherit property of the dead, 128

A-hun-ig-ut, " the bottom day ", 20

Ainu, the, of Japan, use water as barrier against ghosts, 37

"Aka-oa ", friends, 89

Alaska, urine used to prevent return of ghost in, 112

Algonkin Indians, the, obstruct return of dead, 35

Alistrati, treatment of vampire at, 87

All Souls' Day, 4

Amazon, the, the Yaguas on, 133

Ambaca, the people of, use water for purification after funeral, 43

Ambau, Tanoa, King of, 90

Ambrosian MS. of the *Iliad*, drawing depicting maiming of victim by murderer in, 82

America, driving away the dead in, 20 ; obstructing return of dead in, 34 ; use of water as a barrier against the dead in, 46, 47 ; corpse tied up to prevent return of ghost in, 67 ; dead mutilated to prevent

turning in, 31 ; barrier of water used against ghosts in, 50 ; water considered the best preservative against death by dropsy in, 50 ; use of barrier of fire against dead in, 56, 57 ; precautions taken to prevent return of spirit in, 104, 107 ; pebble used to sever connexion with spirit in, 107 ; nets used to catch spirits in, 107, 108

Indian tribes of the Orinoco, the, cut down trees of the dead, 131

Indians, the ancient, tie up corpse to prevent return of ghost, 66

——, the, of North America, mutilate dead to prevent return of ghost, 70 ; of Brazil, their fear of the dead, 115 ; tie up corpse to prevent return of ghost, 115 ; of Nicaragua, destroy property of the dead, 131 ; cut down fruit trees of dead, 131 ; of South America, destruction of property of the dead by, 136

Inheriting property of the dead, 128, 129

Iron, to prevent return of ghost, 104

Jadegi, Wejinecte man, 79

Japan, use of water as barrier against ghosts in, 37

Jesuit travellers on destruction of property of the dead, 126

Jesuits, the, on North American Indians, 22

Kachins, the, drive away the dead, 17 ; the, obstruct return of dead, 29, 35

Kaffirs, the, of South Africa, their use of water for purification, 43 ; of South-East Africa, burn property of the dead, 126 ; of Natal, personal articles buried with dead by, 127

Kakhyen, the, of Upper Burma, take precautions to prevent return of ghost, 103

Kamilaroi tribe, the, drive away the dead, 7

Karens, the, of Burma, their pre-

cautions to separate spirits of living from dead, 104

Kawar, the, of India, use pebble to sever connexion with spirit, 107

Kenta, the, shift camp after a death, 102

Kenya, illness attributed to dead in, 77 ; body of sick man burned in, 77

Khambu caste, in Sikkim, use barrier of water and fire against dead, 54

Kiko-kiko, evil spirit of the dead, 87, 88

Kilimanjaro, Mount, the Wajagga of, 110

Killing the ghost, the practice of, 69, 87-94

—— wives after death of husband, 121

King, new, prevents return of late chief's ghost, 110

King George's Sound, the natives near, tie up corpse to prevent return of ghost, 66

Kingsley, Miss Mary, on purification by fire and water, 60 ; on cutting up of child's body to destroy soul, 93, 94

Kissi, the, of Liberia, mutilate dead to prevent return of ghost, 70

Kiwai Papuans, the, of British New Guinea, their attitude towards the dead, 13 ; obstruct return of dead, 33 ; use water after burial, 46 ; carry corpse to grave head foremost, 100 ; destroy property of the dead, 122

Knisteneaux Indians, the, bury property of the dead, 128

Kobeua Indians, the, of North-West Brazil, destroy property of the dead, 132

Korku, the, a Munda people, take precautions to prevent return of spirit, 107

Koryak, the, of Asia, regard spirits as hostile to the living, 108 ; burn their dead, 108 ; of North-East Asia, burn the property of the dead, cremate their dead, 124

Kpelle, the, obstruct return of dead, 33

Mooretown, burning of property of dead at, 130

Moral effects of destruction of property, 135

Mori-oris, the, of the Chatham Islands, kill ghost, 87

Mosquito Indians, the, use water as a barrier against the dead, 47; bury property of the dead, 130; destroy property of the dead, 130; cut down fruit trees of dead, 130, 131

Mossi, the, of the Western Sudan, mutilate chief's body to prevent return of ghost, 77

Mother's brother's wife in ritual, 105

Motlav, ghost-driving at, 8

Mount Elgon district, in Kenya, natives of, burn body of sick man, 77

Mull, Island of, barricade against ghost in, 116

Munda people, the Korku, 107

Murderers mangle dead to prevent ghost taking vengeance, 81

Mutilation, prevention of return of dead by, 62-4, 67-72, 75-85; of dead to kill ghost, 69; of dead to stop plague, 83

Mytilini, modern, barrier of water used against ghosts in, 48

Names changed, to prevent return of dead, 98

Nassau, Rev. Robert, on water as barrier against dead, 39; on mutilation of dead to prevent return of ghost, 69

Natal, personal articles buried with dead in, 127

Negroes, West African, cut up child's body to destroy soul, 93, 94

Nepal, the Mangars of, 28

Nets used to catch spirits, 107, 108

New Britain, the natives of, drive away the dead, 10

New Guinea, the natives of, drive away the dead, 13; their varying attitude to the dead, 13, 15; obstruct return of dead, 33; use water barrier against ghosts, 41;

use of water after a burial in, 45, 46; precautions taken to prevent return of ghost in, 100; property of the dead destroyed in, 122

New South Wales, driving away the dead in, 7

New Zealand, use of water as barrier against ghosts in, 45

Newcastle, Western Australia, the natives near, tie up corpse to prevent return of ghost, 65

Ngarigo, the, obstruct return of dead, 36

Nias, the natives of, obstruct return of dead, 36; Island of, precautions taken to prevent return of ghost in, 99

Nicaragua, property of dead destroyed in, 131; fruit trees cut down in, 131

Nicobar Islands, barrier of fire against dead in, 57, 58; portable property of dead destroyed in, 123

Niger Delta, the, plantain stem used to prevent return of ghost in, 111

Nigeria, killing the ghost in, 90

——, Northern, new king prevents return of late chief's ghost in, 110

——, Southern, belief in rebirth of dead in, 112

Nilotic Sudan, the, natives of, drive away the dead, 18; body of rain-maker submitted to special treatment in, 109

Niue Island, natives of, destroy property of the dead, 122

Nyanja-speaking peoples, the, their use of water as barrier against ghosts, 45

Nyasaland Protectorate, use of water as barrier against ghosts in, 45; barrier of fire against dead in, 58; precautions taken to prevent return of ghost in, 111

Offering for the dead, 130

Ogowe, the, West Africa, 69

Ojebway Indians, the, drive away the dead, 22

Omahas, the, mutilate body of man killed by lightning, 78

touching of, prevents dreaming, 106

Rome, driving away the dead in, 23

——, ancient, use of barrier of water after a death in, 49 ; barrier of fire used against the dead in, 62

Rook, natives of, use water after burial, 46

Roro-speaking tribes of British New Guinea, the, drive away the dead, 14

Roumanians, the, of Transylvania, their belief concerning vampires, 85

Russia, corpse fastened down to prevent return of ghost in, 67 ; corpse mutilated to prevent return of ghost in, 67 ; precautions taken to prevent return of ghost in, 115

Ruthenia, barrier of fire used against ghosts in, 62

Sahmahei, fermented rice, 105

Sal, tree, 56

San Cristoval, natives of, their attitude to the dead, 9 ; destroy property of the dead, 121

Sântals, the, of Bengal, dangerous ghosts of women among, 72 ; their precautions to prevent return of ghost, 72

Santos, Fr. J. dos, on destruction of property of the dead, 126, 127

Satapatha-Brâhmana, an ancient Indian book, 32 ; water described as barrier against dead in, 38

Savage Island, natives of, destroy property of the dead, 122

Savara, the, of Southern India, drive away the spirit of the dead, 17 ; burn their dead, 124 ; burn property of the dead, 124

Savoy, obstructing return of dead in, 36

Saxo Grammaticus, Danish historian, 82

Scotland, North-East, barrier of water used against ghosts in, 49

Scythians, the ancient, use barrier of water after a death, 49

Semang, the, shift camp after a death, 102

Serbia, precautions against becoming a vampire in, 84

Shaman, 21 ; urine used to prevent return of ghost of, 112, 113

Shan States, use of water after funeral in, 46

Shans, the, of Burma, their precautions to prevent return of ghost, 102

Shuswap, the, drive away the dead, 21 ; obstruct return of dead, 34

Siam, precautions taken to prevent return of ghost in, 102

Sick person, body mutilated, 80

Sickness attributed to the dead, 76, 91, 92

Sikkim, use of barrier of water and fire against dead in, 54

Singhalese, the, use water as barrier against ghosts, 45

Sivaji, Marâtha leader, his fear of ghost, 33

Skulls preserved, 9

Skuñgen Indians, the, of Vancouver Island, remove body by special opening, 113

Slave Coast, the, barrier of fire against dead on, 60 ; Yoruba-speaking peoples of, 125

Slavonians, South, the, use barrier of fire against the dead, 62

Slavs, the, their belief in vampires, 86

Slendang, cloth in which a child is carried, 98

Snow, lime on, regarded as water barrier, 109

Society Islands, the, precautions taken to prevent return of ghost in, 101

Solomon Islands, the, property of the dead destroyed in, 121 ; dead chief's fruit trees cut down in, 121

—— Islanders, the, their beliefs concerning the dead, 9

Songish Indians, the, use water as a barrier against the dead, 46

Sophocles, Scholiast on, records case of murderer maiming victim, 81

THE FEAR OF THE DEAD
IN PRIMITIVE RELIGION
VOL. III

MACMILLAN AND CO., Limited
LONDON · BOMBAY · CALCUTTA · MADRAS
MELBOURNE

THE MACMILLAN COMPANY
NEW YORK · BOSTON · CHICAGO
DALLAS · ATLANTA · SAN FRANCISCO

THE MACMILLAN COMPANY
OF CANADA, LIMITED
TORONTO

THE
FEAR OF THE DEAD
IN PRIMITIVE RELIGION

BY

SIR JAMES GEORGE FRAZER
O.M., F.R.S., F.B.A.

FELLOW OF TRINITY COLLEGE, CAMBRIDGE
ASSOCIATE MEMBER OF THE *INSTITUT DE FRANCE*

VOL. III

MACMILLAN AND CO., LIMITED
ST. MARTIN'S STREET, LONDON
1936

PRINTED IN GREAT BRITAIN
BY R. & R. CLARK, LIMITED, EDINBURGH

PREFACE

THIS volume concludes my study of the Fear of the Dead in Primitive Religion. It forms a sequel to the two volumes of my lectures delivered under the William Wyse Foundation at Trinity College, Cambridge. The subject is the same, and the treatment is continuous. Throughout we are dealing with some of the answers which primitive man has given to the great enigma of death—of death in the widest sense, as the inevitable end, not only of man, but of every living thing. We may smile at some of his answers as childish and absurd, but do we of this generation read the riddle better than he ? May it not be that posterity will smile at some of the solutions of the problem to which our contemporaries, with all the resources of modern science at their disposal, cling as tenaciously as does primitive man to his phantasmagoria of the dead ? The only lesson we can safely draw from the survey of facts here submitted to the reader is a lesson of humility and hope : a lesson of humility, because it reminds us how little we know on the subject, which, of all others, concerns us most nearly ; a lesson of hope, because it suggests the possibility that others may hereafter solve the problem which has baffled us.

J. G. FRAZER

13*th February* 1936

CONTENTS

The fear of the spirits of the dead has led primitive man to take many precautions to keep them at bay. One method commonly and widely adopted is to destroy or desert the house in which the deceased lived and died, and which his spirit will consequently be expected to seek out. Examples from Australia, from the East Indies, from the Straits, Burma, India and Assam, from Lappland, from Africa, and from North, Central and South America.

Stinks are occasionally employed to repel ghosts, as among various Indian tribes of North and South America.

Corpses may be buried in the bed of a stream to prevent the spirits from returning : examples from different parts of Africa. Alaric the Goth was thus buried, and the ashes of the prophet Daniel are reported to have been similarly treated.

The ghost of a dead man may be pegged down into the earth. Examples from India, Cochin-China, and Africa.

By burying the body in certain positions also some people imagine they prevent the return of the spirit. Examples from South America, India, and Siam. For the same purpose a corpse is very often carried out of the house feet foremost, as among some natives of the East Indies, of South America, and of Northern India, as well as among the inhabitants of Germany, Denmark, and Italy.

Sometimes a corpse is blindfolded to blind the spirit. Examples from Australia, Corea and Cambodia. Often a coin is placed on each of the dead person's eyes to blind him, a custom recorded for various parts of the Indian Archipelago and Europe. The masks found covering faces in the ancient royal graves of Mycenae may have had a similar purpose. Such masks for corpses have been employed in different parts of Asia and Europe.

Occasionally all the openings of the head are blocked up, a custom
specially prevalent in the East Indies, but also reported for Africa
and a Turkish tribe in Russia.

Besides attempting to repulse the spirits of the dead by force, primitive
man often tries to mislead them by guile.   Thus, after a death, strict
silence is often enjoined upon the survivors in order to avoid the
attention of the spirit of the deceased.   This custom is prevalent
throughout the Indian Archipelago, and is also practised in Australia,
in North America, and in various parts of Africa.   Similarly it is
often forbidden to mention the name of a dead person for fear of
attracting his ghost.   Examples from Tasmania, Australia, the East
Indies, Siberia, Africa and America.

Mourning costumes have been adopted in the Nicobar Islands
explicitly to disguise the wearers from the recognition of ghosts, and
this may have been the original purpose of mourning costumes
generally.   Examples from Africa, from ancient Greece and Rome,
from the East Indies and America.

The custom of cutting the hair short in mourning is practised
widely.   Examples from the East Indies, ancient Greece and Persia,
America and Asia.   The opposite custom of letting the hair grow
is much rarer, but has been recorded in Africa, Europe and Asia.
The laceration that sometimes accompanies the cutting of the hair
appears to be intended as a sign of grief rather than as a disguise.

Deception of the spirits is sometimes attempted by the use of
effigies of living people.   Examples from Tahiti, East Indies and
Africa.

Other methods of deceiving the ghost are adopted in the Solomon
Islands, in Fiji, in Australia, in New Guinea, in Borneo, in Siberia,
in the East Indies, in Burma, in Indo-China and China and in South
Africa.

The carrying-out of a dead body by a special opening is a common
device to deceive the ghost and frustrate his efforts to return, practised
in Siam, Annam, Indo-China, Burma, China, Siberia, the Indian
Archipelago, India, Baluchistan, Persia and in various parts of
Africa, America and Europe.

The ghosts of the slain are greatly feared by primitive man, and
special precautions are often taken to avoid or pacify them.   Examples from Australia, New Zealand, the East Indies, Burma, India,
Africa, North and South America, and ancient Greece.   In this

connexion it may be suggested that the legend of Orestes, how he recovered sanity by biting off one of his fingers after murdering his mother, may contain a reminiscence of a drastic mode of appeasing the angry ghost of a murdered person.

Persons who have taken their own life are greatly feared after death, and special precautions are often taken to guard against their spirits. Examples from Africa, India, China, Russia, Indo-China, ancient Greece and modern Europe.

All who have died violently are commonly dreaded after death by primitive man. Thus in India various precautions are taken against the spirits of those slain by tigers. Other examples from Burma, the East Indies, Africa and North America.

A special dread is widely entertained of the spirits of women dying in childbed. This dread is particularly prevalent throughout India and the Malay region to the east. It is also recorded in parts of Africa and among the ancient Mexicans.

The ghosts of dead husbands and wives are commonly deemed very dangerous to their surviving spouses, and special precautions are often taken to guard the widow or widower. Examples from East Indies, India, Kamtchatka, Africa, America and Australia.

Adults who die unmarried or without issue are thought to have missed the crowning blessing of this world, and to be ill at ease in the next, so that their spirits are greatly feared as especially dangerous. Various means are adopted of propitiating them. Commonly this takes the form of a marriage of the dead with another dead person, with a living person, or with some animate or inanimate object. Examples from Fiji, the Indian Archipelago, Africa, India, China and Russia. The ancient Greek custom of placing a pitcher on the tomb of all unmarried people may have originated in this way.

Since the soul of a recently deceased person is supposed to be greatly concerned with the disposal of his mortal remains, the bodies of people who die away from home, and therefore cannot be buried in the usual way, occasion much anxiety to their survivors. Commonly their kinsmen attempt to pacify the spirits of such people by holding

CHAPTER I

PRECAUTIONS AGAINST THE RETURN OF GHOSTS

In a former part of this work[1] I endeavoured to show that a belief in the survival of the human spirit after death has been general, if not universal, among those races of lower culture whom we call savages or barbarians, and whom we may legitimately term primitive in a relative sense, by comparison with civilized nations. We saw that in the opinion of primitive man the spirits of the dead continue to exert a great influence on the life of the survivors both for good and evil. It is thought on the one hand, for example, that they can cause the rain to fall and the fruits of the earth to grow, that they can bless women with offspring, that they can give oracles, and aid their living kinsfolk in war. These are substantial benefits, but on the other hand the spirits of the dead are supposed to be touchy and prone to take offence, and to visit offenders with their displeasure in the shape of many grievous calamities, including sickness and death. Naturally,

[1] *The Fear of the Dead in Primitive Religion*, vol. i. (London, 1933), pp. 1 *sqq.*

therefore, primitive man looks on the spirits of the dead with very mixed feelings. The thought of them is associated in his mind with emotions of hope and fear, of love and hate, of attraction and repulsion. It is not possible for us to measure exactly the force and extent of these diverse and conflicting emotions and to gauge the relative proportion in which they stand to each other ; but it is safe to say that if the fear of the dead has not been the predominant motive in the attitude of primitive man to their spirits it has at least been a very potent agent in moulding the early history of religion. As such, it deserves our serious attention, and forms the subject of this work.

The fear of the spirits of the dead has led primitive man to adopt many precautions for the purpose of keeping these formidable beings at bay and removing them to what he deems a safe distance from him. Thus, for example, he often attempts to drive them away by main force, or to dismiss them peaceably under the safe-conduct of an animal or bird, who is supposed to guide the poor wanderers to that bourne from which no traveller returns ; but in case the spirits should nevertheless attempt to force their way back to the land of the living he sometimes erects barriers of fire or water or more solid materials which he hopes may arrest their progress, and so will leave him in peace. Another mode of preventing the return of the spirits is to render their old home as unattractive as possible in the hope that they will thus be prevented from attempting to regain it. With this view it has often been customary to destroy the property of a dead man in order to spare him the temptation of returning to take possession of it from its living proprietor. This destruction of the property of the dead I have illustrated at some length in a previous volume,[1] and I now take up the subject at the point where I broke off.

Some primitive peoples, not content with destroying the property of a dead man, demolish the dwelling in which the death took place, and flee from the spot in order to avoid a possible encounter with the ghost who may be prowling about his desolate home. Other peoples, without destroying the house or hut, content themselves with retiring to a distance from the scene of death, with the same object of avoiding all possible contact with the spirit of the deceased.

Thus, to take examples: in the Mara tribe of Northern Australia, when any person dies, the body is eaten by the relatives, and the bones deposited on a platform in a tree. "As soon as any one dies, the camps arc immediately shifted, because the spirit, of whom they are frightened, haunts its old camping ground."[2] Among the aborigines of the Lower Murray River, when a death took place, it was customary to pull down the wurley or rude temporary hut of the deceased, because no one would inhabit the spot where a death had taken place.[3]

[1] *The Fear of the Dead in Primitive Religion*, vol. ii. pp. 119 *sqq.*
[2] Baldwin Spencer, *Native Tribes* of the Northern Territory of Australia (London, 1914), p. 254.
[3] R. Brough Smyth, *The Ab-*

An English traveller in New Zealand has described his visit to a Maori village which had been totally deserted on the death of the chief. " Here, though everything was in perfect preservation, not a living soul was to be seen : the village, with its neat houses, built of *raupo*, and its court-yards and provision boxes, was entirely deserted. From the moment the chief was laid beneath the upright canoe, on which was inscribed his name and rank, the whole village became strictly *tapu* or sacred ; and not a native, on pain of death, was permitted to trespass near the spot : the houses were all fastened up, and on most of the doors were inscriptions, denoting that the property of such an one remained there. An utter silence pervaded the place. After ascertaining that no natives were in the vicinity of the forbidden spot, I landed and trod the sacred ground ; and my footsteps were probably the first, since the desertion of the village, that had echoed along its palisaded passages." [1] Similarly in the Marshall Islands, when a chief dies, his hut is abandoned and allowed to fall into decay, for no one will dare to enter it.[2]

Among some of the natives in the eastern part of British New Guinea, " after a death has taken place in a house it is usual for the house to be deserted and allowed to fall to pieces ; but sometimes it is so nearly new that it is a pity to have to build

origines of Victoria (Melbourne and London, 1878), i. p. xxx.

[1] G. F. Angas, *Savage Life and Scenes in Australia and New* *Zealand* (London, 1847),i. pp. 278 *sq*.

[2] A. Erdland, *Die Marshall-Insulaner* (Münster, 1914), p. 325.

another, the doorway is closed up and a new doorway made in another wall and the house still used. It seems that the spirit of the dead one will haunt the place, but it can be deceived by this little artifice. As people lie awake at night they will sometimes say they have heard the spirit scratching along the wall trying to find its way into the house."[1] Among the Kai of Northern New Guinea, the house in which a death has taken place is abandoned because the spirit of the deceased is supposed to haunt it.[2] In Misol, a small island to the north-west of New Guinea, when a death has taken place in a house the house is abandoned, and a new one is built elsewhere. The body, wrapped in cloths, is deposited on a scaffold built for it in the forest. From time to time the relations come to inspect the corpse until decomposition is complete. The skeleton is then brought to the place, generally a cave, where the bones of all the dead inhabitants of the village are collected.[3] In the East Indian island of Buru, when a death has taken place in a house, the survivors desert it, and go in search of a dwelling elsewhere.[4]

In the Andaman Islands a dead body is either buried in a grave or deposited on a platform in a tree. When this has been done the men return to the camp, "where the women have been busy packing

[1] H. Newton, *In Far New Guinea* (London, 1914), p. 227.

[2] R. Neuhauss, *Deutsch Neu Guinea* (Berlin, 1911), p. 83.

[3] J. Wanner, "Ethnologische Notizen über die Inseln Timor und Misol", in *Archiv für Anthropologie.* N.F. xii. (1913).

[4] J. G. F. Riedel, *De Sluik— en Kroesharige Rassen tusschen Selebes en Papua* ('s-Gravenhage, 1886), p. 12.

up all belongings.   Plumes of shredded palm-leaf stem (*koro*) are put up at the entrance to the camp to show chance visitors that there has been a death. The camp is then deserted, the natives moving to some other camping ground until the period of mourning is over, when they may, if they wish, return to the deserted village. No one goes near the grave again until the period of mourning is over." [1]

Among the Sakai of Perak, a primitive dwarf race of the Malay Peninsula, when a death took place the house was invariably burned down and the settlement deserted, even at the risk of the loss of standing crops.[2] Among the Mantra of Malacca, after a death in the clearing, nothing more was planted there, and when the crop or plants on the ground had been gathered it was abandoned.[3] Among the Benuas of Malacca the house where a person has died is generally deserted and burnt.[4] The Kachins of Burma, who have attained to a higher level of culture than these wild tribes of the Malay Peninsula, do not destroy a house in which a death has taken place, but merely make a pretence of doing so and of building a new house in another place.[5] It is thus with the growth of civilization, superstition yields to economic consideration.

[1] A. R. Brown, *The Andaman Islanders* (Cambridge, 1922), p. 108.

[2] A. Hale, "On the Sakais", in the *Journal of the Royal Anthropological Institute*, xv. (1886) p. 291; W. W. Skeat and C. O. Blagden, *Pagan Races of the Malay Peninsula* (London, 1906), ii. p. 96.

[3] Skeat and Blagden, *op. cit.* ii. p. 111.

[4] T. J. Newbold, *British Settlements in Malacca* (London, 1839), ii. p. 410.

[5] C. P. Gilhodes, "Mort et funérailles chez les Katchins (Birmanie)", in *Anthropos*, xii-xiii. p. 431.

The Karens of Burma desert a house in which a death has taken place lest the soul (*Kelah*) of some person remaining in it, especially of one of the children, should be induced to accompany the departed, whose soul (*Kelah*) may thereby the more readily return to a wonted spot and call for a friend's soul. Of this many cases are believed to have occurred.[1]

Some of the Ainus, a primitive tribe of Japan, say that "in years long gone by the ancients used to burn down the hut in which the oldest woman of a family had died. This curious custom was followed, so some of them say, because it was feared that the spirit of the woman would return to the hut after death, and, out of envy, malice, or hatred, bewitch her offspring and sons- and daughters-in-law, together with their whole families, and bring upon them various noxious diseases and many sad calamities. Not only would she render them unprosperous, but she would cause them to be unsuccessful in the hunt, kill all the fresh and salt-water fish, send the people great distress, and render them childless. She would curse the labour of their hands, both in the house, the garden, and the forest ; she would blight all their crops, stop the fountains and springs of drinking water, make life a weary burden, and eventually slay all the people and their children. So vicious and ill-disposed are the departed spirits of old women supposed to be, and

[1] Rev. E. B. Cross, "On the Karens", in the *Journal of the* *American Oriental Society*, iv. (1854) p. 310.

so much power for evil are they said to possess. For this reason, therefore, the ancients used to burn down the hut in which an old woman had lived and died ; the principal idea being that the soul, when it returned from the grave to exercise its diabolical spells, would be unable to find its former residence and the objects of its hatred and fiendish intentions. The soul having been thus cheated of its prey, and its malignant designs frustrated, is supposed to wander about for a time in a towering rage, searching for its former domicile ; but of course to no purpose. Eventually the spirit returns, defeated and dejected, to the grave whence it came, and woe betide the person bold or unlucky enough to venture near the spot.

The custom, however, is now being discontinued ; but customs die hard, and part of this one is still seen to survive. Thus, whenever a woman is getting to be very old and likely to die soon, her children build her a tiny hut somewhere near her old home. When finished, she is sent there to reside, where she is provided with food till she dies.   But when she is dead and buried this hut is burned instead of her old house."[1]

Among the Dhanwār, a primitive hill tribe of the Central Provinces of India, when an elder man dies his family usually abandon their hut, because they believe that his spirit haunts it, and would cause the death of anybody who dared to live there.[2]

---

[1] J. Batchelor, *The Ainus and their Folk-Lore* (London, 1901), pp. 130 *sq.*

[2] R. V. Russell, *The Tribes and Castes of the Central Provinces of India* (London, 1916), ii. 498.

Among the Korwas, another tribe of the Central Provinces of India, when a man dies his hut is broken down, and the family does not inhabit it again.[1] Among the Kurmis, yet another tribe of the Central Provinces of India, " there is a belief that the spirit of the deceased hovers round familiar scenes and places, and on this account, whenever possible, a house in which any one has died is destroyed or deserted." [2]   Among the Savaras, an important hill-tribe of Southern India, on certain days every house in which a death has taken place during the last two years is burned down.   After this the ghost of the deceased (*Kulba*) is supposed to give no more trouble, and does not come to reside in the new hut that is built on the site of the burnt one.[3] In Assam, " if a man dies inside a house, no Hindoo can eat in it afterwards, or reside in it, as it has become impure; it is generally pulled down and burned, and a new house erected on the same spot. All Assamese when dying are, therefore, invariably brought out to die in the open air on the bare ground, that the building may be preserved ; and also to ensure the happier liberation from the body." [4]   Far from India the Lapps in the north of Europe used to strew with stones the place in the hut where a person had died, and then to remove their dwelling to another site, doubtless to avoid the spirit of the

---

[1] Russell, *op. cit.* iii. 574.
[2] Russell, *op. cit.* iv. 80 (referring to Gordon, *Indian Folk-Tales*, p. 54).
[3] E. Thurston, *Castes and Tribes* of *Southern India* (Madras, 1909), vi. 328.
[4] J. Butler, *Travels and Adventure in the Province of Assam* (London, 1855), pp. 258 *sq.*

deceased, which they had apparently sought to pin down by a weight of stones piled on the place where he had died.[1]

In Africa the custom of deserting a place in which a death has occurred is very wide-spread. Thus, among the Banyankole, a pastoral people of Uganda, mourning lasts for three or four months. When it ends the survivors remove to some new site, and build another kraal. The old place falls into decay and is soon overgrown and lost to sight.[2] Sometimes when the heir had had time to build a new kraal, the old kraal was not only deserted but broken down and left in its ruins to decay.[3] Among the Basoga, another people of Uganda, when a death has taken place the hut of the deceased is deserted, and never repaired. No one may live in it, though the chief's house may be built near the site.[4] Similarly among the Bateso, another people of Uganda, the house in which a death has taken place is deserted and suffered to fall into decay, and no one attempts to repair it.[5] Among the Nilotic tribes of Kavirondo the hut in which a death has taken place is used for a month. The neighbours then assemble and drink beer, and break down the hut.[6]

Among the negroes of the Slave Coast the dead

[1] C. Leemius, *de Lapponibus Finmarchiae eorumque lingua, vita, et religione pristina commentatio* (Copenhagen, 1767), pp. 499 *sq.*

[2] J. Roscoe, *The Northern Bantu* (Cambridge, 1915), p. 129.

[3] J. Roscoe, *The Banyankole* (Cambridge, 1923), p. 149.

[4] Roscoe, *The Northern Bantu*, p. 227.

[5] Roscoe, *The Northern Bantu*, p. 267.

[6] C. W. Hobley, *Eastern Uganda* (London, 1902). p. 27; Sir H. Johnston, *The Uganda Protectorate*, Second Edition (London, 1904), ii. 793.

are buried in the house. The room in which the dead is buried is no longer used ; but often the roof is removed and the house abandoned. They burn the clothing of the deceased, and destroy the objects which he used in his life.[1]

Among the Ewe-speaking people of Togoland, nine days after a burial the house of the deceased is pulled down, and the remains of it are taken outside of the house and burned.[2] But if the deceased has died a violent death away from home, whether killed in war, or drowned in a river, or fallen from a tree in the forest, nine days after the burial they go to the place where the misfortune overtook him, dig up some of the earth from the spot, put it in two little pots, tie them up with blue stuff, and place the pots on the grave. When they have done this they break down the house of the deceased and burn it. Among these same people when a man has been killed by the bite of a snake a curious ceremonial is observed. His friends shoot the body of the deceased and bring it to a public place in the village, where they bathe it, ornament it, and smear it with white earth. Then they pour palm-wine into his mouth, and continue to fire their muskets for a long time. Nine or eleven days after they break down the house of the deceased. But before doing so they take a small pot with a lid and carry it to the spot where the man was bitten by the snake. There they dig up some earth, put it in the pot, and close the pot. The oldest woman

[1] P. Bouche, *La Côte des Esclaves et le Dahomey* (Paris, 1885), p. 214.

[2] J. Spieth, *Die Ewe-Stämme* (Berlin, 1906), p. 288.

of the family then carries the pot on her head, and followed by the whole population of the village, drumming and firing shots, she goes to the grave of the deceased, on which she places the pot upside down. The firing continues for a long time, and the companions of the deceased then break down his house. Afterwards they entertain the inhabitants of that quarter of the town, and then they play till nightfall.[1] The writer who describes this quaint rite does not explain it ; but we may conjecture that the soul of the deceased is supposed to be taken up in the earth dug up at the spot where he was bitten by the snake, and that having been thus recovered, the soul is safely bottled up in the pot, and finally restored to the deceased at his grave.[2] Among the Bimbians in the valley of the Niger, on the death of a chief or great man, " more or less of the property is left in the house, which is abandoned, and allowed after an interval to go to decay."[3] Among the Yaunde in the Cameroons, when an unexplained death has taken place in a hamlet, the inhabitants abandon it, and shift their abode to a distance, often to a considerable distance. We are told that the motive is to avoid the evil magic which has proved fatal to one of their number ; but we may conjecture that the true reason is to avoid the ghost of the deceased.[4] Among the peoples in the district of

[1] J. Spieth, *op. cit.* 156–158.
[2] J. Spieth, *op. cit.* p. 760.
[3] W. Allen and T. R. H. Thomson, *Narrative of the Expedition to the River Niger in 1841* (London, 1848),

ii. p. 297.
[4] G. Zenker, " Yaunde ", in *Mitteilungen von Forschungsreisenden und Gelehrten aus den Deutschen Schutzgebieten*, iii. p. 69.

Ogowe, when a chief or other man of importance dies, the custom is to abandon the site where the death took place, and to remove the settlement to another place in the forest. A traveller in West Africa tells us that he often met with the remains of such abandoned settlements in the forest. The old houses are either left to fall into decay or are burned down.[1] Among the Wangata of the Belgian Congo when a death occurs they pull down the house in which the deceased died, fell the banana-trees which overshadowed it, and allow the grass to grow on the site.[2] Among the Baholoholo of the Belgian Congo when a death has taken place all the huts of the deceased are burned.[3] The writer who reports the custom supposes that this is done as a measure of hygiene ; but more probably the motive is a fear of the ghost. An old Portuguese writer, Dos Santos, speaking of the Kafirs of South-East Africa, tells us that after a burial they burn the thatched house of the deceased with all it contains, so that no one may possess anything that the dead person made use of in his lifetime, or even touch it, and if it so happens that some one touches anything belonging to the deceased he does not enter his house until he has washed in the river. The ashes of the burnt house with any pieces of wood not quite consumed they put on the top of the grave.[4] With regard to the Barotse, a Bantu tribe of South Africa, we are told

[1] O. Lenz, *Skizzen aus Westafrika* (Berlin, 1878), p. 208.

[2] Lieut. Engels, *Les Wangata* (Brussels, 1912), p. 53.

[3] R. Schmitz, *Les Baholoholo* (Brussels, 1912), p. 223.

[4] Dos Santos, in Theal, *Records of South-eastern Africa* (1901), vii. 307.

that death inspires them with a mortal terror, and that among them consequently the hut of the deceased person is almost always abandoned.[1] Livingstone was told that among the Makonde, another South African tribe, when any one died in a village the whole population deserted it, saying that it was a bad spot.[2] Of the Bantu tribes in South Africa generally the attitude to the spirits of the dead has been described as follows by their historian, Dr. McCall Theal. " There was an idea that something connected with death attached to the personal effects of the deceased, on which account whatever had belonged to him that could not be placed in the grave, his clothing, mats, head-rest, etc., was destroyed by fire. The hut in which he had lived was also burned, and no other was allowed to be built on the spot. If he had been the chief, the whole kraal was removed to another site. Those who touched the corpse or any of the dead man's effects were obliged to go through certain ceremonies, and then to bathe in running water before associating again with their companions. Except in cases of persons of rank, however, very few deaths occurred within kraals. As soon as it was seen that any one's end was near, the invalid was carried to a distance and left to die alone, in order to avert the danger of the presence of the dreaded something that could not be explained."[3]

[1] L. Decle, *Three Years in Savage Africa* (London, 1898), p. 76.

[2] D. Livingstone, *Last Journals* (London, 1874), i. 28.

[3] Dr. G. McCall Theal, *Ethnography of South Africa* (London, 1919), p. 76.

With regard to the Bushmen of South Africa we are told by two French missionaries in the first half of nineteenth century that when a man died his hut was broken down, piled over his grave, and burned.[1] At the other extremity of Africa the nomadic Tuaregs of the north, when a death has taken place, always shift their camp, and avoid everything that might recall the memory of the deceased.[2] Among some tribes at the foot of the Atlas Mountains, when a cadi dies, the new cadi never inhabits the castle or house of his predecessor, unless he happens to be a member of the same family. He always builds a new house for himself. A traveller in these regions has described how he saw many such castles falling into ruins after the death of their last occupants.[3]

Similar customs have been observed for similar reasons by the aborigines in many parts of America, both north and south. Thus the Eskimos think that a hut in which a death has taken place is polluted and dangerous, and they will make no use of anything that is in it at the moment when the dying person breathed his last. Hence when a sick person is obviously dying they hasten to remove him to a small temporary hut which after the death can be abandoned without serious loss.[4] Among the

[1] T. Arbousset and F. Daumas, *Relation d'un voyage d'exploration* (Paris, 1842), p. 503.

[2] H. Duveyrier, *Exploration du Sahara: Les Touareg du Nord* (Paris, 1864).

[3] E. Doutté, *En Tribu* (Paris, 1914), p. 247.

[4] C. F. Hall, *Life with the Esquimaux* (London, 1864), pp. 201, 249. Cf. Lecorre, in *Annales de l'Association de la Propagation de la Foi*, vol. xlvii. (1875) p. 121.

Eskimos of Alaska if there are many deaths about the same time, or an epidemic occurs, everything belonging to the dead is destroyed. The house in which a death occurs is always deserted, and usually destroyed. In order to avoid this, they commonly take a sick person out of the house, and put him in a tent to die.[1] Among the Thompson Indians of British Columbia, "the lodge in which an adult person died was burned. The winter house, after a death had taken place in it, was purified with water in which tobacco and juniper had been soaked, and fresh fir-boughs were spread on the floor each morning. Pieces of tobacco and juniper were also placed in various parts of the house. But if two or more deaths occurred in it at the same time, or in immediate succession, then the house was invariably burned. Most of the household utensils of a deceased person were also burned, as well as the bed on which he had died. The place where the deceased had lain when dying was not occupied for some time. Then an adult male slept on it four nights in succession. After that it was considered safe for any one to lie there."[2] From this account we may see that while these Indians invariably burned a summer hut in which a single death had occurred they spared in a similar case the more solid and therefore more valuable winter house, not burning it down until several deaths in it had con-

[1] W. Dall, *Alaska and its Resources* (London, 1870), p. 146.

[2] J Teit, *The Thompson Indians of British Columbia* (Memoirs of the American Museum of Natural History, vol. ii. The Jesup North Pacific Expedition), 1900, p. 331.

vinced them of the great danger of allowing it to stand. Among these Indians economic considerations have partially tempered the fear of the spirits of the dead. Yet among them that fear is very serious ; for we are told that " nobody could with impunity take possession of the bow and arrows, long leggings, and moccasins of a dead man. If any one appropriated the first of these, the dead man would come back for them, and in taking them away would also take the soul of the man possessing them, thereby causing his speedy death. If either of the other two were appropriated, the one who took them would be visited by a sickness which would cause his feet and legs to swell enormously. It is not safe, except for a person who has a strong guardian spirit, to smoke out of the pipe of a person who has recently died. The tobacco will burn up in it faster than usual. This is a sign that the deceased wishes the pipe." [1] Among the Cree Indians of Canada, when a death has taken place in a tent, the whole camp is shifted for several miles.[2] Among the Apache-Yumas, an Indian tribe of the United States, if a death occurs in a hut, the hut with everything in it is burnt. " As soon as a death is announced, all the huts in the immediate neighbourhood are deserted, and often burned. . . . They dislike to speak of the dead, but refer to him indirectly, and usually in a whisper." [3] Among

[1] J. Teit, *op. cit.* p. 331.
[2] C. Leden, " Unter den Indianern Canadas ", in *Zeitschrift für Ethnologie*, xliv. (1912), p. 816.

[3] W. F. Corbusier, " The Apache-Yumas and Apache-Mojavas ", in *The American Antiquary*, vol. vii. p. 338.

the Navahos, another Indian tribe of the United States, when a death takes place the rafters of the house are pulled down over the remains and the place is usually set on fire. After that nothing would induce a Navaho to touch a piece of the wood, or even approach the immediate vicinity of the place ; even years afterwards such places are recognised and avoided, because they are believed to be haunted by the spirits of the dead. These shades or spirits of the dead are not necessarily malevolent, but they are regarded as inclined to resent any intrusion or the taking of any liberty with them or their belongings.[1] The Tamarahumare Indians of Mexico always destroy a house in which a death has taken place, and they break the baskets and other household utensils which it contained.[2] The Yucatecs, a Maya people of Mexico, used always to forsake a house in which a death had taken place, because they greatly feared the spirit of the dead.[3]

The Anabali and other tribes of the Orinoco in South America have so great a fear of death that as soon as they have buried one of their number near where he lived they immediately abandon their crops, and build a new village at a distance of twelve or fifteen leagues, and when they are questioned for their reason for thus abandoning their crops they answer that since death has entered

---

[1] C. Mindeleff, "Navaho Houses", in the *Seventeenth Annual Report of the Bureau of American Ethnology*, 1895–1896 (1898), p. 475.

[2] C. Lumholz, *Unknown Mexico* (London, 1903), i. p. 384.

[3] H. H. Bancroft, *Native Races of the Pacific States of North America* (London, 1875–1876), ii. 800.

among them they no longer feel secure in that neighbourhood.[1]   Among the Jibaros, a wild Indian tribe of Ecuador, when a death took place the dead used to be deposited in the house, which was then abandoned.   The dead man was given his spear in his hand, and pots of food were placed around him ; then the door was shut and strongly fastened, and the relations departed.[2]   Among the Guarauno Indians, a tribe in the delta of the Orinoco, when a death has taken place the body is placed in the hollowed-out trunk of a tree or in a canoe, wrapped in leaves, and is then left in the house, which is deserted.   When several persons die in the village at short intervals, the village is deserted, because, as they assert, "an evil spirit (*gébu*) has passed by, cursing it."[3]   Here again we may conjecture that the real evil spirits whom they dread are the ghosts of the departed.

Among the Jaguas, an Indian tribe in the upper valley of the Amazon, when a death has taken place the survivors burn the hut of the deceased and build a new one.[4]   In a tribe of Peruvian Indians, whom the German traveller von Tschudi visited, the dead were buried in the huts which they inhabited in life. The relations broke the household utensils of the deceased, deserted the house, and built for themselves a new one in a distant place.   But they

[1] P. J. Gumilla, *Histoire de l'Orénoque* (Avignon, 1758), i. 325.

[2] Dr. Rivet,"Les Indiens Jibaros", in *L'Anthropologie*, xviii. (1907) p. 608.

[3] J. Chaffanjon, *L'Orénoque et le Caura* (Paris, 1889), p. 13.

[4] G. Osculati, *Exploratione delle Regioni equatoriali lungo il Napo ed il fiume delle Amazzoni* (Milan, 1850), p. 209.

buried the weapons and agricultural instruments of their dead kinsman with his body in the grave, because they thought that he would need them in the spirit land.[1] Among the Conibos, an Indian tribe visited by the French traveller Castelnau in the interior of South America, when a death had taken place and the body of the deceased had been buried, the relatives used to break all the household vessels of the departed and then set fire to his house. When the hut was burned down they spread a thick layer of ashes over the spot, in which they expected to find traces of the wandering soul of the deceased.[2] The Tucanos, an Indian tribe in the valley of the Uaupes, a northern tributary of the Amazon, always bury their dead in the huts which they inhabited in life. Then the family immediately desert the hut and go and build another, leaving the old one to decay. In a few years the site of the old house has disappeared, and is overgrown once more by the forest.[3]

Among the Yuracares, an Indian tribe in the interior of South America, visited by the French traveller D'Orbigny, when a death has occurred, and the relatives have buried the deceased, they abandon his hut and his fields.[4] The Calchaquis, an Indian tribe of Brazil to the north of Paraguay, always burned the hut in which a death had taken

[1] J. J. von Tschudi, *Peru—Reiseskizzen aus den Jahren 1838–1842* (St. Gallen, 1846), i. 235.

[2] F. de Castelnau, *Expédition dans les parties centrales de l'Amérique du Sud* (Paris, 1850–1851), ii. 385.

[3] H. A. Coudreau, *La France équinoxiale* (Paris, 1887), ii. 172.

[4] A. D'Orbigny, *L'Homme Américain* (Paris, 1839), i. 359.

place, and they buried the deceased with his eyes open, that he might see to find his way to the other world.[1] The Lengua Indians of Paraguay were wont to burn down the hut in which a death had occurred, and then to destroy and vacate the village, till the eminent English missionary, Mr. Grubb, exacted from them a promise not to follow this ruinous practice. They thought that the souls of the dead returned to the ruined village, to warm themselves at the fires in the chilly morning air, and that if they found the fires extinct they used to throw the ashes about in a rage.[2] Mr. Grubb's evidence on this point is confirmed by the testimony of another English missionary, Mr. L. E. Guppy, who spent many years with the English Mission to the Paraguayan Chaco.[3] Among the Coroados Indians of Brazil when an adult dies they bury him in his hut, and abandon it for another dwelling at a distance, for they fear to be haunted by the spirit of the deceased if they ever visited the place of death.[4] The Tacunas, another Indian tribe of Brazil, bury their dead in pots in the huts which they inhabited. Then they set fire to the huts and burn them with all their contents, unless the children of the deceased care to appropriate their father's weapons, which in that case are spared from the flames.[5]

[1] R. Southey, *History of Brazil* (Second Edition, 1822), i. 395.
[2] W. B. Grubb, *An Unknown People in an Unknown Land* (London, 1911), pp. 124, 165, 169.
[3] T. Koch, " Die Lenguas-Indianer in Paraguay ", in *Globus*, lxxvii. (1900) p. 220.
[4] J. B. von Spix und C. F. Ph. von Martius, *Reise in Brasilien* (Munich, 1823–1831), i. 382.
[5] *Ibid.* ii. 1187.

Another mode of avoiding all contact with the dangerous spirits of the dead is to repel them by stinks, for apparently the spirits are credited with a delicate sense of smell which leads them to shun persons and places infected with foul smells. Thus the Algonquin Indians of Canada used to burn stinking substances in order to repel the hovering spirits of the dead, and for the same purpose they sometimes put stinking stuffs on their own heads in order to guard themselves against the approach of the dreaded ghosts. This curious custom was observed and recorded by Jesuit missionaries in the seventeenth century,[1] and it has persisted down at least to the middle of the nineteenth century among the Ojebway Indians, one of whom has described his observations and experiences for us. After mentioning various modes of repelling the dangerous ghosts of the dead, he goes on, " Lest this should not prove effectual, they will also frequently take a deer's tail and, after burning or singeing off all the hair, will rub the necks or faces of the children before they lie down to sleep, thinking that the offensive smell will be another preventive to the spirit's entrance. I well remember when I used to be daubed over with this disagreeable fumigation, and had great faith in it all. Thinking that the soul lingers about the body a long time before it takes its final departure, they use these means to hasten it away."[2]

---

[1] *Relation des Jésuites dans la Nouvelle-France en 1639* (Quebec, 1858), p. 44.

[2] P. Jones, *History of the Ojebway Indians* (London, N.D.), pp. 99 *sq.*

The Hidatsa Indians of the United States believe that the ghost of a deceased person lingers near his dwelling for four nights after his death. During this time " those who disliked or feared him and do not wish a visit from his shade, scorch with red-hot coals a pair of moccasins, which they leave at the door of the lodge. The smell of the burning leather, they claim, keeps the ghost out ; but the true friends of the dead man take no such precautions."[1] Of the Pampa del Sacramento Indians of South America it is recorded that when a person is dying and at his last gasp, " the women fall upon him, some close his eyes by force, others his mouth, and they throw upon him whatever comes to hand, and literally kill him while he is dying. Meanwhile others run to put out the candle, and dissipate the smoke, lest the soul not knowing how to get out should be entangled in the roof, and lest it should come back again to the same dwelling they collect all sorts of filth round about it, that the stink may drive it away."[2]

A forcible way of preventing the spirits of the dead from returning to plague the survivors is to divert the water of a stream, bury the corpses in the dry bed of the river, and then allow the water to resume its natural course. The double barrier of earth and water may then be regarded as sufficient to prevent the ghosts from escaping to return and molest living folk. This mode of burial has been

[1] Washington Matthews, *Ethnology and Philology of the Hidatsa Indians* (Washington, 1877).

[2] R. Southey, *History of Brazil*, i. Supplementary Notes, p. xxiv.

adopted in various parts of Africa. It has been reported for the dwarfs of West Africa by Mgr. Le Roy, who was personally acquainted with these primitive folk. He says that among the A-Kôa, when a death has taken place, the elders assemble at midnight to decide on the place of burial, while the women and children are sent away from the camp. When a decision has been reached the elders go a long way into the forest till they come to the stream which has been chosen for the burial. There they divert the current of the stream and dig a deep round hole in its bed, taking care to surround the edges of the hole with little posts to prevent the sand or earth from tumbling in. Then they return to the camp to fetch the corpse. They find it wrapped in rough mats or fig-tree bark. Afterwards at midnight they convey the body silently and secretly to its destined grave in the bed of the stream. There they place it upright, with its face turned to the sky and set a large stone over the head with a ridge of clay to prevent the water from penetrating. Then one of the elders pronounces the last farewell to the departed spirit, bidding it to go away to the happy land. After that they allow the stream to resume its course and to flow over the grave of their kinsman.[1]

A similar custom is reported by Du Chaillu for the Obongo, a tribe of West Africa. " The modes of burial of these savages, as related to me by my Ashango companions, are curious. The most com-

---

[1] Mgr. Le Roy, " Les Pygmées ", in *Les Missions Catholiques*, vol. xxix. (1897) pp. 238 *sq.*

mon habit is to place the corpse in the interior of a hollow tree in the forest, filling up the hole with branches and leaves mixed with earth ; but sometimes they make a hole in the bed of a running stream, diverting the current for the purpose, and then, after the grave is covered in, turning back the rivulet to its former course." [1]

In the Watumbe and Wabemba tribes of Tanganyika it is customary to bury great chiefs in the beds of rivers, of which the water has been temporarily diverted to permit of this mode of sepulture. Most of the great chiefs choose their place of burial during their lifetime. At the chosen spot when the water of the river has been diverted they dig the grave in the dry bed. Two of the wives of the deceased chief are then lowered into the grave, and placed in a sitting posture with their legs crossed and firmly tied. The skeleton of the dead chief is deposited in their arms, resting on their knees, and with it is put a vessel of food. They occupy the bottom of the cavity. Near them on each side are lowered two young men, one holding the chief's pipe and the other his fire tongs. The opening is next covered with a mat. Next they throw into the grave a number of slaves in proportion to the dignity of the deceased chief, first killing or stunning them by blows of a club upon their heads. Then the grave is filled up and the earth stamped down. Afterwards the other slaves of the chief are forced to walk over the grave, and each receives the blow of a club

[1] P. B. Du Chaillu, *A Journey to Ashango Land* (London, 1867), p. 321.

on his neck. If he does not succumb under the blow he is free ; but if he succumbs it is because the chief desires his company, so his body is left to lie upon the tomb. After that the water of the river is allowed to resume its course, and to flow over the remains of the dead chief and his victims. When that has been done every one runs upstream and bathes in the river to purify himself ; but the last to arrive is not allowed to enter the river. He is deemed impure and may not enter the village for a month. After a month he purifies himself in the river and may go home.[1]

In his journey across Africa, Commander Cameron visited the country of the Kirua, and learned from them the grandiose fashion in which they used to bury their dead kings. He says, " The first proceeding is to divert the course of a stream, and in its bed to dig an enormous pit, the bottom of which is then covered with living women. At one end a woman is placed on her hands and knees, and upon her back the dead chief, covered with his beads and other treasures, is seated, being supported on either side by one of his wives, while his second wife sits at his feet.

" The earth is then shovelled in on them, and all the women are buried alive, with the exception of the second wife. To her custom is more merciful than to her companions, and grants her the privilege of being killed before the huge grave is filled in.

---

[1] C. Delhaise, *Notes ethno-graphiques sur quelques peuplades du Tanganyika*, Second Edition (Brussels, 1905), pp. 21–22.

" This being completed, a number of male slaves—sometimes forty or fifty—are slaughtered and their blood poured over the grave ; after which the river is allowed to resume its course.

" Stories were rife that no fewer than a hundred women were buried alive with Bambarré, Kasongo's father ; but let us hope that this may be an exaggeration." [1]

Among the Grebos, a tribe of Liberia, persons who have filled the office of high priest (*Bodia*) are usually buried on an island off Cape Palmas if they have died a natural death ; but if they have died through drinking sassy-wood they must be buried beneath a running stream of water.[2] The drinking of sassy-wood is one form of the poison ordeal, which is very common in Africa as the supreme and infallible test in a charge of sorcery. If the accused vomits the poison he is regarded as innocent ; if he fails to vomit it he is guilty and, should the poison not prove fatal on the spot, he is regularly executed as a convicted sorcerer.[3] Thus we see that a Grebo high priest who dies by drinking an infusion of sassy-wood must always be regarded by the natives as a convicted sorcerer, and his ghost will therefore inevitably be deemed exceedingly dangerous. That, therefore, must be the reason for burying his body, not with his fellow high priests on the island, but under the bed of a running stream,

[1] V. L. Cameron, *Across Africa* (New Edition, 1885), pp. 365-366.
[2] Sir H. Johnston, *Liberia* (London, 1906), vol. ii. p. 1076.
[3] J. G. Frazer, *Folk-Lore in the Old Testament* (London, 1918), vol. iii. pp. 307-401.

in the hope that the double barrier of earth and water will prevent his malignant spirit from molesting living folk by his sorcery as he had done in his lifetime by his black art.   In antiquity the Gothic leader Alaric was similarly buried in the bed of a river, which was then allowed to flow over his grave.[1] The object of this burial in his case is not stated.   It may have been to prevent his too powerful spirit from roaming at large to the danger of living folk, or it may have been to guard the grave from desecration by the king's enemies.

Curiously enough, the ashes of the prophet Daniel are reported by an Arab geographer to have been subjected to a similar treatment by order of the khalif Omar ben Khattab.   Having found in the latest of his conquests the traditional site of the grave of Daniel, and being informed that the natives invoked the name of the prophet for the purpose of obtaining rain, the pious khalif took measures to stop this idolatrous rite for the future.   By his order they stopped the course of a river, dug a grave in its dry bed, and there deposited the remains of the prophet in order that for the future no man might know where the ashes of the prophet lay, and so might no longer employ his name in incantations for rain.[2]

A much simpler and less troublesome mode of preventing the return of an unwelcome ghost is to peg his remains down into the earth.   This method is adopted by the Oraons of Orissa for all ghosts

[1] Jordanes, *Getica*, c. xxx. § 158.

[2] Módjem el Bouldan, in C. B. de Meynard, *Dictionnaire géographique, historique, et littéraire de la Perse* (Paris, 1861), p. 327.

except those of their dead ancestors. They imagine that the wooden pegs prevent the ghosts of the dead from rising through the earth to molest them.[1] In Cochin China the troublesome ghost of a stranger can be confined to his grave by knocking a nail or other piece of iron into the earth of the grave at the point where his head reposes.[2] Among the Wawanga in the Baringo district of East Africa when a sick man in his delirium calls out the name of a dead relative the friends of the sick man imagine that his sickness is caused by the ghost of the deceased. Accordingly, to give a quietus to the ghost they sometimes drive a stake into the head of the grave and pour boiling water down after it; or as an alternative they engage a poor old man to undertake the dangerous task of digging up the corpse, after which the bones are burned over a nest of red ants, and the ashes swept up and thrown into a river.[3]

In order to prevent the return of the spirits of the dead some peoples bury the bodies in certain positions which they imagine will produce the desired effect. Among the Chiriguano Indians of the Rio Pilcomayo in South America when a man has been killed by a jaguar they bury him head downwards in the earth to prevent him from turning into a jaguar after death, and in that form committing ravages upon the people.[4] When the Ibibio of

---

[1] S. C. Roy, *Oraon Religion and Customs* (Ranchi, 1928), p. 50.

[2] P. Giran, *Magie et Religion Annamites* (Paris, 1912), pp. 132 *sq.*

[3] Hon. K. R. Dundas, " Notes on the Tribes inhabiting the Baringo District, East Africa Protectorate ", in *Journal of the Royal Anthropological Institute*, xl. (1910) pp. 54 *sq.*

[4] E. Nordenskiöld, *Indianerleben* (Leipzig, 1912), p. 218.

Southern Nigeria wish to prevent the reincarnation of persons whom they regard as undesirable they bury the bodies in the grave with their faces downwards, apparently imagining that their spirits will thus be unable to find their way back to earth. On the contrary, young people are usually buried lying on their side, in an attitude of sleep. " Grown men, on the other hand, are buried lying flat on their backs, ' so that they may be able to see straight before them and soon find their way back to earth'."[1] To prevent the ghost from walking some of the menial tribes of Northern India bury the dead face downwards in the grave.[2] We have already seen that this mode of burial is adopted for the Mehtar, a caste of sweepers in the Punjab.[3] In Siam the corpse is very often placed in the coffin face downwards in order that the spirit of the dead may not be able to find its way back.[4]

For the same purpose a corpse is very often carried out of the house feet foremost. Apparently the notion is that in this posture the eyes of the corpse are turned away from the house and that therefore the ghost will not be able to see his way back to the dwelling. Thus for example in Mabuiag, one of the Torres Straits Islands, a corpse was always carried out of the camp feet foremost, for otherwise it was believed the spirit of the dead would return to haunt

[1] P. A. Talbot, *Life in Southern Nigeria* (London, 1923), p. 144.

[2] W. Crooke, *Natives of Northern India* (London, 1907), p. 216.

[3] J. G. Frazer, *Fear of the Dead* (London, 1934), ii. p. 108.

[4] E. Young, *The Kingdom of the Yellow Robe* (London, 1907), p. 346.

and torment the survivors.[1] The Kiwai Papuans of British New Guinea, on the other hand, carry their dead out head foremost, thinking that otherwise their ghosts will return to the village and make people sick.[2] Thus the practice of the Kiwai differs from that of their neighbours, the natives of Mabuiag, but their intention is the same, namely, to prevent the return of dangerous ghosts. The Pehuenches, a nomadic tribe of Indians in Central Chile, always carry the dead out of a tent feet foremost, for they think that otherwise the wandering ghost might return to its old abode.[3] In Northern India the corpse of an orthodox Hindu is always carried out of the house feet foremost in order that the ghost may not find its way back to the dwelling.[4] Similarly in many parts of Germany people are very careful to carry out their dead feet foremost, believing that otherwise their ghosts would return to the house.[5] In Denmark corpses are always carried out of the house feet foremost, because it is believed that if they were carried out head foremost their ghosts would see their way back to the house and return to haunt it.[6] In Italy, also, it is the general practice to carry a corpse out of the house feet foremost.[7]

[1] A. C. Haddon, in *Reports of the Cambridge Anthropological Expedition to Torres Straits* (Cambridge, 1904), vol. v. p. 248. Cf. Haddon, in *Internationales Archiv für Ethnographie*, vol. vi. (1893) p. 152.

[2] J. Landtman, *The Kiwai Papuans of British New Guinea* (London, 1927), p. 257.

[3] E. Poeppig, *Reise in Chile, Peru, und auf dem Amazonenstrome* (Leip-zig, 1830–1836), i. 392.

[4] W. Crooke, *Natives of Northern India*, p. 217.

[5] A. Wuttke, *Der deutsche Volksaberglaube* (Berlin, 1869), § 736.

[6] Dr. H. F. Feilberg, "The Corpse-Door: A Danish Survival", in *Folk-Lore*, xxiii. (1907) p. 369.

[7] A. de Gubernatis, *Storia Comparata degli Usi Funebri in Italia*, Second Edition (Milan, 1878), p. 52.

Another way of preventing the spirit of the dead from seeing his way back is to blindfold him by bandages or otherwise. Some of the Australian aborigines in the neighbourhood of Lake Alexandrina place bandages round the eyes of their dead, which they fasten behind.[1] The Bana of the Cameroons tie up the eyes of a corpse and fasten the hands and feet before they carry the body out of the house.[2] In Corea people tie blinkers, or rather blinders, on the eyes of a corpse. These are made of black silk, and are fastened with strings at the back of the head.[3] In Cambodia pieces of gold leaf are placed on the eyes, the mouth, and the nose of the corpse, but are removed when the body has been brought to the funeral pyre.[4] The Warangi and Wambugwe tribes of East Africa, when a death has occurred, kill a goat, extract its fat, and rub it on the eyes of the corpse in order that the ghost of the deceased may not see new-born children and injure them by his evil looks.[5] In the Nicobar Islands they do not indeed blindfold the dead, but " one near of kin gently closes the eyes of the corpse in order to give the appearance of sleep, for not only is the glazed fixed look of death held in fear, but the further benefit is gained of darkening the vision of the departed spirit—believed to be still hovering near—

---

[1] E. J. Eyre, *Journals of Expeditions of Discovery into Central Australia* (London, 1845), ii. 345.

[2] G. von Hagen, " Die Bana ", in *Baessler-Archiv*, ii. (1912) p. 108.

[3] J. Ross, *History of Corea*, p. 325.

[4] J. Moura, *Le Royaume de Cambodge* (Paris, 1883), i. 360.

[5] A. Baumann, *Durch Massailand zur Nilquelle* (Berlin, 1894), p. 187.

and thereby preventing it from acting malevolently towards the living."[1]

A common mode of blindfolding a corpse is to place a coin on each of the dead person's eyes. This is done by the Dyaks of Borneo immediately after death, for the avowed purpose of closing the eyes of the ghost, and so preventing him from seeing and injuring the surviving kinsfolk on earth.[2] Among the Galelareese of Halmahera, a large island to the west of New Guinea, if the eyes of a dead person are wide open, they say that he is looking round for a companion, in order to draw him away with him to the spirit land. Hence they are always careful to weight the eyelids of a corpse, generally with a *rijks-dollar*, in order to keep them shut.[3] But if the deceased is suspected of being a were-wolf it is necessary to strew lime on his eyes and to cover his head with a pan ; for then, they say, his eyes are dim and he cannot see to come and visit the survivors with sickness or death.[4] A similar custom has been practised for similar reasons in various parts of Europe. For example in the north-east of Scotland, if the eyes of a corpse did not close, or if they opened a little after being closed, an old penny or halfpenny piece was laid on each eye to keep it

[1] E. H. Man, " Notes on the Nicobarese ", in *The Indian Antiquary*, xxviii. (1899) p. 253 ; *id.* Man, *The Nicobar Islands and their People* (Guildford, N.D.), p. 130.

[2] F. Grabowsky, " Der Tod, das Begräbnis, das Tiwah oder Todtenfest und Ideen über das Jenseits bei den Dajaken ", in *Internationales Archiv für Ethnologie*, ii. (1889) p. 178.

[3] M. J. van Baarda, " Fabelen, verhalen en Overleveringen der Galelareezen ", in *Bijdragen tot de Taal- Land- en Volkenkunde van Nederlandsch-Indië*, xlv. (1895) p. 538.

[4] *Ibid.* p. 541.

closed.[1] A like practice seems to have been observed in some parts of England, as we learn from the words put by Dickens in the mouth of Mrs. Gamp: "When Gamp was summonsed to his long home, and I see him a-lying in Guy's Hospital with a penny piece on each eye, and his wooden leg under his left arm, I thought I should have fainted away. But I bore up."[2] The custom of placing coins on the eyes of the dead is recorded also for Russia, Serbia, and Bulgaria.[3] Modern Jews put potsherds on the eyes of a corpse.[4] The notion that if the eyes of the dead be not closed his ghost will return to fetch away another of the household still exists in Bohemia, Germany, and England.[5]

On the citadel of Mycenae the royal graves of the ancient kings were discovered by Dr. Schliemann in his memorable excavations of the site.[6] In them he found seven golden masks, five of them covering the faces of men, and two the faces of children. The

[1] Rev. W. Gregor, *Notes on the Folk-lore of the North-East of Scotland* (London, 1881), p. 207.

[2] Chas. Dickens, *Martin Chuzzlewit*, ch. xix.

[3] W. R. S. Ralston, *Songs of the Russian People*, Second Edition (London, 1872), p. 318; F. S. Krauss, *Volksglaube und religiöser Brauch der Südslaven* (Munster, 1890), p. 140.

[4] J. C. G. Bodenschatz, *Kirkliche Verfassung der heutigen Juden* (Erlangen, 1748), iv. p. 174.

[5] J. V. Grohmann, *Aberglauben und Gebräuche aus Böhmen und Mähren* (Leipzig, 1864), p. 188; G. Lammert, *Volksmedezin und medezinischer Aberglaube aus Bayern* (Wurzburg, 1869), p. 106; A. Wuttke, *Der deutsche Volksaberglaube*, § 725; T. F. T. Dyer, *English Folk-Lore* (London, 1884), p. 230; A. Schleicher, *Volksthumliches aus Sonnenberg* (Weimar, 1858), p. 52; C. L. Rochholz, *Deutscher Glaube und Brauch* (Berlin, 1867), i. 176. Cf. Witzschel, *Kleine Beiträge zur deutscher Mythologie*, ii. 256; E. Veckenstedt, *Wendische Sagen Märchen, und abergläubische Gebräuche* (Graz, 1880), p. 449.

[6] J. G. Frazer, *Pausanias's Description of Greece* (London, 1898), iii. 107.

masks were clearly portraits of the dead, and the intention with which they were so placed can only be conjectured. In one of the children's masks holes were cut out for the eyes ; but there were no such holes in the men's masks. This perhaps suggests an intention of blinding the eyes of dead men, while allowing a dead child to retain its eyesight. The custom of covering the faces of the dead with masks appears to have prevailed widely in the world, and is still practised in some places. Thus golden masks are regularly placed on the faces of dead kings of Siam and Cambodia ;[1] and among the Shans of Indo-China the face of a dead chief is invariably covered with a mask of gold or silver.[2] In ancient Mexico masks made of gold or turquoise mosaic or painted wood were placed on the faces of dead kings.[3] Among the Ibibio of Southern Nigeria in olden days the faces of chiefs were regularly covered by wooden masks, conventionalized enough, but carved with a certain dignity. In modern times the art of carving these funeral masks has much degenerated. The object of placing them on the faces of dead chiefs is not mentioned by our authority.[4] The Aleutian Islanders used to put masks on the faces of their dead, and as they wore masks at certain dances as a protection against a dangerous spirit who was supposed to descend into a wooden idol, it seems

---

[1] Mgr. Pallegoix, *Description du royaume Thai ou Siam* (Paris, 1854), i. 247 ; J. Moura, *Le Royaume du Cambodge* (Paris, 1883), i. 349.

[2] A. S. Colquhoun, *Among the Shans*, p. 279.

[3] F. S. Clavigero, *History of Mexico*, translated by Cullen (London, 1807), p. 324 ; Bancroft, *Native Races of the Pacific States*, ii. 606.

[4] P. A. Talbot, *Life in Southern Nigeria* (London, 1923), p. 147.

possible that their mortuary masks were intended to guard their dead against some spiritual danger.[1] The masks placed upon the faces of dead kings may perhaps have had a similar protective intention. In ancient Egypt every mummy had its artificial face ; and masks made of gold, silver, bronze and terra-cotta found in Mesopotamia, Phoenicia, the Crimea, Italy, the valley of the Danube, Gaul and Britain, appear to testify to the extent to which a similar custom prevailed both in Western Asia and Europe.[2] Some people, not content with covering the eyes of the dead, block up all the other openings of his head, his ears and mouth, that he may not be able to see, hear or speak. The custom seems to be specially prevalent in the East Indies. Among the people who practise it are the Malays, and the Batak and Achinese of Sumatra.[3] Such practices seem to testify to a great fear of the spirits of the dead. In the Bari tribe of the Nilotic Sudan the rain-maker is a very important personage, and if he dies a natural death his corpse is subjected to a special treatment for the purpose of keeping his precious spirit within his body and so under the control of his son, who succeeds him in the office of rain-maker. To effect this purpose all the orifices in the dead man's body are plugged up to prevent the escape of the soul.

[1] W. H. Dall, *Alaska and its Resources*, p. 389.

[2] O. Benndorf, *Antike Gesichts-helme und Sepulcralmasken* (Wien, 1878) ; R. Andree, *Ethnographische Parallelen und Vergleiche*, Neue Folge (Leipzig, 1889), pp. 120–134.

Cf. J. Abercromby, " Funeral Masks in Europe ", in *Folklore*, vii. (1896) pp. 351–366.

[3] Albert Kruijt, *s.v.* " Indonesians " in *Encyclopaedia of Religion and Ethics* (Edinburgh, 1914), vol. vii. p. 241.

In the words of Mr. Whitehead, " When the rain-maker is dead, he is plugged, his ears are plugged, his nose is plugged, his eye is plugged, his mouth is plugged, he is plugged, his fingers are plugged. And then he is buried. It is done thus so that . . . the spirits may not go out, so that the son may manage the father so that he obeys (him), so that the spirits obey the son." [1]

Among the Chuwash, a Turkish tribe on the Volga in Russia, it is the custom to stop up the nose, ears, and mouth of a corpse with silk, in order that on his arrival in the spirit land the deceased may be able to say that he has seen and heard nothing of what is going on on earth in the land of the living. The writer who records this custom does not say that the eyes of the dead are stopped up, but that they are so seems to be implied by the reason which he gives for the practice. [2]

[1] C. G. and B. Z. Seligman, *Pagan Tribes of the Nilotic Sudan* (London, 1932), p. 292.

[2] H. Vámbéry, *Das Türkenvolk* (Leipzig, 1885), p. 462.

CHAPTER II

DECEIVING THE GHOST

THUS far we have seen that primitive man has resorted to many contrivances for the purpose of banishing the dreaded spirits of the dead to a safe distance and keeping them there ; but often it appears that all his contrivances are vain. The spirits of the dead break the bounds which he has attempted to impose upon them and they return to their old haunts to plague and torment the living. But even when they do so our primitive man is by no means at the end of his resources. Trusting to that intellectual weakness which he appears to impute to the spirits of the dead, he fancies that he can outwit them and escape their attention even when they are hovering about him in the air. This he thinks he can do, in the first place, by remaining strictly silent after a death, in the hope of thus avoiding the attention of the ghost.

The custom of observing strict silence after a death for the purpose of eluding the attention of the ghost is particularly prevalent among the peoples of the Indian Archipelago, or Indonesia, as the islands are now commonly called. On this subject we may quote the testimony of the Dutch missionary, Dr. Albert C. Kruijt, our highest living authority on the customs and religion of Indonesia. " The Indonesians assume that, when a person has died, his soul is angry at renouncing life on earth. Afterwards it gets used to its new condition, but at first it is in a mood dangerous for the survivors. Therefore great care is recommended for the first few days after a death ; this fear has given rise to the institution of mourning customs. During the first days after a death the inhabitants of a village must keep perfectly quiet. No noise must be made, dancing or singing is forbidden, music must not be heard, rice must not be pounded, nor coconuts thrown down from the trees, nor shots fired ; in fact, they go so far as to forbid fishing, sailing on the water, and carrying goods in the usual way. The intention is that no sound should meet the ear of the soul to indicate the way to its home ; people try to conceal themselves from it. Such injunctions are found among all Indonesian peoples." [1]

A remarkable instance of the silence imposed upon mourners for the sake of eluding the attention of the ghost is furnished by the practice of some Australian widows, who are debarred for a certain time, often for a very long time, from speaking after the deaths of their husbands. In the Warramunga tribe of Central Australia the period of silence

---

[1] A. Kruijt, s.v. "Indonesians", in *Encyclopaedia of Religion and Ethics* (Edinburgh, 1914), vol. vii. p. 241.

imposed on widows extends from one to two years, and curiously enough it is not confined to widows. His mother, his sisters, his daughters, his mother-in-law or mothers-in-law, must all equally be dumb and for the same protracted period. More than that, not only his real wife, real mother, real sisters, and real mothers-in-law are subjected to this rule of silence, but a great many more women whom the natives, on the classificatory principle, reckon in these relationships, though we should not do so, are similarly bound over to hold their tongues, it may be for a year, or it may be for two years. As a consequence it is no uncommon thing in a Warramunga camp to find the majority of women prohibited from speaking. Even when the period of mourning is over, some women prefer to remain silent and to use only the gesture language, in the practice of which they become remarkably proficient. Not seldom, when a party of women are in camp, there will be almost perfect silence, and yet a brisk conversation is all the while being conducted among them on their fingers, or rather with their hands and arms, for many of the signs are made by putting the hands or elbows in varying positions. At Tennant's Creek some years ago there was an old woman who had not opened her mouth, except to eat or drink, for twenty-five years, and who has probably since gone down into the grave without uttering another syllable. A similar ban of silence is imposed on widows for a shorter or longer period among other Australian tribes, such as the Unmatjera, the Kaitish, the

Arunta, and the Dieri.[1] The motive for this silence
imposed upon native Australian widows is not
mentioned by our authorities, but we may safely
suppose that it is a fear of attracting the attention
of the jealous ghosts of their husbands, for a similar
rule of silence is imposed on widows in some Indian
tribes of North America, and in one of them, the
Bella Coola tribe of British Columbia, the reason
assigned for it is a fear of the dead husband's ghost,
who if she broke silence would come and lay his
ghostly hand upon her mouth, and she would die.
In this tribe the period of silence imposed upon
widows lasts only four days.[2] But in the Nishinam
tribe of California the period of silence imposed on
widows lasted for several months, sometimes for a
year or more.[3] A similar custom for widows is
recorded for some parts of Africa. In the Kutu
tribe of the Congo widows observe mourning for
three lunar months. They shave their heads, strip
themselves almost naked, daub their bodies all over
with white clay, and pass the whole of the three
months in the house without speaking.[4] Among
the Sihanaka in Madagascar the observances are
similar, but the period of silence is still longer, and

---

[1] Baldwin Spencer and F.J. Gillen,
*The Northern Tribes of Central
Australia* (London, 1904), pp. 525 *sq.*
and *The Native Tribes of Central
Australia* (London, 1899), pp. 500
sq.; J. G. Frazer, *Folk-Lore in the
Old Testament*, iii. pp. 73-80.

[2] Franz Boas, in Seventh Report
of the Committee on the North-West
Tribes of Canada, *Report of the*

*British Association for the Advance-
ment of Science, Cardiff Meeting,*
1891, p. 13 (separate reprint).

[3] Stephen Powers, *The Tribes of
California* (Washington, 1877), p.
327.

[4] *Notes analytiques sur les col-
lections ethnographiques du Musée
du Congo*, tome i. fascicule 2.
Religion (Brussels, 1906), p. 185.

sometimes for a year. During the whole of that time the widow is stripped of all her ornaments and covered up with a coarse mat, and she is given only a broken spoon and a broken dish to eat out of. She may not wash her face or her hands, but only the tips of her fingers. In this state she remains all day long in the house and may not speak to any one who enters it.[1] We may safely assume that all these observances are intended to render the widow unattractive, and even repulsive, to the jealous ghost of her deceased husband, so that he may not come and annoy her by his unwelcome attentions.[2]

Another case of silence imposed upon the living for the sake of eluding the attention of the dead is the widespread rule which forbids the living to mention the names of the dead for a longer or shorter period after their death, lest the ghost of the deceased should hear and answer to his name. Elsewhere I have cited many examples of this common custom:[3] here it may suffice to illustrate the practice with some instances which I have not quoted in my other work. Thus we are told that the very primitive aborigines of Tasmania had "a fear of pronouncing the name by which a deceased friend was known, as if his shade might thus be offended. To introduce, for any purpose whatever, the name of

---

[1] Rabesikanaka (a native Malagese), "The Sihanaka and their Country", *The Antananarivo Annual and Madagascar Magazine*, Reprint of the first Four Numbers (Antananarivo, 1885), p. 326.

[2] Elsewhere I have treated more

at large the subject of the silence imposed upon widows after the deaths of their husbands. See my *Folk-Lore in the Old Testament*, iii. pp. 71-81.

[3] *The Golden Bough, Taboo*, pp. 349-374.

any one of their deceased relatives called up at once a frown of horror and indignation, from a fear that it would be followed by some dire calamity."[1] A similar custom was observed among the aborigines of New South Wales by one of the earliest voyagers to Australia. He says, " They either bury or burn their dead ; in both cases they commit to the grave or the pile the arms and utensils of the deceased, viz. spears, fishing-tackle, canoes, etc. ; even the very name is consigned to oblivion, which they take care never again to mention : the namesake (*Tomelai*) of the deceased assumes, for a time, the name of *Bourang* ; which appears to be the general appellation for those in such circumstances, and signifies that they are at present destitute of a name, their name-father being dead. This title they retain till they become the namesake of another person."[2] The natives of the Andrawilla tribe on the Diamentina, Herbert, and Eleanor Rivers, in East Central Australia, never mention the names of the dead, believing that their spirits would never rest peacefully if their names were spoken.[3] At Buin, at the extreme south of Bougainville, in the Solomon Islands, the old names of the dead are not pronounced. The departed are referred to by new names, " names of the

[1] J. Barnard, " Aborigines of Tasmania ", in *Report of the Second Meeting of the Australasian Association for the Advancement of Science* (1890), p. 605.

[2] J. Turnbull, *A Voyage Round the World in 1800–1804*, Second Edition (London, 1813), p. 87.

[3] F. H. Wells, " The Habits, Customs, and Ceremonies of the Aboriginals on the Diamentina, Herbert, and Eleanor Rivers, in East Central Australia ", in *Report of the Fifth Meeting of the Australasian Association for the Advancement of Science* (1893), p. 519.

other world," which were usually chosen by the deceased in their lifetime.[1] In Dobu, at the southeast extremity of New Guinea, one cause of war was the naming of the dead, for as a rule the dead might only be named in mighty oaths, or by a sorcerer as a last resort to save the life of a dying man.[2] The Kiwai Papuans of British New Guinea avoid mentioning the names of the dead, in particular of those who have recently died, and are feared after death. They say that to do so would be a way of calling on the ghost, who might respond to the call, and cause sickness. It would be impolite, also, to mention a name which might renew the sorrow and evoke the lamentations of the kinsfolk of the departed.[3] Among the primitive aborigines of the Andaman Islands the names of the dead are not mentioned during the period of mourning, which lasts several months. If it is necessary to refer to a dead person he is spoken of as " he who is buried by the big rock," or " he who is laid in the fig-tree ", or otherwise mentioning the place of burial. There is no objection to mentioning the name in other connections ; for example, if a man were called *Buio*, from the name of a species of *Mucuna*, it is not necessary to avoid the word *buio* when speaking of the plant. Further, if there is

[1] R. Thurnwald, " Im Bismarck-archipel und auf den Salomo-inseln, 1906–1909", *Zeitschrift für Ethnologie*, xlii. (Berlin, 1910), p. 129.

[2] W. E. Bromilow, " Some Manners and Customs of the Dobuans of South-East Papua ", in *Report of the Twelfth Meeting of the Australasian Association for the Advancement of Science* (1909), p. 447.

[3] G. Landtman, *The Kiwai Papuans of British New Guinea* (London, 1927), p. 293.

another person alive of the same name as the dead man it is not necessary to avoid the name in referring to the living individual. The custom is that a dead person must not be spoken of unless it is absolutely necessary, and then must not be spoken of by name. After the period of mourning is over the dead person may again be spoken of by name.[1]

The Yakuts of Siberia never mention the name of a dead person except allegorically, and allow the hut in which a death took place to fall into ruins, believing it to be the habitation of demons.[2]

Among the Malagasy or natives of Madagascar it is prohibited under the pain of sacrilege to pronounce the names which their dead relations and chiefs or kings bore in their lifetime. They fear that if they were to pronounce their names the spirits of the dead would hear and return among them, for they have a great dread of entering into any direct relations with the spirits of the deceased. Only a wicked sorcerer plotting the death of somebody would dare to invoke the names of the dead. Further, among some peoples of Madagascar, such as the Sakalavas, it is forbidden under the gravest penalties to use in current language words which form parts of the names of dead kings, or which have a similar sound, such words being replaced by synonyms created for the purpose.[3]

[1] A. R. Brown, *The Andaman Islanders* (Cambridge, 1922), pp. 111, 121.

[2] M. Sauer, *An Account of a Geographical and Astronomical Expedition to the Northern Parts of Russia in 1785–1794* (London, 1802), p. 125.

[3] J. Grandidier, " La Mort et les funérailles à Madagascar ", in *L'Anthropologie*, xxiii. (Paris, 1912) p. 348.

Among the Banyankole, a pastoral people of Southern Uganda, it is a rule never to mention the name of a dead person, " and a child who inherited property from his father was called ' the father of himself ' : thus, if N died leaving a son L who inherited, L was never called the son of N but ' the father of L ', which made it clear to every one that he possessed property inherited from a dead father ".[1] In the same tribe Mr. Roscoe experienced great difficulty in ascertaining the names of dead kings (*Mugabe*), because the name of a dead king is never pronounced after his death, and moreover if it corresponded with some word in ordinary use, that word was dropped out of the language.[2] Among the Barundi, a Bantu tribe of Tanganyika to the west of Lake Victoria-Nyanza, the name of a dead man is never pronounced for fear of attracting his dangerous and mischievous ghost. All persons and things that bear the same name drop it and take new names.[3] For example, after the death of the eldest son of king Kisabo, named Namagongo, the name of the mountain Magongo was changed to Mukidja. Another son of king Kisabo was named *Mafjuguru* which means *spear*. After his death the name for spear was changed from *mafjuguru* to *itschumu*.[4] Among the Bakongo in the valley of the Congo the name of the dead is taboo and never pronounced, " but if it is necessary to refer to the deceased one, they call him ' old what's his name ' (*nkulu nengandi*) or

[1] J. Roscoe, *The Banyankole* (Cambridge, 1923), pp. 151-152.
[2] J. Roscoe, *op. cit.* p. 35.
[3] H. Meyer, *Die Barundi* (Berlin, 1916), p. 114.
[4] Meyer, *op. cit.* p. 186.

'old Peter' (*nkulu Mpetelo*), or 'of the name of Peter' (*ejina dia Mpetelo*). Any photographs of the deceased are torn up, all signs of him removed from the house, and every effort is made to forget him ".[1] Among the Bechuanas of South Africa the name of a dead person was usually never mentioned after his death, lest his spirit might be offended.[2] Similarly among the Bushmen of South-West Africa when a death took place they shifted their camp and never mentioned the name of the deceased afterwards.[3] With regard to the Tuaregs of North Africa we are told that in spite of their undaunted courage " they hate the idea of death. They do not say of any one who has died, ' he is dead ', but *Aba*, he has disappeared. It is a sign of very bad breeding to speak of a dead relative or even to pronounce his name. He must be alluded to as *mandam*, or such an one." [4] Among the Lengua Indians of Paraguay the name of a dead person is never mentioned, and should it be necessary to refer to him, he is spoken of simply as " he who was ".[5] The funeral rites of these Indians are said to aim chiefly at exorcising the dangerous spirits of the dead.[6]

The Onas, an Indian tribe of Tierra del Fuego, think it improper to mention the name of a dead

---

[1] J. M. Weeks, *Among the Primitive Bakongo* (London, 1914), pp. 248 *sq.*

[2] S. S. Dornan, *Pygmies and Bushmen of the Kalahari* (London, 1925), p. 279.

[3] Dornan, *op. cit.* p. 145.

[4] Lieut. Hourst, *French Enterprise in Africa*, translated by Mrs. Arthur Bell (London, 1898), p. 238.

[5] W. B. Grubb, *An Unknown People in an Unknown Land* (London, 1911), p. 170.

[6] Grubb, *op. cit.* p. 168.

man in the presence of his relations. If it is necessary to refer to him they allude to him as "our friend", or "the friend of our father", in the assurance that the allusion will be understood.[1]

Thus far we have seen that by silence primitive man has sought to elude the hearing of the dangerous spirits of the dead; but he has also attempted to evade their sight. Ancient authors tell us that among the barbarous Sacae mourners used to descend into subterranean chambers or pits to evade the light of the sun; but we may conjecture that the real motive was to avoid the ghost of the deceased.[2]

A traveller who visited the steppes of Astrakhan and the Caucasus in the early part of the nineteenth century tells us that after the death of a prince his nurses were compelled to pull out the hair of the head, eyebrows and eyelashes. They were then put in a perpendicular hole in the ground. The head of each of them was covered with a pot, in which there was a hole. They received food, but being obliged to stay in the hole for several weeks, most of them died.[3] The motive of this strange custom is not mentioned by the traveller; but we may conjecture that the intention was to avoid all contact with the dangerous spirit of the dead prince, with whom in his lifetime as his nurses the women had been in a very intimate relation.

---

[1] C. R. Gallardo, *Los Onas* (Buenos Aires, 1910), pp. 355 *sq.*

[2] Aelianus, *Variae Historiae*, ch. xii. 38; Plutarch, *Consolatio ad Apollonium*, c. xxii.

[3] J. Potocki, *Voyage dans les Steps d'Astrakhan et du Caucase* (Paris, 1829), ii. p. 122.

But in order to escape from the dangerous spirits of the dead, primitive man seeks not only to hide himself but also to disguise himself, so that even if the ghost sees him he will fail to recognize him. This appears to be the true explanation of mourning costume ; it is a disguise to protect the mourner against the observation of the ghost of a recently deceased person, for it is in the period immediately succeeding the death that the ghost is deemed to be particularly dangerous. In this matter the behaviour of the Nicobar Islanders, as described by the excellent observer, Mr. E. H. Man, is especially instructive. He says that in these islands after a death " a man takes a short lighted torch, made of dry coconut leaves, which he waves in all directions inside the hut with the object of driving away any evil spirits that may be lurking therein. With the further object of disguising themselves so that the departed spirits may fail to recognize them, and may do them no mischief, all the mourners shave their heads (*ikōah-kōi*), in addition to which the women shave their eyebrows (*ikōah-puyōl-okmât*), and the men eradicate with tweezers any hairs they may have on their upper lips and chins (*itōsh-enhòin*). It is also common for a mourner, for the same reason, to assume some new name for him- or herself, which, in a great measure, accounts for the fact that some individuals have borne several different names in the course of their lives. This dread of the disembodied spirits of their departed relatives and friends is induced by the conviction that they so keenly desire to return to the scenes and associates of their earthly existence that they are utterly unscrupulous as to the means and methods they adopt for the purpose of attaining their object." [1]   This passage seems to me to furnish a clue to the whole custom of mourning costume ; it is essentially a disguise to protect the living against the spirits of the recently deceased. A good instance of disguise assumed to elude the observation of a recently deceased person is furnished by the Ovaherero, a tribe of South-West Africa.   As described by the Rev. G. Viehe, the custom is as follows.   " Before his death, the man informs his relatives regarding what will happen after his decease.   This may be good (*okusera ondaya ombua*) or bad (*okusera ondaya ombi*).   The last is done in the following manner : If the dying man sees a person who is not agreeable to him, he says to him : ' Whence do you come ?   I do not wish to see you here ' (or something to this effect) ; and so saying, he presses the fingers of his left hand together in such a way that the thumb appears between the fingers.   The man spoken to now knows that the other has decided upon taking him away (*okutuaerera*) after his death, which means that he must die.   In many cases, however, he can avoid this threatening danger of death.   For this purpose, he hastily leaves the place of the dying man, and looks for an *onganga* (*i.e.* ' doctor, magician '), in

[1] E. H. Man, *The Nicobar Islands* (Royal Anthropological Institute, N.D.), pp. 141-142.

order to have himself undressed, washed, and greased again, and dressed with other clothes. He is now quite at ease about the threatening of death caused by the deceased ; for, says he, ' Now our father does not know me ' (*Nambano tate ke ndyi i*). He has no longer any reason to fear the dead." [1]

To confirm the interpretation of mourning costume as a disguise to protect mourners against the dangerous spirits of the dead it may be observed that the customs adopted in mourning are often the very reverse of those which obtain in ordinary life, for this reversal of custom may naturally be explained by the intention of baffling and deceiving the ghost, whose dull wits do not allow him to detect the subterfuge. Whatever may be its explanation, this reversal of custom in mourning was long ago noted by the shrewd and learned Plutarch, whose researches into primitive custom and belief entitle him to be called the Father of Folk-lore. Thus in his valuable treatise called *Roman Questions* he tells us that at a Roman funeral the sons of the deceased walked with their heads covered, the daughters with their heads uncovered, thus exactly reversing the ordinary usage, which was that women wore coverings on their heads while men did not. Further he proceeds to say that similarly in Greece men and women during a period of mourning exactly inverted their habits of wearing the hair—the ordinary practice of men being to cut it short, that of women to wear it long. [2]

[1] G. Viehe, "Some Customs of the Ovaherero", in *Folk-Lore Journal*, vol. i. Part III. (Cape Town) p. 51.

[2] Plutarch, *Quaestiones Romanae*, xiv.

Among the ancient Lycians it was a law that in mourning men should dress as women, thus reversing the usual apparel of the sexes.[1] A similar reversal of custom in mourning has obtained among many primitive peoples. Thus we find that savages who ordinarily paint themselves sometimes refrain from doing so after a death.[2] Again, in similar circumstances, tribes which usually go naked put on certain articles of dress. Thus in some parts of New Guinea, where the men go naked and the women wear only a short grass petticoat, women in mourning wear a net over the shoulders and breast.[3] Elsewhere in New Guinea men also wear netted vests,[4] and in another place " when in deep mourning they envelope themselves with a very tight kind of wicker-work dress, extending from the neck to the knees in such a way that they are not able to walk well."[5] On the other hand, when the Mpongwés in Western Africa are in mourning, a woman wears as few clothes as possible, and a man wears none at all,[6] though the tribe is very fond of dress, the usual garb of a man being a shirt, a square cloth falling to the ankles, and a straw hat.[7]

Whether or not these peculiar costumes (or absence of costume) were meant to disguise the

[1] Plutarch, *Consolatio ad Apollonium*, xxii; Valerius Maximus, ii. 6. 13.

[2] P. F. X. de Charlevoix, *Histoire du Paraguay* (Paris, 1756), i. p. 73.

[3] J. Chalmers and W. W. Gill, *Work and Adventures in New Guinea* (London, 1885), p. 35.

[4] Chalmers and Gill, *op. cit.* p. 130.

[5] Chalmers and Gill, *op. cit.* p. 149.

[6] J. G. Wood, *The Natural History of Man* (London, 1874–1880) i. p. 586.

[7] P. B. Du Chaillu, *Equatorial Africa* (London, 1861), p. 9. Cf. J. L. Wilson, *Western Africa* (London, 1856), c. 19.

wearers of them from the ghost of the deceased, certain it is that disguises have been assumed as a means of deceiving spirits. Thus the Mosquito Indians believe that the devil (Wulasha) tries to get possession of the corpse ; so after they have lulled him to sleep with sweet music " four naked men *who have disguised themselves with paint*, so as not to be recognized by Wulasha, rush out from a neighbouring hut " and drag the body to the grave.[1] At the feast held on the anniversary of the death these same Indians wear cloaks fantastically painted black and white, while their faces are correspondingly streaked with red and yellow, perhaps to deceive the devil. Again in Siberia, when a Shaman accompanies a soul to the underworld, he often paints his face red, expressly that he may not be recognized by the devils.[2] In South Guinea, when a woman is sick she is dressed in a fantastic costume, her face, breast, arms, and legs are painted with streaks of white and red chalk, and her head is decorated with red feathers. Thus arrayed she struts about before the door of the hut brandishing a sword.[3] The intention is doubtless to deceive or intimidate the spirit which is causing the sickness. In Guinea, women in their pregnancy also assume a peculiar attire ; they leave off ornaments, allow their hair to grow, wear peculiar cuffs, and in the last eight days their heads are thickly plastered with red clay,

[1] Bancroft, *The Native Races of the Pacific States of North America*, i. pp. 744 *sq.*

[2] W. Radloff, *Aus Siberien* (Leipsig, 1884), p. 55.

[3] J. L. Wilson, *Western Africa*, c. 28.

which they may not leave off till the child is born.[1]
All this is probably done to disguise the women from
the demons who are commonly supposed to lie in
wait for women at such periods.

The customs of blackening the face or body and
of cutting the hair short after a death are very
widespread. But when we find these customs observed after the death, not of a friend, but of a slain
enemy, as is reported of some Indians of Central
America,[2] no one will pretend that they are intended as marks of sorrow, and the explanation that
they are meant to disguise the slayer from the angry
ghost of the slain may be allowed to stand till a
better is suggested. These disguises are meant to
serve the same purpose as the so-called purification of slayers of men and beasts. In fact " mourning " and " purification " run into each other ; this
" mourning " is not mourning, and this " purification " is not purification. Both are simply pieces of
spiritual armour, defences against ghosts or demons.
In regard to " mourning " costume this appears
clearly in the Myoro custom ; when the child of a
Myoro woman in Africa dies, she smears herself with
butter and ashes and runs frantically about, while
the men abuse her in foul language, for the express
purpose of frightening away the demons who have
carried off the child.[3] If the curses are meant to
frighten, are not the ashes meant to deceive the

[1] J. Klemm, *Allgemeine Cultur-
Geschichte der Menschheit* (Leipzig,
1844), iii. pp. 284-285.
[2] Bancroft, *The Native Races of*
the Pacific States of North America,
i. 764.
[3] J. H. Speke, *Journal of the
Discovery of the Source of the Nile.*

demon ? Here the disguise is adopted as a protection, not against the spirit of the dead, but against the devils which carried it off, and it is possible that the same may be true of " mourning " costume in other cases ; but considering the generally vicious and dangerous nature of ghosts, it is probable that " mourning " costume was usually a protection against them, rather than against devils.

The custom of cutting the hair short after a death has been very common all over the world ; examples would be endless. Here I will cite only a single instance. In the Babar Archipelago of the East Indies, when a corpse is being carried to the grave all the inmates of the houses which the funeral procession passes cut locks of their hair and throw them out of the house.[1] This is probably done as a precaution to prevent the ghost of the deceased from entering the house and molesting the inmates, or carrying their souls off with him to the grave. It may be worth while to notice that the Greeks, not content with cutting short the hair of men in mourning, cut off the manes of their horses on the same occasion, and a similar custom was observed in antiquity by the ancient Persians and in modern times by the Comanche Indians. The Comanches cut off the tails as well as the manes. Possibly the Greeks and Persians did so too, but it is only said that they " shaved " their horses, except in Euripides, where the shaving is distinctly confined to the

---

[1] J. H. F. Riedel, *De Sluik- en Kroesharige Rassen tusschen Selebes en Papua*, p. 362.

manes.[1] The Turkish tribes of Central Asia, after the death of a hero, cut off the tails of all his favourite horses, let them go free for a year, and then sacrifice them on his grave.[2] The opposite custom of letting the hair grow long in mourning is much rarer ; it has been practised by the Egyptians, Jews, Chinese, widows on the Slave Coast, and Hindu sons in mourning for a parent.[3] It is also observed by the Japanese,[4] and in some districts among the Ainos.[5] Among the Birhors, a primitive jungle tribe of Chota Nagpur, when a death has taken place in a settlement, no man in the settlement will shave for seven days.[6] The Nairs of Southern India do not shave or cut the hair for a year in mourning.[7] With regard to some of the Indians of Canada we are told by an old Jesuit missionary that when a man had lost a kinsman by death he used to allow his hair to grow long in sign of mourning.[8] Among the Angoni of British Central Africa women usually shave their heads, but in times of sorrow and trouble, and therefore no doubt in mourning, they allow the hair to

---

[1] Euripides, *Alcestis*, 429 ; Plutarch, *Pelopidas*, 33 ; *Alexander*, 72 ; *Aristides*, 14 ; Herodotus, ix. 24 ; Bancroft, *op. cit.* i. 523.

[2] H. Vámbéry, *Das Türkenvolk* (Leipzig, 1885), p. 250.

[3] For Egyptians see Herodotus, ii. 36 ; for Jews, J. Buxtorf, *Synagoga Judaica* (Bâle, 1661), p. 706, and Bodenschatz, *Kirchliche Verfassung der heutigen Juden*, iv. 179 ; for Chinese, J. H. Gray, *China* (London, 1878), i. 286 ; for Slave Coast, P. Bouche, *La Côte des Esclaves et le Dahomey*, p. 218 *sq.* ; for Hindus, S. C. Bose, *The Hindus as They Are* (London and Calcutta, 1881), p. 254.

[4] *Manners and Customs of the Japanese in the Nineteenth Century* (London, 1841), p. 197.

[5] B. Scheube, *Die Ainos* (Yokohama), p. 22.

[6] S. C. Roy, *The Birhors* (Ranchi, 1925), p. 265. According to another account the period of abstinence from shaving is ten days. E. T. Dalton, *Descriptive Ethnology of Bengal* (Calcutta, 1872), p. 220

[7] S. Maheer, *Native Life in Travancore*, p. 173.

[8] *Relations des Jésuites* for 1646, p. 48.

grow. In both men and women, the dirtier they are, the deeper the mourning.[1] The Oigób, a tribe of Masai in East Africa, may not cut their hair for two months after a death. In the third month, on the sixth day after the new moon, the relations, both men and women, cut off the hair of their head and all the rest of their hair, go out before the village, kill several oxen, and eat the flesh in one day.[2] When Mutesa, king of Uganda, died, " the whole country went into mourning, and every one allowed his hair to grow." [3] In ordinary mourning the Hovas of Madagascar let their hair and beards grow. But in mourning for a sovereign the people shave their heads.[4] Among the Chewsurs of the Caucasus men in mourning do not shave.[5] It is reported that in New Caledonia when a man has buried a corpse he allows his beard and hair to grow, and covers his hair with a sort of turban. He never uncovers it, and if he were seen by a woman arranging his hair he would have to perform ablutions in the depths of the forest.[6] In Sardinia the men do not shave for a year after the death of their wives,[7] and in Corsica men in mourning often let their beards

[1] W. M. Kerr, " Journey from Cape Town overland to Lake Nyassa ", in *Proceedings of the Royal Geographical Society*, MS. viii (1886), p. 81.

[2] J. M. Hildebrandt, " Ethnographische Notizen über Wakamba und ihre Nachbarn ", *Zeitschrift für Ethnologie*, x. (1878) p. 405.

[3] R. P. Ashe, *Two Kings of Uganda* (London, 1889), p. 79.

[4] A. Grandidier, " Des rites funéraires chez les Malagaches ", in *Revue d'Ethnographie*, iv. (1885) p. 229.

[5] J. Radde, *Die Chews' uren und ihr Land* (Cassel, 1878), p. 91.

[6] Ch. Lemire, *Voyage à pied en Nouvelle-Calédonie* (Paris, 1884), p. 117.

[7] R. Tennant, *Sardinia and its Resources* (Rome and London, 1885), p. 236.

grow for a long time.[1] We have already seen that
in ancient Greece the men but not the women allowed
their hair to grow long in mourning.[2]

Among many peoples ancient and modern the
custom of cutting the hair short in mourning has
often been accompanied by the laceration of the
body of the mourner in a great variety of ways ;
but there appears to be little or no evidence that this
laceration of the body is designed to deceive the
ghost of the dead by rendering the person of the
mourner unrecognizable. On the contrary there is
some evidence to show that the laceration is intended
to please the ghost of the deceased by proving to
him the sincerity and depth of the mourners' grief.
The Australian evidence in particular points in
this direction. For example among the Arunta of
Central Australia if a man does not cut himself
sufficiently in honour of his dead father-in-law
his wife will be given away to another man in
order to appease the angry ghost of his deceased
father-in-law.[3] Elsewhere I have discussed the
two customs, often conjoined, of cutting the hair
and lacerating the body of the mourner, and
must refer the reader to my discussion for fuller
details.[4]

But the attempts of primitive man to deceive the

<hr/>

[1] F. Gregorovius, *Corsica*, translated by R. Martineau (London,
1855), p. 283.

[2] See above, p. 51. On mourning
costumes cf. my essay " On Certain
Burial Customs as illustrative of the
Primitive Theory of the Soul ", in

Garnered Sheaves (London, 1931),
pp. 42-46.

[3] Spencer and Gillen, *Native
Tribes of Central Australia*, p. 500.

[4] *Folk-Lore in the Old Testament*,
vol. iii. pp. 270-303.

spirits of the dead are by no means limited to the assumption of mourning costume, if that indeed be, as I have suggested, the true explanation of the peculiar garb assumed by mourners. He has many other artful dodges by which he hopes to take advantage of that guilelessness and simplicity of mind which he commonly imputes to the spirits of the departed. One of these consists in the use of effigies which he attempts to palm off upon the spirits as substitutes for the living person, hoping that the threatening spirit will not notice the difference, but will accept the effigy and spare the person. Thus for example in Tahiti after a death the priest who performed the funeral rites took a number of small slips of plantain leaf-stalk, fixed two or three pieces under each arm of the corpse, placed a few on the breast, and then, addressing the dead body, said, " There are your family, there is your child, there is your wife, there is your father, and there is your mother. Be satisfied yonder (that is, in the world of the spirits). Look not towards those who are left in this world."—" The concluding parts of the ceremony were designed to impart contentment to the departed, and to prevent the spirit from repairing to the places of his former resort, and so distressing the survivors." [1] When the Galelareese of Halmahera, an island to the west of New Guinea, bury a corpse, they inter with it the stem of a banana-tree

---

[1] W. Ellis, *Polynesian Researches*, Second Edition (London, 1832), i. 402. With this and what follows compare my exposition of the same subject in *The Golden Bough : Spirits of the Corn and of the Wild*, vol. ii. pp. 97 *sqq.*, which I here closely follow.

for company, in order that the ghost of the dead person may not seek a companion among the living.[1] Just as the coffin is being lowered into the earth, one of the bystanders steps up and throws a young banana-tree into the grave, saying, " Friend, you must miss your companions of this earth ; here, take this as a comrade ". Thus in the Banks Islands, Melanesia, " the ghost of a *vasisgona*, a woman who has died in childbed, cannot go to Panoi " (the spirit land) " if her child lives, for she cannot leave her child. They therefore deceive her ghost by making up loosely a piece of a banana trunk in leaves, and laying it on her bosom when she is buried. Then, as she departs, she thinks she has the child with her ; as she goes the banana stalk slips about in the leaves and she thinks the child is moving ; and this in her bewildered new condition contents her, till she gets to Panoi and finds that she has been deceived. In the meanwhile the child has been taken to another house, because they know that the mother will come back to take its soul. She seeks everywhere for the child in grief and rage without ceasing ; and the ghost of a *vasisgona* therefore is particularly dreaded." [2] In the Pelew Islands, when a woman has died in childbed, her spirit comes and cries, " Give me the child ! " So to deceive her they bury the stem of a young banana-tree with her body, cutting it short and laying it between her

[1] M. J. van Baarda, " Fabelen, verhalen en Overleveringen der Galelareezen ", in *Bijdragen tot de Taal- Land- en Volkenkunde van* *Nederlandsch-Indië*, xlv. (1895) p. 539.

[2] R. H. Codrington, *The Melanesians* (Oxford, 1891), p. 275.

right arm and her breast.[1] The same device is
adopted for the same purpose in the East Indian
island of Timor.[2] In the Niger delta when a
woman has died in childbed a piece of a plantain
stem is forced into the womb of her dead body to
make her fancy that she has her child with her in
the spirit land and so to prevent her ghost from
coming back to claim the living child.[3] Among the
Yorubas of West Africa, when one of twins dies, the
mother carries about, along with the surviving child
a small wooden figure roughly fashioned in human
shape and of the sex of the dead twin. This figure
is intended not merely to keep the live child from
pining for its lost comrade, but also to give the
spirit of the dead child something into which it can
enter without disturbing its little brother or sister.[4]
Among the Tschwi of West Africa a lady observed
a sickly child with an image beside it which she
took for a doll. But it was no doll; it was an effigy
of the child's dead twin which was being kept near
the survivor as a habitation for the little ghost, lest
it should wander homeless and, feeling lonely, call
its companion away after it to the spirit land.[5]
Among the Wajagga, a tribe of the great mountain

[1] J. Kubary, "Die Religion der Pelauer", in A. Bastian's *Allerlei aus Volks- und Menschenkunde* (Berlin, 1888), i. p. 9.

[2] W. M. Donselaar, "Aanteekeningen over het eiland Saleijer", in *Mededeelingen van wege het Nederlandsche Zendlinggenootschap*, i. (1857) p. 290.

[3] Le Comte C. N. de Cardi, " Juju laws and customs in the Niger Delta ", in *Journal of the Anthropological Institute*, xxix. (1899) p. 58.

[4] A. B. Ellis, *The Yoruba-Speaking Peoples of the Slave Coast of West Africa* (London, 1894), p. 80.

[5] Miss Mary H. Kingsley, *Travels in West Africa* (London, 1879), p. 473.

Kilimanjaro in East Africa, it is believed that when a woman dies in childbed her affectionate ghost will return to fetch away her living child with her to the spirit land. So to prevent this from happening they place the shoot of a banana tree in the lap of her corpse when they bury it, hoping that her ghost will accept this substitute and leave her living child in peace.[1]

In San Cristoval, one of the Solomon Islands, there is a very curious custom called *ha'a ariro* or misleading the ghost. When the canoe containing the corpse is carried out of the house, all the children walk under it and back again while it is lifted high up. " Another form of puzzling the ghost, so that it will forget a child and not haunt him, is to take the young nut of a coconut and slice it in two, and then the same with another nut. Then take half of each nut and join them together and put this made-up nut under the right armpit of the dead. The ghost will be so puzzled and taken up with trying to fit together the two halves of what he supposes to be one nut that he will not haunt his child. On the south coast of Arosi half a *reremo* fruit and half a young coconut are thus joined ; in the bush half the fruit of *ahuhu* and half a canarium nut. But the idea is the same." [2] In Ulawa, another of the Solomon Islands, the bodies of the dead are usually taken out in a canoe, and thrown into the sea, weighted with a stone, so as to sink them to the bottom. When this has been done the canoes paddle four or six times round the spot, in order to puzzle the ghost should he seek to follow them.[1] Among the Melanesians of the South-East Solomon Islands, when one of a pair of twins died, a coconut was placed beside the living twin to deceive the ghost of his dead brother or sister, and the coconut was spoken of as " your brother " or " your sister ".[2] In Fiji " the spirits of women who die in childbirth, or before the child is weaned, are greatly dreaded, especially if the child were not born in wedlock. It is a common custom to lay upon the breast of such a woman a piece of a banana stem wrapped in native cloth, and to bury it with her. This is done to cheat her into the belief that it is her baby which she has lying on her breast. The child in the meanwhile is carried secretly to a distant town, that its dead mother may be unable to find it if she discovers the cheat. Other precautions also are taken. In some places bits of bamboo are strung loosely on a cord and fastened to the wrists of a corpse, so that by their rattling they may give warning of her approach if she takes to walking by night. Elsewhere the poor woman is buried with her *liku* or waist-fringe untied, that it may fall down when she rises, and the wretched ghost may be thereby compelled to sit down again with shame and confusion of face.

" In several parts of Fiji, when an old man dies a curious custom is observed. Before the body is carried forth to the burial, it is either lifted up by

[1] C. E. Fox, *op. cit.* pp. 256-257.
[2] W. G. Ivens, *Melanesians of the* *South-East Solomon Islands* (London, 1927), p. 77.

the bearers or laid upon a raised platform. A man (the brother of the child's mother) then takes the son's son of the deceased, passes him rapidly several times hither and thither, and under and over the corpse, and then runs away with him at top speed. This is done in order to bewilder the old gentleman as to the direction in which the child is taken away, it being supposed that he will be very desirous to have his grandson with him where he is, and will therefore seek to kill him. A like custom is observed when the father dies ; but it is the father's father who is especially dreaded, for it is supposed that the relationship between the paternal grandfather and his grandchild is closer than that which exists between the child and his father. This idea can be clearly traced to the former prevalence of descent through females, which indeed is still the rule among some of the Fijian tribes." [1]

Some of the aborigines in Northern Queensland, like many other Australian tribes, deposit their dead on stages at a distance from the camp. Having done so they bark the trees in the neighbourhood so as to make a false trail leading back to the stage where the corpse is lying. This is done in order to lead the wandering spirit of the dead back to his body on the stage, and to prevent him from following his friends back to their camp. [2]

---

[1] L. Fison, " Notes on Fijian Burial Customs ", in *Journal of the Royal Anthropological Institute*, x. (1881) p. 145 ; *id.* L. Fison, *Tales of Old Fiji* (London, 1904), pp. 168 *sq.*

[2] J. C. Muirhead, quoted by Howitt in *Journal of the Royal Anthropological Institute*, xiii. (1884) p. 191.

The Kai tribe of Northern New Guinea often think that a death among them has been caused by the enchantments of a wicked sorcerer in a neighbouring village, and they send out a warlike expedition to take vengeance on him and his village. Sometimes, instead of sending forth a band of warriors to ravage, burn, and slaughter the whole male population of the village in which the wicked sorcerer resides, the people of one village will come to a secret understanding with the people of the sorcerer's village to have the miscreant quietly put out of the way. A hint is given to the scoundrel's next of kin, it may be his brother, son, or nephew, that if he will only wink at the slaughter of his obnoxious relative, he will receive a handsome compensation from the slayers. Should he privately accept the offer, he is most careful to conceal his connivance at the deed of blood, lest he should draw down on his head the wrath of his murdered kinsman's ghost. So, when the deed is done and the murder is out, he works himself up into a state of virtuous sorrow and indignation, covers his head with the leaves of a certain plant, and chanting a dirge in tones of heart-rending grief, marches straight to the village of the murderers. There, on the public square, surrounded by an attentive audience, he opens the floodgates of his eloquence and pours forth the torrents of an aching heart. " You have slain my kinsman," says he, " you are wicked men ! How could you kill so good a man, who conferred so many benefits on me in his lifetime ? I knew nothing of the plot. Had I had an inkling of it, I would have foiled it. How can I now avenge his death? I have no property with which to hire men of war to go and punish his murderers. Yet in spite of everything my murdered kinsman will not believe in my innocence! He will be angry with me; he will pay me out; he will do me all the harm he can. Therefore do you declare openly whether I had any share whatever in his death, and come and strew lime on my head in order that he may convince himself of my innocence." This appeal of injured innocence meets with a ready response. The people dust the leaves on his head with powdered lime; and so, decorated with the white badge of spotless virtue, and enriched with a boar's tusk or other valuable object as the price of his compliance, he returns to his village with a conscience at peace with all the world, reflecting with satisfaction on the profitable transaction he has just concluded, and laughing in his sleeve at the poor deluded ghost of his murdered relative.

Sometimes the worthy soul who thus for a valuable consideration consents to waive all his personal feelings, will even carry his self-abnegation so far as to be present and look on at the murder of his kinsman. But true to his principles he will see to it that the thing is done decently and humanely. When the struggle is nearly over and the man is down, writhing on the grass with the murderers busy about him, his loving kinsman will not suffer them to take an unfair advantage of their superior numbers to cut him up alive with their knives, to chop him with their axes, or to smash him with their clubs. He will only allow them to stab him with their spears, repeating of course the stabs again and again till the victim ceases to writhe and quiver, and lies there dead as a stone. Then begins the real time of peril for the virtuous kinsman who has been a spectator and director of the scene ; for the ghost of the murdered man has now deserted its mangled body, and, still blinded with blood and smarting with pain, might easily and even excusably misunderstand the situation. It is essential, therefore, in order to prevent a painful misapprehension, that the kinsman should at once and emphatically disclaim any part or parcel in the murder. This he accordingly does in language which leaves no room for doubt or ambiguity. He falls into a passion ; he rails at the murderers ; he proclaims his horror at their deed. All the way home he refuses to be comforted. He upbraids the assassins, he utters the most frightful threats against them ; he rushes at them to snatch their weapons from them and dash them in pieces. But they easily wrench the weapons from his unresisting hands. For the whole thing is only a piece of acting. His sole intention is that the ghost may see and hear it all, and being convinced of the innocence of his dear kinsman may not punish him with bad crops, wounds, sickness, and other misfortunes. Even when he has reached the village, he keeps up the comedy for a time, raging, fretting, and fuming at the irreparable loss he has sustained by the death of his lamented relative.

Similarly when a chief has among his subjects a particular sorcerer whom he fears, but with whom he is professedly on terms of friendship, he will sometimes engage a man to murder him. No sooner, however, is the murder perpetrated than the chief who bespoke it hastens in seeming indignation with a band of followers to the murderer's village. The assassin, of course, has got a hint of what is coming, and he and his friends take care not to be at home when the chief arrives on his mission of vengeance. Balked by the absence of their victim the avengers of blood breathe out fire and slaughter, but content themselves in fact with smashing an old pot or two, knocking down a deserted hut, and perhaps felling a banana-tree or a betel-palm. Having thus given the ghost of the murdered man an unequivocal proof of the sincerity of their friendship, they return quietly home.[1]

Among the Sea Dyaks of Borneo, when a death has taken place in a village, the body, wrapped in mats and covered over with a light framework of wood, is carried out of the house on the shoulders of four men. As they descend the house-ladder, ashes from the fire burnt near the corpse are thrown after them by the people who are left in the house. This is done in order that the dead man's ghost may not

---

[1] Ch. Keysser, "Aus dem Leben der Kaileute", in R. Neuhauss, *Deutsch Neu Guinea* (Berlin, 1911), iii. pp. 148-149. Cf. J. G. Frazer, *Belief in Immortality*, i. pp. 280-282. In the text I have reproduced my English version from the latter work.

know his way back to the house, and may thus be unable to trouble his friends afterwards.[1] This Dyak custom has been described by a Dyak in his native language. His account, as translated by an English missionary, runs thus : " The burial takes place in the early hours of the morning, at the first sign of twilight. As soon as the corpse is carried away from the house ashes are strewn over the footprints of the bearers. These ashes are supposed to prevent the soul of the deceased from finding its way back again to the house, should it desire to return and haunt the living."[2] From this we see that a returning ghost is believed to follow the tracks of the bearers who carried his body from the house to its last resting-place. That is why it is necessary to conceal the footprints of the bearers by ashes or otherwise.

Among the Tungus, a people of Siberia, on returning from a funeral ceremony the mourners try to efface the footprints they have made in the snow, or else cut down trees so that they fall across the way, in order to prevent the return of the ghost.[3] In this case the effacing of the footprints is an alternative to blocking the path by the trunks of fallen trees. The custom of erecting physical barriers to prevent the return of the ghost has been illustrated in a former part of this work.[4]

[1] E. H. Gomes, *Seventeen Years among the Sea Dyaks of Borneo* (London, 1911), pp. 135-136.

[2] Leo Nyuak, " Religious Rites and Customs of the Iban or Dyaks of Sarawak ", translated by Very Rev. Edm. Dunn, in *Anthropos*, i. (1906) p. 669.

[3] M. A. Czaplicka, *Aboriginal Siberia* (Oxford, 1914), pp. 155-156, referring to Mordvinoff, *The Natives of the Turukhansk Country*.

[4] *The Fear of the Dead in Primitive Religion*, ii. pp. 27-52.

In ancient India, when a corpse was carried to the pyre, a branch was tied to the body in such a way that it brushed and effaced the footprints of the bearers in order that death, or rather the ghost of the dead man, might not find his way back to the house.[1]

In South Nias, an island off the west coast of Sumatra, the corpse is coffined outside of the village, in order that the spirit of the dead may not find its way back to the village to fetch somebody there. For this reason there is, also in North Nias, no regular path to the cemeteries, but on each occasion of a burial a path is cleared to the cemetery.[2]

Among the Karens, a tribe of Burma, when a corpse has been burned on the pyre they bring back the skull and the bones of the arms and legs to the house. After that they adopt a sort of inverted form of action and speech. They winnow some rice on a sieve turned upside down and, addressing the spirit of the dead, they say, " See, it is necessary to clean the rice before cooking it." Then they set it beside the bones of the deceased. Next the priest takes the skull in his hands and, showing it a vessel of water, says, " If you are cold, bathe yourself " ; and showing it next burning coals, says, " If you are warm, heat yourself." And in addressing the ghost he adopts an inverted form of speech in which everything is designated by a name the reverse of

[1] H. Oldenberg, *Die Religion des Veda* (Berlin, 1894), p. 573.
[2] N. C. Rappard, " Het eiland Nias en zijne Bewoners ", in *Bij-dragen tot de Taal- Land- en Volkenkunde van Nederlandsch-Indië*, lxii. (1909) p. 573.

the real one. Thus he calls the north the south, and the south the north, and he calls the west the east, and the east the west. He speaks of the sky as the earth, and of the earth as the sky. In his speech the trees have their roots in the air and their branches in the earth. All this the priest does, as the missionary who reports the custom rightly thought, for the purpose of so confusing the ghost that he will not wander and trouble the survivors. At the conclusion of his address the priest places the skull and the bones in a miniature house or reliquary, in which it is apparently hoped that the spirit of the dead will continue to reside peaceably.[1]

Among the Palaungs of Burma a very curious mode of deceiving the ghost of a dead child has been recorded by an excellent observer, Mrs. Leslie Milne. She says : " The following is a very gruesome way of making an amulet. When a woman dies with her child unborn, she is rolled in a mat and buried as soon as possible. In the evening of the same day the man who wished to make the amulet goes with three or four other men to the grave where the woman has been buried. It would be in a lonely place, far from the graves of others, for it is believed that people who have died a violent death, or on whom great misfortunes have fallen, must have committed some terrible crime in their last existence to come to such a terrible end. When the man (who wishes to have the amulet) and his

[1] J. B. Bringaud, " Un chapitre de l'ethnographie des Birmans Karins ", in *Missions Catholiques*, xxviii. (1896) p. 521.

friends reach the grave, they first make a little shrine of grass or bamboo; then they stick a few flowers and flags of paper into it and set a bunch of bananas before it. These offerings are to appease the spirit of the dead woman. Stripping himself absolutely naked, the man then goes to the grave and digs out the earth until he reaches the mat in which the body of the dead woman is rolled. This he cuts open, then he operates on the body of the woman so as to be able to bite off the little finger of the unborn child. Having done this, he hurriedly replaces the mat, and shovels in the earth to fill up the grave. His companions, who have brought sticks with them, now give him a severe beating, to show that they are not to blame for what their companion has done, and also to make the spirit of the dead woman believe that the man who has violated her grave is being well punished for his temerity. They then withdraw, and the man dresses himself and goes home, carrying with him the little finger of the baby. He makes a large fire in the entrance-room of his house and sits as near to it as possible, as a Palaung woman would sit who had recently given birth to a child. He wraps himself in a blanket so that his clothes are hidden. He does this in order to make the child's ghost—if it has followed him to the house—believe that he is its mother. He has previously prepared cooked rice and bananas. In the middle of the night—as Palaungs believe—the ghost of the baby comes into the room to demand its finger. It is appeased at intervals all through the night by offerings of rice and bananas. The ghost is supposed to come for seven nights, and each night a fresh offering of rice and bananas is made. The seven days being over, it is hoped that the child's spirit has gone to eat the fruit of forgetfulness, or has become a *kar-man* in the jungle, therefore no more offerings are made to it. The man then gilds the finger, and Palaungs say that any one at whom he points it—especially a girl whom he loves—can refuse him nothing."[1]

Often in funerals the bearers of the corpse, in carrying it to the grave or the pyre, perform certain strange evolutions, for the purpose of so confusing the spirit of the dead that he will not be able to find his way back to his old home. Thus, for example, among the Chams of Indo-China, who burn their dead, "when at length the great day arrives the priests construct a catafalque adorned with paper figures, the mourners line up in procession behind, and all proceed to the appointed place. Every villager dons his white scarf—white being the colour of mourning—brandishes a spear, sword, or flag, and joins in the cortège. The bearers perform the most remarkable evolutions with the body, carrying it now feet first, now head first, or turning it round and round in order to confuse the spirit and prevent it from finding its way back. This essential object is also secured by a priest, known on

[1] Mrs. Leslie Milne, *The Home of an Eastern Clan* (Oxford, 1924), p. 266. In the Palaung language *kar-man* denotes a spirit of the dead inhabiting a tree, water, air, earth or stone : see Mrs. Leslie Milne, *op. cit.* p. 342.

these occasions as *Po Damôeun* or ' Lord of Sorrow ', who remains in the house of the deceased shuts himself in, and calls on every object, animate and inanimate, to prevent the soul from entering and molesting the living ".[1] At a funeral in Burma, when a corpse is being carried to the pyre to be burnt, the bearers of the bier engage in grotesque dances, sometimes allowing it to advance, and sometimes to recede, as if its possession were being contested ; and at the pyre, before they lay the coffin on the wood, they sway it backwards and forwards seven times before the sacred *Bo* tree.[2] The writers who describe this ceremony do not explain the reasons for the grotesque dances and other movements of the bearers ; but probably their motive was the usual one of confusing the ghost, and so preventing his return. Among the Bataks of Sumatra, before carrying a corpse out of a house, the bearers first walk backwards and forwards several times, as if to confuse the dead and prevent him from finding his way back again.[3] In the Adelaide tribe of the Australian aborigines, when a man dies " a rude bier is prepared by fastening together ten or twelve branches, so as to form the radii of a circle ; and, when the body is lifted upon this bier, the ground upon which the man died is dug up by his wives or women related to him, with their long

---

[1] Commandant Baudesson, *Au pays des superstitions et des rites* (Paris), p. 249 ; Captain H. Baudesson, *Indo-China and its Primitive People*, p. 313. I quote from the English translation.

[2] M. and B. Ferrars, *Burma* (London, 1900), p. 195.

[3] J. Freiherr von Brenner, *Besuch bei den Kannibalen Sumatras* (Würzburg, 1894), p. 235.

sticks, occasionally assisted by the men. A little heap of earth is thus formed, supposed to contain the ' wingko ', or breath that has left the body, and which this digging is intended to set free. While this is being done, the bier is raised upon the shoulders of several men, each one taking a branch, and some facing one way, others another. They move slowly off from the spot, stopping at intervals, and performing a quick rotatory motion in one direction, and, when they can do so no longer, in the opposite one. All this while a man stands under the centre of the bier, assisting to support it with his head ; and, after each rotation, he addresses the deceased, asking him how and why he died, who killed him, etc. The group of men surrounding the bier and its supporters are all armed with their spears and other weapons, and the women carry their long sticks and bags. Sometimes the bearers move forward as if by a consentaneous impulse, and, at others, one of the bystanders beckons to a spot to which the body is immediately borne, and the rotations are repeated. Even the presence of the feather of some rare bird upon the ground will attract their attention to that particular place, and the circumvolutions will there be renewed with increased energy. If there happens to be large trees in the neighbourhood, they walk quickly up to one and then another, resting the bier against them ; and, on every such occasion, the deceased is interrogated as before. Between every act of rotation, their march is more extended ; so that they thus by degrees proceed farther from the place where the death occurred, until at last they walk off altogether to a distant locality, in which it is resolved to bury the body ; the ceremony occasionally continuing more than one day. The place of burial being fixed upon, the earth or sand is loosened by the digging-sticks, and thrown out by the hands ; the body is laid in the grave on one side, and the hole being filled up again, is usually covered with branches and bark of trees ".[1] The writer who describes these burial rites does not explain the motive for the rotations and other odd behaviour of the bearers ; but probably we shall not err in supposing that their aim is to lure the spirit of the dead far away from his old home, and so to bewilder him on his last journey that he will never find his way back to trouble his family and friends.

The peasants of Ho-nan, in China, fear the ghosts of young children even more than the ghosts of grown men, for when they die children receive no ancestral honours in the domestic shrine, and accordingly their ghosts are angry and seek to avenge themselves on their family by killing the cattle or the fish on which the people live. However, their relations have a mode of guarding themselves against these dangerous spirits. When a child is sick, and at the point of death, they expose or drown or bury the little sufferer, and the man who carries the dying child to its last home is careful not to walk

[1] W. Wyatt, " Some Account of the Manners and Customs of the Adelaide and Encounter Bay Tribes ", in *The Native Tribes of South Australia* (Adelaide, 1879), pp. 164-165.

in a straight line. He moves in a zigzag, going and returning, pacing now to the east and now to the west, describing a confusion of triangles, in order that in this labyrinth of broken lines the ghost of the child may never be able to trace its way home. So the family in the house are quite at their ease, thinking that they will never be troubled by the depredation of their child's ghost on the domestic cattle and fish.[1]

The Koryaks, a primitive tribe in the extreme north-east of Siberia, burn their dead, and when they have placed a body on the pyre they take measures to prevent the dangerous spirit of the deceased from following them back to the house. Mr. Jochelson, who witnessed the cremation of a girl's body, has described their precautions as follows : " When the clothes were burned, and the child's head appeared, her grandfather took a pole, and, thrusting it into the body, said, 'Of yonder magpie pricked ' (*A'nalan vaki'tha ti'npinen*) ; or, in a free translation, ' This is the magpie of the underworld which pricked '. He imitated the actions of the magpie of the world of the dead, in order to inform the deceased that she was passing to another world, and must not return to the house. The further actions of the dead girl's grandfather had the same end in view. When the flames of the pyre were dying away, he broke some twigs from the alder and willow bushes that were growing near by,

[1] A letter of the missionary Delaplace, dated Moncy-te-Fou, 25 September 1851, in *Annales de la* *Propagation de la Foi*, xxiv. (1852) pp. 250 *sqq.*

and strewed them around the pyre. These twigs represented a dense forest which was supposed to surround the burning-place. We left the place while the pyre was still burning. Before leaving, the grandfather went around the pyre, first from right to left, them from left to right, in order so to obscure his tracks that the deceased would not be able to follow him. Then, stepping away from the pyre towards the houses, he drew with his stick a line in the snow, jumped across it, and shook himself. The others followed his example. The line was supposed to represent a river which separated the village from the burning-place. All these actions are identical with episodes in the tales of the ' magic flight '. After being taken out of the house, the deceased is apparently regarded as a spirit hostile to the living." [1]

Often the bearers of a corpse, before they convey the body to the grave or pyre, walk or run with it at full speed round the house, in order to confuse the spirit of the dead, and thus to prevent him from returning to his old dwelling. Thus, for example, in Siam the bearers carry the coffin thrice round the house, running at full speed, for they believe that if they did not take this precaution, the spirit of the dead would recall the road by which he had passed, and would return during the night to play some mischievous prank upon his family.[2] In

[1] Waldemar Jochelson, *The Kor-yaks* (Memoir of the American Museum of Natural History: The Jesup North Pacific Expedition) (Leiden and New York, 1905), i. p. 112.

[2] " Lettre de Mgr. Bruguière, évêque de Capse, à M. Bousquet,

Minahassa, a district in the north of the island of
Celebes, before a corpse is carried to the grave, it is
borne thrice round the house where the death took
place. The bearers who carry it walk or run at a
quick pace, with comic gestures which excite the
amusement rather than the sorrow of the spectators.
The corpse is seated on a chair placed on the bier,
and if the deceased was a mother one of her daughters will sit on the bier with bells fastened to her
body which jingle with the movements of the bier.
The jingle of the bells may be intended to hasten the
departure of the mother's ghost to the spirit land.[1]

Among some of the Indians of Bolivia, when a
death has taken place in a house, it is customary to
shift the door to the other side of the house in order
that the returning ghost may not be able to find it,
and to effect an entrance into the dwelling.[2] A
similar precaution to baffle a returning ghost is
reported from various parts of Africa. After a
death has taken place, and the body has been
buried, the Barundi of Tanganyika adopt various
precautions to prevent the return of the dreaded
ghost. In the hut where the death occurred they
shift the entrance to the other side of the hut, renew

---

vicaire-général d'Aire ", in *Annales
de la Propagation de la Foi*,v. (1831)
p. 174. Cf. Mgr. Pallegoix, *Description du royaume Thai ou Siam*
(Paris, 1854), p. 245, and E. Young,
The Kingdom of the Yellow Robe,
p. 246.
[1] " Een blik op de Minahassa ",
in *Tijdschrift voor Nederlandsch-
Indië*, 1845, Part IV, p. 330 ; N.

Graafland, *De Minahassa* (Rotterdam, 1867), i. p. 331.

[2] *Exploraciones y noticias hidro-
graficas de los Rios del Norte de
Bolivia* : Segunda Parte (La Paz,
1890), p. 20. Cf. Chr. Nusser-Asport,
" Padre Armentias Reise in den
Bolivianischen Provinz Caupolican ",
in *Globus*, lx. (1891) p. 120.

the hearthstone, and move the place of the bed and all the other furniture in the hut, all no doubt to deceive the ghost so that even if he returned to the hut he could not recognize his old dwelling.[1] A similar precaution taken by some of the Kafirs of South Africa is reported by Mr. Dudley Kidd. He says : " Another strange case was told me. At the funeral of a small child the people buried the blankets and ornaments used by the child, and then went and fetched the door of the hut in which the baby had lived. This also they buried, substituting a new door for the old one ; they said they did so to bamboozle the spirit of the baby. When it came wandering round at night it would find a new door on the hut, and would think it had made a mistake ; whereupon it would wander about until it found the old familiar door in the earth, and it would then settle down contentedly, and not trouble the people in the kraal."[2]

A common, almost a world-wide way of deceiving a ghost, is to carry his body out of the house, not by the door, but through a special opening in a wall of the house, which is immediately afterwards closed up. The belief seems to be that the returning ghost can enter his old home only through the opening by which his body was carried out, so that when he arrives at the opening and finds it blocked up he is puzzled, and being unable to find the door he cannot enter the house. A custom of this kind has been

[1] H. Meyer, *Die Barundi*, p. 114.

[2] Dudley Kidd, *The Essential Kafir* (London, 1904), p 251.

reported from many parts of the world, both in ancient and modern times, and the explanation of it which has just been given is assigned for it by many of the peoples who practise it. But sometimes the true original reason is forgotten and a mistaken reason substituted for it. In the east, where the houses are often raised above the ground on piles, the corpse is often passed through a hole in the floor instead of through a hole in the wall, but the intention is the same. Sometimes it is not all the dead who are thus carried out, but only the remains of those whose ghosts are specially dreaded, particularly the corpses of women who have died in childbed. We will now take examples of this curious custom, arranging them so as to illustrate the geographical. diffusion of the practice. We have already seen that the custom obtains in Siam, for the purpose of excluding the ghost of the dead from the house.[1]

In Laos, a province of Siam, it is especially the bodies of women dying in childbed which are thus taken out of the house by a special opening; in their case the corpse is taken out through a hole in the floor, and not in the wall of the house.[2] The people of

[1] See above, *Fear of the Dead in Primitive Religion*, vol. ii. p. 102, and for the authorities see Bruguière in *Annales de l'Association de la Propagation de la Foi*, v. (Lyons and Paris, 1831) p. 180 ; Mgr. Pallegoix, *Description du royaume Thai ou Siam* (Paris, 1854), p. 245 ; Sir John Bowring, *The Kingdom and People of Siam* (London, 1857), i. 122 ; E. Young, *The Kingdom of the Yellow Robe*, p. 246. Mr. P. A. Thomson thinks that the custom is observed from a fear that if the corpse were not carried through a special opening the spirit of the dead would refuse to go out through the door and so would remain in the house. See P. A. Thomson, *Lotus Land* (London, 1906), p. 136. This explanation appears to be erroneous. Why should a dead man refuse to go out by the door which he has gone out so often in his lifetime ?

[2] Carl Bock, *Temples and Elephants* (London, 1884), p. 262.

Annam, which borders on Siam, sometimes observe a similar custom. The writer who reports it says that the Annamites resort to every kind of device to prevent the spirits of the dead from returning to the house. For this purpose the funeral procession follows a roundabout way to the tomb, thinking so to deceive the spirit, and to complete his confusion the bearers of the bier turn it about several times. Or they take the corpse out of the house, not by the door, but by a special opening, sometimes breaking a hole in a wall of the house for the purpose.[1] The Moï, a primitive race who inhabit the mountainous region of Indo-China, from China on the north to Cambodia on the south, observe a similar custom for a similar reason. The writer who reports it says that among them, when a death has taken place, " the bearers take up the body, convey it rapidly through every room in the house, and after wrapping it in large palm leaves secure it to a stout bamboo pole. The next matter is to get it out of the house in such a way that it will never know the point of exit. Otherwise the spirit will surely find its way back and continue to haunt the living. Accordingly, an opening is very carefully made in the thatched walls or roof, so that the breach will close of itself when the corpse has passed through." [2] The Kachins of Burma carry out the corpses of women dying in childbed not through the door of the house but through an opening made for the purpose in a wall

---

[1] P. Giran, *Magie et religion Annamites* (Paris, 1912), p. 393.
[2] Captain Baudesson, *Indo-China* and its Primitive People, p. 170; *id.* Commandant Baudesson, *Au pays des superstitions et des rites*, 127.

or in the floor of the house. This they do to prevent the return of her dangerous ghost, and for the same purpose they resort to other devices, which we shall have occasion to notice later on.[1] We have already seen that for a similar purpose the Shans of Burma take out the corpse of a woman dying in childbed through a hole in the wall of the house, and that the Palaungs of Burma lower the corpses of such women through a hole in the floor, always for the sake of preventing the return of the much-dreaded ghost.[2]

In China it seems to have been an ancient practice to knock down part of the wall of a house for the purpose of carrying out a corpse, for the custom is alluded to in the Lî-Kî, one of the sacred books of the Chinese.[3] The custom is said to have been particularly observed for members of the royal family ; when one of them died ancient usage required that the corpse should be carried out of the palace, not through the door, but through a breach made for the purpose in the wall.[4] At Mukden in Mongolia, the body of a dead child " must not be carried out of a door or window, but through a new or disused opening, in order that the evil spirit which causes the disease may not enter. The belief is that the Heavenly Dog, which eats the sun at the time of an

[1] Ch. Gilhodes, " Naissance et enfance chez les Katchins (Birmanie) ", in *Anthropos*, vi. (1911) pp. 872 *sq.*

[2] *The Fear of the Dead*, vol. ii. pp. 112 *sq.*, referring to Mrs. Leslie Milne, *The Shans at Home*, p. 96, and *The Home of an Eastern Clan*, pp. 304 *sq.*

[3] *The Sacred Books of China*, translated by James Legge, Part III., *The Lî-Kî*, i.-x. (Oxford, 1885) pp. 144 *sq.* (Book II. Sect. I. Part II. 33) (*Sacred Books of the East*, vol. xxvii.).

[4] J. F. Lafitau, *Mœurs des sauvages amériquains* (Paris, 1724), ii. 401 *sq.*, citing Le Comte, *Nouv. mémoires de la Chine*, vol. ii. p. 187.

eclipse, demands the bodies of children, and that if they are denied to him he will bring certain calamity on the household."[1] This explanation of the custom is apparently an afterthought which has displaced the original motive, the fear of the ghost of the dead child and a desire to prevent it from returning to the house. In the extreme east of Siberia the primitive Reindeer Koryaks do not carry out their dead by the usual door, but under the edge of the tent-cover, which is lifted up for the purpose.[2] Among the primitive Chukchee, neighbours of the Koryaks on the north, a corpse is usually drawn up through a hole in the roof or in the back of the tent, and then all traces of the passage are removed, to prevent the possible return of the dead.[3] The Samoyeds of Siberia carry out the dead, not through the door of the hut, but through an opening made by lifting up the roof or covering of the hut, for they think that, were the corpse carried out by the door, the ghost of the deceased would soon return to fetch away another of the family.[4]

The custom with which we are here concerned has been observed by various peoples of the Indian Archipelago, for example, by the Gajos of Sumatra.[5]

[1] Mrs. Bishop, *Korea and Her Neighbours* (London, 1898), pp. 239 sq.

[2] W. Jochelson, *The Koryak* (New York and Leiden, 1908), pp. 110 sq. (The Jesup North Pacific Expedition: Memoir of the American Museum of Natural History).

[3] W. Bogaras, *The Chukchee* (publication of the Jesup North Pacific Expedition, vol. vii. Memoir of the American Museum of Natural History) (New York, 1904-1910), p. 525. Cf. M. A. Czaplicka, *Aboriginal Siberia* (Oxford, 1914), pp. 146 sq.

[4] P. S. Pallas, *Reise durch verschiedene Provinzen des russischen Reichs* (St. Petersburg 1771-1776), iii. 75 ; Middendorff, *Reise in den aussersten Norden und Osten Siberiens*, iv. 1464.

[5] C. Snouck Hurgronje, *Het Gajo-*

Among the Kayans in the interior of Borneo, whose houses are raised above the ground on piles, the coffin containing the corpse is lowered to the ground with rattans, either through the floor, planks being taken up for the purpose, or under the eaves at the side of the gallery. " In this way they avoid carrying it down the house-ladder ; and it seems to be felt that this precaution renders it more difficult for the ghost to find its way back to the house."[1] Among these Kayans it is especially the bodies of women dying in childbed which are carried out by removing boards in the back wall of the dwelling, for the ghosts of these women are here, as usual, much dreaded, and special precautions have to be taken to prevent their return.[2] The Toradyas of Central Celebes usually pass a corpse out of the house by the window, but if the window is too small to permit of the passage of the body they break an opening through a wall of the house, and so pass the corpse through it. The dead body of a child is passed out of a house through a hole in the floor.[3] The Buginese of South Celebes never carry a corpse out of the house by the ordinary door, but always break a hole in one of the walls of the house for the purpose.[4] Among the Buginese and Macassars of South

land en zijne Bewoners (Batavia, 1903), p. 313.

[1] C. Hose and W. McDougall, The Pagan Tribes of Borneo (London, 1912), i. 35. Cf. W. H. Furness, The Home-life of Borneo Head-hunters (Philadelphia, 1902), p. 52.

[2] Dr. A. W. Nieuwenhuis, Quer durch Borneo (Leiden, 1904), p. 91.

[3] N. Adriani and A. C. Kruijt, De Bare'e-sprekende Toradja's van Midden-Celebes (s'Gravenhage, 1912), i. p. 236 ; ii. pp. 97, 99.

[4] Adriani and Kruijt, op. cit. vol. i. p. 356.

Celebes there is in the king's palace a window reaching to the floor through which on his decease the king's body is carried out.[1] That such a custom is only a limitation to kings of a rule which once applied to everybody becomes all the more probable, when we learn that in the island of Saleijer, which lies to the south of Celebes, each house has, besides its ordinary windows, a large window in the form of a door, through which, and not through the ordinary entrance, every corpse is regularly removed at death.[2] In Bali, a small island to the north of Java, when a queen of the island died, " the body was drawn out of a large aperture made in the wall to the right-hand side of the door, in the absurd opinion of *cheating the devil*, whom these islanders believe to lie in wait in the ordinary passage."[3] Probably the true original motive of the custom was to prevent the dead queen's ghost from coming back to disturb her successor on the throne. In Fiji, when a certain king died, the side of the house was broken down to allow the body to be carried out, though there were doorways wide enough for the purpose close at hand.[4] The missionary who records the fact could not learn the reason of it, but here

[1] B. F. Matthes, *Bijdragen tot de Ethnologie van Zuid-Celebes* (The Hague, 1875), p. 139 ; *id.*, " Over de *ádá's* of gewoonten der Makassaren en Boegineezen ", *Verslagen en Mededeelingen der Koninklijke Akademie van Wetenschappen*, Afdeeling Letterkunde, Derde Reeks, ii. (Amsterdam, 1885) p. 142.

[2] W. M. Donselaar, " Aantekeningen over het eiland Saleijer ",

Mededeelingen van wege het Nederlandsche Zendelinggenootschap, i. (1857) p. 291.

[3] Prevost, quoted by John Crawford, *History of the Indian Archipelago* (Edinburgh, 1820), ii. 245. Cf. Adolf Bastian, *Die Volker des östlichen Asien*, v. (Jena, 1869), p. 83.

[4] Thomas Williams, *Fiji and the Fijians*, Second Edition (London, 1860), i. 197.

again we may suppose that the carrying out of the royal body through a breach in the wall of the house was a precaution to prevent the deceased monarch's ghost from coming back to haunt and trouble his successor on the throne.

In India, among the Birhors, a primitive tribe of Chota Nagpur, " a woman dying within twenty-one days of childbirth or a child dying within twenty-one days of birth may never be admitted into the community of ancestor-spirits, as their spirits are always dangerous. In their case, therefore, a new doorway to the hut is opened to take their corpses to the grave. These corpses are buried in a place apart from where other corpses are buried." [1] Speaking of the Hindoos, a French traveller in India of the eighteenth century says that instead of carrying the corpse out by the door they make an opening in the wall by which they pass it out in a seated posture, and the hole is closed up after the ceremony.[2] Among various Hindoo castes it is customary, if a death occurs on an inauspicious day, to remove the corpse from the house not through the door, but through a temporary hole made in the wall.[3] Another high authority on India gives us more precise information as to those unlucky days which necessitate this change in the ordinary mode of burial. He tells us that the Hindoos attribute to the moon a kind of zodiac composed of twenty-seven constellations

[1] S. C. Roy, *The Birhors* (Ranchi, 1925), p. 266.
[2] Sonnerat, *Voyage aux Indes orientales et à Chine* (Paris, 1782), i. p. 86.
[3] E. Thurston, *Ethnographic Notes in Southern India* (Madras, 1906), p. 226.

which preside each over one of the twenty-seven
days of its periodic course. The five last days of
the moon are all deemed more or less disastrous.
Woe to the relatives of a person who dies on one of
these ill-omened days. The corpse of the unfortunate must not be carried out through the door or
the window : it is absolutely necessary for the
purpose to make a hole in the wall of the house,
through which the corpse is passed out.[1] In
Travancore the body of a dead rajah " is taken out
of the palace through a breach in the wall, made
for the purpose, to avoid pollution of the gate, and
afterwards built up again so that the departed spirit
may not return through the gate to trouble the
survivors".[2] Another writer describes as follows
this mode of carrying out the corpse of a dead rajah
of Travancore. " Before the body is taken from
the palace, a hole is made in the wall of the compart-
ment where it rested, and through this the corpse
is conveyed outside. This is a custom even with
the Sûdras, the reigning family of Travancore being
Kshatrias. What the exact superstition, or idea, is,
I am not in a position to say, but I fancy that there
is a belief that if the corpse is conveyed through the
door, other deaths will immediately follow."[3] We
may suppose that such a death would be ascribed to
the maleficent influence of the deceased rajah's ghost,
who might have effected an entrance into the palace

---

[1] Abbé J. A. Dubois, *Mœurs,
institutions et cérémonies des peuples
de l'Inde* (Paris, 1825), ii. 225.
[2] S. Mateer, *Native Life in
Travancore* (London, 1883), p. 137.
[3] A. Butterworth, " Royal Families in Travancore ", in the *Indian
Antiquary*, xxxi. (1902) p. 251.

by the ordinary door. Among the Brahuis, a Dravidian-speaking people of Baluchistan, if the door of a house faces south they think that it will be very unlucky to carry out a corpse for burial through the door on the third or fourth day of the new moon. Hence on any such day it is necessary to make a breach in the wall of the house facing the door, for the sake of carrying out through it the corpse of the deceased.[1] The Lepchas of Sikkim take a corpse out of the house by a hole made in the floor. Their houses are generally built on pillars or wooden posts.[2] Among the Persians the custom of carrying out a corpse through a breach in the wall of a house would seem to be very ancient, for in their sacred book, the *Zend-Avesta*, it is prescribed that, when a death has occurred, a breach shall be made in the wall and the corpse carried out through it by two men, who have first stripped off their clothes.[3]

Among the Sakalava and Antimerina of Madagascar, when a sovereign or a prince of the royal family dies within the enclosure of the king's palace, the corpse must be carried out of the palace, not by the door, but by a breach made for the purpose in the wall ; the new sovereign could not pass through the door that had been polluted by the passage of a dead body.[4] Here again we may suppose that as in Celebes and Travancore the rule for the burial of

[1] Denys Bray, *Life-History of a Brahui* (London, 1913), p. 123.

[2] J. A. H. Louis, *The Gates of Thibet* (Calcutta, 1894), p. 114.

[3] *The Zend-Avesta*, Part I., *The Vendidâd*, translated by James Darmesteter (Oxford, 1880), p. 95 (Fargard, viii. 2, 10), *Sacred Books of the East*, vol. iv.

[4] Arnold van Gennep, *Tabou et totémisme à Madagascar* (Paris, 1904), p. 65, quoting Dr. Catat.

sovereigns is or has been formerly the rule for the burial of their subjects likewise; kings are commonly conservative of ancient usages.

In Africa the custom of carrying the dead out of a house by an opening made specially for the purpose is practised by many tribes in many parts of the continent. Thus, for example, "the Ashantis, and some others of the northern tribes, bury their dead outside, and the body is taken out of the house through a hole which is made in the wall, for a corpse may not pass through any door. This superstition appears to have been borrowed from the Mohammedan peoples inland, for it is held by the Fulas, Houssas, Dagombas, and others, and also by the Mandingos and Jolloffs far to the north; while it is unknown to the southern Tshi-speaking tribes."[1] Among the Ewe-speaking peoples of Togo the body of a priest may not be carried out through the door of a house; a hole is made in the roof of the house, and the priest's corpse is pushed through it. The German missionary who reports the custom thinks that this is done to prevent the priest's ghost from finding the door of the house and so entering and troubling the survivors.[2] Among the Ibibios of Southern Nigeria " a woman who dies in giving birth to twins, or before the end of her year of purification after such an event, may not be carried to her last resting-place through the house-door, any more than she may go out by it on leaving home to

[1] A. B. Ellis, *The Tschi-speaking Peoples of the Gold Coast of West Africa* (London, 1887), pp. 239 *sq.*

[2] J. Spieth, *Die Ewe-Stämme* (Berlin, 1906), p. 756.

spend the prescribed twelve moons in the twin women's town. Such sad exiles must pass through a hole purposely broken in the wall, by which exit the unfortunate babes are also carried forth. Further, the body of a twin mother may on no account be borne along a road by which ordinary people pass to and fro, but only by a little path specially cut through the bush to the place where it is to be flung. The reason given for this prohibition is much the same as that given in Cambodia for carrying a dead body feet foremost, *i.e.* ' that it may not see the house, in which event other sickness and other deaths would result'. Ibibios say, too, that should the ghost return and try to enter her former home she would be unable to do so since the place by which the body was carried forth has been blocked up, and wraiths can only enter by the same way through which their bodies were borne forth."[1] The general Nigerian custom at a burial is described briefly as follows, by another authority : " Superstition does not permit of the corpse being carried through a door, and a hole for its egress has to be made in the wall ".[2] Among the Bambara, a tribe in the upper valley of the Niger, this mode of carrying a corpse out of a house to burial appears to be reserved for the bodies of social outcasts.[3] Among the Mossi, a tribe of the Western Sudan, a corpse is regularly

[1] D. Amaury Talbot, *Woman's Mysteries of a Primitive People* (London, 1918), p. 215.
[2] Lieut.-Col. A. F. Mockler-Ferryman, *British Nigeria* (London, 1912), p. 234.
[3] Abbé Jos. Henry, *L'Âme d'un peuple africain: les Bambara* (Münster, 1910), p. 231.

carried out of the hut, not by the door, but through an opening made for the purpose in the wall of the hut.[1] Among the Bubis of Fernando Po, when an eminent person dies the corpse is carried out of the house, not by the door, but by a hole broken through that wall of the house near which the dying man lay.[2] Among the Wajagga of Mount Kilimanjaro in East Africa, the dead body of a childless woman is never carried out of the hut by the door, but always through a breach made in the opposite wall of the house. She is buried in the depth of the forest ; but never in a place which the natives expect to cultivate. Apparently they think that the corpse of a childless woman would render the ground barren. It is safe therefore to infer that the carrying out of her body through a special opening in the hut is intended to prevent her dangerous ghost from returning to blight her friends and the land.[3] Similarly among the Kavirondo, near neighbours of the Wajagga, " when a woman dies without having borne a child, she is carried out of the back of the house. A hole is made in the wall and the corpse is ignominiously pushed through the hole and carried some distance to be buried, as it is considered a curse to die without a child. If the woman has given birth to a child, then her corpse is carried out through

[1] P. E. Mangin, " Les Mossi ", in *Anthropos*, ix. (1909) p. 729.

[2] L. Janikowski, " L'Ile de Fernando-Poo, son état actuel et ses habitants ", in *Bulletin de la Société* *de Geographie*, vii. (1886) p. 563.

[3] B. Gutmann, " Trauer und Begräbnis-Sitten der Wadschagga ", in *Globus*, lxxxix. (1906) p. 200.

the front door and buried in the veranda of the house." [1]

In describing a burial among the Ngoni (Angoni) of Nyassaland a missionary tells how the bearers carried out the corpse, not through the door of the hut, but by a hole broken through the wall of the hut, and then laid it in the grave. " All the dishes, pots, clothes, and articles of personal use belonging to the deceased were buried with him. But no metal goods were buried, whether hoes, or arrows, or brass ornaments. It was feared that these would give the ghost opportunity to return with anger to hurt the friends." [2] Among the Atonga of Nyassaland the dead are carried out of a hut, not by the door, but by a special opening opposite the door, which has been broken through the wall of the hut. [3] Among the Thonga, a Bantu tribe of South-East Africa, a corpse may not be carried out of a hut by the door : it must be passed out through a hole made in the wall of the hut on the right-hand side if the deceased is a man, or presumably on the left-hand side if the deceased be a woman. It is buried in a grave either behind the hut or in the neighbouring forest. [4] A missionary who has described the customs and religion of the Bantu tribes of South-East Africa between Cape Colony and Natal tells us that the dead body of a chief is never carried out

[1] Rev. N. Stam, " The Religious Conceptions of the Kavirondo ", in *Anthropos*, v. (1910) p. 361.
[2] D. Fraser, *Winning a Primitive People* (London, 1914), p. 158.
[3] Rev. A. C. MacAlpine, in A.

Werner, *The Natives of British Central Africa* (London, 1906), p. 161.
[4] H. A. Junod, *The Life of a South African Tribe*, Second Edition (London, 1927), i. 138.

of the hut by the door, but always by a special opening made for the purpose in the wall of the hut.[1] Among the Basutos, another Bantu tribe of South Africa, a corpse is carried out of the hut, not through the door, but through an opening made in the wall of the hut opposite to the door.[2] So among the Bechuanas, another Bantu tribe of South Africa, a corpse is not carried out of the hut by the door, for that is reserved for the use of the living. It is carried out through an opening made in the fence, and buried in the cattle kraal.[3] Describing the burial customs of the South African tribes among which he laboured, the missionary Dr. Moffat says that "the body is not conveyed through the door of the fore-yard or court connected with each house, but an opening is made in the fence for that purpose".[4] The Hottentots of South Africa, who are not a Bantu tribe, practise a similar custom. They carry a corpse out of a hut, not by the door, but by an opening specially made for the purpose in the wall of the hut.[5] According to the French missionaries, Arbousset and Daumas, some of the Bushmen observe a similar custom ; when a person dies they wrap up his body in his ordinary attire,

[1] Rev. Jas. Macdonald, *Light in Africa* (London, 1890), p. 166. Cf. Dudley Kidd, *The Essential Kafir* (London, 1904), p. 247.

[2] Rev. E. Casalis, *The Basutos* (London, 1861), p. 202.

[3] "Extrait du Journal des Missions evangeliques", in *Bulletin de la Société de Géographie*, xx. (1833) p. 196. Cf. C. G. Andersson, *Lake Ngami, or Explorations and Dis-coveries*, Second Edition (London, 1856), p. 446.

[4] R. Moffat, *Missionary Labours and Scenes in Southern Africa* (London, 1842), p. 307.

[5] P. Kolben, *The Present State of the Cape of Good Hope* (London, 1731–1738), i. 316 ; Adolph Bastian, *Der Mensch in der Geschichte* (Leipzig, 1860), vol. ii. pp. 322 *sq.*

and carry it out of the hut, not by the door, but by
a large opening made in the wall.[1]

A like burial custom has been observed for like
reasons by many of the aboriginal inhabitants of
America, both Eskimo and Indian. Thus, for
example, among the Greenlanders " if a person dies
in the house, his body must not be carried through
the ordinary entry of it, but conveyed out at the
window ; and if he dies in a tent, he is brought out
at the back part of it. At the funeral, a woman
lights a stick in the fire, brandishing the same and
saying, *piklerrukpok*, that is, Here is no more to be
got."[2] Among the Eskimos of Hudson Bay, when
a death has taken place in a snow house (*igloo*) or a
tent the relatives try to bury it before the sun has
risen. But if the sun has risen while the corpse is
still in the house or tent the body must be kept there
for three or five days. At the end of that time the
corpse must be carried out, not by the door, but by
a special opening made in the wall of the house or
by raising a corner of the tent.[3] With regard to
the Eskimos of the Ungava District in the Hudson
Bay Territory we are told that " the nearest relatives
on approach of death remove the invalid to the outside of the house, for if he should die within he must
not be carried out of the door but through a hole cut
in the side wall, and it must then be carefully closed

[1] T. Arbousset and F. Daumas, *Relation d'un voyage d'exploration* (Paris, 1842), pp. 502 *sq.*

[2] Hans Egede, *Description of Greenland*, Second Edition (London, 1818), pp. 152 *sq.* Cf. David

Crantz, *History of Greenland* (London, 1767) i. 237.

[3] Mgr. A. Turquetil, " Notes sur les Esquimaux de Baie Hudson ", in *Anthropos*, xxi. (1926) p. 432.

to prevent the spirit of the person from returning ".[1] To the same effect Rink, who seems to have spent much of his time in Greenland, in speaking of the Eskimos in general, says, " the bodies of those who died in a house were carried out through a window, or if in a tent, underneath the back part."[2] When C. F. Hall was living with the Eskimos of Cumberland Inlet, a young child died in a snow house (*igloo*). In order to bury the body a passage was cut through the wall of the snow house, and through this opening the little body was carried by its mother, accompanied or followed by Hall and the other mourners.[3] Among the Eskimos of Hudson Strait, with whom Captain G. F. Lyon wintered, " the dead are in most cases carried through the window, in preference to the door of a snow hut, which, after the three days of mourning have expired, is forsaken, at least by the family of which the deceased had formed a part ".[4]

Among the Unalit Eskimos of Bering Strait a corpse is usually removed from the house by being raised with cords through the smoke-hole in the roof ; but is never passed through the doorway. Should the smoke-hole be too small to allow of the passage of the corpse, an opening is made in the rear

[1] Lucien M. Turner, " Ethnology of the Ungava District, Hudson Bay Territory ", in *Eleventh Annual Report of the Bureau of Ethnology* (Washington, 1894) p. 191.

[2] H. J. Rink, *Tales of the Eskimo* (London, 1875), p. 55.

[3] C. F. Hall, *Narrative of the Second Arctic Expedition made by Charles F. Hall* (Washington, 1879), p. 265.

[4] Capt. G. F. Lyon, *The Private Journal of Captain G. F. Lyon, of H.M.S. Hecla, during the recent voyages of discovery under Captain Parry* (London, 1824), p. 369.

of the house, and the body is carried through it.[1] Among the Tuski, an aboriginal but not Indian tribe of Alaska, "those who die a natural death are carried out through a hole cut in the back of the hut or *yaráng*. This is immediately closed up, that the spirit of the dead man may not find his way back." [2] Among the Tlingit Indians of Alaska, when a chief dies his body is taken out of the house by an opening made in the back wall of the dwelling.[3] Among the Haida Indians of Queen Charlotte Island, British Columbia, when a chief died his body was carried out to the grave through an opening made for the purpose in a wall of the house. His near relatives and friends cut their hair short and put pitch on their faces in sign of mourning. If he was a great chief all the people of the town sometimes followed their example.[4] Among the Kwakiutl Indians of British Columbia a corpse " must not be taken out of the door, else other inmates of the house would be sure to die soon. Either a hole is made in one of the walls, through which the body is carried out, or it is lifted through the roof. It is placed behind the house to be put into the box that is to serve as a coffin. If it were placed in the coffin inside the house, the souls of the other inmates would enter

---

[1] E. W. Nelson, "The Eskimo about Bering Strait", in the *Eighteenth Annual Report of the Bureau of American Ethnology* (1896–1897), Part I. (Washington, 1899) p. 310.

[2] W. H. Dall, *Alaska and its Resources* (London, 1871), p. 382.

[3] Aurel Krause, *Die Tlinkit-Indianer* (Jena, 1885), p. 225.

[4] J. R. Swanton, *Contributions to the Ethnology of the Haida* (The Jesup North Pacific Expedition: Memoir of the American Museum of National History) (Leiden and New York, 1905), pp. 52, 54.

the coffin too, and then all would die soon."[1] Among the Lkuñgen Indians, in the south-east part of Vancouver Island, after a death the corpse is at once carried out of the house through an opening which has been made by removing some boards of the back wall of the house. They think that the ghost would kill every one in the house if the corpse were allowed to remain in it.[2]

Concerning some of the Indians of Canada near the St. Lawrence River, we are told by a Jesuit missionary of the seventeenth century that among them a corpse was never carried out of a hut by the door, but always through a hole made in a wall of the hut by removing some of the bark.[3] The Ojebway Indians greatly fear the spirits of the lately deceased. Hence they bury their dead as soon as possible. They do not carry them out of the doorway, but cut a hole in the bark of the lodge and thrust the body out, for they fear that if the dead person remained in the house his spirit would carry off the souls of the survivors, and they would die. Hence they not only pull down the whole house and put out the fire, but are very careful not even to light the new fire in the new house with a spark or sticks from the old one. A new fire and new wood must be taken. Nor do they build the new lodge

---

[1] Franz Boas, "Notes on the Kwakiutl", in *Eleventh Report on the North-Western Tribes of Canada* (Report of the British Association for 1890), Sixth Report on the Indians of British Columbia, p. 574.

[2] Franz Boas, *Sixth Report of the Committee on the North-Western Tribes of Canada* (Report of the British Association for 1890), p. 23.

[3] *Relation des Jésuites*, 1633, p. 11; *id.*, 1634, p. 23 (Canadian reprint, Quebec, 1858).

on the old spot, but choose another place as far from it as possible.[1]

Among the Catios Indians of Columbia in South America a corpse may not be carried out of the house by the usual house-ladder, lest the spirit of the deceased should find his way back to the house ; but the missionaries who report the custom and the reason for it do not inform us through what part of the hut a corpse is passed out.[2] The custom of blocking up the entrance to a hut for the purpose of excluding the returning ghost of a recently deceased person has been well described by the missionary, Mr. Grubb, in a particular case among the Lengua Indians of Paraguay. After speaking of the death of an old man among these Indians he says, " The people had built their shelters on the forest side of my hut, but, although they had promised not to destroy the village nor vacate it, they had taken the precaution to pull down their booths and re-erect them on the farther side of my hut, so that, whatever happened, I, at any rate, should be between them and the ghost, and therefore be the first to suffer. The witch-doctor, the most intelligent man of the party, had, a week or two previously, under strong persuasion from me, erected for himself quite a superior kind of hut, with a small opening for a door. His wife and family, however, although they did not remove the hut, made very considerable

---

[1] J. G. Kohl, *Kitchi-Gami: Wanderings round Lake Superior* (London, 1860), p. 106 n.

[2] Joseph and Maria Schilling, " Religion und soziale Verhältnisse der Catios-Indianer in Kolumbien ", in *Archiv für Religionswissenschaft* (Leipzig), xxiii. (1925) p. 296.

alterations to it, the chief of which was that they securely blocked up the doorway, making it appear like a part of the wall, and opened a small gap on the opposite side instead. As the old wizard afterwards explained to me, this was done on purpose to puzzle the ghost. He, while in the body, knew the house well, but the alterations were so considerable that it was supposed his ghost would not recognize it, and would be especially nonplussed when it made for the entrance to find a solid wall."[1]

In Europe the custom of carrying the dead out of the house by a special opening which is then closed to prevent their ghosts from re-entering the dwelling has been observed by several peoples at various times, both ancient and modern. Thus among the Cheremiss of Russia, "old custom required that the corpse should not be carried out by the door but through a breach in the north wall, where there is usually a sash window. But the custom has long been obsolete, even among the heathen, and only very old people speak of it. They explain it as follows : to carry it out by the door would be to show the *Asyrèn* (the dead man) the right way into the house, whereas a breach in the wooden wall is immediately closed by replacing the beams in position, and thus the *Asyrèn* would in vain seek for an entrance."[2] With regard to the

[1] W. B. Grubb, *An Unknown People in an Unknown Land*, pp. 165 *sq.*

[2] S. K. Kusnezow, " Über den Glauben vom Jenseits und den Todtencultus der Tscheremissen ", *Internationales Archiv für Ethnographie*, ix. (1896) p. 157.

Russian custom we are told that "the corpse was often carried out of a house through a window, or through a hole made for the purpose, and the custom is still kept up in many parts ".[1] In Denmark corpses used to be carried out of the house, not through the door, but through an opening made in the wall for the purpose, especially in the wall of the principal room. After the corpse had been carried through, the opening was immediately bricked up before the mourners returned from the grave. Such customs used to be common among the Danish peasantry : each peasant house commonly had its corpse-door of this sort, which could be distinguished from the outside at the gable end of the house. The practice is now nearly, if not totally, extinct.[2] "In Sweden it is said that all the gates along the road through which a corpse has been carried to the churchyard are hung upside down, so that they open the opposite way. And if a ghost has begun to haunt a house, it is generally sufficient to alter the position of the door, then he has to remain outside. It is impossible for him to find his way in again."[3] It was an old Norse rule that a corpse might not be carried out of the house by the door which was used by the living ; hence a hole was made in the wall at the back of the dead man's head and he was taken out through it backwards, or a hole was dug in the ground under the south wall and the body was drawn out through

---

[1] W. R. S. Ralston, *The Songs of the Russian People* (London, 1872), p. 318.

[2] Dr. H. F. Feilberg, "The Corpse-Door : a Danish Survival ", in *Folk-Lore*, xviii. (1907) pp. 364-375.

[3] Dr. Feilberg, *op. cit.* p. 369.

it.[1] The practice is repeatedly alluded to in the old Norse sagas.[2] Old German law required that the corpses of criminals and suicides should be taken out of a house through a hole under the threshold.[3] In the Highlands of Scotland the corpses of suicides used to be carried out of the house not through the door but through an opening made between the thatched roof and the top of the wall. They were buried, along with the bodies of unbaptized children, outside the common churchyard.[4] In Mecklenburg "it is a law regulating the return of the dead that they are compelled to return by the same way by which the corpse was removed from the house. In the villages of Picher, Bresegard, and others the people used to have moveable thresholds at the house-doors, which, being fitted into the door-posts, could be shoved up. The corpse was then carried out of the house under the threshold, and therefore could not return over it."[5] In Perche, a province of France, the bodies of still-born children are not taken out by the door, but are passed through a window for burial. The reason for the custom is not explained, but probably the original motive was to prevent the return of their unhappy spirits to the house.[6]

[1] W. Weinhold, *Altnordisches Leben* (Berlin, 1856), p. 476.

[2] Dr. Feilberg, *loc. cit.*

[3] J. Grimm, *Deutsche Rechtsalterthümer*[3] (Gottingen, 1881), pp. 726 *sq.*

[4] J. G. Campbell, *Superstitions of the Highlands and Islands of Scot-land* (Glasgow, 1900), p. 242.

[5] Karl Bartsch, *Sagen, Märchen, und Gebräuche aus Meklenburg* (Vienna, 1879–1880), ii. § 358.

[6] F. Chapiseau, *Le Folk-lore de la Beauce et du Perche* (Paris, 1902), i. 164.

CHAPTER III

DANGEROUS GHOSTS

I. *Ghosts of the Slain*

HITHERTO I have spoken for the most part of the spirits of the dead in general, as if all these spirits were equally feared by primitive man. That is by no means the case. He distinguishes sharply between ghosts and ghosts, particularly according to the death they died, and some of them he deems much more dangerous than others and takes special precautions against them. In general the spirits of all who have died a violent death are classed among the dangerous ghosts. Their span of life has been cut prematurely short: they feel that they have been wronged, and seek to avenge themselves on the authors of their death if they can discover them. And since, in their wrath, they do not always discriminate nicely between the innocent and the guilty, they may become a danger, not only to individuals, but to a whole community. Among these the spirits of the slain are the most commonly feared,

and with these we shall begin our survey of dangerous ghosts.[1]

The Arunta of Central Australia, like many
other savage tribes, think that a death among them
is often caused by the nefarious arts of a sorcerer in
a neighbouring tribe, and they send out a party of
men to take vengeance by killing the supposed culprit. When they have accomplished their mission
of blood by taking the life of the reputed sorcerer,
the avengers return to their own camp, which may
be a long way distant. On the whole of the return journey they think they are followed by the
spirit of the man whom they have murdered. It
takes the form of a little bird called the *chichurkna*,
and may be heard crying like a child in the distance
as it flies. If any of the slayers should fail to hear
its cry, he would become paralysed in his right arm
and shoulder. At night-time especially, when the
bird is flying over the camp, the slayers have to lie
awake and keep the right arm and shoulder carefully hidden, lest the bird should look down upon
and harm them. When once they have heard its
cry their minds are at ease, because the spirit of the
dead then recognizes that he has been detected, and
can therefore do no mischief. On their return to
their friends, as soon as they come in sight of the
main camp, they begin to perform an excited war-
dance, approaching in the form of a square and

---

[1] With what follows compare *The
Golden Bough : Taboo and the Perils
of the Soul*, pp. 177 *sqq.*; *Psyche's
Task* (*The Devil's Advocate*), pp.
113 *sqq.* Much of the evidence cited
in these passages is here repeated,
with the addition of some fresh
examples.

moving their shields as if to ward off something which was being thrown at them. This action is intended to repel the angry spirit of the dead man, who is striving to attack them. Next, the men who did the deed of blood separate themselves from the others, and forming a line, with spears at rest and shields held out in front, stand silent and motionless like statues. A number of old women now approach with a sort of exulting skip and strike the shields of the man-slayers with fighting-clubs till they ring again. They are followed by men who smite the shields with boomerangs. This striking of the shields is supposed to be a very effective way of frightening away the spirit of the dead man. The natives listen anxiously to the sounds emitted by the shields when they are struck ; for if any man's shield gives forth a hollow sound under the blow, that man will not live long, but if it rings sharp and clear, he is safe. For some days after their return the slayers will not speak of what they have done, and continue to paint themselves all over with powdered charcoal, and to decorate their foreheads and noses with green twigs. Finally, they paint their bodies and faces with bright colours, and become free to talk about the affair ; but still of nights they must lie awake listening for the plaintive cry of the bird in which they fancy they hear the voice of their victim.[1]

The Fijians used to bury the sick and aged alive,

---

[1] Spencer and Gillen, *Native Tribes of Central Australia*, pp. 493-495 ; *id., Northern Tribes of Central Australia*, pp. 563-568.

and having done so they always made a great uproar with bamboos, shell-trumpets and so forth in
order to scare away the spirits of the buried people
and prevent them from returning to their homes ;
and by way of removing any temptation to hover
about their former abodes they dismantled the
houses of the dead and hung them with everything
that in their eyes seemed most repulsive.[1] When
the cannibal Melanesians of the Bismarck Archipelago have eaten a human body, they shout, blow
horns, shake spears and beat the bushes for the
purpose of driving away the ghost of the man or
woman whose flesh has just furnished the banquet.
Before doing so they considerately offer to their
victim's ghost a portion of his or her own flesh.[2]
When a Maori warrior had slain his foe in combat,
he tasted his blood, believing that this preserved
him from the avenging spirit (*atua*) of his victim ;
for they imagined that " the moment a slayer had
tasted the blood of the slain, the dead man became
a part of his being and placed him under the protection of the *atua* or guardian spirit of the deceased ".[3]   In the Pelew Islands the relations of a
man whose head has been taken by enemies are
secluded and purified for fear of the ghost, which is
angry with them ; after the purification the ghost

[1] John Jackson, in J. E. Erskine's
*Journal of a Cruise among the
Islands of the Western Pacific*
(London, 1853), p. 477.

[2] George Brown, D.D., *Melanesians and Polynesians* (London,

1910), pp. 142, 145.

[3] J. Dumont D'Urville, *Voyage
autour du monde et à la recherche
de la Pérouse* (Paris, 1832–1833), iii.
305.

goes away to the land of the enemy and pursues his murderer.[1]

Among the Kiwai of British New Guinea, " the warrior who has killed is, as only might be expected, in continual danger from the ghosts of those he has slain. Consequently he must for a month refrain from intercourse with women and eat no crabs, crocodile, sago, or pig. If he did, the ghost would enter into his blood and he would certainly die. As a further precaution against the power of ghosts, food and a bowl of *gamada* are set aside and flung away with a warning to the dead to return to their own place." [2] Among the tribes at the mouth of the Wanigela River, in New Guinea, " a man who has taken life is considered to be impure until he has undergone certain ceremonies : as soon as possible after the deed he cleanses himself and his weapon. This satisfactorily accomplished, he repairs to his village and seats himself on logs of sacrificial staging. No one approaches him or takes any notice whatever of him. A house is prepared for him which is put in charge of two or three small boys as servants. He may eat only toasted bananas, and only the centre portion of them —the ends being thrown away. On the third day of his seclusion a small feast is prepared by his friends, who also fashion some new perineal beads for him. This is called *ivi poro*. The next day the man dons all his best ornaments and badges for

[1] J. Kubary, *Die socialen Einrichtungen der Pelauer* (Berlin, 1885), pp. 126 *sq.*

[2] W. N. Beaver, *Unexplored New Guinea* (London, 1920), p. 174.

taking life, and sallies forth fully armed and parades the village. The next day a hunt is organized, and a kangaroo selected from the game captured. It is cut open and the spleen and liver rubbed over the back of the man. He then walks solemnly down to the nearest water, and standing straddle-legs in it washes himself. All the young untried warriors swim between his legs. This is supposed to impart courage and strength to them. The following day, at early dawn, he dashes out of his house, fully armed, and calls aloud the name of his victim. Having satisfied himself that he has thoroughly scared the ghost of the dead man, he returns to his house. The beating of flooring-boards and the lighting of fires is also a certain method of scaring the ghost. A day later his purification is finished. He can then enter his wife's house." [1]

In the Namau district of British New Guinea, on returning to their village after a raid, warriors who had slain their enemies took great precautions to drive away the vengeful ghosts of their enemies, which had followed them to the village. These precautions were often witnessed by a missionary who has graphically described them as follows : " In Namau the spirits of enemy warriors were regarded very seriously, and dealt with very systematically on the night immediately after a fight. They were supposed to follow their dead bodies back to the village of the victors, and there conceal themselves

[1] R. E. Guise, " On the Tribes inhabiting the Mouth of the Wanigela River, New Guinea ", in the *Journal of the Royal Anthropological Institute*, xxviii. (1899) pp. 213 *sq*.

in every possible nook and cranny to await a favourable opportunity to torture the men who had overthrown them in the fight. As soon as night had set in the old men provided themselves with coconut-palm flares and torches, paraded the village from end to end, pushed their flares into every possible hiding-place of a spirit until they were satisfied that they had rid their village of their presence. I have a dim recollection that this practice was observed by the Ibi tribes in the long ago, but I have no data by me to confirm it. Whereas I saw the driving-out of the spirits in the Namau villages, as described above, so frequently that, alas, I cannot forget it."[1] One such ceremony witnessed by him in a village of the Purari delta is described by the same observer as follows : " Darkness I have said ; but there was no darkness in the village that night other than the darkness of heathenism, and it was terrible indeed. Fires were kindled on every open space ; torches of coconut palms were lit and carried into every dark recess of the village ; drums were beaten ; conch shells were blown ; everybody yelled who had a yell left ; all this was done to drive away the spirits of the victims from the village."[2]

Among the Orokaiva, in the east of British New Guinea, a native who has slain an enemy has to perform a number of curious rites. Among other things he has to climb into a tree and submit to be severely bitten by a vicious species of green ant

---

[1] J. H. Holmes, *In Primitive New Guinea* (London, 1924), p. 184.
[2] J. H. Holmes, *op. cit.* p. 174.

which haunts its branches. Also a coconut was broken over his head, and he was soused with its milk. Mr. Williams, who reports these and the other observances and restrictions imposed upon a man-slayer among the Orokaiva, was informed directly that they are meant to drive away the *asisi*, or spirit, of the slain man.[1]

Among the Kai of Northern New Guinea, when a party of warriors has stormed a village, and killed many of the inmates, they beat a hasty retreat, in order to reach their own, or a friendly village, before nightfall. Their reason for haste is the fear of being overtaken in the darkness by the ghosts of their slaughtered foes, who, powerless by day, are very dangerous and terrible by night. Restlessly through the hours of darkness these unquiet spirits follow like sleuth-hounds in the tracks of their retreating enemies, eager to come up with them and by contact with the bloodstained weapons of their slayers to recover the spiritual substance which they have lost. Not till they have done so can they find rest and peace. That is why the victors are careful not at first to bring back their weapons into the village, but to hide them somewhere in the bushes at a safe distance. There they leave them for some days until the baffled ghosts may be supposed to have given up the chase and returned, sad and angry, to their mangled bodies in the charred ruins of their old home. The first night after the return of the warriors is always the most anxious time ; all the

[1] F. E. Williams, *Orokaiva Society* (London, 1930), p. 175.

villagers are then on the alert for fear of the ghosts ; but if the night passes quietly, their terror gradually subsides and gives place to the dread of their surviving enemies. As the victors in a raid are supposed to have more or less of the soul-stuff or spiritual essence of their slain foes adhering to their persons, none of their friends will venture to touch them for some time after their return to the village. Everybody avoids them and goes carefully out of their way, and any ache or ailment which he or she may experience during this time is set down to indirect contact with one of the slayers.[1] Similarly the Yabim of Northern New Guinea dread the spirit of a murdered man because he is believed to haunt his murderer and to do him a mischief. Hence they drive away such a dangerous ghost with shouts and the beating of drums ; and by way of facilitating his departure they launch a model of a canoe, laden with taro and tobacco, in order to transport him with all comfort to the land of souls.[2] When the Bukaua of Northern New Guinea have won a victory over their foes, and have returned home, they kindle a fire in the middle of the village and hurl blazing brands in the direction of the battle field, while at the same time they make an ear-splitting din, to keep at bay the angry spirits of the slain.[3] Similarly in the Doreh district of Dutch New

[1] Ch. Keysser, " Aus dem Leben der Kaileute ", in R. Neuhauss, *Deutsch Neu Guinea*, iii. (Berlin, 1911) pp. 64 *sq.*, 147 *sq.*, 132.

[2] K. Vetter, in *Nachrichten über*

Kaiser Wilhelms-Land und den Bismarck-Archipel, 1897, p. 94.

[3] S. Lehner, " Bakaua ", in R. Neuhauss, *Deutsch Neu Guinea*, iii. p. 444.

Guinea, if a murder has taken place in the village, the inhabitants assemble for several evenings in succession and utter frightful yells to drive away the ghost of the victim in case he should be minded to hang about the village.[1] In Windessi, Dutch New Guinea, when a party of head-hunters has been successful, and they are nearing home, they announce their approach and success by blowing on triton shells. Their canoes are also decked with branches. The faces of the men who have taken a head are blackened with charcoal. If several have taken part in killing the same victim, his head is divided among them. They always time their arrival so as to reach home in the early morning. They come rowing to the village with a great noise, and the women stand ready to dance in the verandahs of the houses. The canoes row past the *room sram* or house where the young men live, and as they pass the murderers throw as many pointed sticks or bamboos at the wall or roof as there were enemies killed. The day is spent very quietly. Now and then they drum or blow on the conch ; at other times they beat the walls of the houses with loud shouts to drive away the ghosts of the slain.[2]

In Timor, an island of the Indian Archipelago, when a warlike expedition has returned in triumph bringing the heads of the vanquished foe, the leader of the expedition is forbidden by religion and custom

---

[1] H. von Rosenberg, *Der malay-ische Archipel* (Leipsic, 1878), p. 461.

[2] J. L. D. van der Roest, " Uit het leven der Bevolkung van Windessi ", in *Tijdschrift voor Indische Taal- Land- en Volkenkunde*, xl. (1890) pp. 157 *sq.*

to return at once to his own house. A special hut is prepared for him, in which he has to reside for two months, undergoing bodily and spiritual purification. During this time he may not go to his wife nor feed himself ; the food must be put in his mouth by another person.[1] That these observances are dictated by fear of the ghosts of the slain seems certain ; for from another account of the ceremonies performed on the return of a successful head-hunter in the same island we learn that sacrifices are offered on this occasion to appease the soul of the man whose head has been taken. The people think that some misfortune would befall the victor were such offering omitted. Moreover, a part of the ceremony consists of a dance accompanied by a song in which the death of the slain man is lamented and his forgiveness is entreated. "Be not angry", they say, "because your head is here with us ; had we been less lucky, our heads might now have been exposed in your village. We have offered the sacrifice to appease you. Your spirit may now rest and leave us at peace. Why were you our enemy? Would it not have been better that we should remain friends? Then your blood would not have been spilt and your head would not have been cut off."[2]

The Bare'e-speaking Toradyas of Central Celebes

---

[1] S. Muller, *Reizen en Onderzoekingen in den Indischen Archipel* (Amsterdam, 1857), ii. 252.

[2] J. S. G. Graamberg, "Eene maand in de binnenlanden van Timor", in *Verhandelingen van het Bataavisch genootschap van Kunsten en Wetenschappen*, xxxvi. (1872) pp. 208, 216 *sq.*

are greatly concerned about the souls of men who
have been slain in battle.   They appear to think
that men who have been killed in war instead of
dying by disease have not exhausted their vital
energy and that therefore their departed spirits are
more powerful than the common ruck of ghosts ;
and as on account of the unnatural manner of their
death they cannot be admitted into the land of souls
they continue to prowl about the earth, furious with
the foes who have cut them off untimely in the prime
of manhood, and demanding of their friends that
they shall wage war on the enemy and send forth
an expedition every year to kill some of them.   If
the survivors pay no heed to this demand of the
bloodthirsty ghosts, they themselves are exposed to
the vengeance of these angry spirits, who pay out
their undutiful friends and relatives by visiting them
with sickness and death.   Hence with the Toradyas
war is a sacred duty in which every member of the
community is bound to bear a part ;   even women
and children, who cannot wage real war, must wage
mimic warfare at home by hacking with bamboo
swords at an old skull of the enemy, while with their
shrill voices they utter the war-whoop.[1]

In the Andaman Islands, if a man has killed
another in a fight between two villages or in a private
quarrel, he leaves his village and goes to live in the
jungle, where he must stay for some weeks, or even
months.   His wife may attend him in his seclusion.

---

[1] N. Adriani and Alb. C. Kruijt, *De Bare'e-sprekende Toradjas van
Midden-Celebes*, i. 285, 290 *sq.*

For several weeks the homicide must observe several taboos. He may not handle a bow or arrow. He may not feed himself or touch food with his hands, but must be fed by his wife or a friend. He must keep his neck and upper lip covered with red paint, and must wear plumes of shredded *Tetrathera* wood in his belt before and behind, and in his necklace at the back of his neck. If he breaks any of these taboos it is believed that the spirit of the man whom he killed will make him ill. After this he undergoes a kind of purification. His hands are first rubbed with white clay, and then with red paint. He is then rid of the taboos; he may handle bows and arrows, and feed himself with his own hands; but he retains the plumes of shredded wood for a year of so.[1]

Among the Kachins of Burma, when a man has committed a murder it is necessary for him to take immediate precautions against the spirit of his victim, which will become a malignant *nat*, and will assuredly follow the murderer and wreak its vengeance on him. Because of this danger he may not enter his or any other village until a certain ceremony has been performed. Near the sacred grove (*num-shang*) of the village the sacred *kumbang* grass is planted in the ground. Next to it, in the direction of the village, a wooden rice-pounder is laid; next to the pounder, one of the smooth stones used for sharpening *dahs* (large knives); and finally a small fire. A sacrifice must be offered to the spirit of the

---

[1] A. R. Brown, *The Andaman Islanders*, pp. 133, 164.

murdered man, and the most effective is that of a dog ; but if a dog is not available and the matter is urgent, a fowl or a pig will answer the purpose. The sacrificial animal is killed over the pounder, and the murderer steps over the *kumbang* grass, the pounder, the sacrificed animal, the stone and the fire. Having done so, he bends back the grass in the direction away from the pounder, and he may then enter the village and his home, both of them now being considered secure from the unpleasant attentions of the murdered man's ghost. Under no circumstances will anybody use or even touch the pounder, stone, or, if a pig or fowl has been sacrificed, the flesh of the sacrificed animal. These remain lying in the sacred grove.[1]

The Lushai of North-Eastern India believe that if a man kills an enemy the ghost of his victim will haunt him and he will go mad, unless he performs a certain ceremony which will make him master of the dead man's soul in the other world. The ceremony includes the sacrifice of an animal, whether a goat, a pig, or a mithran.[2]

Among the Lakhers, a tribe of head-hunters in the same region, as soon as the warriors have returned from a successful raid, all those who have been lucky enough to take an enemy's head must perform a certain ceremony called the *Ia*, the object

[1] W. J. S. Carrapiett, *The Kachin Tribes of Burma* (Rangoon, 1929), pp. 29, 69.
[2] Lieut.-Col. J. Shakespear, " The Kuki-Lushai clans ", in the *Journal of the Royal Anthropological Institute*, xxxix. (1909) p. 380; *id., The Lushei Kuki Clans* (London, 1912), pp. 78 *sq.*

of which is twofold : first to render the spirit of the slain, which is called *saw*, harmless to his slayer, and secondly to ensure that the spirit of the slain shall be the slave of the slayer in the next world. It is believed that unless the *Ia* ceremony is performed over the heads of men killed in war, their ghosts (*saw*) will render their slayers blind, lame, or paralysed, and that if by any lucky chance a man who has omitted to perform the *Ia* ceremony escapes these evils, they will surely fall upon his children or his grandchildren. Again, if the *Ia* ceremony is not performed the spirit of the slain man will not accompany his slayer to the spirit land as his slave, but will go to a special abode of the dead where dwell the spirits of all those who have died violent deaths. The *Ia* ceremony varies somewhat from village to village ; but it always includes a dance round either the captured head or an artificial head carved out of a gourd. On the night of the ceremony and all the next day dancing and singing continue. The following day is a holiday (*aoh*). No work is done in the village, and no one leaves it. The next day each man who has taken a head kills a pig, and then goes and bathes and thoroughly cleanses himself of all bloodstains, so that the spirits of the dead shall not be able to recognize their slayers. While the *Ia* ceremony is in progress the man performing it may not sleep with his wife. Not till he has cleansed himself may he resume conjugal relations. The belief is that during the *Ia* ceremony the spirit of the deceased is hovering round, and if it saw the man who had slain him sleeping with his wife, it would say, "Ah, you prefer women to me ", and would inform all the spirits, and the man who had done what is forbidden would not be allowed to take any more heads. In the village of Chapi some special precautions are taken to guard the slayer against the vengeful ghost of the man whom he has slain. On the return of the warriors from a raid, a dog is sacrificed by each warrior who has taken a head, and its skull is hung up above the head of the man slain. This is a preliminary precaution to guard the slayer against the angry ghost of the man whom he has slain. They think that the dog's ghost will bark at the dead man's ghost, and so hinder him from harming his slayer. After that the warriors enter the village and perform the rest of the *Ia* ceremony, by sacrificing a pig and dancing round an artificial head. Then in the evening each man who has taken a head goes into his house with the cook, the rice-beer maker, the drummers and the person who played the gongs at the *Ia* feast, and they must all remain inside the house for five days. On the morning of the sixth day the man who has taken a head rises at cockcrow and goes and bathes in the nearest stream. He then returns to his house and in front of it plants two chestnut poles. The persons who have kept him company inside the house during these five days hold on to the chestnut poles, and the head-taker says, " The spirit of the man I have killed has now departed ". Then they sacrifice a pig and eat it, so finishing the ceremony. The reason why the cook, the rice-beer maker, the drummer and the gong-player are shut up for five days with the head-taker is that it is believed that if they go home before the whole ceremony is finished they will take the deceased's ghost with them and will become ill. During these days it is taboo for the head-taker to sleep with his wife. If he did so he would take no more heads, for the reason already given.

Among these Lakhers, a man who has taken a head in war, although by doing so he has acquired great renown, is none the less regarded as unclean. On his return to the village a head-taker is taboo (*pana*) until the *Ia* ceremony has been performed to lay the dangerous ghost of the man killed ; and it is not until a formal purification—at which the hands and feet are washed in the blood of the pig sacrificed and the whole body is washed in water—has been accomplished, that a head-taker resumes his ordinary family and social relations. The temporary separation of a head-taker from the rest of the community is especially marked among the Sabeu, the tribe inhabiting the Chapi group of villages. Among this tribe the ghost (*saw*) of the deceased is regarded as so powerful that it is believed that it will do harm to all who helped the head-taker to perform the *Ia* ceremony and to their family unless they remain with him apart until the ghost (*saw*) has finally been laid and the head-taker cleansed. All Lakhers share this view, but their ceremonies are less elaborate than those of the Sabeu. It is not only men who have taken heads in war who are bound to cleanse and purify themselves, murderers are also under the same obligation. Although head-taking on a raid is deemed meritorious, while murder is regarded as a social sin, it makes no difference to the fact that after taking human life a man must purify himself ; but even after purification a murderer labours under certain social disadvantages, while a head-taker does not.[1]

Among the Oraons of Chota Nagpur in India the angry spirit of a murdered man is propitiated by sacrifice, and is sometimes reckoned among the ancestral spirits of his murderer. For example, " in village Siligain two Oraons, related to each other as cousins, had a quarrel over a piece of land ; and one of them, in a sudden fit of anger, thrust his axe into the bowels of the other man. The man, thus struck, at once ran to his assailant's house and, pressing his wounded stomach with his hands, sat down at one corner of the hut and exclaimed, 'Here I establish myself,' and then ran out again to the field in dispute and dropped down dead. To this day, the descendants of the murderer propitiate the murdered man's spirit. After the harvest, the first sheaf of paddy from the field on to which he dropped down dead is offered to the spirit of the murdered man at the same corner of the house where he sat down before his death. The descendants of the murdered man too are allowed access to the same

[1] N. E. Parry, *The Lakhers* (London, 1932), pp. 213-218.

spot for making similar offerings."[1] In Travancore the ghosts of murderers who have been hanged are thought to be especially dangerous and are believed to haunt the place of execution and its neighbourhood. To prevent this it used to be customary to cut off the criminal's heels with a sword or to hamstring him as he was turned off.[2]

In Africa also the belief is very widespread that the ghosts of the slain are dangerous to their slayers, or to the community in general, and special precautions are taken to guard against them. For this purpose among the Kabyles of North Africa a murderer tries to leap seven times over the grave of his victim within three or seven days, believing that if he can do so he will be safe from the pursuit of the ghost. Hence the fresh grave of a murdered man is carefully guarded.[3] Among the Ibibio of Southern Nigeria, when a murderer thinks that he is haunted to his hurt by his victim's angry ghost, he offers a dog in sacrifice to the offended spirit. Should the sacrifice prove unavailing he catches a male lizard, and, with this carefully caged, goes to a place where cross-roads meet. There, by the wayside, he makes a tiny gallows, and taking out the lizard from its prison, passes it three times round his head, crying, " Here I give you a man instead of me. Take him and leave me free." After this he places a noose round the neck of the lizard and hangs it upon the miniature gallows, hoping that the ghost will accept

[1] S. C. Roy, *Oraon Religion and Custom* (Ranchi, 1928), pp. 69 *sq.*

[2] Rev. S. Mateer, *The Land of Charity* (London, 1871), pp. 203 *sq.*

[3] J. Liorel, *Kabyle du Jurjura* (Paris, N.D.), p. 441.

the lizard instead of himself or another human victim.[1]

The Yendang, a tribe of Northern Nigeria, were formerly head-hunters like all their neighbours. Among them men who had taken heads were obliged to have their bodies washed in beer by an old man in order to safeguard themselves from pursuit by the ghosts of their victims.[2]   Again, among the Katab, another tribe of Northern Nigeria, who were also of old head-hunters, when a warrior had taken a head he used to make off with it at full speed, and when he was free from pursuit one of his friends made him drink immediately a concoction of the bark of the locust and male shea-trees, at the same time striking him on the chest and back with locust-bean leaves.   These rites were designed to protect the warrior from assault from the dead man's ghost.[3] The Chiwai, another tribe of Northern Nigeria, used also to be head-hunters, like all their neighbours. Among them all heads taken had to be brought immediately to the priestly chief of the village.   The heads were boiled, and pieces of the flesh eaten by the priest, after which the skulls were deposited in the sacred hut of the village.   During the performance of these rites each man who had taken a head remained in concealment, and he was anointed with a filthy mixture, which included the intestines of a porcupine, in order to ward off pursuit by the dead

---

[1] P. A. Talbot, *Life in Southern Nigeria*, p. 245 ; *id.*, *The Peoples of Southern Nigeria* (London, 1926), iii. 866.

[2] C. K. Meek, *Tribal Studies in Northern Nigeria* (London, 1931), i. 487.

[3] C. K. Meek, *op. cit.* ii. 69.

man's ghost.[1] Among the Yungur, another tribe of head-hunters in Northern Nigeria, it was customary for a warrior on taking a head to lick off the blood from his weapon in order to prevent his victim's ghost from pursuing him.[2] Among the Igara, yet another tribe of head-hunters in Northern Nigeria, a warrior who had taken a head used to propitiate the spirit of his dead foe annually by pouring the blood of a sacrificed pullet over his enemy's skull before he might eat of the new yams.[3] And in this tribe when a man had taken a head it was deemed necessary for him to perform a purificatory rite for the purpose of warding off the angry ghost of his victim. With this object the slayer partook of a magical medicine, which was made up by grinding into powder a portion of the lips, nose, eyes, eyebrows, genital organs, liver and heart of his enemy, together with various herbs. The eating of this concoction was considered to destroy the power of the ghost of his dead foe to harm the eater.[4]

The Dinka, a pastoral people of the Upper Nile, believe that a homicide is likely to be haunted by his victim's ghost, and in consequence to grow thinner and weaker until he dies.[5] Among the Shilluk, another tribe of the Upper Nile, warriors used to engage the services of a medicine man to invoke their ancestors that the spirits of their slain enemies might

[1] C. K. Meek, *op. cit.* ii. 156.
[2] C. K. Meek, *op. cit.* ii. 458.
[3] Capt. J. R. Wilson-Haffenden, *The Red Men of Nigeria* (London, 1930), p. 215.

[4] Capt. J. R. Wilson-Haffenden, *op. cit.* pp. 216 *sq.*
[5] C. G. and B. L. Seligman, *Pagan Tribes of the Nilotic Sudan* (London, 1932), p. 177.

do them no harm. For this purpose a sheep was sacrificed, and part of its entrails buried in a pot as an offering to the spirits of the underworld.[1] Among the Lango, a Nilotic tribe of Uganda, on the morning after a battle every man who has slain an enemy brings a goat or a sheep for a sacrifice, because the killing of an enemy entails great dangers from his ghost. The ghost is supposed to have a deadly influence on his slayer, afflicting him with attacks of giddiness and frenzy, during which he may do himself or the bystanders mortal mischief. It makes his brain reel, and dances in his head until he is not responsible for his actions. For this reason, and also lest in the heat of the conflict a leprous or cancerous man has been speared, the slayers sacrifice goats and sheep, which may be of any colour, unless the slayer feels the influence of a ghost already beginning to affect him, in which case he must kill a black goat. The whole community joins in eating the meat of the sacrificial victims. The undigested matter from the intestines of the slaughtered goats is smeared over the bodies of the warriors to protect them from the ghosts of their dead enemies, and all the bones are burned to ashes, which the warriors throw broadcast to the winds. The ghost of the slain man has also to be appeased by making cicatrices on the bodies of his slayers. This has to be done by the slayer himself: he cuts rows of these scars on his shoulder and upper arm, the number of

[1] W. Hofmayr, *Die Shilluk* (Vienna, 1925), p. 230; *id.*, C. G. Seligman, *op. cit.* p. 97.

the scars varying according to his ability to stand the pain up to three and a half rows. Finally each slayer has to shave his head in a particular fashion called *atira*.[1]

Among the Nilotic people of Kavirondo, to the east of Lake Victoria Nyanza, when a warrior has killed another in battle he is isolated from his village, lives in a separate hut for about four days, and is fed by an old woman because he may not touch food with his hands. On the fifth day he is escorted to the river by another man, who washes him. A white goat is killed and cooked by the attendant, who feeds the man with the meat. The goat-skin is cut into strips and put upon the slayer's wrists and round his head, and he returns to his temporary home for the night. The next day he is again taken to the river and washed, and a white fowl is presented him. He kills it and it is cooked for him, and he is again fed with the meat. He is then pronounced to be clean, and may return to his home. It sometimes happens that a warrior spears another man in battle and the latter dies from the wound some time after. When he dies the relatives go to the warrior and inform him of the death, and he is separated at once from the community until the ceremonies above described have been performed. The people say that the ceremonies are necessary in order to release the ghost of the dead man, which is bound to the warrior who slew him and is only

[1] J. H. Driberg, *The Lango, a Nilotic Tribe of Uganda* (London, 1923), pp. 110 *sq.*

released on the fulfilment of the ceremonies. Should a warrior refuse to fulfil the ceremonies, the ghost will ask, " Why don't you fulfil the ceremonies and let me go ? " Should the man still refuse to comply, the ghost will take him by the throat and strangle him.[1]

Among these Nilotic people of Kavirondo the ceremonial treatment of a murderer closely resembles the treatment of a warrior who has killed a foe in battle, and the reason is that both treatments are dictated by a fear of the ghost of the slain. When a murder has been committed the murderer seldom seeks safety in flight, and often confesses his guilt without any trial. But he must undergo a ceremony of purification. He is first separated from the members of his village and lives in a hut with an old woman who attends to his wants, cooks for him and also feeds him, for he may not touch food with his own hands. The seclusion lasts three days, after which a man who is himself a murderer, or has at some time killed a man in battle, leads the murderer to a stream and washes him all over. He then kills a goat and cooks the meat, takes four sticks and places a piece of meat on each stick and gives the man the meat to eat from each stick in turn. When the meat has been eaten, he gives him four pieces of porridge made into balls and put on the sticks. After this the goat-skin is cut into strips, which are put round the neck and round each wrist of the murderer. This ceremony is performed by the two

[1] J. Roscoe, *The Northern Bantu* (Cambridge, 1915), p. 289.

men who are alone at the river, and after it the murderer is free to return home. It is said that until this ceremony is performed the ghost cannot take its departure for the place of the dead, but hovers about the murderer.[1]

Among the Basoga, a Bantu people of Uganda, on the northern shore of Lake Victoria Nyanza, when a murder has been committed by a member of another clan, the clan whose member has been killed seeks to capture a member of the offending clan and kill him. Sometimes they succeed in capturing one of its members, most often a youth in the road. They drag him away to the grave of the murdered man and there cut his throat and leave the body lying at the grave as an atonement to the ghost of the murdered.[2] Among the Bagesu, a cannibal tribe of Mount Elgon in Kenya, when a murderer belongs to the same clan as his victim he must leave his village and find a new home, even though the case may be settled amicably. But before quitting the village the murderer has to take a goat, kill it, smear his chest with the contents of the stomach, and take the remainder and throw it upon the roof of the house of the murdered man to appease the ghost of his victim.[3]

Among the Banyankole, a pastoral people of Southern Uganda, "a warrior who had killed a man was treated like a murderer or a hunter who had killed a lion, leopard, antelope, or hyaena (because

[1] J. Roscoe, *op. cit.* p. 281.   [2] J. Roscoe, *op. cit.* p. 243.
[3] J. Roscoe, *op. cit.* p. 98.

these animals belonged to the gods) ; he was not allowed to sleep or eat with others until he had been purified, for the ghost of the man was upon him ".[1] Among the Bakitara, a powerful tribe of Uganda, when a rebellious prince had been killed it was necessary that he should be speared, even after his death, by a man of royal blood, for no ordinary man might shed royal blood, and the prince's ghost might be a dangerous enemy to the man who had done such a deed.[2] Similarly among the Bakunta, a small tribe on the shores of Lake Edward in Uganda, the princes of the royal family often rose in rebellion against the king. If the king was killed in the fight, the man who did the deed was raised to a position of authority and importance at the time, but when later any misfortune or illness attacked members of the royal house, the priests would declare that the ghost of the last monarch desired vengeance on his murderer, and the dead king's successor would be persuaded to arrest and kill the man whose act had put him on the throne. If it was the rebellious prince who had been killed, the same treatment would be meted out to his slayer, for none might shed royal blood with impunity.[3]

Among the Kikuyu, a Bantu tribe of Kenya, when a man has killed a person of his own clan, it is deemed necessary to perform certain ceremonies for the purpose of guarding him against the dangerous

[1] J. Roscoe, *The Banyankole* (Cambridge, 1923), p. 161.

[2] J. Roscoe, *The Bakitara or Banyoro* (Cambridge, 1923), p. 314.

[3] J. Roscoe, *The Bagesu and other Tribes of the Uganda Protectorate* (Cambridge, 1924), p. 159.

ghost of his victim. Among other things, the elders go to the local sacred fig-tree and kill a sheep there. They deposit some of the fat, the chest bone, the intestines, and the more important bones at the foot of the tree. The rest of the carcase is eaten by the elders. They say that the ghost of the murdered man will visit the tree that night in the shape of a wild cat and eat the meat, and that this offering will prevent the ghost of the deceased from coming back to his village and troubling the occupants.[1] Among the Bantu tribes of Kavirondo, when a man has killed an enemy in warfare he shaves his head on his return home, and his friends rub a medicine, which generally consists of goat's dung, over his body to prevent the spirit of the slain man from troubling him.[2] Exactly the same custom is observed for the same reason by the Wageia of Tanganyika.[3] With the Ja-Luo of Kavirondo the custom is somewhat different. Three days after his return from the fight the warrior shaves his head. But before he may enter the village he has to hang a live fowl, head uppermost, round his neck; then the bird is decapitated and its head is left hanging round his neck. Soon after his return a feast is made for the slain man, in order that his ghost may not haunt his slayer.[4] When a Ketosh warrior of

[1] C. W. Hobley, " Kikuyu Customs and Beliefs ", in *Journal of the Royal Anthropological Institute*, xl. (1910) pp. 438 *sq.*

[2] Sir H. Johnston, *The Uganda Protectorate*, ii. 723 ; C. W. Hobley, *Eastern Uganda*, p. 20.

[3] M. Weiss, *Die Völkerstämme im Norden Deutsch-Ostafrikas* (Berlin, 1910), p. 198.

[4] Sir H. Johnston, *The Uganda Protectorate*, ii. 794 *sq.* ; C. W. Hobley, *Eastern Uganda*, p. 31.

Kenya who has killed a foe in battle returns home, " it is considered essential that he should have connection with his wife as soon as convenient ; this is believed to prevent the spirit of his dead enemy from haunting and bewitching him ".[1]

Among the Ba-Yaka, a Bantu people of the Congo Free State, a man who has been killed in battle is supposed to send his soul to avenge his death on the man who killed him ; but the slayer can escape the vengeance of the dead by wearing the red tail-feathers of the parrot in his hair, and painting his forehead red.[2]

Among the Boloki, a people of the Upper Congo, " a homicide is not afraid of the spirit of the man he has killed when the slain man belongs to any of the neighbouring towns, as disembodied spirits travel in a very limited area only ; but when he kills a man belonging to his own town he is filled with fear lest the spirit shall do him some harm. There are no special rites that he can observe to free himself from these fears, but he mourns for the slain man as though he were a member of his own family. He neglects his personal appearance, shaves his head, fasts for a certain period, and laments with much weeping."[3] By this display of sorrow he doubtless hopes to soften the heart of his victim's ghost, and so to induce him to spare his slayer.

[1] C. W. Hobley, " British East Africa ", in *Journal of the Anthropological Institute*, xxxiii. (1903) p. 353.

[2] E. Torday and T. A. Joyce, " Notes on the Ethnography of the Ba-Yaka ", in the *Journal of the Royal Anthropological Institute*, xxxvi. (1906) pp. 50 *sq.*

[3] J. H. Weeks, *Among Congo Cannibals* (London, 1913), p. 268.

Among the Angoni, a Zulu tribe settled to the north of the Zambesi, warriors who have slain foes on an expedition smear their bodies and faces with ashes, and hang garments of their victims on their persons. This costume they wear for three days after their return, and rising at break of day they run through the village uttering frightful yells to banish the ghosts of the slain, which otherwise might bring sickness and misfortune on the people.[1] Among the Ila-speaking peoples of Northern Rhodesia, who were head-hunters, the warrior who had taken a head in battle had afterwards to undergo purification. The doctor or medicine-man put a little medicine on the tongue of the slayer that the ghost of the man he had slain might not trouble him. This he did to each of the warriors who had taken a head in battle. Further, each warrior was bathed in the fumes of certain medicines burnt in a sherd. The ashes were afterwards placed in a koodoo horn and planted at the threshold of his hut to drive off the ghost of the person he had killed.[2]

In these tribes a man who has committed a murder is believed to be possessed by the ghost of his victim, which renders him very uneasy in his mind ; but the ghost can be expelled by the taking of an emetic or by cupping, and so the slayer's peace of mind can be restored ; he has either vomited up the ghost or ejected him in the blood of

<hr />

[1] C. Wiese, " Beiträge zur Geschichte der Zulu im Norden des Zambesi ", in *Zeitschrift für Ethnologie*, xxxii. (1900) pp. 197 *sq.*

[2] Rev. E. W. Smith and Capt. A. M. Dale, *The Ila-speaking Peoples of Northern Rhodesia* (London, 1920), i. 179.

his body.[1] Among the Awemba, a tribe of Northern Rhodesia, "according to a superstition common among Central African tribes, unless the slayers were purified from blood-guiltiness they would become mad. On the night of return no warrior might sleep in his own hut, but lay in the open *nsaka* in the village. The next day, after bathing in the stream and being anointed with lustral medicine by the doctor, he could return to his own hearth, and resume intercourse with his wife."[2] In all such cases the madness of the slayer is probably attributed by the natives to the ghost of the man he has slain, which has taken possession of him.

Among the Thonga, a Bantu tribe of South Africa, about Delagoa Bay, "to have killed an enemy on the battlefield entails an immense glory for the slayer ; but that glory is fraught with great danger. They have killed. . . . So they are exposed to the mysterious and deadly influence of the *nuru* and must consequently undergo a medical treatment. What is the *nuru* ? *Nuru*, the spirit of the slain which tries to take its revenge on the slayer. It haunts him and may drive him to insanity : his eyes swell, protrude, and become inflamed. He will lose his head, be attacked by giddiness, and the thirst for blood may lead him to fall upon members of his own family and to stab them with his assegay. To prevent such misfortunes, a special medication is required, the slayers must *lurulula tiyimpa ta bu*,

[1] Smith and Dale, *op. cit.* ii. pp. 136 *sq.*
[2] J. H. West Sheane, "Wemba Warpaths ", in *Journal of the African Society*, No. 41 (October, 1911), pp. 31 *sq.*

take away the *nuru* of their sanguinary expedition.
. . . In what consists this treatment ? The slayers
must remain some days at the capital. They are
taboo. They put on old clothes, eat with special
spoons, because their hands are ' hot ', and off special
plates (*mireko*) and broken pots. They are forbidden
to drink water. Their food must be cold. The chief
kills oxen for them ; but if the meat were hot it
would make them swell internally ' because they are
hot themselves, they are defiled (*ba na nsila*) '. If
they eat hot food, the defilement would enter into
them. ' They are black (*ntima*). This black must
be removed.' During all this time sexual relations
are absolutely forbidden to them. They must not
go home to their wives. In former times the Ba-
Ronga used to tattoo them with special marks from
one eyebrow to the other. Dreadful medicines were
inoculated in the incisions, and there remained
pimples ' which gave them the appearance of a
buffalo when it frowns '. After some days a medicine-
man comes to purify them, ' to remove their black '.
There seems to be various ways of doing it, according to Mankhelu. Seeds of all kinds are put into a
broken pot and roasted, together with drugs and
psanyi [1] of a goat. The slayers inhale the smoke
which emanates from the pot. They put their hands
into the mixture and rub their limbs with it, especially the joints. . . . Insanity threatening those who
shed blood might begin early. So, already on the

[1] *Psanyi* is half-digested grass found in the stomachs of sacrificed goats. See Henri A. Junod, *The* *Life of a South African Tribe*, Second Edition (London, 1927), i. 477 *sqq.*

battlefield, just after their deed, warriors are given a preventive dose of the medicine by those who have killed on previous occasions. . . . The period of seclusion having been concluded by the final purification, all the implements used by the slayers during these days, and their old garments, are tied together and hung by a string to a tree, at some distance from the capital, where they are left to rot."[1]

Among the Basutos of South Africa ablution is especially performed on return from battle. It is absolutely necessary that the warriors should rid themselves, as soon as possible, of the blood they have shed, or the ghosts of their victims would pursue them incessantly, and disturb their slumbers. They go in procession, and in full armour, to the nearest stream. At the moment they enter the water a diviner, placed higher up, throws some purifying substance into the current. The spears and battle-axes also undergo the process of washing.[2]

Among the Thompson Indians of British Columbia, when a man had killed his enemy he used to blacken his own face, believing that if he failed to do so the ghost of his victim would blind him.[3] On the evening of the day on which they had tortured a prisoner to death, the American Indians used to run through the village with hideous yells, beating with sticks on the furniture, the walls, and the roofs of the huts to prevent the angry ghost of

---

[1] H. A. Junod, *op. cit.* i. 477 *sqq.*
[2] Rev. E. Casalis, *The Basutos* (London, 1861), p. 258.
[3] J. Teit, *The Thompson Indians*, p. 357.

their victim from settling there and taking vengeance for the torments that his body had endured
at their hands.[1] " Once," says a traveller, " on
approaching in the night a village of Ottawas, I
found all the inhabitants in confusion : they were
all busily engaged in raising noises of the loudest
and most inharmonious kind. Upon inquiry, I
found that a battle had been lately fought between
the Ottawas and the Kickapoos, and that the object
of all this noise was to prevent the ghosts of the
departed combatants from entering the village." [2]
Amongst the Omaha Indians of the United States
a murderer whose life had been spared by the kinsmen of his victim had to observe certain stringent
rules for a period which varied from two to four
years. He must walk barefoot, and he might eat
no warm food, nor raise his voice, nor look around.
He had to pull his robe around him and to keep it
tied at the neck, even in warm weather ; he might
not let it hang loose or fly open. He might not
move his hands about, but had to keep them close
to his body. He might not comb his hair, nor
might it be blown about by the wind. No one would
eat with him, and only one of his kindred was allowed
to remain with him in his tent. When the tribe
went hunting, he was obliged to pitch his tent about
a quarter of a mile from the rest of the people,
" lest the ghost of his victim should raise a high

[1] P. F. X. de Charlevoix, *Histoire de la Nouvelle-France* (Paris, 1744), vi. 77, 122 *sq.* ; J. F. Lafitau, *Mœurs des sauvages ameriquains*, ii. 279.

[2] W. H. Keating, *Narrative of an Expedition to the Source of the St. Peter's River* (London, 1825), i. 109.

wind which might cause damage."[1] The reason here alleged for banishing the murderer from the camp of the hunters gives the clue to all the other restrictions laid on him : he was haunted by the ghost and therefore dangerous. Speaking specially of the Creek Indians in the south-east of the United States, James Adair, who knew them well, tells us that after a successful expedition the Indians cut the scalps into several pieces and place them on the tops of the winter houses of their deceased relations, whose deaths, if by the hand of the enemy, they esteem not revenged until then ; and thus their ghosts are enabled to go to their intermediate place of rest, till after a certain time they return to live for ever in that tract of land which pleased them best when in their former state. They dance for three days and nights for their victory, and for the happiness of sending the spirits of their killed relations from the eaves of their houses which they haunted, mourning with plaintive notes, like owls in winter.[2] From observing the great respect paid by the Indians to the scalps they had taken, and listening to the mournful songs which they howled to the shades of their victims, the painter Catlin was convinced that " they have a superstitious dread of the spirits of their slain enemies, and many conciliatory offices to perform, to ensure their own peace."[3]

---

[1] Rev. J. Owen Dorsey, " Omaha Sociology ", in *Third Annual Report of the Bureau of Ethnology* (Washington, 1884), p. 369.

[2] James Adair, *History of the American Indians* (London, 1775), p. 397.

[3] G. Catlin, *North American Indians*, Fourth Edition (London, 1844), i. 246.

Among the Natchez, an Indian tribe of the lower Mississippi, young braves who had taken their first scalps were obliged to observe certain rules of abstinence for six months. They might not sleep with their wives, nor eat flesh ; their only food was fish and hasty-pudding. If they broke these rules, they believed that the soul of the man they had killed would work their death by magic, that they would gain no more successes over the enemy, and that the least wound inflicted on them would prove mortal.[1]

The Indians of British Guiana in South America believe that an avenger of blood who has slain his man must go mad unless he tastes the blood of his victim ; in order to avert this consequence the Indian man-slayer resorts on the third night to the grave of his victim, pierces the corpse with a sharp-pointed stick, and withdrawing it sucks the blood of the murdered man. After that he goes home with an easy mind, satisfied that he has done his duty and that he has nothing more to fear from the ghost.[2] Among the Lengua Indians of Paraguay a murderer is not only put to death, but his body is burned, and his ashes scattered to the four winds. These Indians believe that after this treatment his spirit cannot take human form, and remains in the after-world shapeless and unrecognizable, and

---

[1] " Relation des Natchez ", Voyages aux Nord (Amsterdam, 1737), ix. 24 ; Lettres édifiantes et curieuses (Paris, 1780-1783), vii. 26 ; Charlevoix, Histoire de la Nouvelle-France.

[2] Rev. J. H. Bernau, Missionary Labours in British Guiana (London, 1847), pp. 57 sq. ; R. Schomburgk, Reisen in British Guiana (Leipsic, 1847-1848), ii. 497 ; W. H. Brett, Indian Tribes of Guiana (London, 1868), pp. 358 sq

therefore unable to mingle with its kindred spirits, or to enjoy such social intercourse as exists.[1] In that disabled and melancholy state the spirit of the murderer must clearly be incapable of harming the survivors.

Like so many savages, the ancient Greeks believed that the soul of any man who had just been killed was angry with his slayer and troubled him ; hence even an involuntary homicide had to depart from his country for a year until the wrath of the dead man had cooled down ; nor might the slayer return until sacrifice had been offered and ceremonies of purification performed. If his victim chanced to be a foreigner, the homicide had to shun the country of the dead man as well as his own.[2] The legend of the matricide Orestes, how he roamed from place to place pursued and maddened by the ghost of his murdered mother, reflects faithfully the ancient Greek conception of the fate which overtakes the murderer at the hands of the ghost.[3]

But it is important to observe that to Greek thinking not only does the hag-ridden homicide go in terror of his victim's ghost ; he is himself an object of fear and aversion to the whole community on account of the angry and dangerous spirit which dogs his steps. It was probably more in self-defence than out of consideration for the man-

---

[1] W. B. Grubb, *An Unknown People in an Unknown Land*, p. 120.
[2] Plato, *Laws*, ix. 8, pp. 865D-866A ; Demosthenes, xxiii. pp. 683 sq. ; Hesychius, s.v. ἀπενιαυτισμός.

[3] Aeschylus, *Choephor*, 1021 sq. ; *Eumenides*, 85 sqq. ; Euripides, *Iphig.in Tauri*, 940 sqq.; Pausanias, ii. 31. 8, viii. 34. 1-4.

slayer that Attic law compelled him to quit the country. This comes out clearly from the provisions of the law. For in the first place, on going into banishment the homicide had to follow a prescribed road:[1] obviously it would have been hazardous to let him stray about the country with a wrathful ghost at his heels. In the second place, if another charge was brought against a banished homicide, he was allowed to return to Attica to plead in his defence, but he might not set foot on land ; he had to speak from a ship, and even the ship might not cast anchor or put out a gangway. The judges avoided all contact with the culprit, for they judged the case sitting or standing on the shore.[2] Plainly the intention of this rule was literally to insulate the slayer, lest by touching Attic earth even indirectly through the anchor or gangway he should blast it by a sort of electric shock, as we might say ; though doubtless the Greeks would have said that the blight was wrought by contact with the ghost, through a sort of effluence of death. For the same reason if such a man, sailing the sea, happened to be wrecked on the coast of the country where his crime had been committed, he was allowed to camp on the shore till a ship came to take him off, but he was expected to keep his feet in sea-water all the time,[3] evidently to neutralize the ghostly infection, and prevent it from

[1] Demosthenes, xxiii. pp. 643 *sq.*
[2] Demosthenes, xxiii. pp. 645 *sq.* ; Aristotle, *Constitution of Athens*, 57 ; Pausanias, i. 28. 11 ; Pollux, viii. 120 ; Helladius, quoted by Photius ; *Bibliotheca*, p. 535A, lines 28 *sqq.*, ed. I. Bekker (Berlin, 1824).
[3] Plato, *Laws*, ix. 8, p. 866C, D.

spreading to the soil. For the same reason, when the turbulent people of Cynaetha in Arcadia had perpetrated a particularly atrocious massacre and had sent envoys to Sparta, all the Arcadian states through which the envoys took their way ordered them out of the country ; and after their departure the Mantineans purified themselves and their belongings by sacrificing victims and carrying them round the city and the whole of their land.[1] So when the Athenians had heard of a massacre at Argos, they caused purificatory offerings to be carried round the public assembly.[2] No doubt the root of all such observances was a fear of the dangerous ghost which haunts the murderer and against which the whole community as well as the homicide himself must be on its guard. The Greek practice in these respects is clearly mirrored in the legend of Orestes ; for it is said that the people of Troezen would not receive him in their houses until he had been purified of his guilt,[3] that is, until he had been rid of his mother's ghost.

At a sanctuary of the goddesses of madness—the Maniae—in Arcadia, on the road from Megalopolis to Messene, a curious legend ran that on his wanderings Orestes came thither and there, maddened by the murder of his mother, bit off one of his fingers, whereupon the black Furies of his murdered mother, who had driven him crazy, appeared to him white,

---

[1] Polybius, iv. 17-21.
[2] Plutarch, *Praecept. ger. reipub.*   xvii. 9.
[3] Pausanias, ii. 31. 8.

and he was at once healed of his madness.[1] The legend perhaps contains a reminiscence of a drastic mode of appeasing the angry ghost of a murdered person, to which Greek murderers may sometimes have resorted. In savage society, as we have seen, man-slayers are often supposed to be driven mad by the ghosts of their victims, and have resort to many ceremonies for the purpose of ridding themselves of these dangerous spirits. With this object Greek murderers may sometimes have sacrificed a finger. The sacrifice of a finger, or rather the joint or joints of a finger, in mourning and on other occasions, has been a common custom in many parts of the world, including Australia, Polynesia, India, Africa, and America.[2]

---

[1] Pausanias, viii. 34. 2, with my commentary upon the passage in *Pausanias's Description of Greece*, iv. pp. 355-357.

[2] See my note on Pausanias, *loc. cit.* For further references to the custom see J. C. van Eerde: "Fingermutilatie in Centraal Nieuw-Guinea", in *Tijdschrift van het Koninklijk Nederlandsch Aardrijkskundig Genootschap*, 2de Serie, Deel xxviii. (1911) pp. 49-65; P. J. de Smet, *Western Missions and Missionaries* (New York, 1863), p. 135. (at the first peal of thunder in spring); G. B. Grinnell, *Blackfoot Lodge Indians* (London, 1893), pp. 194, 258; J. Mathew, *Eaglehawk and Crow* (London and Melbourne, 1899), p. 120; Chevron, in *Annales de l'Association de la Propagation de la Foi*, xiv. (1842) p. 192 (sacrifice for a sick parent in Fiji); *op. cit.* xvii. (1845) pp. 74 *sqq.* (in Australia, sacrifice to serpents, fish, or kanga-roos in infancy); *op. cit.* xviii. (1846) p. 6 (Wallis Island, Pacific: a general custom); *op. cit.* xxiii. (1851) p. 314 (Mandan and Big-Belly Indians, North America: in mourning for children or grand-children); *op. cit.* xxxii. (1860) p. 95 (Futuna Island, Pacific: Sacrifice at illness or death of parent); Max Bartels, "Isländischer Brauch und Volksglaube in Bezug auf die Nach-kommenschaft", in *Zeitschrift für Ethnologie*, xxxii. (1900) p. 74 (Ice-and: mother bites off child's finger to prolong child's life); Mgr. Le Roy, "Les Pygmées", in *Les Missions Catholiques*, xxix. (1897) p. 90 (Ba-Bongo of Upper Ogowe River, Africa: mutilation of chil-dren's fingers after death of first-born child); Buchanan Hamilton, cited in *The Indian Antiquary*, xxiv. (Bombay, 1895) p. 303 (Mysore, India: amputation of mother's finger joints at betrothal of her

II. *Ghosts of Suicides*

The spirits of persons who have taken their own life are commonly regarded with dread and fear,

daughter) ; A. W. Howitt, *Native Tribes of South-East Australia* (London, 1904) pp. 746 *sq.* (Australia, tribes of eastern coast : amputation of joints of little finger or whole little finger of all women in childhood) ; Dudley Kidd, *The Essential Kafir* (London, 1904) pp. 203, 262 *sq.* (Africa, Kafirs : amputation of finger in mourning or childhood or to give strength. Amputated joint placed in roof to counteract evil magic of enemies) ; A. Karasek, " Beiträge zur Kenntnis des Waschambaa ", in *Baessler-Archiv* (Berlin and Leipzig), i. (1911) p. 171 (Africa, the Wachamba : mother amputates joint of her little finger and drops the blood into the eye of her child to heal malady of eyes. If hut falls on man and he escapes unhurt he amputates a joint of his little finger, buries it, and sacrifices a goat) ; E. Thurston, *Ethnographic Notes in Southern India* (Madras, 1906), pp. 390-396 (India, Mysore : amputation of first joints of third and fourth fingers of mother's right hand before her daughter's ears are pierced as a preparation for marriage) ; *id.*, Thurston, *Castes and Tribes of Southern India* (Madras, 1909), v. pp. 75 *sqq.* ; *Ethnographic Survey of Mysore* (Preliminary Issue), No. xv. pp. 8 *sq.*, 10 *sq.* ; Rev. A. G. Morice, " The Great Déné Race ", in *Anthropos*, i. (1906) p. 724 (N. America, Déné Indians : in mourning for child or husband) ; *Voyage de la Pérouse autour du monde* (Paris, 1797), iii. 254 (Tonga and other Polynesian islands : in mourning for dead relative or friend);

Labillardière, *Relation du voyage à la recherche de la Pérouse* (Paris, 1800), p. 151 (Tonga : to heal sickness) ; Rev. G. Brown, " Notes on a Recent Journey to New Guinea and New Britain ", in *Seventh Report of the Australasian Association for the Advancement of Science*, 1898 ; *id.*, G. Brown, *Melanesians and Polynesians* (London, 1910), pp. 241, 394 (New Guinea, New Britain, and Eastern Polynesia : amputation of finger-joints in mourning, and for benefit of sick friends) ; John Williams, *Narrative of Missionary Enterprises in the South Sea Islands* (London, 1838), pp. 470 *sq.* ; L. Degrandpré, *Voyage à la côte occidentale d'Afrique* (Paris, 1801), ii. pp. 93 *sq.* (Africa : amputation of finger-joints among Bushmen as cure for sickness) ; Father Betaillon, in *Annales de la Propagation de la Foi*, xiii. (1841) p. 20 (Wallis Island, Pacific : little fingers amputated in mourning and thrown on bier) ; J. B. Stair, *Old Samoa* (London, 1897), p. 117 (Samoa : amputation of finger or finger-joints in mourning) ; J. E. Erskine, *Journal of a Cruise among the Islands of the Western Pacific* (London, 1863), p. 123 (Tonga Island : in mourning and depreciation of sickness) ; R. W. Williamson, *The Mafulu* (London, 1912), p. 247 and note (New Guinea : in woman's mourning for children and other relatives) ; Baldwin Spencer, *Native Tribes of Northern Australia* (London, 1914), p. 10 (North Australia, Larakia Tribe : amputation of joint of index finger of woman by her mother in

and special precautions are taken by the living to guard against these dangerous ghosts. Among the Ewe tribes of Togo in West Africa, when a man is in great anger or trouble, he will sometimes go into the forest and hang himself on a tree. When this becomes known, if it is night, no one but the relations of the suicide will go to look for the body ; but next morning other people will go in search of it. They do it, however, in great fear, and hang magic strings about them, while others smear their faces with a magical powder, in order that the ghost of the suicide may not molest them. If a man hangs himself at midday, after previously making an unsuccessful attempt at suicide, the neighbours will not go to look for him, or if they go it is a mere pretence, and they leave to his relatives the trouble of finding his body. For they believe that the man who should first set eyes on the suicide would be unlucky and troubled by the dead man's ghost. Hence the people will not approach the body. When one of the searchers catches sight of the body he throws grass upon it, saying, " I pity you, I pity you ". Then the others come up, and

childhood, or at a later time) ; John Turnbull, *A Voyage Round the World in 1800–1804*, Second Edition, (London, 1813), p. 100 (Australia, New South Wales : amputation of first two joints of little finger of right hand of female child in infancy. Severed part thrown into sea, that the woman may thereafter be fortunate in fishing) ; David Collins, *Account of the English Colony in New South Wales*, Second Edition (London, 1804), pp. 358 *sq.* ; J. Irle, *Die Herero* (Gutersloh, 1906), p. 155 (South-West Africa, in tribe Bergdamra : first joint of little finger of left hand of every child amputated at birth as tribal mark) ; G. W. Stow, *Native Races of South Africa* (London, 1905), pp. 129, 152. See further my discussion of the subject in *Folk-Lore in the Old Testament*, iii. 198-241.

cut down the tree on which the man has hanged himself. After that they cut off the branch on which he hanged himself. On this branch they lay the corpse, and drag it ruthlessly over stones and through thorns to the place set apart for the burial of persons who have died a violent death (*Blutmenschen*). There they dig a small hole, shove the body in, and huddle it up in all haste. Should one of them have pity on the dead man he may fire a few shots from his musket. If a man has hanged himself in the neighbourhood of a village, they thrust a stake through his breast, carry him like a pig into the forest, and there give him a hasty burial. But if the man was unpopular, then they drag his body along the ground to the place of burial.

The branches of the tree on which he hung himself are then cut off and laid on his grave, in order that his remains may not be dragged out by wild beasts. After the burial the relations of the suicide must pay a fine of cowries and a goat to the villagers, because their kinsman has defiled the village by the manner of his death. A portion of the cowrie fine is used to defray the expenses of purifying the village from the defilement it has incurred through the death of the suicide. What remains of the fine is distributed among the villagers. Nine days later the people assemble to hold the final ceremony. They have bought palm-wine and collected provisions for the purpose. The brothers of the deceased on his father's side spread a new mat upside down on the road, and heap provisions of all kinds upon it, of which some of the people freely partake. Then they fill a small pot with palm wine, smear it with white earth, and bind its neck with the bark of the raffia palm. Next they cut three pieces of firewood, and put them together as if to form a hearth, and they place the pot upon the wood, but kindle no fire. In the evening they take the pot, together with all the provisions that lie upon the mat, carry them away, and set them down at the edge of the path near the suicide's grave. After that they go home and fire two musket shots, which ends the death ceremony. Afterwards the priests, for a fee, call the spirit of the suicide into the house of the earth-gods (*Trōhaus*). Arrived there, the spirit of the suicide makes his excuses to the deities for his crime. He may say, for example, that spirits have driven him mad, and so goaded him into crime. Or he may say that his dead brothers, who have also died unhappy deaths, have lured him to his doom, in order to have his company in the spirit land.

Among these people, when a man has taken his life, smarting under an insult which has been offered to him by a kinsman, his body is not buried until his relatives have paid a fine to the villagers, because his spirit is believed to render the ground barren, and to hinder the rain from falling, so that the whole tribe suffers from the effects of his crime. The member of his family who insulted the deceased is also called to account and must pay a fine before the body of his kinsman may be laid in the earth.

If the motive to suicide has been shame at the failure to keep a solemn promise which the man made in his life, his body is denied honourable burial, and the place where he did the deed must be purified by a sacrifice to the earth god (*trõ*).[1]

The Baganda of Central Africa were very superstitious about suicides. They took innumerable precautions to remove the body and destroy the ghost, lest he should cause trouble to the living. Shame for crime committed sometimes led to suicide, but this occurred rarely in any section of the community, and most rarely among women. When a man committed suicide, he hanged himself on a tree in his garden or in his house. In the former case the body was cut down, and the tree felled also, then both the tree and the corpse, the latter tied to a pole like the carcase of an animal, were taken to a distant place where cross-roads met, and the body was burned, the tree being used for firewood. When the suicide had taken place in the house the dwelling was pulled down, and the materials were taken with the body and burned in the road. People feared to live in a house in which a suicide had taken place, lest they too should be tempted to commit the same crime. Those who had burned the corpse afterwards washed their hands carefully at the place of burning with sponges made from plantains, and threw them on the pyre. When women passed the place where a suicide had been burned, they threw grass or sticks upon the heap, to prevent the ghost from

[1] J. Spieth, *Die Ewe-Stämme* (Berlin, 1906), pp. 272-277.

entering into them and being reborn. The intention
in burning the body was, if possible, to destroy the
ghost. If the suicide had been a man of no social
importance his body was regularly burnt to ashes
on a piece of waste land beside the road, or at
cross-roads, in order to destroy the ghost.[1] If,
however, he had been a person of some position,
and his relatives claimed the body, it was first
charred by fire before it was handed over to them.
Everyone passing the spot where the corpse of a
suicide had been burned took the precaution to
throw some grass, or a few sticks, on the place, so
as to prevent the ghost from catching him, in case it
had not been destroyed.[2]

Among the Wachagga of Mount Kilimanjaro in
East Africa the bodies of suicides are buried like
those of other people, but the place where the crime
was committed must be purified or, to use the expression of our authority, " pacified " by being
sprinkled with water drained from the blossom of a
certain sacred yellow flower. Further, they take the
noose of the rope with which the man had hanged
himself, and bringing a goat, hang it in the noose,
and then offer it in sacrifice. In this way they
attempt to appease the ghost of the suicide, and to
prevent him from tempting other people to imitate
his crime.[3] Among the Wachamba of Usambara

[1] J. Roscoe, *The Baganda* (London, 1911), pp. 20 *sq.*

[2] J. Roscoe, *op. cit.* p. 289.

[3] B. Gutmann, *Dichten und*
Denken der Dschagganeger (Leip-
zig, 1909), p. 141. Cf. Gutmann,
" Trauer und Begräbnis-sitten der
Wadschagga ", in *Globus*, lxxxix.
(1906) p. 200.

in Central Africa, the bodies of suicides do not receive a regular burial, but are huddled away in holes in the rocks or in the forest. There a tree is felled, and laid over his body. With the exception of his axe, knife, spear and sword the property of the deceased, and especially his clothing, is thrown away in the wood. If he had hanged himself on a tree, the tree is torn up by the roots. They take a goat and kill it, and having extracted the entrails they throw them together with the animal's bones into the hole from which the tree has been torn up. If the tree were not thus torn up, it is believed that the children and relatives of the suicide would immediately die. If the suicide was committed in a hut in the field, the hut is at once burned.[1] The Sakalava of Madagascar have so firm a belief in a life after death that they will sometimes threaten that after their decease their ghosts will haunt and persecute such as had offended them in life. When the persons so threatened hear it they seek to effect a reconcilement, fearing apparently that the persons who threaten them might make good their threats by taking their own lives, and then attacking such as had given umbrage in life. A traveller in the south of Madagascar has reported that when the Mahafali desire to avenge themselves speedily on their enemies they will sometimes take their own lives in order that their ghosts may at once take vengeance on their foes. Among the young men of the Mahafali tribe this

---

[1] A. Karasek, " Beiträge zur Kenntnis der Waschambaa ", in *Baessler-Archiv*, i. (1911) pp. 190 *sq.*

belief has been known to create a regular epidemic of suicides.[1]

Suicide as a method of wreaking a ghostly vengeance after death for a wrong done in life has been practised as a regular part of their profession by the Chārans, a sub-division of the Bhāts, a caste of bards and genealogists in India, who are found all over the Central Provinces and Birār. By profession they were bards and heralds, and they travelled from court to court without fear of molestation from robbers or enemies. But the mere reverence for their calling would not have sufficed to protect them from the attacks of robbers and others. They derived a greater security from their readiness to mutilate, starve or kill themselves, rather than yield up any property committed to their care ; and it was a general belief that their ghosts would then haunt the persons whose ill-deeds had forced them to take their own lives. It was on this fear of their ghosts that the Chārans relied, nor did they hesitate a moment to sacrifice their lives in defence of any obligation they had undertaken or of property committed to their safe-keeping. When plunderers carried off any cattle belonging to the Chārans, the whole community would proceed to the spot where the robbers resided ; and if restoration of the property were not made they would cut off the heads of several of their old men and women. In such cases many instances occurred of a man dressing

<hr />

[1] H. Russillon, *Un culte dynastique avec évocation des morts* chez les Sakalavas de Madagascar (Paris, 1912), pp. 47 sq.

himself in cotton-quilted cloths, steeped in oil, which he set on fire at the bottom, and thus danced against the criminal until he himself dropped down dead and was burned to ashes. To do this was to perform the ceremony of *trāga* against the male-factor.

The following account of a suicide and actual haunting of his ghost is reported by Mr. R. V. Russell from the *Rāsmālā*. A Chāran asserted a claim against the chief of Siela in Kathiawar, which the latter refused to pay. The bard then went to Siela, taking forty of his caste with him, with the intention of sitting *Dharna*, as the ceremony is called, at the chief's door, and preventing any one from coming out or going in until the claim was settled. However, the chief, having got wind of it, ordered the gates of the town to be closed against them. The Chāran to whom the debt was due thus remained outside the walls, and for three days he abstained from food. Finally, after sacrificing the life of several of his company he dressed himself in clothes wadded with cotton steeped in oil, and having set fire to them burned himself to death. But as he died he cried out : " I am now dying ; but I will become a headless ghost in the palace, and will take the chief's life and cut off his prosperity". After this sacrifice the rest of the bards returned home.

On the third day after the creditor's suicide his ghost (*Bhūt*) threw the chief's wife downstairs, so that she was much injured. Many people too beheld the headless phantom in the palace. At last the ghost entered the chief's own head and set him trembling. At night he would throw stones at the palace, and he killed a female servant outright. At length, in consequence of the many acts of violence committed by the ghost of the suicide, none dared to approach the chief's palace even by broad daylight. In order to exorcize the ghost Fakirs and Brahmans were summoned from many different places ; but whoever attempted the cure was immediately assailed by the ghost in the chief's body, and that so furiously that the courage of the exorcizer failed him. Moreover the ghost would cause the chief to tear the flesh off his own arms with his teeth. Besides this, several persons died of injuries received at the hands of the ghost ; but nobody had the power to expel him. At last a foreign astronomer came, who had a great reputation for charms and magic, and the chief sent for him and paid him honour. The sage tied all round the house threads which he had charged with a charm ; then he sprinkled charmed milk and water all round ; then he drove a charmed iron nail into the ground at each corner of the mansion, and two at the door. He purified the house and continued his charms and incantations for forty-one days, each day making sacrifices at the cemetery to the ghost of the suicide. He himself lived in a room in the chief's house which was securely fastened up ; but people say that while he was muttering his charms stones would fall and strike the windows. Finally the astrologer brought the chief, who had been living in a separate room, and tried to exorcize the ghost that was possessing him. The patient began by being very violent, but a sound thrashing which the astrologer and his assistants administered unsparingly at last reduced the sufferer to a better frame of mind. A sacrificial fire-pit was made and a lemon placed between it and the chief. The astrologer commanded the ghost to enter the lemon. But the ghost, speaking from the chief's body, said, "Who are you? If one of your gods were to come, I would not quit this man for him." Thus they went on from morning till noon. At last they came outside, and, by burning various kinds of incense and sprinkling many charms, they induced the ghost to enter into the lemon. When, thus inspired, the lemon began to bounce about, the whole of the spectators praised the astronomer, crying out, " The ghost has gone into the lemon ! The ghost has gone into the lemon ! " The chief himself who had been possessed was now perfectly satisfied that the ghost had gone out of him and into the lemon. The astronomer then drove the lemon out of the city, followed by drummers and trumpeters, and if the lemon diverged from the right path, the astrologer with a tap of his wand would guide it back into the way it should go. On the track they sprinkled mustard and salt and finally buried the lemon in a pit seven cubits deep, throwing into the hole above it mustard and salt, and above these dust and stones, and filling in the space between the stones with lead. At each corner too, the astrologer drove in an iron nail, two feet long, which he had previously charmed. The lemon thus buried and nailed down, the people returned home, and we are told, and without being unduly credulous we may readily believe, that nobody ever saw that ghost again.[1]

Akin to the process of *trāga* is the process of *Dharna*, which was commonly practised by a creditor to extort payment from a recalcitrant debtor. The ordinary method of *Dharna* was for the creditor to sit starving himself at the door of the person from whom redress was sought until the debtor consented to pay his debt, from fear of being haunted by his creditor's ghost if he starved himself to death. Or instead of threatening to starve himself to death the creditor might stand at his debtor's door with an enormous weight on his head, and to declare that if payment were refused he would stand there till he died. This seldom failed to produce the desired effect, but if he actually died under the weight, the debtor's house was razed to the ground and he and his family were sold for the benefit of the creditor's heirs.[2]

In China a similar dread of the ghosts of suicides has prevailed, and has led to similar practices. We are told that among the Chinese "the firm belief in ghosts and their retributive justice has still other effects. It deters from grievous and provoking injustice, because the wronged party, thoroughly sure of the avenging power of his own spirit when

[1] R. V. Russell, *The Tribes and Castes of the Central Provinces of India* (London, 1916), ii. pp. 259-262.

[2] R. V. Russell, *op. cit.* ii. pp. 265 *sq.*

disembodied, will not always shrink from converting himself into a wrathful ghost by committing suicide. It is still fresh in our memory how such a course was followed in 1886 by a shopkeeper in Amoy, pressed hard by a usurer, who had brought him to the verge of ruin. To extort payment, this man ran off with the shutters of his shop, thus giving its contents a prey to burglars ; but in that same night the wretch hanged himself against his persecutor's door-post, the sight of his corpse setting the whole ward in commotion at daybreak, and bringing all the family he had storming to the spot. The usurer, frightened out of his wits, had no alternative but to pay them a considerable indemnification, with an additional sum for the burial expenses, on which they pledged their promise to abstain from bringing him up before the magistrate. Pending those noisy negotiations, the corpse remained untouched where it hung. Thus the usurer had a hairbreadth escape from jail, flagellation and other judicial woes, but whether he slipped also through the hands of his etherized victim, we were never told. It impressed us on that occasion to hear from the Chinese that occurrences of this kind were very far from rare, and they told us a good many, then fresh in everybody's memory."[1]

Again we read that " the prevalence of suicide is a feature of Mukden as of most Chinese cities. Certain peculiarities of Chinese justice render it a

[1] J. J. M. De Groot, *The Religious System of China* (Leiden, 1901), vol. v. Book II. pp. 450 *sq.*

favourite way of wreaking spite upon an employer or neighbour, who is haunted besides by the spirit of the self-murderer. Hence servants angry with their masters, shopmen with their employers, wives with their husbands, and above all daughters-in-law with their mothers-in-law, show their spite by dying on their premises, usually by opium, or eating the tops of lucifer matches! It is quite a common thing for a person who has a grudge against another to go and poison himself in his courtyard, securing revenge first by the mandarin's inquiry and next by the haunting terrors of his malevolent spirit. Young girls were daily poisoning themselves with lucifer matches to escape from the tyranny of mothers-in-law and leave unpleasantness behind them." [1] With regard to the Chinese fear of the ghosts of suicides we are informed that they are taught in their almanacs that if on any given day and hour of any month they feel headache or pain in their bones " it is because they have unwittingly come in contact, at some corner of their house within or without, with the ghosts of men or women who have committed suicide by drowning or hanging or poison. In consequence of this impolite approach to the spirits, the god of the furnace is ill at ease, or the ancestors of the man are disturbed. The remedy is to make an apology to the ghost so rudely offended, and to present a propitiatory offering consisting of two or five hundred paper cash, a paper horse on which the ghost is requested to ride away, and a

[1] Mrs. Bishop, *Korea and Her Neighbours* (London, 1898), i. 241.

bowl of water and rice as an inducement to commence the journey requested."[1]

The Wotyaks, a people of Asiatic affinities settled in Russia, stand in great fear of the spirits of the dead, and in particular of the ghosts of suicides. Hence when a man has a grudge at somebody he will sometimes hang himself in his enemies' courtyard, or stab himself to death, in order that after his death his ghost may haunt and persecute his foe. The writer who reports this custom suggests that the peaceable disposition of the Wotyaks is partly to be explained by this fear of the spirits of the dead, fear being apparently among them a more potent motive than love in their attitude towards the departed.[2]

With regard to the Bannavs, a people of Indo-China inhabiting the mountains between Tonkin and Siam, we are told that suicide has a stigma in their penal code. The suicide is buried in a corner of the forest far from the graves of his brethren, and all who have assisted at the burial are required to purify themselves afterwards in a special manner.[3] Though we are not informed of it by our authority we may assume that this purification is intended to free the mourners from the dangerous influence of the suicide's ghost.

In ancient Greece it was customary at Athens to cut off the right hand of a suicide and bury it

[1] J. Preston, " Charms and Spells in use amongst the Chinese ", in *China Review*, vol. ii. (1873–1874) p. 169.

[2] Max Buch, *Die Wotjaken* (Helsingfors, 1882), 147 *sq.*

[3] Le Compte in M. H. Mouhot, *Travels in the Central Parts of Indo-China* (London, 1864), ii. pp. 27 *sq.*

apart from his body, no doubt in order to disarm his ghost, by depriving him of the use of his right hand.[1] Similar precautions have been taken in modern Europe to prevent the ghosts of suicides from doing a mischief to the living. In England a person against whom a coroner's jury had found a verdict of suicide used to be buried at cross-roads with a stake driven through the body, no doubt to prevent the ghost from walking, and attacking the survivors.[2] In Pomerania and West Prussia the ghosts of suicides are much feared. Such persons are buried, not in the churchyard, but at the place where they took their lives, and every passer-by must cast a stone or a stick on the spot, or the ghost of the suicide will haunt him by night and give him no rest. Hence the piles of sticks or stones accumulated on the graves of these poor wretches sometimes attain a considerable size.[3] With regard to the customs and beliefs concerning suicides in Denmark, Dr. Feilberg, an excellent authority on the folk - lore of his native land, writes as follows: " Whilst on the subject I will mention a custom of earlier times when burying suicides ; the dead person was not carried through the churchyard gate, but lifted over the outer mound, dragged down on the opposite side, and placed to the north of the church. In times still further back a rope was

[1] Aeschines, *In Ctesiphontem*, 244. Cf. E. Westermarck, *The Origin and Development of the Moral Ideas* (London, 1908), ii. 248.

[2] Westermarck, *op. cit.* ii. 256.

[3] A. Treichel, " Reisig- und Stein-häufung bei Ermordeten oder Selbstmördern ", in *Verhandlungen der Berliner Gesellschaft für Anthropologie, Ethnologie und Urgeschichte* (1888), p. 569, bound up with *Zeitschrift für Ethnologie*, xx. (1888).

attached to the body, it was then dragged by wild horses and buried wherever the rope happened to break, or else the corpse was thrown among carrion in the gallows ditch, whereby one also interfered with the suicide after death. For no poor human soul can find rest unless the funeral rites have been properly observed, and to these belong more especially according to the popular belief, the having prayers read over him, and being buried in consecrated ground. When manners became milder, the suicide was allowed to rest in the churchyard, but was to be buried either before sunrise or after sunset. I myself have been present on such occasions. The grave, to distinguish it from those of the honest dead, might be dug from north to south instead of from east to west. That is an insult, and has been done towards other dead (besides suicides) to tease them. The intended insult has always been felt by the person in question, and been revenged by malicious haunting. When one compares all the many other examples which point in the same direction, I have no doubt that when the suicide's coffin is carried in over the mound, it is to prevent its ghost finding its way out of the churchyard, as it will be stopped by the hedge."[1] In Bulgaria the bodies of suicides may not be buried at all in the churchyard.[2] A similar prohibition to bury the bodies of suicides within a churchyard used to be strictly observed in the north-east of Scotland. On this

---

[1] Dr. H. F. Feilberg, " The Corpse Door ", in *Folk-Lore*, xviii. (1907) pp 369 *sq.*

[2] A. Strauss, *Die Bulgaren* (Leipzig, 1898), p. 455.

subject the Rev. Walter Gregor, a high authority on the folk-lore of that district, writes as follows. " Peculiar horror was manifested towards suicides. Such were not buried in the churchyard. It is not much over half a century since a fierce fight took place in a churchyard in the middle of Banffshire, to prevent the burial of a suicide in it. By an early hour all the strong men of the parish who were opposed to an act so sacrilegious were astir and hastening to the churchyard with their weapons of defence—strong sticks. The churchyard was taken possession of, and the walls were manned. The gate and more accessible parts of the wall were assigned to picked men. In due time the suicide's coffin appeared, surrounded by an excited crowd, for the most part armed with sticks. Some, however, carried spades sharpened on the edge. Fierce and long was the fight at the gate, and not a few rolled in the dust. The assailing party was beaten off. A grave was dug outside the churchyard, close beneath the wall, and the coffin laid in it. The lid was lifted, and a bottle of vitriol poured over the body. Before the lid could be again closed, the fumes of the dissolving body were rising thickly over the heads of actors and spectators. This was done to prevent the body from being lifted during the coming night from its resting-place, conveyed back to its abode when in life, and placed against the door, to fall at the feet of the member of the family that was the first to open the door in the morning. The self-murderer's grave was on the boundary of two lairds' lands, and was marked by a single stone or a small cairn, to which the passing traveller was bound to cast a stone. It was the prevailing idea that nothing would grow over the grave of a suicide, or on the spot on which a murder had been com-mitted. After the suicide's body was allowed to be buried in the churchyard, it was laid below the wall in such a position that one could not step over the grave. This was done under the belief that, if a woman *enceinte* stepped over such a grave, her child would quit this earth by her own act." [1] In Scotland the bodies of suicides are now buried on the north side of the churchyard with the head to the east whereas all other dead are buried with their feet to the east. The fisher folk think that after such a burial the herring will forsake the coast for seven years. Hence sometimes they dig up the corpse by night and bury it on the shore at low water mark, or on the top of a mountain out of sight of the sea, that the herring may not be scared. Such burials have occurred on the top of Aird Dubh, and also on a mountain bounding Inverness and Ross-shire.[2] At Lochbroom, in Scotland, the people believe that if the body of a suicide be interred within any burial ground which is within sight of the sea or of culti-vated land this would prove disastrous both to fishing and agriculture, or, in the words of the people, would cause " famine (or dearth) on sea and land " ; hence the custom has been to bury suicides in out-

[1] W. Gregor, *Notes on the Folk-lore of the North-east of Scotland* (London, 1881), pp. 213 *sq.*

[2] C. F. Gordon Cumming, *In the Hebrides* (London, 1883), p. 185.

of-the-way places among the lonely solitudes of the mountains.[1]

III. *Ghosts of Persons who have died a violent death other than murder or suicide*

The souls of persons who have been killed either by others or by themselves are by no means the only spirits of the dead whom primitive man regards with a more than ordinary degree of apprehension. In his list of peculiarly dangerous ghosts he includes the spirits of all who have died a violent death other than murder or suicide; for, their natural term of life having been prematurely cut short, he believes that they are indignant and ready to visit their displeasure on all and sundry, without discriminating nicely between the innocent and the guilty. In countries like India, where wild beasts abound, and are the causes of many deaths, the real terror of such a death is augmented or even redoubled in the minds of the natives by the purely imaginary terror of the victim's ghost. Thus, for example, among the Baigas, a primitive Dravidian people of the Central Provinces in India, when a man has been killed by a tiger, a Baiga priest goes to the spot and there makes a small cone out of the blood-stained

---

[1] E. Westermarck, *op. cit.* ii. 255, citing Ross in *Celtic Magazine*, xii. p. 350 *sq.* On the customs and superstitions as to suicide, see further A. Wuttke, *Der deutsche Volksaberglaube der Gegenwart* (Berlin, 1869), § 756; Dr. R. Lasch, " Die Behandlung der Leiche des Selbstmörders ", in *Globus*, lxxvi. (1899) pp. 63 *sqq.*; E. Westermarck, *op. cit.* ii. pp. 229-264.

earth. This must represent a man, either the dead man or one of his living kinsmen. His companions having retired a few paces, the priest goes on his hands and knees and performs a series of antics which are supposed to represent the tiger in the act of destroying the man, at the same time seizing the lump of blood-stained earth in his jaws. One of the party then runs up and taps him on the back with a small stick. This perhaps means that the tiger is killed or otherwise rendered harmless ; and the Baiga immediately lets the mud cone fall into the hands of one of the party. It is then placed in an ant-hill and a pig is sacrificed over it. The next day a small chicken is brought to the place, and when a mark supposed to be the dead man's name has been made on its head with red ochre, it is thrown back again into the forest, the priest crying out, "Take this and go home". The ceremony is supposed to lay the dead man's ghost, and at the same time to prevent the tiger from doing any further damage. The Baigas believe that the ghost of the victim, if it is not charmed to rest, will reside on the head of the tiger and incite him to further deeds of blood, rendering him also secure from harm by his preternatural watchfulness.[1] Among the Bhatra, another primitive tribe in the Central Provinces in India, when a man has been killed by a tiger his spirit must be propitiated. The priest ties strips of tiger-skin to his arms, and the feathers

[1] R. V. Russell, *The Tribes and Castes of the Central Provinces of India*, ii. 84 ; and Capt. J. Forsyth, *The Highlands of Central India* (London, 1871), pp. 362 *sq.*

of the blue jay to his waist, and thus disguised jumps about pretending to be a tiger. A package of two hundred pounds of rice is made up, and the priest sits on it and finally takes it away with him. If the dead man had any ornaments they must all be given, however valuable, lest his ghost should hanker after them and return to look for them in the shape of a tiger. The large quantity of rice given to the priest is also probably intended as a provision of the best food for the dead man's spirit, lest it be hungry and come in the shape of a tiger to satisfy its appetite upon the surviving kinsfolk. The laying of ghosts of persons killed by tigers is thus a very profitable affair for the priests.[1] The Dumāl are an agricultural caste of the Central Provinces in India who have recently been transferred to Orissa and Bihār. Among them if two or more persons in a family have been killed by tigers, a magician is called in, and he pretends to be the tiger, and to bite someone in the family, who is carried as a corpse to the burial-ground, there buried for a short time, and then taken out again. All the ceremonies of mourning are observed for him for one day. This proceeding is believed to secure immunity for the family from further attacks ; doubtless also it is thought to appease the ghosts of the men whose bodies have been devoured by tigers. In return for his services the magician gets a share of everything in the house corresponding to what he would receive, supposing

[1] Russell, *op. cit.* ii. 274 *sq.*

he were a member of the family, on a partition.[1] Among the Gonds of Bastar, a great Dravidian tribe of India, when a man has been killed by a tiger and his widow marries again, she goes through the ceremony not with her new husband but with a lance, axe, or sword, or with a dog. It is believed that the tiger into which her first husband's spirit has entered will try to kill her second husband, but owing to the precaution taken he will either simply carry off the dog or will himself get killed by an axe, sword or lance.[2] Among these Gonds also the soul of a man who has been devoured by a tiger must be specially propitiated, and ten or twelve days are occupied in bringing it back. To ascertain when the soul has come back a thread is tied to a beam and a copper ring is suspended from it, being secured by twisting the thread round it and not by a knot. A pot full of water is placed below the ring. Songs are then sung in propitiation of the spirit, and a watch is kept day and night. When the ring falls from the thread and drops into the water it is believed that the soul has come back. If the ring delays to fall they implore the dead man to come back and ask where he has gone to and why he is tarrying. Animals are sacrificed to the ring and their blood poured over it, and when it finally falls they rejoice greatly and say that the dead man has come back. A man who has been killed by a tiger or a cobra may receive general veneration, for the purpose of propitiating his spirit, and so may

[1] Russell, *op. cit.* ii. 536.   [2] Russell, *op. cit.* iii. 81.

become a village god.[1] Among the Halbas, a caste of cultivators and farm-servants in the Central Provinces of India, if a person has been killed by a tiger, the people go out, and if they find any remains of the body these are burned on the spot. The priest is then invoked to call back the spirit of the deceased, which is deemed a most essential precaution. In order to do this he suspends a copper ring on a long thread above a vessel of water and then burns butter and sugar on the fire, muttering incantations, while the people sing songs and call on the spirits of the dead man to return. The thread swings to and fro, and at length the ring falls into the pot, and this is accepted as a sign that the spirit has come and entered the vessel. The mouth of the vessel is immediately covered and it is buried or kept in some secure place. The people believe that unless the dead man's spirit is thus secured it will accompany the tiger and lure solitary travellers to destruction. This is done by calling out and offering them tobacco to smoke, and when they go in the direction of the voice the tiger springs out and kills them. "The malevolence thus attributed to persons killed by tigers is explained by their bitter wrath at having encountered such an untimely death and consequent desire to entice others to the same."[2] The Kalanga, a caste of cultivators in the Central Provinces of India, make offerings to the spirits of their dead in a certain month of the year; but they make no such offerings to the

[1] Russell, *op. cit.* iii. 95.   [2] Russell, *op. cit.* iii. 195 *sq.*

spirits of persons who have died a violent death. The spirits of these latter must be laid lest they should trouble the living, and this is done in the following manner : a handful of rice is placed at the threshold of the house, and a ring is hung by a thread so as to touch the rice. A goat is then brought up, and when it eats the rice the spirit of the dead person is believed to have entered into the goat, which is thereupon killed and eaten by the family so as to dispose of him once for all. If the goat will not eat the rice it is forced to do so. The spirit of a man who has been killed by a tiger must, however, be laid by the sorcerer of the caste, who goes through the ceremony of pretending to be a tiger and of mauling another sorcerer.[1] Among the Kawars, a primitive tribe in the Central Provinces in India, when a man has been killed by a tiger they perform a ceremony called " Breaking the string " or the connexion which they believe the animal establishes with a family on having tasted its blood. Otherwise they think that the tiger would gradually kill off all the remaining members of the family of his victim. In this ceremony the village medicine-man (*Baiga*) is painted with red ochre and soot to represent the tiger, and proceeds to the place where the victim was carried off. Having picked up some of the blood-stained earth in his mouth, he tries to run away to the jungle, but the spectators hold him back until he spits out the earth. This represents the tiger being forced

[1] Russell, *op. cit.* iii. 308.

to give up his prey. The medicine-man then ties a string round all the members of the dead man's family standing together. He places some grain before a fowl saying, " If my charm has worked, eat of this " ; and as soon as the fowl has eaten some grain the medicine-man states that his efforts have been successful and the attraction of the man-eater has been broken. He then breaks the string and all the party return to the village. A similar ceremony is performed when a man has died of snake-bite.[1] In both cases the ceremony is probably supposed to appease the angry ghosts of the persons killed by a tiger or a cobra.

Among the Kir, a caste of cultivators in the Central Provinces of India, great respect is paid to the spirit of a relative who has died a violent death, or died as a bachelor or without progeny, the spirits of such persons being always prone to trouble their living kinsfolk. In order to appease them songs are sung in their praise on important festivals, the members of the family staying awake the whole night, and wearing their images on a silver piece round the neck. When they eat and drink they first touch the food with the image by way of offering to the dead, so that their spirits may be appeased and refrain from harassing the living.[2] The Kurmis, a great cultivating class of Hindustan, believe that the spirits of their dead return to their old homes in the dark fortnight of the month Kunwār (September-October). On the thirteenth day of that

---

[1] Russell, *op. cit.* iii, 398–399. [2] Russell, *op. cit.* iii. 483.

fortnight come the spirits of all those who have died
a violent death, as by a fall, or have been killed
by wild animals or snakes.   The spirits of such persons are supposed, on account of their untimely end,
to entertain a special grudge against the living.[1]
Among the Panwar, a famous Rajput clan found
in the Central Provinces of India, when a man has
been killed by a tiger (*bagh*) he is deified and worshipped as the tiger god (*Bagh Deo*).   A hut is made
in the yard of the house, and an image of a tiger
placed inside and worshipped on the anniversary
of the man's death.   The members of the household will not afterwards kill a tiger, because they
think that the animal has become a member of the
family.   A man who dies from the bite of a cobra
(*nag*) is similarly worshipped as the cobra god (*Nag
Deo*).   The image of a snake made of silver or iron
is venerated by the family, and the members of it
will not kill a snake.   If a man is killed by some
other animal, or by drowning or a fall from a tree,
his spirit is worshipped as the forest god (*Ban Deo*)
with similar rites, being represented by a little lump
of rice and red lead.[2]   Before sacrificing to their beneficent ancestral spirits, the Sansia or Uria—a caste
of masons and navvies in the Central Provinces of
India—are wont to offer two sacrifices to the spirits
of ancestors who have died a violent death or have
committed suicide, and to the spirits of relatives
who died unmarried, for fear lest these unclean and
malignant spirits should seize and defile the offer-

---

[1] Russell, *op. cit*. iv. 79 *sq*.   [2] Russell, *op. cit*. iv. 346 *sq*.

ings made to the kindly ancestral spirits.[1]   Among the Savars, a primitive tribe of the Central Provinces in India, if a man has died a violent death, a small platform is raised in his honour under a teak tree, in which the ghost of the dead man is supposed to take up its residence, and nobody thereafter may cut down that tree.   In such a case the Uriya Savars take no special measures unless the ghost of such a man appears to somebody in a dream and asks to be worshipped as Baghiapat (tiger-eaten) or Masan (serpent-bitten).   When this happens they consult a sorcerer, and take such measures as he may prescribe to appease the dead man's ghost.[2]

The Oraons, a primitive aboriginal tribe, inhabiting the secluded plateau of Chota Nagpur in Northern India, believe that the spirits of persons who have been killed by tigers assume the form of tigers and prowl about at night near their old homes which they seek to enter.   To drive away these unquiet spirits the help of a spirit-doctor is called in.   A man not belonging to the family is made to personate the tiger.   His body is painted in colours like those of the tiger, coloured earth being used for the purpose.   A tail is also provided.   Thus arrayed, the man stands in the manner of a tiger on his hands and legs, to which four ropes are tied. Four men hold him by the ropes, and he is led on, all the while fretting and fuming and snarling and gnashing his teeth and otherwise imitating the manner of a tiger.   The spirit-doctor follows the

[1] Russell, *op. cit.* iv. 498.   [2] Russell, *op. cit.* iv. 507.

mock tiger, and makes a show of driving it away. As this sham tiger is driven away from the village the ghost of the tiger's victim is supposed to be simultaneously banished from the neighbourhood. A fowl or some other sacrifice as dictated by the spirit-doctor is offered to the tiger-ghost by the spirit-doctor, as a further inducement for him to go away. Then the sham tiger is bathed and brought back home. At the house a feast is provided for the family and fellow-villagers.[1]

Among the Kachins of Burma the souls of persons who have died a violent or unnatural death do not receive the usual funeral honours, because it is believed that they have become malignant spirits ready and willing to cause harm and misfortune to the living. In these cases the body is invariably cremated, never buried, and no time is lost in disposing of the corpse. All the usual marks of respect are omitted, and the priest does not even go through the ceremony of sending off the spirit to the spirit land. The place for the cremation is chosen as far from the village as possible. All the property of the deceased goes with him, and food and some fire from the house are placed beside the open hollow in which his body has been cremated. A white cord is drawn round four saplings stuck in the ground near the property. The spirits of all such persons go west, in the direction of the setting sun, so the priest gives no directions as to the route to

[1] S. C. Roy, *Oraon Religion and Custom* (Ranchi, 1928), p. 98. Cf. S. C. Roy, " Magic and Witchcraft on the Chota Nagpur Plateau ", in the *Journal of the Royal Anthropological Institute*, xliv. (1914) p. 346.

be followed. Nevertheless every Kachin house contains an image of the Gumgun nat ; that is, the spirit of an ancestor who has met with a violent or unnatural death and whose spirit has returned to its former home or the home where kinsfolk are living, and requires propitiation, and can in turn help the living. The altar to the spirit is usually placed against the left-hand walling of each house nearest the back entrance. The altar may not be touched : any stranger interfering with it would give great offence and might meet with violence.[1] Among the Palaungs of Burma, when anyone dies a mysteriously sudden death, or is killed, his body is buried as quickly as possible in a lonely part of the jungle at some distance from the village. The grave is generally dug beside a large tree, because the spirits of all people dying suddenly are believed to remain near their bodies, haunting the place where they are buried. Their time to die had not yet come, and the spirit could not yet go to eat of the fruit of forgetfulness. Such a spirit is wicked, hurtful, and jealous, and the only hope for its happiness is to give it the chance of a pleasant and shady tree for its home. The funeral customs, such as tying coins to the wrist, are the same as usual ; but if the person has been found dead in the jungle, his corpse would not be brought back to the village, but would be buried near where he died.[2] There is a general belief among the Burmese and Shans that

[1] W. J. S. Carrapiett, *The Kachin Tribes of Burma* (Rangoon, 1929), pp. 46, 78.

[2] Mrs. Leslie Milne, *The Home of an Eastern Clan*, p. 304.

the spirits of human beings who have been killed by an elephant ride on the animal's head, warning him of his approach to pitfalls and hunters, and guiding him to where he may kill people, so as to add to their own ghostly company.[1] In Cambodia all persons who die a natural death are buried according to the course of the sun with their heads to the west ; but all who die a violent death or by accident—such as by a fall—or drowning, or murder, or suicide, or the sting or bite of wild animals, are buried across the course of the sun, with their heads to the north, in order to prevent their spirits from returning to afflict their families.[2] In Korea the spirits of all those who die sudden or violent deaths are believed to become evil demons who haunt and torment the living in endless ways.[3]

Like so many other peoples, the Kiwai Papuans of British New Guinea greatly fear the ghosts of persons who have met with a violent death, or have otherwise died in some unusual way. The spirits of people who have been drowned or killed by a crocodile or a snake, and also those of suicides, are greatly feared because they will try to entice friends into a like death. The spirit of a man killed by a crocodile is called *síbara-adíri*. It is thought to carry on its back a " ghost-crocodile ", which it may throw upon another man, who is then doomed

[1] H. S. Hallett, *A Thousand Miles on an Elephant in the Shan States* (Edinburgh and London, 1890), pp. 377 *sq.*

[2] M. S. Aymonier, " Notes sur les coutumes et croyances super-stitieuses des Cambodgiens ", in *Excursions et reconnaisances*, No. 16 (Saigon, 1883), p. 202.

[3] Mrs. Bishop, *Korea and its Neighbours*, ii. 242.

to be killed in the same way. The "ghost-crocodile" is believed to be carried by the man's ghost all the way to the land of the dead ; and this may reveal the cause of death to people who have the faculty of seeing spirits. Such an apparition forbodes a similar death to anyone to whom it appears, but this fate can be averted if some friend of the man involved contrives to separate the crocodile from its bearer ; otherwise it is inevitable. In order to lay the ghost of a man killed by a crocodile the people build a small hut, like that erected on graves, at the place where the man met his death, and put food inside. They wish the spirit to remain there, and say to him, " Do not come back to where people are living. You are now a ghost : stay here, this is your house." If this is not done, the ghost, who does not wish to be alone, will come and fetch one of his friends to suffer the like fate. Another means of protection against such a fate is this : a man will burn part of a crocodile's tail to ashes and mix them with clay, and out of this form a ball, which he throws far away into the river. Or he fastens the piece of crocodile's tail to a stick, wades into the water with it, and fixes the stick to the bottom. In both cases he utters the following spell : " You are a crocodile spirit. Go far away, and stay there for ever." This adjuration prevents the crocodile ghost from attacking people.[1]

Among the Wandamba of Tanganyika in East Africa, if the hunter of an elephant has the mis-

---

[1] G. Landtman, *The Kiwai Papuans of British New Guinea*, pp. 283 *sq.*

fortune to be killed by an animal, his companions bury him on the spot, and the chief medicine-man puts some powder and medicine into the dead man's hands, and also pours a little on the ground at the foot of an adjacent tree, and sweeps round the grave vowing vengeance on the animal, for the death of their friend. Then the party go off, and when they have killed the elephant the head medicine-man puts a little powder into the palm of his hand and blows it away to let the dead man know that he had been avenged. Afterwards he returns to the hunter's grave with some of the elephant's blood, which he pours on the powder to appease the spirit of the deceased.[1] The curious rites which the Ewe people of Togo perform after the death of a person who has been killed by snake-bite have already been described.[2]

Among the Huron Indians of Canada, when any-one died by drowning or cold it was believed that Heaven was angry with the people, and must be appeased by sacrifice. They summoned the inhabitants of the neighbouring villages and held a feast and distributed presents freely, thinking that the matter concerned the whole country. The corpse was carried to the cemetery and laid on a mat. On one side of it a grave was dug in the ground and on the other side a fire was made for the sacrifice. At the same time several young men chosen by their

[1] A. G. O. Hodgson, " Some Notes on the Hunting Customs of the Wandamba of the Wanga Valley, Tanganyika ", in the *Journal of the* *Royal Anthropological Institute*, lvi. (1926), p. 64.

[2] See above, p. 11.

relations took their stand round about the corpse with their knives in their hands. The priest, who was described as the protector of the deceased, marked with charcoal the parts of the corpse which were to be cut. The young men set to work with their knives hacking off the fleshy parts. Finally they cut open the body and drew out the entrails and threw them on the fire together with the fleshy parts which they had severed. Then they laid the mangled remains in the grave. While the young men were hacking at the corpse women went round them, encouraging them to ply their work well for the good of the whole country, at the same time putting beads as a further encouragement into the mouths of the operators. Sometimes the mother of the deceased, bathed in tears, joined the party, lamenting the death of her son in a doleful chant. By these rites the Hurons believed that they appeased the wrath of Heaven ; but if they were to omit them they thought that any accidents or misfortunes that might befall them were the effects of Heaven's displeasure at the sacrilege.[1]

IV. Ghosts of Women dying in Childbed

The ghosts of women dying in childbed are commonly believed to be dangerous in a peculiarly high degree, and very special precautions are taken

[1] *Relations des Jésuites*, 1636 (Canadian reprint, Quebec, 1858) p. 108. P. F. X. de Charlevoix, *Histoire de la Nouvelle - France* (Paris, 1744), v. 110.

to guard against them.[1]   The belief and the practice
consequent upon it are particularly prevalent in some
parts of India, and all over the Malay region to the
east.   Thus the Hindus of the Punjab believe that
if a mother dies within thirteen days of her delivery,
she will return in the guise of a malignant spirit to
torment her husband and family.   To prevent this
some people drive nails through her head and eyes,
while others also knock nails on either side of the
door of the house.[2]   A gentler way of attaining the
same end is to put a nail or a piece of iron into the
clothes of the poor dead mother.[3]   The ghost of
such a woman is called a Churel.   She is particularly
malignant towards members of her own family.
She appears in various forms, sometimes she is fair
in front and black behind, but she invariably has her
feet turned round, heels in front and toes behind.
However she generally assumes the form of a beautiful woman and seduces youths at night, especially
the handsome.   She carries them off to some kingdom of her own, and if they venture to eat the food
offered to them there she keeps them till they lose
their manly beauty.   Then she sends them back to
the world grey-haired old men, where, like Rip Van
Winkle, they find all their friends dead long ago.[4]
Among the Gurao, a caste of village priests in the

[1] Cf. *Psyche's Task* (*The Devil's
Advocate*), pp. 133 *sqq.*, where some
of the evidence here cited has been
previously adduced.

[2] H. A. Rose, " Hindu Birth
Observances in the Punjab", in
*Journal of the Royal Anthropological
Institute*, xxxvii. (1907) pp. 225 *sq.*

[3] G. F. D'Penha, " Superstitions
and Customs in Salsette ", in *The
Indian Antiquary*, xxviii. (1899)
p. 115.

[4] W. Crooke, *Popular Religion
and Folk-lore of Northern India*
(Westminster, 1896), i. pp. 269 *sq.*

Central Provinces of India, when the corpse of a woman who has died in childbed is being carried to the burning ground various rites are observed to prevent her spirit from becoming a malignant ghost (*Churel*) and troubling the living. A lemon charmed by a magician is buried under her corpse and a man follows the body strewing the seeds *rala*, while nails are driven into the threshold of the house.[1] Among the Kurmis, the representative cultivating caste of Hindustan, if a woman has died in childbirth, or after the birth of a child and before the performance of the sixth-day ceremony of purification, her hands are tied with a cotton thread when she is buried, in order that her spirit may be unable to rise and trouble the living. It is believed that the souls of such women become evil spirits (*Churels*). Thorns are also placed over her grave for the same purpose.[2] In Bombay it is believed that the souls of women dying in childbed enter the order of ghosts variously known as *Chudels*, *Vantris*, or *Takshamis*. In order that the spirit of such a woman may not return from the cremation ground, mustard seeds are strewn along the road behind her bier, for a belief prevails that her ghost can only succeed in returning if she can gather all the mustard seeds thus strewn on the way. In some places loose cotton-wool is thrown over the bier so as to be scattered all along the road to the cemetery. It is thought that the ghost can only return to the house if she can collect

---

[1] R. V. Russell, *Tribes and Castes of the Central Provinces*, ii. pp. 180 *sq.*

[2] R. V. Russell, *op. cit.* iv. 78.

all the cotton scattered behind her in one night. This is deemed an impossible task, and consequently her friends at home entertain no fear of the return of the ghost when once the cotton has been scattered. To prevent the return of such a ghost, some people pass underneath the bier the legs of the cot on which the woman lay in her confinement, while others drive in an iron nail at the end of the street immediately after the corpse has been carried beyond the village boundary. In some places the nail is driven into the threshold of the house. Even after these ceremonies have been observed to prevent the return of the ghost of such a woman, other rites are performed, and a number of Brahman women feasted on the twelfth and thirteenth day after death to propitiate her departed soul, for the fear of the mischief she may do is very strong.[1] In Travancore the spirits of women who die in pregnancy are believed to become demons. Their bodies accordingly are carried away to some distant spot in the jungle, and there incantations are pronounced over them to prevent their ghosts from returning and molesting the survivors.[2]

The Oraons of Chota Nagpur are firmly convinced that every woman who dies in pregnancy or childbirth becomes an evil and dangerous spirit (*bhut*), who, if steps are not taken to keep her off, will come back and tickle to death those whom she loved best in life. " To prevent her, therefore, from

---

[1] R. E. Enthoven, *The Folk-Lore of Bombay* (Oxford, 1924), p. 197.

[2] S. Mateer, *Native Life in Travancore* (London, 1883), p. 90.

coming back, they carry her body as far away as they can, but no woman will accompany her to her last resting-place lest similar misfortune should happen to her. Arrived at the burial-place, they break the feet above the ankle, twist them round, bringing the heels in front, and then drive long thorns into them. They bury her very deep with her face downwards, and with her they bury the bones of a donkey, and pronounce the *anathema* ' If you come home may you turn into a donkey : ' and the roots of a palm-tree are also buried with her ; and they say, ' May you come home only when the leaves of the palm-tree wither', and when they retire they spread mustard-seeds all along the road saying, ' When you come home, pick up all these '. They then feel pretty safe at home from her nocturnal visits, but woe to the man who passes at night near to the place where she has been buried. She will pounce upon him, twist his neck, and leave him senseless upon the ground, until brought to by the incantations of a sorcerer." [1]

To complete this account of the quaint rites observed in such cases by the Oraons I will subjoin the report of another highly-competent witness, the Indian ethnologist, Mr Sarat Chandra Roy, who has made a special study of the tribe. " A *Churil* or *Churel* or *Malech* is the ghost of a woman dying in pregnancy or childbirth or within a few days of it.

[1] Rev. P. Dehon, " Religion and Customs of the Uraons ", in *Memoirs of the Asiatic Society of Bengal*, vol. i. No. 9 (Calcutta, 1906), pp. 139 *sq.*

A *Churil* spirit, it is said, carries a load of coal upon its head, imagining it to be its baby. It is believed that if a *Churil* spirit sees any man passing by its. grave it pursues him and takes delight in tickling him under the arms and, if possible, throwing him down senseless and embracing him. If, however, the man perceives the approach of a *Churil* by its spectral figure which is sometimes visible or by the rustling and shaking of the branches of some neighbouring tree, and calls out the *Churil* by the name which it formerly bore in life, and asks—' So-and-so [names], is it you ? ' the spirit forthwith decamps. Or, when the *Churil* attacks him, if the man can take away her load of charcoal, the spirit is said to lose its power and to burst into tears. Drunken wayfarers are naturally easy victims of this spirit. It is with the object of preventing such spirits from moving about, that the feet of women dying in childbed are broken and turned backwards and thorns inserted on the soles of their feet. When a *Churil* is visible, its feet appear, it is said, to be inverted with the heels forward. A person, particularly a drunken man, supposed to have been chased and tormented by a *Churil*, is sometimes so seriously affected that it requires the services of a spirit-doctor (*Mati* or *deonra*) to cure him by exorcising the spirit. When the trouble caused by a *Churil* is not more serious than a griping of the stomach or such other ailment, a few mustard-seeds, two grains and a half of some pulse, a little iron-slag and a bit of charcoal are thrown outside the house in the direction of the spot where the *Churil* was met with."[1]

Among the Birhors, another primitive tribe living in the jungles of Chota Nagpur, the spirit of a woman who has died within twenty-one days of childbirth may never be admitted into the community of ancestor-spirits, because such a spirit is always dangerous. In her case, therefore, a new doorway in the hut is opened through which her corpse is carried out to the grave. Such a corpse is buried in a place apart from the ground where other corpses are interred. Women and not men bury such corpses : the men only dig the grave and go away. Thorns are thrust into the woman's feet to prevent her ghost from leaving the grave. The corpse in the grave is formally made over by the spirit-doctor (*mati*) to the charge of some spirit of a hill or jungle of the neighbourhood. In doing so the spirit-doctor works himself up to a state of supposed possession, and says, " O, Spirit of such-and-such hill or forest ! [names] We make over so-and-so [names the deceased] to you. Guard her well and let her remain here." The spirit-doctor, or rather, as is believed, the spirit speaking through the mouth of the spirit-doctor, says, " I do take charge ". If the first spirit asked to take charge does not make such a reply, another spirit is similarly invoked, and so on, until some spirit agrees to take charge of the dangerous corpse.[2]

[1] S. C. Roy: *Oraon Religion and Customs* (Ranchi, 1928), pp. 96-97. Cf. E. T. Dalton, *Descriptive Ethnology of Bengal* (Calcutta, 1872), p. 258.

[2] S. C. Roy, *The Birhors* (Ranchi, 1925), pp. 267 *sq.*

Speaking of the much-dreaded spirits of these unhappy women in Bengal generally, Sir Edward Gait, a high authority on the subject, observes, " But the most malevolent of all spirits is the Churel or Kichin, the spirit of a woman who dies in childbirth. Her feet are turned backwards, she has no mouth, and she haunts filthy places. She is specially feared by women, whom she attacks during the menstrual period, or at the time of parturition. Sometimes she falls in love with young men, before whom she appears in the form of a beautiful girl neatly decked and dressed with ornaments, and whom she eventually kills by a slow process of emaciation. Like other similar spirits, she can only be ejected by exorcism. The fear of the Churel is by no means confined to the Hindus. It is even more dreaded by the aboriginal tribes, and amongst the Bhuiyas of Keonjhar, if a woman should die before delivery, the embryo is extracted from the corpse and the bodies are burnt on the opposite banks of a hill stream. As no spirit can cross water, and the mother cannot become a witch unless united to her child, this precaution is believed to avert all risk of evil to the villagers." [1]

Among the Lushais of North-Eastern India, when a woman dies in childbed, the relatives offer a sacrifice to her departed soul, " but the rest of that village treat that day as a holiday and put a small green branch on the wall of each house on the out-

[1] Sir E. A. Gait, in *Census of India*, 1901, vi. Bengal: Part I. (Calcutta, 1902) p. 199.

side near the doorpost to keep out the spirit of the dead woman ".[1]   The Lakhers, a tribe of the same region, think that the ghost of a woman who has died in childbed becomes a dangerous spirit, to be classed with the spirits of all who have died an un-natural death.   Her corpse may not be carried out of the house by the doorway, but through a hole cut in the back wall.   This is done because, as the spirits of women who have died in childbed do not follow the road taken by the spirits of those who have died natural deaths, but have to go by another path to the *Sawvawkhi*, the place reserved in the spirit land for the souls of all who have died an unnatural death, it is thought that the corpse should not leave the house by the ordinary path, but should also take a different path to the grave.[2]

The Kachins of Burma are so afraid of the ghosts of women dying in childbed that no soooner has such a death taken place than the husband, the children, and almost all the people in the house take to flight lest the ghost should bite them.   They bandage the eyes of the woman with her own hair to prevent her from seeing anything ; they wrap the corpse in a mat and carry it out of the house, not by the ordinary door, but by an opening made for the purpose either in the wall or in the floor of the room where she breathed her last.   Then they convey the body to a deep ravine where foot of man seldom penetrates, and there, having heaped her

[1] Lieut.-Col. H. G. W. Cole, " The Lushais ", in *Census of India*, 1911, vol. iii. Assam : Part I. (Shillong, 1912) p. 140.
[2] N. E. Parry, *The Lakhers* (London, 1932), pp. 406-408.

clothes, her jewellery, and all her belongings over her, they set fire to the pile and reduce the whole to ashes. "Thus they destroy all the property of the unfortunate woman in order that her soul may not think of coming to fetch it afterwards and to bite the people in the attempt." When this has been done the officiating priest scatters some burnt grain of a climbing plant (*shāmien*), inserts in the earth the pestle which the dead woman used to husk the rice, and winds up the exorcism by cursing and railing at her ghost, saying, "Wait to come back till this grain sprouts and this pestle blossoms, till the fern bears fruit, and the cocks lay eggs". The house in which the woman died is generally pulled down, and the timber may only be used as firewood or to build small hovels in the fields. Till a new house can be built for them, the widower and the orphans receive the hospitality of their nearest relatives, a father or a brother; their other friends would not dare to receive them from fear of the ghost. Occasionally the dead mother's jewels are spared from the fire and given away to some poor old crones who do not trouble their head about ghosts. If the medicine-man who attended to the woman in life and officiated at the funeral is old, he may consent to accept the jewels as the fee for his services; but in that case no sooner has he got home than he puts the jewels in the hen-house. If the hens remain quiet, it is a good omen and he can keep the trinkets with an easy mind; but if the fowls flutter and cackle, it is a sign that the ghost is sticking to the jewels, and in a fright he restores them to the family. The old man or old woman into whose hands the trinkets of the dead woman thus sometimes fall cannot dispose of them to other members of the tribe, for nobody who knows where the things come from would be so rash as to buy them. However, they may find purchasers among the Shans or Chinese, who do not fear Kachin ghosts.[1]

With regard to these customs and beliefs of the Kachins, another writer, who knows the tribe well, tells us that when a woman has died in childbed her body is cremated, and saplings are then procured and rude representations of the male organ of generation are carved at one end of each. These are stuck in the ground, and bending towards the spot where cremation took place. In returning from the grave or cremation ground precautions have to be taken against any assault by the dead woman's dangerous spirit. A long bamboo is procured, and split in half for about half way or more of its length. One half is fixed in the ground, the other half lying loose. Between the two halves a wedge is inserted about three or four inches off the ground, thus forming a triangle with the wedge as base. All who have attended the funeral pass through the triangle, the medicine-man and the butcher bringing up the rear. Either of these two knock away the wedge after passing over it and the two halves of the bamboo close with a snap. Those

[1] Ch. Gilhodes, " Naissance et enfance chez les Katchins (Birmanie) ", in *Anthropos*, vi. (1911) pp. 872 *sq.*

who have guns fire as many shots as they can into the bamboo to frighten and drive away the malignant spirit.[1] The passage of the mourners through the split bamboo is no doubt another mode of eluding the pursuit of the ghost ; when the two halves of the bamboo have closed with a snap the gate has been shut in her face.

Another writer who travelled in Burma in the second half of the nineteenth century has described somewhat differently the customs and beliefs on this subject observed and held by the Kachins, or Kakhyens, as he calls them. His account runs as follows. " Funeral rites are also denied to those who die of small-pox and to women dying in child-birth. In the latter case the mother and her child are believed to become a fearful compound vampire. All the young people fly in terror from the house, and divination is resorted to, to discover what animal the evil spirit will devour, and another with which it will transmigrate. The first is sacrificed, and some of the flesh placed before the corpse ; the second is hanged, and a grave dug in the direction to which the animal's head pointed when dead. Here the corpse is buried, with all the clothes and ornaments worn in life, and a wisp of straw is burned on its face, before the leaves and earth are filled in. All property of the deceased is burned on the grave, and a hut erected over it. The death dance takes place, to drive the spirit from the house, in all cases.

[1] W. J. S. Carrapiett, *The Kachin Tribes of Burma* (Rangoon, 1929), p. 47.

The former custom appears to have been to burn the body itself, with the house and all the clothes and ornaments used by the deceased. This also took place if the mother died during the month succeeding childbirth, and, according to one native statement, the infant also was thrown into the fire, with the address, ' Take away your child ' ; but if previously any one claimed the child, saying, ' Give me your child ' it was spared, and belonged to the adopting parent, the real father being unable at any time to reclaim it." [1]

The Shans of Burma believe that the death of a woman with her unborn child is the greatest misfortune that can befall her own and her husband's family. It is thought that the spirit of the dead woman becomes a malignant ghost, who may return to haunt her husband's home and torment him, unless precautions are taken to keep her away. In the first place, her unborn child is removed by an operation ; then the bodies of mother and child are wrapped in separate mats and buried without coffins. If this be not done, the same mishap may befall the woman in her future life, and the widower will suffer from the attacks of her ghost. When the corpses are being removed from the house, part of the mat wall in the side of the house is taken down, and the dead woman and her baby are lowered to the ground through the opening. The hole through which the bodies have passed is immediately filled with new mats, so that the ghost may not know how

---

[1] J. Anderson, *Mandalay to Momien* (London, 1876), pp. 145 *sq.*

to return. In such a case no guests are invited, and there is no burial ceremony, though a funeral feast may be given on the anniversary of the death.[1]

The Palaungs of Burma regard the spirits of women dying in childbed as the most terrifying of all unhappy spirits. After such a death has taken place in a house, the woman's body is hurriedly washed and dressed in new clothes, and the usual food and other things are placed beside her in a new mat, which is wrapped round her body. The corpse is then lowered through a hole which has been cut in the flooring-boards of the room where she died. And as the desire of every one is to remove her body from the house and the village as quickly as possible for burial, a coffin is not made. The unborn child may be removed by an operation, wrapped in another mat, and buried by itself, but this is seldom done. As soon as the body has been lowered, the floor is washed and the hole is closed with new boards. This, they hope, will prevent the return of the spirits of the unfortunate mother and child. The husband does not attend the funeral, but goes to spend days, or even weeks, at the monastery. It is now the practice to dig a grave of the usual shape in a lonely part of the jungle, and when earth has been heaped above the body, a banana-tree, the emblem of fertility, is sometimes planted beside it. In olden times a grave was made in the shape of a well, and the woman's body was buried in a standing

---

[1] Mrs. Leslie Milne, *The Shans at Home* (London, 1910), p. 96. Cf. *The Fear of the Dead in Primitive Religion*, ii. pp. 102 *sq.*

position, a large terra-cotta pot, inverted, being placed on her head, so as to rest on her shoulders. When a pregnant woman dies, no woman still capable of child-bearing and no girl should go into the house of the dead woman, until the body has been removed. When the funeral has taken place the mourners in the house may be visited by girls and young unmarried women, who should accept no food there until seven days have passed. They fear that if they eat in the house before the spirit of the dead woman has gone to eat of the fruit of forgetfulness, a similar fate may befall them should they marry.[1]

In Cambodia it is believed that the spirits of women who die in childbed become malignant spirits who torment living folk in a variety of ways. They are called *khmoch-preai* (the wicked dead). They cause all kinds of sicknesses, they turn into beasts of prey, they throw stones and sand at the mango-trees in the garden in order to frighten the people in the house. No one is safe from their ravages. The first prince of the blood, the highest authority but one in the land, has been heard to complain bitterly of the depredations committed in his garden by these wicked spirits.[2]

The ghosts of women dying in childbed are much dreaded by the Malays of the peninsula and of the Indian Archipelago; it is supposed that they appear in the form of birds with long claws and are

[1] Mrs. Leslie Milne, *The Home of an Eastern Clan* (Oxford, 1924), pp. 304 *sq.*

[2] J. Moura, *Le Royaume du Cambodge* (Paris, 1883), ii. 178.

exceedingly dangerous to their husbands and also to pregnant women. Such a ghost is called a *pontianak*. She is commonly seen in the form of a huge bird uttering a discordant cry. She haunts forests and burial-grounds, appears to men at midnight, and is said to emasculate them. She afflicts children and pregnant women, causing abortions.[1] A common way of guarding against such dangerous ghosts is to put an egg under each armpit of the corpse, to press the arms close against the body, and to stick needles into the palms of the hands. The people believe that the ghost of the dead woman will be unable to fly and attack people ; for she will not spread out her arms for fear of letting the eggs fall, and she will not clutch anyone for fear of driving the needles deeper into her palms. Sometimes, by way of additional precaution, another egg is placed under her chin, thorns are thrust into her fingers and toes, her mouth is stopped with ashes or beads, and her hands, feet, and hair are nailed to the coffin.[2]

[1] T. J. Newbold, *British Settlements in the Straits of Malacca* (London, 1839), ii. 191.

[2] Van Schmidt, " Aanteekeningen nopens de zeden, etc., der bevolking van de eilanden Saparoea, etc.", *Tijdschrift voor Neêrlands Indië*, v. Tweede Deel (Batavia, 1843), pp. 528 *sqq.* ; G. Heijmering, " Zeden en gewoonten op het eiland Timor ", *Tijdschrift voor Neêrlands Indië*, vii. Negende Aflevering (Batavia, 1845), pp. 278 *sq.* note ; B. F. Matthes, *Bijdragen tot de Ethnologie van Zuid - Celebes* (The Hague, 1875), p. 97 ; W. E. Maxwell, " Folk-lore of the Malays ",

Journal of the Straits Branch of the Royal Asiatic Society, No. 7 (June, 1881), p. 28 ; W. W. Skeat, *Malay Magic* (London, 1900), p. 325 ; J. G. F. Riedel, *De sluik- en kroesharige Rassen tusschen Selebes en Papua* (The Hague, 1886), p. 81 ; B. C. A. J. van Dinter, "Eenige geographische en ethnographische aanteekeningen betrefende het eiland Siaoe ", *Tijdschrift voor Indische Taal- Land- en Volkenkunde*, xli. (1899) p. 381 ; A. C. Kruijt, " Eenige ethnographische Aanteekeningen omtrent de Toboengkoe en de Tomori ", *Mededeelingen van wege het Nederlandsche Zendelinggenootschap*, xliv.

Besides these precautions, which are universal in the Malay region, the Achinese of Sumatra give the corpse of such a woman an entangled ball of cotton and a needle without an eye ; when the ghost wants to go off, she must first sew trousers from her shroud, but spends the time in disentangling the cotton and seeking the eye of the needle.[1]

The fear of these dangerous spirits of women dying in childbed is deeply felt and widely held by the natives of Nias, an island lying to the west of Sumatra.[2] In Lolowaoe, a village in the mountains of Western Nias, the natives say that such a spirit, named *matianak*, appears like the shadow of a woman with her hair wound about her head. Only the priests have the faculty of recognizing such spirits. The *matianak* lives by choice on the banks of rivers, and feeds on fish, crabs, and other water creatures. She has a grudge not only at women, but also will not leave men in peace. In the evening she sallies forth and tries to catch some man, whom she then drags to her abode beside the river. There she

(Rotterdam, 1900) p. 218 ; *id.*, *Het Animisme in den Indischen Archipel* (The Hague, 1906), p. 252 ; G. A. Wilken, *Handleiding voor de verglijkende Volkenkunde van Nederlandsch-Indië* (Leyden, 1893), p. 559 ; J. H. Meerwaldt, " Gebruiken der Bataks in het maatschapplijk leven ", *Mededeelingen van wege het Nederlandsche Zendelinggenootschap*, xlix. (1905) p. 113 ; N. Adriani and A. C. Kruijt, *De Bare'e-sprekende Toradjas van Midden-Celebes* (The Hague, 1912), ii. pp. 113 *sq.* The common name for these ghosts is *pontianak*. For a full account of them, see A. C. Kruijt, *Het Animisme in den Indischen Archipel*, pp. 245 *sqq.*

[1] A. C. Kruijt, " Indonesians ", in Hastings' *Encyclopaedia of Religion and Ethics* (Edinburgh, 1914), vii. 241.

[2] J. W. Thomas and L. N. N. A. Chatelin, " Godsdienst en bijgeloof der Niassers ", in *Tijdschrift voor Indische Taal- Land- en Volkenkunde*, 1881, p. 133, and E. Modigliani, *Un Viaggio a Nias* (Milan, 1890), pp. 554, 630.

ducks her victim under the water till he loses consciousness. When he comes to himself, she orders him to climb a high coconut palm and fetch her a coconut. In the oil which she extracts from the nut she boils a human head and therewith prepares an ointment, with which the man must smear his body. Then he is fully in the power of the spirit (*matianak*) and ready to comply with her sexual desires. On the other hand, the *matianak* will also be helpful to her victim. The ointment which he gets from her enables him to steal without being perceived. When he comes to a house which he wishes to rob, he has only to measure at the doorway a space equal to that between his little finger and thumb and to smear on it the ointment which he received from the *matianak*. That enables him to enter the house without being observed by the inmates. Also if he has a grudge against anybody, he may give his knife to the *matianak*, and with it she will rip up the belly of the hated person, so that he or she dies.

It is at evening that these evil spirits go about. Hence, to guard oneself against their attacks, it is well, when you are walking at evening, to brandish a knife or a stick from time to time; this keeps them off. Or the wayfarer throws leaves behind him; the demon stops to pick them up in order to make an ointment out of them, and she loses so much time in picking up the leaves that she cannot overtake the wayfarer.

According to the natives of Eastern Nias it is especially against pregnant women that the *matianak* has a grudge: she causes them to fall sick or to miscarry.   In order to keep the demon from his pregnant wife, a husband will, in the eighth month of her pregnancy, plant a leafy branch of a *damo* tree at a cross-road close to the house.   The leaves flutter in the wind, thus showing their white glistening under-sides.   That frightens the *matianak* so that she dare not approach the house.   Besides that, at the back of the house, close to the woman's chamber, a banana-tree is planted to bar the road against the *matianak*.   The people also place idols, with grim faces, at the entrance of the house and beside the woman's bed, the intention of which must be to frighten the *matianak*.   If the woman is safely delivered, a thank-offering is made to these idols, but if she dies in childbed the idols which have been made are thrown away.   Otherwise they are kept. The natives of Eastern Nias think that the *matianaks* also attack men, wrenching the arms out of their bodies and then inserting them in the reverse way, so that the palms of the hands are turned outwards.[1]

Among the Toradyas of Central Celebes, as additional precautions against the ghost of a woman dying in childbed, an old woman will smear chalk on the cheeks of the corpse, and sometimes the stem of a banana-tree is placed in the coffin with her, to make her think it is her child, and so to soothe and pacify her perturbed spirit.[2]

---

[1] J. P. Kleiweg de Zwaan, " De 'Pontianak' of Nias ", in *Tijdschrift van het Koninklijk Nederlandsch Aardrijkskundig Genootschap,* Tweede Deel, Serie xxix. (1912)

pp. 25 *sqq.*

[2] N. Adriani and A. C. Kruijt, *De Bare'e-sprekende Toradjas van Midden-Celebes,* ii. 114.

We have already seen that a similar mode of contenting the maternal longings of a dead mother is adopted in some parts of Melanesia, including Fiji, and also in the Pelew Islands.[1]

Once more, among the Kayans or Bahaus of Central Borneo, " the corpses of women dying in childbed excite a special horror ; no man and no young woman may touch them ; they are not carried out of the house through the front gallery, but are thrown out of the back wall of the dwelling, some boards having been removed for the purpose."[2] Indeed, so great is the alarm felt by the Kayans at a miscarriage of this sort that when a woman labours hard in childbed, the news quickly spreads through the large communal house in which the people dwell ; and if the attendants begin to fear a fatal issue, the whole household is thrown into consternation. All the men, from the chief down to the boys, will flee from the house, or, if it is night, they will clamber up among the beams of the roof and there remain in terror ; and, if the worst happens, they remain there till the woman's corpse has been removed from the house for burial. In such a case the burial is carried out with the greatest despatch. Old men and women, who are indifferent to death, will undertake the work, and they will extract a large fee for their services. The body, wrapped in a mat, is buried in a grave dug in the earth among the tombs, instead of being laid in a coffin raised on

---

[1] See above, pages 59, 60, 61

[2] A. W. Nieuwenhuis, *Quer durch Borneo* (Leyden, 1901-1907), i. 91.

a tall post ; for the spirit of the woman who dies in childbirth goes, with the spirits of those who fall in battle, or die by violence of any kind, to Bawang Daha (the lake of blood).[1]

The Kiwai of British New Guinea think that the spirits of women dying in childbed are very dangerous ghosts, threatening in particular their husbands, to whom their misfortune is attributed. The spirit of the dead baby is also feared. Not until long afterwards, when the spirits are thought to have gone away, will the husband venture out hunting.[2]

Among the Ewe-speaking peoples of Togo, in West Africa, when a woman dies in childbed they carry her body into the forest, and remain beside it overnight. During the night they light a fire, discharge shots, beat drums, and sing till morning breaks. Then they wash the corpse, spread banana leaves upon the ground, cover them with a mat, and lay the body on the mat. Then they smear the dead woman's face with white earth. And whoever comes to see her takes white earth in his left hand, and strews it on her body, saying three times " I pity thee ". This they do till the time comes for the burial. If the child is still in her womb a man is charged with the duty of cutting open her body at the edge of the grave, so that the dead mother may see her babe. If the child is barely in life they kill it by dashing its head against a tree. But if they see that the child may live they take it home and

[1] C. Hose and W. McDougall, *The Pagan Tribes of Borneo* (London, 1912), i. 155.

[2] G. Landtman, *The Kiwai Papuans of British New Guinea* (London, 1927), p. 284.

rear it. If the child is a male they call it *Kpeme*. They say that only male children, and not female, kill their mothers at birth. The bodies of women who have died in childbed are buried in a special place (*Atsiamanya*). Nine days after the burial the funeral rites are performed, the woman's house is broken up and the materials are burned on the road outside the town, in order that no evil influence may attach to the timbers. The inhabitants of the town receive a fine of forty *hoca* of cowrie shells from the relations of the deceased. Then they take a small dog and a toad, tie them to the end of a palm branch, and drag them through the town. This ceremony is called '*kplo gbo me* (sweeping the town, purifying it from evil spirits). Behind them a bell is rung all the time, till they have completed the round of the town. If this rite were not performed, no solemn purification (*busu*) would thereafter be possible.[1] From this account we gather that among these people the death of a woman in childbed is supposed to affect the whole town with a pollution which must be effaced before life can resume its normal course. The ghost of such a woman must therefore be deemed particularly virulent.

The Ibibio of Southern Nigeria regard with fear and horror the bodies of women who have died in childbed. Such corpses are carried out and thrown away or propped against the foot of a tree in the Bad Bush. In the neighbourhood of Awa the mouths

---

[1] J. Spieth, *Die Ewe-Stämme* (Berlin, 1906), p. 278

of such women are stopped with pitch, while some pitch, mixed with thorns, is also placed at times under the armpits, to prevent them from troubling the living. Otherwise their ghosts, who are thought to hate the whole human race because they have been denied burial, are said to take upon themselves the form of a beautiful woman to lure a man to his destruction. Such a man at his death will find himself surrounded by the ghoul-wife and her demon offspring, and will be prevented from joining his relatives and friends in the ghost town. When the bearers who have carried out the corpse of such a woman and disposed of it in the forest return to the village, they may not enter their own houses, but must wait outside that of the dead woman until the members of her family have brought out and sacrificed a dog, a cock, and some eggs. Magic leaves are ground between stones and rubbed over the bodies of the corpse-bearers, while the kinsmen of the deceased pray that so sad a fate may never again overtake one of their house. The fowl's head is struck off, and its blood is sprinkled over the bearers, who chant meanwhile : " Let not the evil thing pass from me to any woman ". Until the sacrifices have been made and the prayers offered, none who took part in carrying the corpse may touch a woman lest the influence which had proved fatal to the deceased should be communicated by them to the living.[1]

<hr />

[1] D. Amaury Talbot, *Woman's Mysteries of a Primitive People,* pp. 214 *sq.* P. Amaury Talbot, *The Peoples of Southern Nigeria,* iii. 512.

Among the Ila-speaking peoples of Northern Rhodesia, when a woman dies in pregnancy, it is deemed necessary to cut out the child from her womb, and to bury it separately from the mother, for otherwise they believe that the mother's ghost will rise from the grave and kill people.[1]

The ancient Mexicans believed that the spirits of women who died in childbed were turned into dangerous and malevolent goddesses, who roamed about in the air, but descended from time to time on the earth for their errands of mischief. They haunted, above all, the cross-roads. On such descents they afflicted children with various maladies, including paralysis, by penetrating into the bodies of the sufferers. Hence parents forbade their children to leave the house on days when they thought the goddesses descended to earth, lest their offspring should be harmed by these evil deities. Paralysis was explained by them as due to the possession of the sufferer's body by one of these malignant beings. To appease these dreaded goddesses the ancient Mexicans held festivals in their honour, at which they offered them loaves baked in the shape of butterflies and thunder-bolts, cakes called *tamalli*, and roasted maize. The images of these goddesses represented them with white faces and white hands, arms, and legs, as if they were smeared with white earth. Their ears were golden, and the tresses of their hair curled like

---

[1] Rev. E. W. Smith and Capt. A. M. Dale, *The Ila-Speaking Peoples* *of Northern Nigeria* (London, 1920), ii. 115.

those of great ladies. Their robes were striped with black, and their petticoats parti-coloured.[1] Oratories of these goddesses were erected in all the wards of the city. In them their images stood, and these were covered with paper on the days when the deities were supposed to descend. Usually the spirits of women dying in childbed were thought to live in the palace of the sun in the western part of the sky, and to accompany the sun daily from midday till his setting in the west. But on certain days of certain months they were believed to descend to earth, and to afflict children with paralysis and other maladies. It was on these days, which were well known from the calendar, accordingly, that parents were careful to keep their children at home, that they might not encounter the dangerous goddesses.[2]

V. *Ghosts of dead Husbands or Wives*

The ghosts of dead husbands and wives are commonly deemed very dangerous to their surviving spouses, whom they are thought to haunt in a variety of ways. This they are thought to do especially when the surviving partner has taken to himself or herself a second wife or husband, for the ghost is naturally jealous of the second wife or husband, and seeks to wreak her spite against the new

---

[1] Bernardino de Sahagun, *Histoire générale des choses de la Nouvelle-Espagne*, traduite et annotée par D. Jourdanet et Remi Simeon (Paris, 1880), pp. 20 *sq.*

[2] Sahagun, *op. cit.* pp. 433-437, 80, 81, 255, 269. Cf. H. H. Bancroft, *The Native Races of the Pacific States of North America*, iii. 362-364.

bride or bridegroom. Hence special precautions are commonly taken to guard the widower or widow against the dangerous spirit of his or her departed spouse.[1]

Thus, for example, among the Nufoors of Dutch New Guinea, when a widow marries for a second time, she walks into the forest with her new husband, followed by a number of widows or married women, who cut branches and twigs from the trees and throw them at the newly wedded pair. This they do for the purpose of driving away the jealous ghost of the widow's late husband, who is supposed to pursue and endanger one or both of them. For the same reason the widow must put off her mourning garb and give it to another widow, because it is believed that the ghost of her late husband adheres to the garments, and that if she did not put them off he might, out of jealousy, visit her or her new husband with sickness. When the couple have ended their walk the female friends who accompanied them and plied them vigorously with branches and twigs receive a present of chopping-knives and petticoats, and that ends the marriage ceremony.[2]

At Issoudun in British New Guinea a French

---

[1] With what follows, compare *Psyche's Task* (*The Devil's Advocate*), pp. 142-149; *Folk-Lore in the Old Testament*, i. 523-529. See also E. S. Hartland, *Ritual and Belief*, chapter "The Haunted Widow", pp. 194 *sqq.*; and E. Westermarck, *The History of Human Marriage* (Fifth Edition, London, 1921), i.

[2] pp. 326 *sqq.*

[2] J. B. van Hasselt, "Die Noerforezen", in *Zeitschrift für Ethnologie*, viii. (1876) p. 182 *sq.*; *id.*, "Eenige aanteekeningen de bewoners der N. Westkust van Nieuw Guinea", in *Tijdschrift voor Indische Taal- Land- en Volkenkunde*, xxi. (1886) p. 585.

missionary has painted a melancholy picture of the sad lot of a native widower haunted and hag-ridden by the ghost of his dead wife. His miseries begin with the moment of his wife's death. He is immediately stripped of all his ornaments, abused and beaten by his wife's relations, his house is pillaged, his gardens devastated, there is no one to cook for him. He sleeps on his wife's grave till the end of his mourning. He may never marry again. By the death of his wife he loses all his rights. It is civil death for him. Old or young, chief or plebeian, he is no longer anybody; he does not count. He may not hunt or fish with the others ; his presence would bring misfortune ; the spirit of his dead wife would frighten the fish or the game. He is no longer heard in the discussions. He has no voice in the council of elders. He may not take part in a dance ; he may not own a garden. If one of his children marries, he has no right to interfere in anything or to receive any present. If he were dead he could not be ignored more completely. He has become a nocturnal animal. He is forbidden to show himself in public, to traverse the village, to walk in the roads and paths. Like a boar he must go in the grass or the bushes. If he hears or sees anyone, especially a woman, coming from afar, he must hide himself behind a tree or a thicket. If he wishes to go hunting or fishing by himself, he must go at night. If he has to consult anyone, even the missionary, he does it in great secrecy, and at night. He seems to have lost his voice, and only speaks in a whisper. He is painted black from head to foot. The hair of his head is shaved, except two tufts which flutter on his temples. He wears a skull-cap which covers his head completely to the ears; it ends in a point at the back of his neck. Round his waist he wears one, two, or three sashes of plaited grass; his arms and legs from the knees to the ankles are covered with armlets and leglets of the same sort; and round his neck he wears a similar ornament. His diet is strictly regulated, but he does not observe it more than he can help, eating in secret whatever he is given or he can lay his hands on. " His tomahawk accompanies him everywhere and always. He needs it to defend himself against the wild boars and also against the spirit of his dead wife, who might take a fancy to come and play him some mischievous prank; for the souls of the dead come back often, and their visit is far from being desired, inasmuch as all the spirits without exception are bad and have no pleasure but in harming the living. Happily people can keep them at bay by a stick, fire, an arrow, or a tomahawk. The condition of a widower, far from exciting pity or compassion, only serves to render him the object of horror and fear. Almost all widowers, in fact, have the reputation of being more or less sorcerers, and their mode of life is not fitted to give the lie to public opinion. They are forced to become idlers and thieves, since they are forbidden to work: no work, no gardens: no gardens, no food: steal then they must, and that is a trade which cannot be plied without some audacity and knavery at a pinch." [1]

Among the Kiwai Papuans of British New Guinea, when a widow marries again several ceremonies are performed, which appear to be based on a fear of her late husband's ghost. One day just before sundown the pair go to the forest, where they have connexion close to a spider's web spun between them and the village. When the man gets up, he walks home right through the web, breaking it, and at a little distance his wife follows in his tracks. On entering their house they carefully bar the door after them. In the morning when they go back to the bush the spider will have restored its web, and then the past is " shut away ". Another practice is this. The man and widow go to the place where she and her former husband had connexion the last time. There she cooks a little food—a taro root or some sago. They break off the top shoot of a young bamboo, provide themselves each with a little piece of the stem underneath, and replace the shoot. The small pieces of bamboo are put into two portions of the food. They then have connexion, and during the act they put into each other's mouth the two bits of food containing the bamboo. Their intention is to link up their marriage with the first one, at the spot where this had been broken off, and to prevent the new husband from dying as his predecessor had done. The "spirit-smell" still

[1] Father Guis (de la Congrégation du Sacré Cœur d'Issoudun, missionaire en Nouvelle-Guinée), " Les Canaques, mort-deuil ", in *Les Missions Catholiques*, xxxiv. (Lyons, 1902) pp. 208 *sq.*

adheres to the woman, and they want to " wash it away ". As the bamboo grows on, the loose shoot on top, which represents the dead husband, is thrown off, and the stem underneath, symbolizing the new husband, keeps on growing. Before returning home they split the middle part of a certain creeper (*nu-rúde*), leaving the base and top intact, then the man and woman crawl through the opening, which closes behind them, and in this way they " shut the road against the ghost of the dead husband ". These observances are not kept by the bushmen at marrying a widow, hence many of them suffer from shortness of breath, which is supposed to be caused by the first husband's ghost.

If the first husband has been taken by a crocodile, the following rite is observed. The pair go to the place where the accident happened ; there the woman takes off her grass petticoat and breaks her *sógére* (a plaited grass necklace), the last sign of her mourning, throwing them away into the water. After the two have had connexion, the woman stands up astride with her back towards the water, and her husband crawls between her legs from behind. She then puts on a new petticoat and walks home behind her husband. They keep the door of their house carefully closed till next morning. An analogous rite is performed in the case of the first husband having been killed by a snake. The couple have connexion close to the haunt of the snake. Then they fill a coconut bowl with water from some swamp near by, frequented by the creature, and both drink

it. A nipa leaflet is partly split in the same way as
the creeper in the observance described above, and
the two sides are kept apart by means of a transverse
stick. The man first crawls through the leaf, knocking down the stick, and after him the woman in the
same way, the stick having been replaced. On their
return home the door is kept shut after them. There
is a third similar rite performed if the widow's first
husband has been killed by a wild boar. At a place
where the boar has rooted in the ground the woman
lies down nude, and the man pours over her genitals
some water brought in a coconut-bowl from a hole
made by the pig. The woman gets up and drinks
the rest of the water in the bowl, the man not drinking any. After a couple of days the pair go back
to the same place and have connexion there. On
their return to the village the people—men, women,
and children—previously summoned by the husband, sit down on the ground, forming a circle, in
the middle of which husband and wife seat themselves. The circle of friends round the newly
married pair is said to fence or guard them, presumably against the ghost of the deceased husband.
The pair remain within the enclosure until sunset,
when they go into their house and secure the door.[1]

Among the Toradyas of Central Celebes, a
widow, after the death of her husband, may not leave
the house until a certain ceremony has been performed over her. A rough fence of umbrellas and
cotton is rigged up round about her, and within this

---

[1] G. Landtman, *The Kiwai Papuans of British New Guinea*, pp. 252 *sq.*

circle a priest performs over her certain rites, which are believed to fasten her soul in her body, and so to prevent it from following her husband's ghost to the spirit land.[1] These Toradyas think, or used to think, that every period of mourning for the dead must be terminated by a human sacrifice, offered to the spirit of the dead, either to divert the wrath of the ghost from the living, or to carry his property to him in the spirit land. In time of war the scalp of a slain enemy might be used for the purpose. When a village in which a death had taken place was not at war, they tried to obtain a human victim by purchase from a neighbouring tribe and, if they succeeded, they hacked him or her to death. Sometimes they employed as victims persons accused of witchcraft. If all other means failed, as a last resort they undertook a warlike expedition against hereditary foes at a distance. A widower must bring back a human head for his dead wife, even if he had to remain absent for three years or more before he could procure it. If he came back without it he was put to public shame by his fellow-villagers.[2] So keen apparently was the dead woman's ghost to obtain the bloody trophy.

In India it is, as usual, at the marriage of a widow or widower that the jealous ghost of the deceased spouse is particularly dreaded and that, accordingly,

[1] A. C. Kruijt, " Het koppen-snellen der Toradjás van Midden-Celebes, en zijne beteekenis ", in *Verslagen en Mededeelingen der Koninklijk Akademie van Wetenschappen*, Vierde Reeks, Derde Deel. xxv. (Amsterdam, 1899) p. 188.

[2] N. Adriani and A. C. Kruijt, *De Bare's Sprekende Toradjas van Midden-Celebes* (The Hague, 1912), pp. 105-107.

special precautions are adopted to guard against his or her unwelcome attentions. Thus among the Barai, a caste of betel-leaf growers and sellers in the Central Provinces, when a man marries a widow he offers a coconut at the shrine of a certain deity called Maroti. The nut is afterwards placed on a plank and kicked away by the widow's new husband, in token of his thus dismissing summarily the ghost of her dead spouse. Later on the coconut is buried in order to lay the spirit of the deceased.[1] Again among the Bhāmta, a caste of thieves and growers of hemp in the Central Provinces, if a man marries a second wife after the death of the first, the new wife wears on her neck an image of the first wife, and offers it the *hom* sacrifice by placing some melted butter (*ghi*) on the fire before taking a meal. In cases of doubt and difficulty she often consults the image by speaking to it, while any chance stir of the image due to the movement of her body is interpreted as a sign of the approval or disapproval of the dead wife.[2] Thus the second wife attempts to appease the jealous spirit of her predecessor in the affections of her husband. Among the Kunbi, the great agricultural caste of the Marathi country, the ceremony of widow-marriage is largely governed by the idea of escaping or placating the wrath of the first husband's ghost. It always takes place in the dark fortnight of the month, and always at night. Sometimes no women are present, and if they do

---

[1] R. V. Russell, *The Tribes and Castes of the Central Provinces of* India, ii. 195.

[2] R. V. Russell, *op. cit.* ii. 237.

attend they must be widows, for it would be a very bad omen for a married woman or an unmarried girl to witness the ceremony. This, it is thought, would shortly lead to her becoming a widow herself. The bridegroom goes to the widow's house with his male friends, and two wooden seats are set side by side. On one of the seats is placed a betel-nut, which represents the deceased husband of the widow. The new bridegroom advances with a small wooden sword, touches the nut with its tip, and then kicks it off the seat with his right toe. The barber picks up the nut and burns it : this is believed to lay the deceased husband's ghost and to prevent his interference with the new union. The bridegroom then takes the seat from which the nut has been displaced and the woman sits on the other side to his left. He puts a necklace of beads round her neck and the couple leave the house and go to the husband's village. It is considered unlucky to see them as they go away, as the second husband is regarded in the light of a robber. Sometimes they stop at a stream on the way home, and, taking off the woman's clothes and bangles, bury them on the bank. An exorcist may also be called in, who will confine the late husband's spirit in a horn by putting in some grains of wheat, and after sealing up the horn deposit it with the clothes. When a widower or widow marries for a second time, and is afterwards attacked by illness, it is ascribed to the ill-will of their former partner's spirit. The metal image of the first husband or wife is then made and worn as an amulet on the arm or round the neck, to protect the wearer against the ghost of the deceased spouse.[1] Among the Mahars, an impure caste of menials, labourers and village watchmen in the Maratha country, when a man marries a widow, and she is proceeding to her new husband's house, she is stripped of her old clothes, necklace and bangles, and these are thrown into a river or stream, and she is given new ones to wear. This is done to lay her first husband's ghost, who may be supposed to hang about the clothes which she formerly wore as his wife, and when they are thrown away or buried the exorcist mutters spells over them in order to lay the spirit of the deceased spouse.[2]

Similarly among the Mana, a Dravidian caste of cultivators and labourers in the Central Provinces, when a widow is to be married again, and is proceeding for that purpose to her new husband's house, she stops by the bank of a stream, and here her clothes are taken off and buried by an exorcist for the sake of laying her first husband's spirit and preventing him from troubling the new household.[3] Among the Mang-Gorari, a criminal subdivision of the Mang caste in the Central Provinces and Berar, if a widow survived two or three husbands and then married again, she had to go through the ceremony holding a fowl under her arm, and the bird was afterwards killed to appease the ghost or ghosts of her late husband or husbands.[4] Among

[1] R. V. Russell, op. cit. iii. pp. 27 sq.
[2] R. V. Russell, op. cit. iv. 135.
[3] R. V. Russell, op. cit. iv. 175
[4] R. V. Russell, op. cit. iv. 193.

the Panwar, a famous Rajput clan, when a widow marries again the stool on which she sat at the ceremony is afterwards stolen by her new husband's friends. After the wedding, when she reaches the boundary of his village the axle of her cart is removed, and a new one made of ebony wood (*tendu*) is substituted for it. The discarded axle and the shoes worn by the husband at the ceremony are thrown away, and the stolen stool is buried in a field. The wood of the *tendu* or ebony tree is chosen because it has the valuable property of keeping off spirits and ghosts. When a child is born a plank of this wood is laid along the door of the room to keep the spirits from troubling the mother and the new-born infant. In the same way, no doubt, this wood keeps the ghost of the first husband from entering with the widow into her second husband's village.[1] Among the primitive Bhils, Mavchis and Konkanis of India, when a man's wife has died and he marries again, custom requires him to carry at the ceremony a large stone engraved with the image of a woman. After the marriage ceremony this stone is buried in the cemetery, in such a way that the image of the woman still shows above the surface. The object of this rite is to fix the ghost of the deceased wife and to prevent it from wandering.[2]

Among the Somavansi Kshatriyas in Bombay " there is a strong belief that when a woman marries another husband, her first husband becomes a ghost

[1] R. V. Russell, *op. cit.* iv. 345.
[2] J. Abbott, *The Keys of Power* (London, 1932), p. 244.

and troubles her. This fear is so strongly rooted in their minds that whenever a woman of this caste sickens she attributes her sickness to the ghost of her former husband, and consults an exorcist as to how she can get rid of him. The exorcist gives her some charmed rice, flowers and basil leaves, and tells her to enclose them in a small copper box and wear it round her neck. Sometimes the exorcist gives her a charmed coconut which he tells her to worship daily, and in some cases he advises the woman to make a copper or silver image of the dead and worship it every day." [1] So in Northern India when a man marries again after the death of his first wife he wears " what is known as the Saukan Maura, or second wife's crown. This is a little silver amulet, generally with an image of Devî engraved on it. This is hung round the husband's neck, and all presents made to the second wife are first dedicated to it. The idea is that the second wife recognizes the superiority of her predecessor, and thus appeases her malignity. The illness or death of the second wife or of her husband soon after marriage is attributed to the jealousy of the ghost of the first wife, which has not been suitably propitiated." [2]

In the Bombay Presidency most high-caste people, on the death of their first wives, take an impression of their feet on gold leaves or leaf-like tablets of gold

---

[1] W. Crooke, *The Popular Religion and Folk-Lore of Northern India* (Westminster, 1896), i. 235 *sq.*, quoting J. M. Campbell's *Notes on the Spirit Basis of Belief and Custom*, p. 171.

[2] W. Crooke, *op. cit.* i. 236.

and cause their second wives to wear them round the neck. These impresses of feet are called mourning footprints. Among the lower castes the hands or the feet of the second wife are tattooed in the belief that this prevents the deceased wife from causing injury to the second wife.[1] A similar purpose, no doubt, is served by the golden footprints of a first wife which the second wife of a high-caste man wears as an amulet on her neck.

The Bhandari are a caste of toddy-drawers, who are scattered all over the Bombay Presidency. They permit the marriage of widows with the sanction of the *panch* or head man of the caste. " The ceremony is performed at night in an unoccupied outhouse. The details vary in the different localities according to local usages. In the Ratnágiri district, where the caste is most numerous, it is celebrated as follows. The ceremony of *oválani* (waving a platter containing lighted wicks, a pice, a coconut, rice grains and a cock) is first performed by a *Bhagat* (exorcist) in order to free the widow from the dominion of the spirit of her deceased husband, who is supposed to haunt her. The materials of the *oválani*, except the cock, which is taken by the *Bhagat*, are carefully packed together and sent to the house of the widow's deceased husband in order to be lodged at the foot of the *tulsi* (sweet basil) plant in front of the house, as it is supposed that these *oválani* materials collected together carry back with them the spirit of the deceased husband. The *Bhagat* himself is possessed

---

[1] R. E. Enthoven, *Folk-Lore of Bombay* (Oxford, 1924), p. 196.

of his favouring spirit while he is performing the ceremony. Thus possessed, he promises good to the pair, and conjures the spirit of the widow's deceased husband by means of the *oválani*. Thus freed, the widow is presented to her husband by another widow who acts as her bridesmaid. She applies paste made of flour of *udid* (black gram) to the left knee of the latter, and puts some grains of rice on it. Next, her new husband presents her with a new dress and ornaments which she puts on in the presence of the assembly. This completes the ceremony. A dinner is then held, and a present of Rs. 5 is made to the caste *panch* who sanctioned the marriage. On the following morning before daybreak the widow's new husband, accompanied by his friends and followed by her, leaves the house to return home. The widow takes a cock under her arm. When the procession reaches the boundary of the village the cock is immolated, and its head, together with a lock of hair from the widow's head and a bit of the new robe worn by her are buried under a rock. The body of the cock is taken away and eaten by the *Bhagat*, who accompanies the pair till they reach home. This ceremony is also performed by the *Bhagat* and is intended to be an offering to the guardian spirit of the village resident on the boundary, who is expected to take charge of the spirit of the deceased husband. Not unnaturally the deceased husband is believed to be very jealous of the second husband, and all the efforts of the *Bhagat* are directed towards annihilating his influence, in case he may be hovering near

in the spirit with evil intentions."[1] Among the
Gabit, a caste of fishers on the Bombay coast, the
marriage of a widow is celebrated in an uninhabited
house on the village boundary, or in a temple of
Vetál or Bhutnáth. At the ceremony "in order to
prevent disturbance from the spirit of the widow's
deceased husband, a cock, a coconut and rice
grains are first offered to him."[2] Among the Mahar,
a tribe of the Bombay Presidency, at the remarriage
of a widow, when the ceremony is over and the newly-
wedded pair are starting for the bridegroom's house,
but before they reach it, a cock is killed and a piece
of the widow's robe is cut off and Rs. 2 with a *ser* of
rice grains and a coconut or five *Nagchampa* leaves
tied in a piece of cloth are sent to the house of the
widow's deceased husband and placed in the basin
of the sweet basil plant in the courtyard. This offering is made to appease the spirit of the widow's deceased husband.[3] Among the Nhavi, the barber caste
of the Bombay Presidency, when a widow has been
remarried, on the night of the marriage day, and
before daybreak, the newly-wedded pair start for the
bridegroom's home, the wife holding a cock under
her arm. At the same time a man of the caste leaves
for the widow's deceased husband's house taking
with him a coconut, some fruit, rice grains and
one rupee. On arriving there, he places these things
either in the house or in the courtyard, unseen by anybody. When the procession of the remarried couple

[1] R. E. Enthoven, *The Tribes and Castes of Bombay* (Bombay, 1920), i. 101-102.

[2] R. E. Enthoven, *op. cit.* i. 349.

[3] R. E. Enthoven, *op. cit.* ii. 415.

reaches the boundary of the widow's village, the cock under the widow's arm is sacrificed and a coconut is broken. The body of the cock and the coconut are given to a *virakti* (worshipper of a village deity). Next, another cock is placed under the widow's arm, and the procession proceeds on its way. When they reach the boundary of the bridegroom's village, another coconut is broken and the cock under the widow's arm is killed by a *virakti*, and the head of the cock together with a hair from the widow's head and a bit of her robe are buried under a rock. The body of the cock is taken away and eaten by the *virakti*, who is also paid some money for his services by the bridegroom. " All these efforts are directed to preventing the spirit of the widow's deceased husband from troubling the second husband. When the party reach home, a jar filled with water is placed on the threshold of the door. The widow takes it on her head and enters the house, thus ending the ceremony." [1] By this last act the widow may perhaps be supposed to place a barrier of water between herself and the ghost of her late husband.

Among the Ramoshi, a very numerous caste of the Bombay Presidency, the remarriage of a widow is celebrated on a dark night. Only men attend the ceremony. As it is considered unlucky for married unwidowed women to hear the service, the ceremony is celebrated in a deserted place. The widow and her new husband separate after the ceremony, and do not see each other or any of the caste

[1] R. E. Enthoven, *op. cit.* iii. pp. 132 *sq.*

for a day. " If a woman has lost three husbands and wishes to marry a fourth, she holds a cock under her left arm when the ceremony is being performed. The priest reads the service first in the name of the cock, and then of the man, the object evidently being that, in case the spirits of her former husbands or rather the spirit of her first husband who killed the next two for meddling with his property, be inclined to do any harm, it may fall on the cock and not on the man." [1]   Among the Teli, a caste of oilmen in the Bombay Presidency, the marriage of widows is permitted. In the Ratnágiri district, before the marriage of a widow takes place a bundle of cloth containing a rupee, a coconut, and a betelnut is sent to the widow's late husband's house, and a coconut and a cock are waved off her face to free her from molestation by her deceased husband's spirit. [2]   Among the Parit, a caste of washermen in the Bombay Presidency, when a widow has been married again she or her new husband sacrifices a cock every year to appease the wrath of her deceased husband's ghost. [3]

Among the Savaras, an important hill-tribe of Southern India, whoever marries a widow must perform a religious ceremony, during which a pig is sacrificed. The flesh, with some liquor, is offered to the ghost of the widow's deceased husband, and prayers are offered by the priest to propitiate the ghost, so that it may not torment the woman and her

[1] R. E. Enthoven, *op. cit.* iii. 301.   [3] R. E. Enthoven, *op. cit.* iii. 176.
[2] R. E. Enthoven, *op. cit.* iii. 374.

second husband. "Oh man!" says the priest, addressing the deceased by name, "here is an animal sacrificed to you, and with this all connexion between this woman and you ceases. She has taken no property belonging to you or your children. So do not torment her within the house or outside the house, in the jungle or on the hill, when she is asleep or when she wakes. Do not send sickness on her children. Her second husband has done no harm to you. She chose him for her husband, and he consented. Oh man! be appeased; oh! unseen ones; oh! ancestors, be you witnesses." The animal sacrificed on this occasion is called *long danda* (inside fine), or fine paid to the spirit of a dead person inside the earth.[1]

Among the Kamchadals or Koryaks of Kamtchatka in north-eastern Asia no man would marry a widow before a ceremony called "removing the sin from her" had been performed. The ceremony consisted in her having sexual intercourse with a stranger, who had to be paid for his services, for his office was considered disgraceful, and until the advent of the Russians it was difficult to find any man who would undertake the duty; but after the coming of the Cossacks there was no lack of men willing to take upon themselves the sin of a handsome young widow.[2] Our authorities for this custom

---

[1] E. Thurston, *Castes and Tribes of Southern India* (Madras, 1909), vi. 321.

[2] S. Krascheninnikow, *Beschreibung des Landes Kamtschatka* (Lemgo, 1766), p. 259; G. W. Steller, *Beschreibung von dem Lande Kamtschatka* (Frankfurt and Leipzig, 1774), p. 346.

do not explain what the sin of the widow consisted in, but we may conjecture with a fair degree of probability that it was the offence which she gave to the ghost of her late husband by her first act of sexual intercourse after his death. This view is accepted by competent modern authorities who have touched upon the custom.[1]

In Africa the fear of the ghost of a dead husband or a dead wife is strongly pronounced among the Ewe-peoples of Togo. At Agome, in Togoland, a widow is bound to remain for six weeks in the hut where her husband lies buried. She is naked, her hair is shaved off, and she is armed with a stick with which to repel the too pressing familiarities of her husband's ghost; for were she to submit to them she would die on the spot. At night she sleeps with the stick under her, lest the wily ghost should attempt to steal it from her in the hours of slumber. Before she eats or drinks she always puts some coals on the food or in the beverage, to prevent her dead husband from eating or drinking with her; for if he did so she would die. If any one calls to her she may not answer, for her dead husband would hear her, and she would die. She may not eat beans or flesh or fish, nor drink palm-wine or rum, but she is allowed to smoke tobacco. At night a fire is kept up in the hut, and the widow throws powdered peppermint leaves and red pepper on the

---

[1] W. Jochelson, *The Koryak*, ii. 752 (Jesup North Pacific Expedition, Memoir of the American Museum of Natural History) (Leyden and New York, 1908); E. Westermarck, *The History of Human Marriage* Fifth Edition, London, 1921), i. 327.)

flames to make a stink, which helps to keep the
ghost from the house. Among these people widowers
observe a similar seclusion after the death of their
wives, but only for eight days, and we are not told
that they resort to the same means of repelling the
ghosts of their deceased spouses.[1]

Among the Ibibio of Southern Nigeria, when a
widow begins to contemplate a second marriage she
is terrified lest the ghost of her late husband should
return and seek to draw her after him to the spirit
land. Should she suspect that the ghost is actually
preparing to do so, she consults a member of the
secret society called Idiong, who has a great reputation for second sight. By his advice food is cooked
and placed in a corner of the room. The priest takes
up a position immediately before this, and stands
calling upon the name of the ghost. Close to the
place where the food is laid some member of the
family crouches, holding a strong pot, preferably of
iron, tilted forward ready to invert over the one in
which the food is served. When the ghost is supposed to be partaking of the food in the first pot the
wizard makes a sign and the second pot is inverted and
clapped over the first pot, and the two are bound fast
together, thus entrapping the spirit of the woman's
late husband, and so presumably preventing him
from offering any obstacle to her second marriage.

[1] Lieutenant Herold, " Bericht
betreffend religiöse Anschauungen
und Gebräuche der deutschen Ewe-
Neger ", Mitteilungen von For-
schungsreisended und Gelehrten aus
den deutschen Schutzgebiet, v. Heft 4
(Berlin, 1892), p. 155 ; H. Klose,
Togo unter deutscher Flagge (Berlin,
1899), p. 274.

If, on the contrary, a widow loved her late husband very much, she will cook food for him after his death and place it secretly in a corner of her room so that his spirit may be induced to return and enjoy it.[1] Among the Baganda of Central Africa, when a man wished to marry a widow he first paid the deceased husband a barkcloth and a fowl, which he put into the little shrine at the dead man's grave : in this way he imagined that he could pacify the ghost.[2]

Among the Wajagga of Mount Kilimanjaro in East Africa, when a man marries a widow he purchases the right to do so from her late husband by sacrificing a goat to his ghost, for the dead man is supposed to retain all the rights that he had in life. The sacrifice is offered at evening in the cattle kraal. When the goat has been killed the contents of the stomach are extracted, carried into the hut, and laid upon one of the stones of the hearth. The bridegroom and the widow crouch beside the hearth, and together draw the hearthstone out of the earth. Thereupon the bridegroom repeats his adjuration to the ghost of the widow's late husband to the following effect : " To-day I take over thy kraal and thy children, in order that I may look after them and bring them up, and that they may bring offerings to thee. If I know any black or white root that could have killed you, may I perish by this stone. It was thy fate, I had no share in thy death, let me live and

---

[1] D. Amaury Talbot, A Woman's Mysteries of a Primitive People, pp. 174 sq.

[2] J. Roscoe, The Baganda (London, 1911), p. 97.

thrive in this place. And if I beget a child by thy wife, let it grow up with its brothers and sisters that they may be a credit to the members of their age-grade." They think that if this satisfaction were not offered to the spirit of the dead husband his ghost might take offence and kill the widow. In his address to the ghost at offering the sacrifice the new husband is careful to insist that he by no means wishes to intrude upon the rights of his predecessor. He begs to be allowed to purchase and pay for his predecessor's rights. He promises to care for his predecessor's cattle and to rescue them should they fall into the hands of the enemy. In return for the sacrifice of the goat, the ghost is requested to transfer all his rights to the new husband, in order that he may go out and in the kraal in safety, and to help him to rear the dead man's orphan children.[1]

Among the Dinkas of the Upper Nile, before a widow may marry again a sacrifice must be offered to appease the spirit of her late husband. A brother of the deceased (and it may be the very brother who is about to marry her) kills a bull from the dead man's herd and the blood is collected in a gourd. The blood and the meat are boiled and eaten by the widow and her children, the woman's clan taking one hind leg and the clan of the deceased the rest. After this satisfaction has been given to the ghost of her dead husband, the widow is free to marry again.[2]

[1] B. Gutmann, *Das Recht der Dschagga* (Munchen, 1926), pp. 52 sq.
[2] C. G. and B. Z. Seligman, *Pagan Tribes of the Nilotic Sudan* (London, 1932), p. 164.

Speaking of the natives of Congo in West Africa a French writer of the eighteenth century tells us that according to their belief the ghost of a dead husband lights upon the head of his widow. Hence when a husband has breathed his last, his widow rushes to some river or tank with a minister of their sect, whose special function it is to perform the rite. There the widow is tied with cords and flung several times into the river, in the belief that this will drown the soul of her late husband and prevent it from returning to torment her. As soon as she returns from the river she is free to marry again. But if a widow does not thus drown her husband's ghost, she must stay at home clad in old, torn, dirty, dark-coloured robes, doubtless in order to elude the attention of her late husband's ghost.[1] In Loango, a province of West Africa to the south of the Congo, widows fear to be visited at night by the ghosts of their dead husbands. They think that as a consequence of such a visit they would either die or give birth to monsters. To guard against such a visit a wizard will provide a widow with a magic bolt with which to close the door of the hut against the ghost, or with a magic cord to fasten round her bed at night. Or he may shift the door of the house to another side of the dwelling, in order to baffle the ghost. If all these precautions fail to allay the widow's anxiety her friends will remove her secretly by night to another house, taking her by a

---

[1] J. B. Labat, *Relation historique de l'Éthiopie occidentale* (Paris, 1732), i. 404.

roundabout way which the ghost cannot follow, and effacing her footsteps, in order that the ghost may not track her to her new abode. With a view to leaving no tell-tale footprints behind they will sometimes carry the widow, or put sandals on her feet if she walks, for in this last case the ghost will not be able to recognize the widow's own footprints. In addition to all these precautions a widow is always provided with a magic cudgel which she lays between her legs when she sleeps at night, to be employed in self-defence against the ghost should he succeed in approaching her.[1]

Among the Wabemba or Awemba, a Bantu tribe of the Congo Free State and North-Eastern Rhodesia, before a widower may marry again he must appease the spirit of his dead wife by scraping with his fingers a little hole at the head of her grave and pouring into it a libation of beer, doubtless to slake the thirst of the ghost.[2] Among the Mashona of Southern Rhodesia, when a man's wife has died he may not marry again until after the obsequies for his dead wife have been fully performed. His father-in-law could accuse him of witchcraft if he took another wife while the ghost of his dead wife still hovered about unappeased. It was thought that such wickedness might cause the ghost to strike her own people : she could not strike him or his.[3]

[1] P. Güssfeld, J. Falkenstein, E. Pechuël-Loesche, Die Loango-Expedition ausgesandt von der deutschen Gesellschaft zur Erforschungen Aquatorial-Africas, 1873–1876 (Stuttgart, 1907), iii. 2, 308 sq.

[2] C. Delhaise, Notes ethnographiques sur quelques peuplades du Tanganyika (Brussels, 1905), p. 10.

[3] C. Bullock, The Mashona (Johannesburg, 1928), p. 261.

The Amazulu of Southern Africa believe that a widow is sometimes visited and troubled by the ghost (*Itongo*) of her dead husband. If such a ghostly visit takes place during her pregnancy, and she afterwards miscarries, the ghost of her dead husband is laid because he has done her an ill turn. Should the ghost trouble her when she has gone to another man without being as yet married, leaving her late husband's children behind, the ghost of her dead husband will follow her and ask, " With whom have you left my children ? What are you going to do here ? Go back to my children. If you do not assent I will kill you." In such a case the vengeful ghost of the dead husband is at once laid in that village because he harasses his widow.[1]

The following is a native account of the method of laying a dead husband's troublesome ghost *(Itongo)* which is practised by the Amazulu. " If a woman has lost her husband, and she is troubled excessively by a dream, and when she is asleep her husband comes home again, and she sees him daily just as if he was alive, and so she at last wastes away, and says, ' I am troubled by the father of So-and-So ; he does not leave me ; it is as though he was not dead ; at night I am always with him, and he vanishes when I awake. At length my bodily health is deranged ; he speaks about his children, his property, and many little matters.' Therefore at last they find a man who knows how to bar out

[1] Rev. C. Calloway, *The Religious System of the Amazulu* (Natal, Capetown and London, 1868), p. 161.

that dream for her. He gives her medicine and says, ' There is medicine. When you dream of him and awake, chew it ; do not waste the spittle which collects in your mouth while dreaming ; do not spit it on the ground, but on this medicine, that we may be able to bar out the dream.' Then the doctor comes and asks if she has dreamt of her husband ; she says she has. He asks if she has done what he told her ; the woman says she has. He asks whether she has spit on the medicine the spittle that collected in her mouth while dreaming ; she says she has. He says, ' Bring it to me then ; and let us go together to the place where I will shut him in'. The doctor treats the dream with medicines which cause darkness ; he does not treat it with white medicines ; for among us black men we say there are black and white *ubulawo* ; therefore the doctor churns for the woman black *ubulawo*, because the dream troubles her. So he goes with her to a certain place to lay the *Itongo* ; perhaps he shuts it up in a bulb of *inkomfe*.[1] The bulb has a little hole made in its side, and the medicine mixed with the dream-spittle is placed in the hole, and it is closed with a stopper ; the bulb is dug up, and placed in another hole, and the earth rammed round it, that it may grow. He then leaves the place with the woman, saying to her, ' Take care that on no account you look back ; but look before you constantly till you get home. I say the dream

---

[1] " *Inkomfe*, a bulbous plant, the leaves of which contain a strong fibre, and are used for weaving ropes."

will never return to you, that you may be satisfied
I am a doctor. You will be satisfied of that this
day. If it returns, you may tell me at once.'
And truly the dream, if treated by a doctor who
knows how to bar the way against dreams, ceases.
And even if the woman dreams of her husband, the
dream does not come with daily importunity; she
may dream of him occasionally only, but not constantly as at first. The people ask her for a few
days after how she is. She replies, ' No, I have
seen nothing since. Perhaps it will come again.'
They say, ' Formerly was there ever a time when
he did not come ? ' The woman says, ' There was
not. There used to be not even one day when he
did not come. I am still waiting to know whether
he is really barred from returning.' The doctor
prevails over the dead man as regards that dream ;
at length the woman, says ' O ! So-and-So is a
doctor. See, I no longer know anything of So-and-
So's father. He has departed from me for ever.'
Such then is the mode in which dreams are stopped."[1]

In America also the ghosts of dead husbands and
wives have been much dreaded by the Indian
tribes. Thus among the Delaware Indians a
widow should not marry within a year of her
husband's death, for the Indians say that he does
not forsake her before that time, and then his soul
goes to the land of spirits. During this year she
must live by her own industry. She is not allowed
to buy any meat, for the Indians think their guns

---

[1] Rev. Canon Calloway, *op. cit.* pp. 318 *sqq.*

would fail and shoot no deer if a widow should eat of the game they have killed. After the first year is over, the friends of her deceased husband clothe and provide for her and her children.[1] Among the Ojebway Indians, when a man has died, " it is often the custom for the widow, after the burial is over, to spring or leap over the grave, and then run zig-zag behind the trees, as if she were fleeing from someone. This is called running away from the spirit of her husband, that it may not haunt her. In the evening of the day on which the burial has taken place, when it begins to grow dark, the men fire off their guns through the hole left at the top of the wigwam. As soon as this firing ceases, the old women commence knocking and making such a rattling at the door as would frighten away any spirit that would dare to hover near. The next ceremony is, to cut into narrow strips, like ribbon, thin birch bark. These they fold into shapes, and hang round inside the wigwam, so that the least puff of wind will move them. With such scarecrows as these, what spirit would venture to disturb their slumbers ? "[2] Among the Menomonie Indians, if a widow contemplates a second marriage, she is careful not to look back at the grave of her first husband, but returns to her lodge by some devious and circuitous road. This she does, the Indians say, to prevent the ghost of her dead

---

[1] G. H. Loskiel, *History of the Mission of the United Brethren among the Indians of North America* (London, 1794), pp. 64 *sq.*

[2] Rev. Peter Jones, *History of the Ojebway Indians* (London, N.D.), pp. 99 *sq.*

husband following her. Sometimes the widow is accompanied by a person, who, walking behind her, flourishes a bundle of twigs over the widow's head, as if driving away flies. This is done, no doubt, to drive away the dead husband's ghost.[1]

Among many tribes of British Columbia the conduct of a widow and widower for a long time after the death of their spouse is regulated by a code of minute and burdensome restrictions, all of which appear to be based on the notion that these persons, being haunted by the ghost, are not only themselves in peril, but are also a source of danger to others. Thus among the Shushwap Indians of British Columbia widows and widowers fence their beds with thorn bushes to keep off the ghost of the deceased ; indeed they lie on such bushes, in order that the ghost may be under little temptation to share their bed of thorns. They must build a sweat-house on a creek, sweat there all night, and bathe regularly in the creek, after which they must rub their bodies with spruce branches. These branches may be used only once for this purpose; afterwards they are stuck in the ground all round about the hut, probably to fence off the ghost. The mourners must also use cups and cooking-vessels of their own, and they may not touch their own heads or bodies. Hunters may not go near them, and any person on whom their shadow were to fall would at once be ill.[2] Again among the Tsetsaut

[1] Narrative of the Captivity and Adventures of John Tanner, during Thirty Years' Residence among the Indians (London, 1830), p. 292.

[2] Franz Boas, in Sixth Report on the North-Western Tribes of Canada,

Indians, when a man dies his brother is bound to marry the widow, but he may not do so before the lapse of a certain time, because it is believed that the dead man's ghost haunts his widow and would do a mischief to his living rival. During the time of her mourning the widow eats out of a stone dish, carries a pebble in her mouth, and a crab-apple stick up the back of her jacket. She sits upright day and night. Any person who crosses the hut in front of her is a dead man. The restrictions laid on a widower are similar.[1] Among the Lkuñgen or Songish Indians, in Vancouver Island, widow or widower, after the death of husband or wife, are forbidden to cut their hair, as otherwise it is believed that they would gain too great power over the souls and welfare of others. They must remain alone at their fire for a long time, and are forbidden to mingle with other people. When they eat, nobody may see them. They must keep their faces covered for ten days. For two days after the burial they fast and are not allowed to speak. After that they may speak a little, but before addressing anyone they must go into the woods and clean themselves in ponds and with cedar branches. If they wish to harm an enemy they call out his name when they first break their fast, and they bite very hard in eating. That is believed to kill their enemy, probably (though this is not said) by directing the

p. 92 (*Report of the British Association for the Advancement of Science*, Leeds, 1890, separate reprint).

[1] Franz Boas, in *Tenth Report on* the *North-Western Tribes of Canada*, p. 45 (*Report of the British Association for the Advancement of Science*, Ipswich, 1895, separate reprint).

attention of the ghost to him. They may not go near the water or eat fresh salmon lest the fish might be driven away. They may not eat warm food, else their teeth would fall out.[1] Among the Bella Coola Indians the bed of a mourner is protected against the ghost of the deceased by thorn-bushes stuck into the ground at each corner. He rises early in the morning and goes out into the woods, where he makes a square with thorn-bushes, and inside of this square, where he is probably supposed to be safe from the intrusion of the ghost, he cleanses himself by rubbing his body with cedar-branches. He also swims in ponds, and after swimming he cleaves four small trees and creeps through the clefts, following the course of the sun. This he does on four subsequent mornings, cleaving new trees every day. We may surmise that the intention in creeping through the cleft trees is to give the slip to the ghost. The mourner also cuts his hair short, and the cut hair is burnt. If he did not observe these regulations, it is believed that he would dream of the deceased, which to the savage mind is another way of saying that he would be visited in sleep by his ghost. Amongst these Indians the rules of mourning for a widower or a widow are especially strict. For four days he or she must fast, and may not speak a word, else the dead wife or husband would come and lay a cold hand on the mouth of the offender, who would die. They may not go

---

[1] Franz Boas, in *Sixth Report on the North-Western Tribes of Canada*, pp. 23 *sq.* (*Report of the British* *Association for the Advancement of Science*, Leeds, 1890, separate reprint).

near water, and are forbidden to catch or eat salmon for a whole year. During that time also they may not eat fresh herring or candle-fish (*olachen*). Their shadows are deemed unlucky, and may not fall on any person.[1]

Among the Thompson Indians of British Columbia, widows or widowers, on the death of the husbands or wives, went out at once and passed through a patch of rose-bushes four times. The intention of this ceremony is not reported, but we may conjecture that it was supposed to deter the ghost from following for fear of scratching himself or herself on the thorns. For four days after the death widows and widowers had to wander about at evening or break of day wiping their eyes with fir-twigs, which they hung up in the branches of trees, praying to the Dawn. They also rubbed their eyes with a small stone taken from under running water, then threw it away, while they prayed that they might not become blind. The first four days they might not touch their food, but ate with sharp-pointed sticks, and spat out the first four mouthfuls of each meal, and the first four of water, into the fire. For a year they had to sleep on a bed made of fir-branches on which rose-bush sticks were also spread at the foot, head and middle. Many also wore a few small twigs of rose-bush on their persons. The use of the rose-bush was no doubt to keep off the ghost, through fear of the prickles. They were

---

[1] Franz Boas, in *Seventh Report on the North-Western Tribes of Canada*, p. 13 (*Report of the British Association for the Advancement of Science*, Cardiff, 1891, separate reprint).

forbidden to eat fresh fish and flesh of any kind for a year. A widower might not fish at another man's fishing-place or with another man's net. If he did, it would make the station and the net useless for the season. If a widower transplanted a trout into another lake, before releasing it he blew on the head of the fish, and after chewing deer-fat he spat some of the grease out on its head, so as to remove the baneful effect of his touch. Then he let it go, bidding the fish farewell, and asking it to propagate its kind. Any grass or branches upon which a widow or widower sat or lay down withered up. If a widow were to break any sticks or branches, her own hands or arms would break. She might not cook food nor fetch water for her children, nor let them lie down on her bed, nor should she lie or sit where they slept. Some widows wore a breech-cloth made of dry bunch-grass for several days, lest the ghost of her dead husband should have connexion with her. A widower might not hunt or fish, because it was unlucky both for him and for other hunters. He did not allow his shadow to pass in front of another widower or of any person who was supposed to be gifted with more knowledge or magic than ordinary.[1] Among the Lillooet Indians of British Columbia the rules enjoined on widows and widowers were somewhat similar. But a widower had to observe a singular custom in eating. He ate his food with the right hand passed underneath his right leg, the knee

[1] James Teit, " The Thompson Indians of British Columbia ", pp. 332 *sq.* (*The Jesup North Pacific Expedition, Memoir of the American Museum of Natural History,* 1900).

of which was raised.[1] The motive for conveying
food to his mouth in this roundabout fashion is not
mentioned : we may conjecture that it was to baffle
the hungry ghost, who might be supposed to watch
every mouthful swallowed by the mourner, but who
could hardly suspect that food passed under the knee
was intended to reach the mouth.

Among the Kwakiutl Indians of British Columbia,
we are told, " the regulations referring to the mourning period are very severe. In case of the death of
husband or wife, the survivor has to observe the
following rule : for four days after the death the
survivor must sit motionless, the knees drawn up
toward the chin. On the third day all the inhabitants of the village, including children, must take a
bath. On the fourth day some water is heated in a
wooden kettle, and the widow or widower drips it
upon his head. When he becomes tired of sitting
motionless, and must move, he thinks of his enemy,
stretches his legs slowly four times, and draws them
up again. Then his enemy must die. During the
following sixteen days he must remain on the same
spot, but he may stretch out his legs. He is not
allowed, however, to move his hands. Nobody must
speak to him, and whosoever disobeys this command
will be punished by the death of one of his relatives.
Every fourth day he takes a bath. He is fed twice
a day by an old woman at the time of low water,
with salmon caught in the preceding year, and given

[1] James Teit, " The Lillooet
Indians " (Leyden and New York,
1906), p. 271 (*The Jesup North*
Pacific Expedition, Memoir of the
American Museum of Natural His-
tory).

to him in the dishes and spoons of the deceased. While sitting so, his mind is wandering to and fro. He sees his house and his friends as though far, far away. If in his visions he sees a man near by, the latter is sure to die at no distant day ; if he sees him very far away, he will continue to live long. After the sixteen days have passed he may lie down, but not stretch out. He takes a bath every eighth day. At the end of the first month he takes off his clothing, and dresses the stump of a tree with it. After another month has passed he may sit in a corner of the house, but for four months he must not mingle with others. He must not use the house door, but a separate door is cut for his use. Before he leaves the house for the first time he must three times approach the door and return, then he may leave the house. After ten months his hair is cut short, and after a year the mourning is at an end." [1]

Though the reasons for the elaborate restrictions thus imposed on widows and widowers by the Indians of British Columbia are not always stated, we may safely infer that, one and all, they are dictated by fear of the ghost of the deceased, who, haunting the surviving spouse, surrounds him or her with a dangerous atmosphere, a contagion of death, which necessitates his seclusion both from the people themselves and from the principal sources of their food supply, especially the fisheries, lest the infected person should poison them by his malignant presence.

[1] Franz Boas, in *Fifth Report on the North-Western Tribes of Canada*, pp. 43 *sq*. (*Report of the British Association for the Advancement of Science*, Newcastle-on-Tyne, 1889, separate reprint).

In Australia also the ghost of a dead husband is sometimes said to haunt his widow for a certain time after his death. Thus in the Unmatjera and Kaitish tribes of Central Australia a widow's hair is burnt off and she covers her body with ashes from the camp fire, and keeps renewing them through the whole time of her mourning. If she does not do this the ghost (*atnirinja*) of her late husband, who constantly follows her about, will kill her and strip all the flesh off her bones. In addition, her late husband's younger brother would be justified by tribal custom in severely thrashing, or even killing her, if during her period of mourning he were to meet her without tokens of respect for her late husband's spirit.[1]

VI. *Ghosts of the Unmarried and Childless Dead*

In primitive society adults who die unmarried are regarded as unfortunate because they have missed what is generally esteemed the crowning blessing of life. It is thought that their ghosts are therefore very unhappy in the spirit land : they repine at their solitary lot, and may seek to repair it either by finding a mate for themselves among the living, or by appealing to their surviving friends to furnish them with one. Thus in one way or another the spirits of the unmarried dead may become very

---

[1] (Sir) Baldwin Spencer and F. J. Gillen, *The Northern Tribes of*   *Central Australia* (London, 1914), pp. 507 *sq.*

troublesome to the kinsfolk whom they have left on earth. To appease their importunate desires many peoples have resorted to a ceremony of posthumous marriage, either of the dead to the dead, or of the dead to the living, or of the dead to some substitute for a living mate.

The Fijians, for example, were strongly impressed with the notion of the unhappiness of the unmarried dead in the spirit land; hence when a man died they used to strangle his widow in order that her spirit should attend him to the spirit land. "An excuse for the practice of widow-strangling may be found in the fact that, according to Fijian belief, it is a needful precautionary measure; for at a certain place on the way to Mbulu (Hades) there lies in wait a terrible god called Nangga-nangga, who is utterly implacable towards the ghosts of the unmarried. He is especially ruthless towards bachelors, among whom he persists in classing all male ghosts who come to him unaccompanied by their wives. Turning a deaf ear to their protestations, he seizes them, lifts them above his head, and breaks them in two by dashing them down on a projecting rock. Hence it is absolutely necessary for a man to have at least one of his wives, or at all events a female ghost of some sort, following him.

"Women are let off more easily. If the wife die before her husband, the desolate widower cuts off his beard, and puts it under her left armpit. This serves as her certificate of marriage, and on her producing it to Nangga-nangga he allows her to pass."[1]

In Savoe, an island of the Indian Archipelago, the people marry very young, often when they are mere children. These early marriages are connected with the religious ideas of the people. For they think that the souls of those who die unmarried do not go to the spirit land, which is in Soemba. The Savoenese Charon, by name Ama Piga Laga, refuses to ferry unmarried persons over to the place where the dead live. Hence the souls of the unwedded dead are doomed to roam about Savoe. They run along the shore lamenting : rest and peace they never find.[2]

In Africa the Bavenda, a Bantu tribe of the Northern Transvaal, have a curious mode of providing the unhappy ghost of a dead bachelor with a substitute for a wife. The method has been described as follows : " There is one interesting rite in connexion with the spirit world that is still occasionally performed. There is a Tshivenda expression—'*u lubumbukavha ?*'—which has the same meaning as the English ' Are you daft ? ' or ' Are you all there ? ' This word *luhumbukavha* (simpleton), is also used to describe any young man above the age of puberty who dies before he has been given a wife ; he is a poor foolish fellow, having left the

[1] L. Fison, " Notes on Fijian Burial Customs ", in *Journal of the Royal Anthropological Institute*, x. (1881) p. 139.

[2] J. K. Wijngaarden, " De zede-lijke toestanden op Savoe ", in *Mededeelingen van wege het Nederlandsche Zendelinggenootschap*, xxxvi. (1892) p. 407.

world ignorant of the all-important subject of sex and parenthood, and dying before he has fulfilled the purpose for which he was born. If he is not pacified he may become a source of endless trouble to his lineage. So he is given an old used hoe-handle (*gulelwa*), with a cotton string tied near the hole, to symbolize a wife, the string being her waist-band and the hole the female genitalia. A girl, never the deceased man's sister, fixes this symbol at a fork in the path in a well-cleared open space where the young man's spirit can clearly see it, with the handle pointing towards him as he faces his old village. The handle is fixed with four pegs made of the *tshiralala* tree (from *uralala*, to wander about), or of the *tshilivhalo* (from *ulivhala*, to forget). Two are knocked into the ground on each side of the head and tied to it with a string made of wild cotton which has been treated with a mixture made from the roots of the *vhulivhadza* (from *u livhadza*, to make forget), and the *mpeta* (to dissolve or tie up), with powder from the hedgehog quill, *thoni* (bashfulness). These preparations, as can be seen by their names, are used to confuse the young man's spirit so that it will forget its anger, become bashful and ashamed, and run away before reaching the village. When the handle is properly fixed, a woman of the dead man's lineage, generally the *makhadzi* (father's sister), pours beer into the hole of the hoe, saying : ' To-day we have found you a wife ; the wife is here. Do not worry us any more. If you are annoyed with us, come here.' This ends the ceremony, and the spirit of the young man is supposed to be satisfied for ever.   A similar rite is, very rarely, performed after the death of a girl dying unmarried, having reached the age of puberty. Such a girl is called *luphofu*, the blind one, as she has died without any knowledge of sexual life.   A peg is driven through the hole in the hoe handle that is provided for the comfort of her spirit, to symbolize the male organ.   The two rites are identical in all else."[1]

Among the Wajagga of Mount Kilimanjaro in East Africa, when an adult man dies unmarried his family looks out for a woman whom they may marry to his ghost in the spirit land.   His father goes to a man whose daughter has died unmarried, and says to him, " Give me your dead daughter for my dead son, who is alone ".   The father of the unmarried girl kills a goat, and brings the animal's head to the father of the unmarried youth.   The father buries the animal's head as a symbol of the maiden's head under the sepulchral monument, and sets over it the three stones which are usually placed on a woman's grave in reference to the stones of her domestic hearth, at which the woman used to be busied in her lifetime.   In doing so he says to his dead son, " To-day you have your marriage ".   In addition, the usual offerings are made to the dead. If the father of the dead youth is poor, he pays only

[1] H. A. Stayt, *The Bavenda* (London, 1931), pp. 241 *sq*.   Cf. Rev. E. Gottschling, " The Bavenda, a Sketch of their History and Customs ", in the *Journal of the Royal Anthropological Institute*, xxxv. (1905) p. 381.

a symbolical bride-price to the girl's father, by handing him a piece of wood, instead of the usual beer and the goat. After this marriage of the dead the father of the dead bride says, " Now I must help my daughter to cook ". He then brings small portions of food to the parents of the dead bridegroom, who are now deemed the parents-in-law of his dead daughter, and they eat the food which he brings them. Among rich people it sometimes happens that the father of the dead bachelor himself marries a living woman as a wife for his deceased son. The marriage is celebrated in the ordinary way, but without any mention of the dead man. But the wife is called the wife of the dead man. For example, if the father were called *Muro*, and the son were called *Nsau*, the bride is called the wife of *Nsau*, and any children she may have are called the children of *Nsau*. The first male child born to her is known by the name of his living father, as if the father were the grandfather of the infant, and the first-born female child is known by the name of her mother, as if she were her grandmother, in accordance with the custom of the Wajagga, who name first-born children after their grandparents and not after their parents. The present case is only an apparent exception to the rule that the name of a father has never been borne by his son.[1]

Among the Akamba, a Bantu tribe of Kenya, if a young unmarried man is killed away from his

[1] B. Gutmann, *Dichten und Denken der Dschagganeger* (Leipzig, 1909), pp. 81 *sq*. Cf. Hon. Chas. Dundas, *Kilimanjaro and its People* (London, 1924), pp. 249 *sq*.

village, his spirit (*muimu*) will return there and speak to the people through the medium of an old woman in a dance, and say, "I am So-and-So speaking, and I want a wife ". The youth's father will then make arrangements to buy a girl from another village and bring her to his, and she will be called the wife of the deceased, speaking of him by name. She will presently be married to a brother of the dead man, but she must continue to live in the village where the deceased had his home. If at any time her living husband beats or ill-treats her, and she in consequence runs away to her father, the spirit of her dead husband will come and pester the people of the village and they will have bad luck. The ghost will probably ask, through the usual medium, why his wife has been ill-treated and driven away. The head of the family will then take steps to induce the girl to return for fear of the wrath of the spirit of his deceased son.[1] Among the Shilluk, a tribe of the Upper Nile, if a chief or other distinguished man dies, after betrothal but before marriage, so that his relations might fear the vengeance of his dissatisfied ghost, the father of the betrothed girl takes her to the grave and marries her to the dead man. He says to the dead man, " Herewith I bring you my daughter, that you may marry her ". The bride is then considered to be related to all her dead husband's kinsfolk, but the relationship is not so strict as to exclude her subsequent marriage to a

[1] C. W. Hobley, " Further Researches into Kikuyu and Kamba Religious Beliefs and Customs ", in *Journal of the Royal Anthropological Institute*, xli. (1911) p. 422.

living man. At her marriage to her dead husband offerings are made to the spirits of many of her great ancestors now deceased, just as they would be entitled to receive them if they were still in life. That is a right of the kinsfolk which they do not lose even by death.[1] Among the Dinkas, another tribe of the Upper Nile, when an unmarried man dies his brother must marry a woman especially to raise up seed to the deceased. Should he fail to do so his dead brother's spirit would cause his living brother's children to die, or prevent the birth of children if none had been born already. If a man has several dead unmarried brothers he must take a wife for each before he may take one for himself.[2] A similar custom prevails among the Nuer, another tribe of the same region. If an unmarried man dies a wife must be found who will bear children to him lest his spirit should be angry.[3]

The Baigas, a primitive Dravidian tribe of the Central Provinces in India, think that the souls of unmarried persons become malignant spirits (*bhuts*) after death, and in that form haunt trees, while the souls of the married dead dwell in streams.[4] The Bhats, another caste of the Central Provinces in India, think that the spirit of a Brahman boy who died unmarried will haunt any person who steps over his grave in an impure condition or otherwise

---

[1] W. Hofmayr, *Die Shilluk* (St. Gabriel bei Wien, 1925), p. 293. Cf. C. G. and B. Z. Seligman, *The Pagan Tribes of the Nilotic Sudan* (London, 1932), pp. 68 *sq.*

[2] Seligman, *op. cit.* p. 164.
[3] Seligman, *op. cit.* p. 220.
[4] R. V. Russell, *The Tribes and Castes of the Central Provinces of India*, ii. 86.

defiles it, and when a man is haunted in such a manner it is called *Brahm laga*. Then an exorcist is called, who sprinkles water over the possessed man, and this burns the Brahm Deo or spirit inside him as if it were burning oil. The spirit cries out, and the exorcist orders him to leave the man. Then the spirit tells him how he has been injured by the man, and refuses to leave him. The exorcist asks the spirit what he requires on condition of leaving the man, and the spirit asks for some good food or something else, and is given it. Then the exorcist takes a nail and goes to a *pipal* tree, and orders the spirit to go into the tree. The spirit obeys, and the exorcist drives the nail into the tree. After that the spirit remains imprisoned in the tree until somebody takes the nail out, whereupon he will come out of the tree and haunt the man who drew out the nail.[1] The Kirs, another caste of the Central Provinces in India, are of opinion that the souls of persons who die unmarried, or without children, are always prone to trouble their living kinsfolk.

To appease these unquiet spirits songs are sung in their praise on important festivals, the members of the family staying awake all night and wearing the images of the dead on silver pieces round their necks. When they eat and drink they first touch the food with the image by way of offering it to the dead, so that their spirits may be appeased and refrain from harassing the living.[2] We have already seen

---

[1] R. V. Russell, *op. cit.* ii. pp 266 *sq.*   [2] R. V. Russell, *op. cit.* iii. 483.

that, before the Sansia—another caste of the Central Provinces—sacrifice to the beneficent spirits of ancestors, they offer sacrifice to the spirits of the unmarried dead, lest these malignant beings should seize and defile the offerings made to the beneficent ancestors.[1] Among the Savars, a primitive tribe of the Central Provinces, if a person dies without a child a hole is made in a stone and his soul is conjured into it by a sorcerer (*gunia*). A few grains of rice are placed in the hole, and it is then closed with melted lead to imprison the ghost, and the stone is thrown into a stream, so that it may never be able to get out and trouble the family.[2] Among the Segidi, the Telugu caste of toddy-drawers and distillers in India, if an adult man dies unmarried, a ceremony of marriage is performed between the corpse and a plantain tree, and if an unmarried woman dies she is married to a sword.[3]

This custom of performing a marriage ceremony for the benefit of persons who died unmarried appears to be not uncommon in India, the intention being to satisfy and pacify the ghost of the deceased, and to prevent him from troubling the survivors with his importunate attentions. On this subject Mr. Abbott writes as follows : " One more form of mock marriage is the marriage of a dead person to a ruī-tree or branch. Brahmins do this when a *Brahmacari* " (a boy who has taken his thread ceremony) " dies before marriage ; *Lingāyats* perform

[1] See above, page 168.

[2] R. V. Russell, *op. cit.* iv. 507.

[3] *Central Provinces, Ethnographic Survey*, iv., Draft Articles on Tamil and Telugu Castes (Allahabad, 1907), p. 67.

this marriage both when a girl dies a virgin and when a man dies unmarried. When the deceased is a girl a male ruī is used, and a female tree when the deceased is a man. Sometimes the body is taken to a standing ruī-tree in the cremation ground ; sometimes a twig of the tree is brought to the house where the dead body lies. The twig and the corpse are smeared with turmeric powder and covered with yellow clothes ; the two are tied together with thread, *aksat* (unbroken rice) is thrown on them and sacrificial *hom* (fires) are performed. The tree after being uprooted or the twig is burnt and the obsequies for thirteen days are performed in the usual way. The basis of this form of mock marriage is the belief that anyone dying with unsatisfied desires returns to this world as a ghost in a vain attempt to satisfy his desires. This fear has created in India quite a number of dreaded ghosts." The dreaded ghost of a Brahman boy who has died unmarried is called *Munjā*.[1]

These ceremonies of mock marriage performed for the satisfaction of the ghosts of persons who have died unmarried appear to be particularly common in the south of India. Thus among the Gānigas, an oil-pressing class of the Canarese people, if a young man dies a bachelor, the corpse is married to an arka plant (*Calotropis gigantea*), and decorated with a wreath made of the flowers thereof.[2] Again among the Siviyar, when an adult person dies

[1] J. Abbott, *The Keys of Power* (London, 1932), pp. 291 *sq.*

[2] E. Thurston, *Castes and Tribes of Southern India* (Madras, 1909), ii. 267.

unmarried, the corpse is made to go through a mock marriage with a human figure cut out of a palm leaf.[1] So among the Vāniyan, oil-pressers among the Tamils, if a man dies a bachelor, a mock ceremony of marriage is performed for his benefit. The corpse is wedded to the arka plant (*Calotropis gigantea*), and decorated with a wreath made of the flowers thereof.[2] Among the Kōmatis, the great trading caste of the Madras Presidency, if a man and woman have been living together and the man dies unmarried his corpse is formally married to the living woman. When the death has been announced a priest is summoned and the ceremony proceeds. It has been described as follows by an eye-witness : " The dead body of the man was placed against the outer wall of the verandah of the house in a sitting posture, attired like a bridegroom, and the face and hands besmeared with turmeric. The woman was clothed like a bride, and adorned with the usual tinsel ornament over the face, which, as well as the arms, was daubed over with yellow. She sat opposite the dead body, and spoke to it in light unmeaning words, and then chewed bits of cocoanut and squirted them on the face of the dead man. This continued for hours, and not till near sunset was the ceremony brought to a close. Then the head of the corpse was bathed, and covered with a cloth of silk, the face rubbed over with some red powder, and betel leaves placed in the mouth. Now she might consider herself married, and the funeral

---

[1] Thurston, *op. cit.* vi. 391.   [2] Thurston, vii. 315.

procession started." [1] Again among the Todas,
a primitive pastoral people of the Nīlgiri Hills in
Southern India, ceremonies of marriage are performed for the benefit of the ghosts of the unmarried
dead. One such ceremony was witnessed by Mr.
Edgar Thurston, one of our best authorities on the
ethnology of Southern India. He writes as follows :
" At the funeral of an unmarried Toda girl, which
I witnessed, the corpse was made to go through a
form of marriage ceremony. A small boy, three
years old, was selected from among the relatives of
the dead girl, and taken by his father in search of a
grass and the twig of a shrub (*Sophora glauca*),
which were brought to the spot where the corpse
was lying. The mother of the dead child then
withdrew one of its hands from the putkūli (cloth)
in which it was wrapped, and the boy placed the
grass and the twig in the hand, and limes, plantains,
rice, jaggery, honey-comb and butter in the pocket
of the putkūli, which was then stitched with needle
and thread. The boy's father then took off his
son's putkūli, and covered him with it from head to
foot. Thus covered, the boy remained outside the
hut till the morning of the morrow, watched through
the night by near relatives of himself and his
dead bride." [2] Once more, among the Maravars, a
Dravidian tribe in the extreme south of India, if a
man and woman are too poor to afford the cost of
the complete marriage rites, they content themselves

[1] E.   Thurston,   *Ethnographic
Notes in Southern India* (Madras,
1906), p. 105.

[2] Thurston, *op. cit.* pp. 105 *sq.*
Cf. W. H. R. Rivers, *The Todas*
(London, 1906), pp. 391 *sqq*

with tying the *tāli* or marriage knot, and then begin to cohabit. But the other ceremonies must be performed at some time, or, as the phrase goes, " the defect must be cured ". Should the husband happen to die before he can afford to cure the defect, his friends and kinsfolk will at once borrow money, and the marriage will be duly completed in the presence and on behalf of the corpse, which must be placed on one seat with the woman, and made to represent a bridegroom. The *tāli* is then taken off, and the widow is free to marry again.[1]

Among the Chinese settled in Siam, if a young man is betrothed to a girl and dies before marriage, his betrothed may claim to be married to him, or rather to the ancestral tablet which represents him in the domestic shrine at his father's house. In such a case the ceremony of marriage is the same as that performed for a living bride and bridegroom.[2] In China itself the marriage of the dead to each other was practised by the Hak-ka, a native Chinese race in the province of Canton. Among them if a boy dies before his parents have had time to choose a bride for him, they seek, among their neighbours and friends, someone who has lost a daughter of the same age. When they find what they want the parents of both families meet and contract a solemn matrimonial engagement in the name of their dead children. The marriage ceremony is celebrated in exactly the same way as it would be if the bride and

---

[1] Thurston, *op. cit.* p. 106.
[2] Mgr. Bruguière, in *Annales de* *l'Association de la Propagation de la Foi,* v. (1831) 185.

bridegroom were living and not dead. They think that thus they unite the spirits of the two children in a spiritual wedlock.[1]

But indeed this custom of marrying the dead to the dead, or the living to the dead, has been a national institution in China from antiquity down to modern times. It is entirely in harmony with that system of ancestor worship which forms the theoretical basis of Chinese society, for they think that the spirit of a man who has died unmarried and childless is not only unhappy in itself, but involves his family in the deepest misfortune and degradation by depriving them of anyone who can offer to their shades the things which they need for their happiness and welfare in the world beyond the grave.[2]

Evidence of the great antiquity of the custom in China has been adduced by the late J. J. M. De Groot in his classical work on the religious system of China. He writes : " The books of the Empire literally abound with passages which show that re-uniting women with their pre-deceased husbands in the grave has constantly prevailed in China as a regular custom. . . . Human immolations at burials naturally imply the prevalence of a conception that it is urgently necessary to be accompanied into the next life by a wife or concubines, to prevent one's being doomed there to the dreary life of a solitary widower. Consequently, it is only natural that in ancient China there existed the curious custom of

---

[1] Dr. Eitel, " Les Hak-Ka ", trans. by M. G. Dumoutier, in *L'Anthropologie*, v. (1893) 175.

[2] E. Westermarck, *The Origin and Development of the Moral Ideas*, ii. 400.

placing deceased females in the tombs of lads who had died before they were married. The prevalence in those times of such *post-mortem* weddings for the next world is revealed to us by the following passage in the *Cheu li*: ' The Officer charged with the Preparation of Marriages is to prevent women already buried from being transferred to other tombs, to be thus given in marriage to deceased minor youths '. The legislators of the time, disliking the sacrilegious removal of women from their graves, deemed themselves in duty bound to forbid the practice in question ; but they do not appear to have included in their veto such marrying of deceased women at the time of their burial. The latter weddings may *a fortiori* be supposed to have been very common ; and that they were firmly rooted in the then customs and manners of the people may be inferred from the fact that they have prevailed ever since, being frequently mentioned in the books of all ages. This point is of sufficient interest to deserve illustration by a short series of quotations.

" In the Memoirs of the Three Kingdoms we read : ' The daughter of Ping Yuen died when still young, at the same time as Ts'ang-shu, the favourite son of the Emperor T'ai Tsu (A.D. 220–227), breathed his last. The Emperor tried to have them buried in the same grave, but Yuen refused his consent, saying that such burials were not recognized by the laws of morals. Therefore the deceased prince was betrothed to a deceased daughter of the family Chen, and she was placed with him in the same grave.

And when Shuh, the young daughter of the emperor Ming of the same dynasty (A.D. 227–239), had died, he buried together with her one Hwang, a grandson of the brother of the empress Chen, conferred the posthumous title of Imperial Prince upon him, and appointed for him a Continuator with the hereditary rank of a noble.' This event becomes all the more curious when we are told that this Hwang was a mere baby. It is in fact stated in the Standard Annals of that time that the magnate Ch'en Khiün rebuked the emperor for having the obsequies of this child, though not a year old, conducted with the same ceremonies as appertained to up-grown people. *Post-mortem* marriages in those times being concluded even in the Imperial family, and between infants so very young, we may safely draw the conclusion that they were the order of the day between adults among the people.

" To convince our readers that such marriages were of frequent occurrence in ensuing ages, we need not make a large number of quotations. A couple of instances, drawn from the Imperial court-life, will suffice. ' P'ing Ch'ing, son of Muh Ch'ung, died when he was still young. During the reign of Hiao Wen (A.D. 471–499), the Imperial princess Shi-p'ing died in the Palace. The posthumous dignity of Prince Consort was then conferred upon P'ing-Ch'ing, and he was united with the Princess in marriage for the World of Shades.' Three centuries afterwards ' the Imperial concubine Wei caused her deceased younger brother Siün, after the dignity of Prince of Jü-nan had been conferred upon him, to be united in marriage for the next life with a deceased daughter of (Siao) Chi-chung, and she had them buried together in one grave. But after this lady Wei had been defeated (in an attempt to usurp the throne), Chi-chung opened the grave, took his daughter's coffin out of it and brought it home ', thus showing that the ties of relationship with a traitress to the cause of lawful government were cut off by him.

" An interesting account of the manner in which such *post-mortem* marriages were concluded at a period when the Sung dynasty governed the Empire, is given by a contemporary work in the following words : ' In the northern parts of the Realm it is customary, when an unmarried youth and an un-married girl breathe their last, that the two families each charge a match-maker to demand the other party in marriage. Such go-betweens are called : match-makers for disembodied souls. They ac-quaint the two families with each other's circum-stances, and then cast lots for the marriage by order of the parents on both sides. If they augur that the union will be a happy one, (wedding) garments for the next world are cut out and the match-makers repair to the grave of the lad, there to set out wine and fruit for the consummation of the marriage. Two seats are placed side by side, and a small streamer is set up near each seat. If these streamers move a little after the libation has been performed, the souls are believed to approach each other ; but if one of them does not move, the party represented thereby is considered to disapprove of the marriage. Each family has to reward its match-maker with a present of woven stuffs.   Such go-betweens make a regular livelihood out of these proceedings. . . .'

" The following instance of a marriage between deceased persons, which occurred in the fourteenth century, must not be passed unnoticed, because it proves more clearly than any other case on record that in times relatively modern the old conception still obtained that a wife's place is at the side of her deceased husband in the life hereafter, and that she may not suffer another woman to occupy her place there.   ' Madam Yang was a native of Sü-ch'ing in Tung-p'ing (province of Shantung).   Her husband Kwoh San marched off from Siang Yang with the army, and she, being left behind, served her parents-in-law so perfectly that she obtained a great repute for filial devotion.   In the sixth year of the period Chiyuen (A.D. 1340) her husband died in his garrison. Then her own mother laid schemes for taking her home and marrying her again, but, bitterly wailing, she took such an oath that these schemes were not carried out.   After some time, when the mortal remains of her husband were brought home, her father-in-law said : ' She, having been married to him only a short time, and being still young, will certainly marry again in the end ; ought I to leave my son under the ground in a state of loneliness ? ' But when he was on the point of requesting a fellow villager to give him the bones of his deceased daughter, that he might bury them in the same grave with his son, Madam Yang being informed of his project became still more overwhelmed by grief, and refused all food. Five days afterwards she hung herself, upon which she was buried with her husband in the same grave. . . .

"Yang Yung-siu, an author who lived under the Ming dynasty, asserts that the custom of uniting dead persons in marriage was prevalent in his time. 'Nowadays', he writes, 'it is still practised among the people, and it is not forbidden by anybody or anything. Consequently such marriages must have prevailed under former dynasties.' Whether the custom still exists at the present time we are not able to say, as no case has come under our notice whilst in China. But, considering that it has flourished for so many ages, we can scarcely believe it has entirely died out even now." [1]

That the custom of marrying the dead to the dead in China persisted in full blast down to the second half of the nineteenth century we know from the evidence of the Rev. J. H. Gray, Archdeacon of Hongkong, who personally witnessed the ceremony and described it as follows : "One other marriage custom, as absurd as it is wicked, remains to be noted. In China, not merely the living are married, but the dead also. Thus the spirits of all males who die in infancy or in boyhood are in due course of time married to the spirits of females who have been

---

[1] J. J. M. De Groot, *The Religious System of China* (Leyden, 1894), vol. ii. Book I., pp. 802-806.

cut off at a like early age. If a youth of twelve years
dies, it is customary when he has been dead six or
seven years for his parents to seek to unite his spirit
in wedlock with that of a girl whose birth and death
corresponded in point of time with those of their son.
For this purpose application is made to a go-between,
and when a selection has been made from this func-
tionary's list of deceased maidens, an astrologer is
consulted. When the astrologer, having cast the
horoscopes of the two departed spirits, has pronounced the selection judicious, a lucky night is set
apart for the solemnization of the marriage. On
that night, a paper figure representing a bridegroom
in full marriage costume is placed in the ceremonial
hall of his parents' house ; and at nine o'clock, or
in some instances later, a bridal chair, which is
sometimes made of a rattan-frame covered with
paper, is despatched in the name of the spirit of the
youth to the house of the parents of the deceased
girl, with a request that they will be so good as to
allow the spirit of their daughter to seat itself therein
for the purpose of being conveyed to her new home.
As one of the three souls of which the body of a
Chinese is supposed to be possessed, is said after
death to remain with the ancestral tablet, the tablet
bearing the name of the girl is removed from the
ancestral altar and placed in the bridal chair, where
it is supplemented by a paper figure meant to represent the bride. The bridal procession is headed
by two musicians, one of whom plays upon a lute
and the other upon a tom-tom, and sometimes the

wearing apparel which belonged to the deceased girl, and which for the future is to be in the keeping of the parents of the departed youth, is carried in it. On the arrival of the procession, the tablet and the effigy are removed from the bridal chair, and placed, the former on the ancestral altar, and the latter on a chair close to that occupied by the effigy of the bridegroom. A table covered with various kinds of viands is placed before the effigies, while five or six priests of Taou are engaged in chanting prayers to the spirits, calling upon them to receive one another as husband and wife, and to partake of the wedding repast. At the close of this ceremony the effigies are burned, together with a great quantity of paper clothes, paper money, paper man-servants and maid-servants, fans, tobacco-pipes, and sedan chairs. I was once present at such a ceremony. It took place at the house of a China friend named Cha Kum-hoi, who resided in the Kwong-ga-lee street of the western suburb of Canton. The immediate occasion of this marriage was, it so happened, the illness of this gentleman's wife, which was attributed by the geomancer or fortune-teller to the angry spirit of her son, who was importunate to be married. A matrimonial engagement was therefore immediately entered into on behalf of the deceased son, and was solemnized as I have described it." [1]

The latest notice of a marriage of the dead in China which I have met with dates from 1891. It runs as follows : " A writer in the *North China*

---

[1] J. H. Gray, *China* (London, 1878), i. pp. 216 *sqq.*

Daily News records a case of something like a *post-mortem* marriage, in which a Chinese girl, recently deceased, was married to a dead boy in another village. ' It not unfrequently happens ', he explains, ' that the son in the family dies before he is married, and that it is desirable to adopt a grandson. The family cast about for some young girl who has also died recently, and a proposition is made for the union of the two corpses in the bonds of matrimony. If it is accepted, there is a combination of a wedding and a funeral, in the process of which the deceased bride is taken by a large number of bearers to the cemetery of the other family and laid beside her husband.' " [1]

A similar custom of marrying the dead to the dead prevailed among the Tartars, and has been described by Marco Polo as follows : " If any man have a daughter who dies before marriage, and another man have had a son also die before marriage, the parents of the two arrange a grand wedding between the dead lad and lass. And marry them they do, making a regular contract ! And when the contract papers are made out they put them in the fire, in order (as they will have it) that the parties in the other world will know the fact, and look on each other as man and wife. And the parents thenceforward consider themselves sib to each other just as if their children had lived and married. Whatever may be agreed on between the parties

---

[1] *Folk-lore*, vol. ii. (1891), quoting *Pall Mall Gazette*, 5th November 1890.

as dowry, those who have to pay it cause to be painted on pieces of paper and then put these in the fire, saying that in that way the dead person will get all the real articles in the other world." [1] The same custom is also vouched for the Tartars by Alexander Guagninus.[2]

Among the Ingush of the Caucasus when a man's son dies another man whose daughter is dead will go to him and say, " Your son may need a wife in the other world, I will give him my daughter. Pay me the price of the bride." Such an obliging offer is never refused, though the price of a bride is sometimes as much as thirty cows.[3]

A similar custom of marriages contracted for the benefit of the dead has been known, and to a limited extent appears still to survive, among some Slav peoples. On this subject Mr. Ralston writes as follows : " Strongly impressed with the idea that those whom the nuptial bond had united in this world were destined also to live together in the world to come, they so sincerely pitied the lot of the unmarried dead, that, before committing their bodies to the grave, they were in the habit of finding them partners for eternity. The fact that, among some Slavonian peoples, if a man died a bachelor a wife

[1] Marco Polo, translated by Col. H. Yule, Second Edition (London, 1875), i. 259 *sq.*

[2] " De Religione Muscovitarum omniumque Ruthenorum ", printed in *De Russorum, Muscovitarum, et Tartarorum religione, sacrificiis, nuptiarum, funerum ritu* (Spirae libera civitate, 1582), p. 253.

[3] J. von Klaproth, *Reise in den Kaukasus und nach Gorgien,* i. 616 *sq* ; Potocki, *Voyage dans les Steps d'Astrakhan et du Caucase* (Paris, 1829), i. 127 (who, however, merely copies Klaproth).

was allotted to him after his death rests on the authority of several witnesses, and in a modified form the practice has been retained in some places up to the present day. In Little Russia, for instance, a dead maiden is dressed in nuptial attire, and friends come to her funeral as to a wedding, and a similar custom is observed on the death of a lad. In Podolia, also, a young girl's funeral is conducted after the fashion of a wedding, a youth being chosen as the bridegroom who attends her to the grave, with the nuptial kerchief twined around his arm. From that time her family consider him their relative, and the rest of the community look upon him as a widower. In some parts of Servia, when a lad dies, a girl dressed as a bride follows him to the tomb, carrying two crowns ; one of these is thrown to the corpse, and the other she keeps, at least for a time.[1]

It was an ancient Greek custom to place on the tombs of all unmarried persons, whether male or female, a pitcher of a peculiar shape called the "bath-bearer " (*loutrophoros*). Examples of such pitchers have been found. In shape they are tall and slender, with a high neck and high handles on either side. Some of the ancient interpreters, who wrote after the custom had fallen into disuse, supposed that the " bath-bearers " placed on the tombs of the unmarried were figures of boys or girls carrying such pitchers ;[2] but archaeological discoveries have

[1] W. R. S. Ralston, *The Songs of the Russian People* (London, 1872), pp. 309 *sq.*

[2] Harpocration and Suidas, *s.v.* " λουτρόφορος " : Pollux, viii. 66.

confirmed the view of Eustathius in his great commentary on Homer [1] that it was the pitcher itself, or at all events a representation of it carved in relief, which was thus used to mark the graves of maids and bachelors. The intention was, according to Eustathius, to intimate that the person on whose grave one of these pitchers stood had never enjoyed the bath which a Greek bride and bridegroom took on their wedding day, and for which the water was fetched from a special spring by a boy who was a near kinsman.[2] It may be suggested that the custom of placing such a pitcher, so intimately connected with marriage, on the grave of an unmarried person, was originally part of a ceremony designed to provide his or her spirit with a spouse in the spirit land, by means of a marriage ceremony, like that which we have seen celebrated for the same purpose by so many peoples in so many lands.[3]

VII. *Ghosts of the Unburied Dead*

In primitive society it is generally believed that the soul of a recently deceased person is much concerned with the disposal of his mortal remains. He desires that his surviving relatives should treat them with all due respect, by interring or otherwise disposing of them in the traditional manner, includ-

---

[1] Eustathius, *Commentary on Homer, Iliad*, p. 1293, referring to *Iliad* xxiii. 141.

[2] Harpocration and Suidas, *loc. cit.*, Photius, *Lexicon. s.v.* " λουτρά ": Pollux, iii. 43, who may be wrong in saying that the water was fetched by a girl.

[3] Cf. my commentary on Pausanias, Book X. chapter xxxi. 9 (vol. v. pp. 388 *sqq.*).

ing the performance of rites intended to please and satisfy the ghost. If this satisfaction is not accorded to him his spirit is perturbed and dissatisfied, and may visit his displeasure on his undutiful kinsfolk. Every effort therefore is made by the survivors to find the mortal remains and to lay them to rest with every mark of reverence and honour. But sometimes the body cannot be found, as for example when a person has been drowned at sea, or devoured by wild beasts in the forest, or has furnished the materials of a cannibal feast to his enemies in war. In all such cases the ghost is supposed still to claim his satisfaction, and to meet his imperious desires his friends have recourse to a simple device : they make an effigy of him, or try to find some personal relic of his, and over the one or the other they perform all the funeral rites just as if the substitute were the real body of the deceased. This is thought fully to satisfy the desires of the ghost, who accordingly leaves the survivors in peace.

Thus among the Maoris of New Zealand, when a chief was killed in battle, and his body eaten by his foes, his spirit was supposed to enter the stones of the oven with which his body had been cooked, which retained their heat so long as it remained in them. His friends repeated their most powerful spells to draw his spirit out of the stones, and bring it within the sacred grove (*wahi tapu*), for it was thought that otherwise it could not rest, but would wander about inflicting injury upon the living, all spirits being considered maliciously inclined towards the survivors. So when any were slain in battle, if the body could not be obtained, the friends endeavoured to procure some of the blood, or fragments of their garments, over which they uttered their spells (*karakia*), and thus brought the wandering soul within this spiritual fold. These places are still looked upon with much fear, as the spirits are thought occasionally to wander from them and cause sickness.[1]

Of the natives of Samoa we are told that the unburied dead caused great concern. " No Roman was ever more grieved at the thought of his unburied friend wandering a hundred years along the banks of the Styx than were the Samoans while they thought of the spirit of one who had been drowned, or of another who had fallen in war, wandering about neglected and comfortless. They supposed the spirit haunted them everywhere, night and day, and imagined they heard it calling upon them in a most pitiful tone, and saying, ' Oh, how cold ! oh, how cold ! ' Nor were the Samoans, like the ancient Romans, satisfied with a mere *tumulus inanis* at which to observe the usual solemnities ; they thought it was possible to obtain the soul of the departed in some tangible transmigrated form. On the beach, near where a person had been drowned, and whose body was supposed to have become a porpoise, or on the battlefield, where another fell, might have been seen, sitting in silence, a group of

[1] Rev. R. Taylor, *New Zealand and its Inhabitants* (London. 1870), p. 221.

five or six, and one a few yards before them with a sheet of native cloth spread out on the ground in front of him. Addressing some god of the family he said, ' Oh, be kind to us ; let us obtain without difficulty the spirit of the young man ! ' The first thing that happened to light upon the sheet was supposed to be the spirit. If nothing came it was supposed that the spirit had some ill-will to the person praying. That person after a time retired, and another stepped forward, addressed some other god, and awaited the result. By and by something came ; grasshopper, butterfly, ant or whatever else it might be, it was carefully wrapped up, taken to the family, the friends assembled, and the bundle buried with all due ceremony, as if it contained the real spirit of the departed." [1]

The Nufoors of Dutch New Guinea make wooden images (*korwar*) of their dead, conjure the spirits of the deceased into them, and then preserve the images in their houses, and consult the inspired images from time to time as oracles. In general they make images only of persons who have died at home. But in the island of Ron such images are also made of persons who have died away from home or have fallen in battle. In such cases the difficulty is to compel the soul to quit its mortal remains far away and come to animate the image. However, the natives of Ron have found means to

---

[1] G. Turner, *Samoa a Hundred Years Ago and Long Before* (London, 1884), 150 *sq.* Cf. Rev. S. Ella, " Samoa ", in *Report of the* *Australasian Association for the Advancement of Science*, Hobart (1892), p. 641, who substantially repeats Turner's account.

overcome this difficulty. They first carve the wooden image of the dead person and then call his soul back to the village by setting a great tree on fire, while the family assemble round it, and one of them, holding the image in his hand, acts the part of medium, shivering and shaking and falling into a trance after the approved fashion of mediums in many lands. After this ceremony the image is supposed to be animated by the soul of the deceased, and it is kept in the house with as much confidence as any other.[1]

Among the Galelareese of Halmahera, an island to the west of New Guinea, when some one dies away from home, in a foreign land, as soon as the relations get news of the death they shear their hair and bathe as soon as possible, undertaking at the same time all the obligations incidental to mourning. They now consult whether to celebrate the death-feast at once, or to wait until the bones of the deceased have been brought back from the foreign land. If they decide to celebrate it at once, they make ready and decorate a mourning chamber in the house, and there on the sleeping bench they lay, instead of the corpse, a puppet (*gari*) into which the soul of the deceased has been temporarily conjured by the seers. After that the usual death-feast takes place. The ceremony of decorating the grave is usually deferred until the bones have been brought back

---

[1] F. S. A. de Clercq, " De Westen Noordkust van Nederlandsch Nieuw-Guinea ", in *Tijdschrift van het Kon. Nederlandsch Aardrijks-kundig Genootschap*, 2de Serie, x. (1893), p. 621. As to these images of the dead (*korwar*), see *Belief in Immortality*, i. pp. 309 *sqq.*

from abroad.[1]   In the district of Tobelo in North Halmahera, when men who are famous for their bravery die elsewhere and it is desired to secure their souls for the village, a symbolical burial takes place for the purpose of making the soul to stay in the neighbourhood of the dwelling.   For this purpose a puppet is made with a peeled coconut for a head, a pillow for a body, and long rolled-up leaves for limbs.   This puppet is placed either on a hurdle in the chief house of the village or in the little soulhouse (*goma ma-taoe*), and a funeral banquet is held for four days.   Then the puppet is wrapped in a mat and buried.   That the soothsayer conjures the soul into the puppet is not expressly stated by our authority, but is highly probable.[2]   The Alfoors of Poso in Central Celebes make offerings for the spirits of persons who have been drowned or devoured by crocodiles, and whose bodies consequently have not been found.   In such cases the Tolage of the same region make a wooden image (*pemia*) of the missing person, which serves as a substitute for the body.   The Popebats do not make such images: they only think of the missing person at the festival. As to persons whose heads have been carried off by enemies in a raid, some tribes replace the missing articles with coconuts, others celebrate the festival over the headless bodies.[3]

[1] M. J. van Baarda, " Een apologie voor de Dooden ", in *Bijdragen tot de Taal- Land- en Volkenkunde van Nederlandsch-Indië*, lxix. (The Hague, 1914), pp. 86 *sq.*

[2] F. S. A. de Clercq, " Dodadi Ma-Taoe en Goma Ma-Taoe, of Zielenhuisjes in het district Tobelo op Noord-halmahera ", in *Internationales Archiv für Ethnographie*, ii. (1889), p. 211.

[3] A. C. Kruit, " Een en ander

Among the Ibans or Dyaks of Sarawak in Borneo, in the case of persons who die far away from home, as soon as the news of the death arrives at the village the clothes, ornaments, and other articles of the deceased are heaped together in the *Ruai* (common room) and covered over with a blanket so as to represent a corpse laid out. This is called the *Rapoh* and all the usual mortuary rites are performed for the simulated corpse, just as if it were the body of the deceased. In the early morning this simulated corpse is taken to the burial ground, and the articles of dress are hung about among the trees.[1] In Bali, a small island to the north of Java, when the body of a deceased person cannot be found his friends make an image of him out of wood or the leaves of a certain tree, and celebrate the mortuary rites over it, instead of over the actual corpse.[2]

The Annamites believe that when a tiger has taken a man, the soul of the deceased rides on the animal's back and guides him back to his house, where he hopes to find offerings. To prevent this the people are very careful, as soon as anybody has been carried off by a tiger, to go in search of his remains. When they find any part of the corpse, or merely his turban or tobacco pouch, they make paper effigies of the tiger and the man, burn them,

aangaande het geestelijk en maatschappelijk leven van den Poso Alfoer ", in *Mededeelingen van wege het Nederlandsche Zendelinggenootschap*, xxxix. (1895), p. 32.

[1] L. Nyuak, " Religious Rites and Customs of the Iban or Dyaks of Sarawak ", translated by Rev. E. Dunn in *Anthropos*, i. (1906), p. 171.

[2] G. A. Wilken, " Het Animisme bij de Volken van den Indischen Archipel ", in *De Verspreide Geschriften van G. A. Wilken* (The Hague, 1912), iii. pp. 61 *sq.*

and carefully bury all the remains they have discovered. The soul of the deceased, which had been
supposed to inhabit the tiger, now passes into the
grave, and his family sleeps quiet.[1]

Among the Black Taï, a tribe of mountaineers in
Tonkin, when the body of a deceased relative cannot
be found, as may happen after a battle, they collect
some articles that belonged to him, and with these as
representatives of the dead man they proceed to the
ceremony of cremation, and to the erection of a tomb,
just as if they were in possession of the corpse.[2]

Among the Red Karens of Burma, when a man
dies far from home and the body cannot be found,
the funeral cannot take place until the spirit of the deceased has been recalled and has given his consent.
The usual feast is held at home, and in the centre
of the room hangs a bullock bell suspended from the
roof. Dancing and beating of gongs goes on until
the spirit announces his arrival and approval by
tinkling the bullock-bell. If the spirit delays his
coming guns are fired to hasten and guide him on
his way. He never fails to arrive sooner or later.
At the man's house the whole ceremony of funeral
is gone through. An effigy made of straw and cloth
is placed in the coffin to represent the body of the
deceased and the usual rites are performed as if this
were the actual corpse.[3]

[1] R. P. Cadière, "Croyances et
Dictons populaires de la Vallée du
Nguôn-son, Province de Quang-binh
(Annam)", in Bulletin de l'École
Française d'Extrême-Orient, i. (1901,
Hanoi), pp. 135 sq.

[2] Col. E. Diguet, Les Monta-
gnards du Tonkin (Paris, 1908), p. 89.
[3] J. G. Scott and J. P. Hardiman,
Gazetteer of Upper Burma and the
Shan States (Rangoon, 1900), Part
I, vol. i. p. 528. In this passage the

Among the Khasis of North-Eastern India, if a man dies far from home, for example in a foreign country, whose body has not been burnt in accordance with custom, and whose bones have not been collected, the members of his clan, or his children, take three or five seeds or cowries (*sbai*) to a place where three roads meet. Here they summon the spirit of the departed in a loud voice, and throw up the seeds or cowries into the air, and when they fall to the ground they say, " Come, now, we will collect you " (the idea being that the seeds represent the bones of the deceased). Having collected the seeds, they place them on a bier and perform the service for the dead just in the same way as if a real corpse were to hand. If possible a portion of the dead person's clothes should be burned with the seeds in the bier, and it is for this reason that the coats or cloths of Khasi coolies, who die when employed as porters on military expeditions at a distance from their homes, are brought back by their friends to give to the relatives.[1] According to another account in such a case the Khasis look in the direction of the place in which the dead man died, and call upon his spirit to come back and enter a shell, which is then burned instead of the body, or if they know exactly the place where the man died they go thither, and on their return they scatter leaves on the path to guide the spirit of the deceased back to his home, and they stretch strings over streams to help the

writers speak of " The guardian spirit of the deceased ", but the real reference seems to be to the dead man's spirit or ghost.

[1] Lt.-Col. P. R. T. Gurdon, *The Khasis* (London, 1914), pp. 136 *sq.*

returning soul to cross the water.[1] In other parts of India the custom of burning or burying an effigy to represent a deceased person when his body cannot be found appears to be both ancient and widespread. Thus, for example, "the Garuḍa-purāṇa directs that if a man dies in a remote place, or is killed by robbers in a forest and his body is not found, his son should make an effigy of the deceased with Kuśa grass and then burn it on a funeral pile with similar ceremonies ".[2] According to another account in such a case the effigy should be made of 360 leaves of the *Butea frondosa* and as many threads, to represent the members of the body, and having been smeared with meal it was burned on a pyre.[3] An ancient Indian book of ritual, the *Grihya Sûtra*, ordained that when the corpse could not be found, 360 stems of *Palâsa* should be wrapped up in a black goat-skin, such as was regularly spread under the corpse on the pyre, and the rest of the funeral ceremonies performed as if the corpse were present.[4] Other ancient Indian texts direct that when the body of a long-deceased person could not be found, but the place of his death was known, some dust should be gathered from the spot, or a garment should be spread out on the bank of a stream, and the name

[1] A. Bastian, " Hügelstämme Assams ", in *Verhandlungen der Berliner Gesellschaft für Anthropologie* (1881), p. 150.

[2] Monier Williams, *Religious Thought and Life in India* (London, 1883), p. 300.

[3] A. Bastian, *Die Völker des oest-lichen Asien*, vi. 12 n. referring to Colebrooke.

[4] Max Müller, " Die Todten-bestattung bei den Brahmanen ", in *Zeitschrift der deutschen morgenländischen Gesellschaft*, ix. Abhang, p. xxxvi.

of the deceased called out. After such an invocation any animal or insect that lighted on the garment
was to be treated as if it were the corpse itself.[1]
This ancient Indian rite closely resembles the custom
which, as we have seen, the Samoans were wont to
observe in similar cases. In modern India, when
a person is drowned and his body cannot be found,
a rite known as Palasvidhi is performed. An effigy
of the deceased is made, in which twigs of the Palâsa
tree represent the bones, a coconut or Bel fruit the
head, pearls or cowrie shells the eyes, and a piece
of birch bark or the skin of a deer the cuticle. It is
then filled up with Urad pulse instead of flesh and
blood, and a presiding priest recites a spell to bring
life into the image, which is symbolized by putting
a lighted lamp close to the head. When the light
goes out, life is believed to be extinct and the funeral
rites are performed in the regular way, the only
exception being that the period of impurity for the
mourners lasts for three instead of ten days.[2]
Among the Sunār, a caste of goldsmiths and silver-
smiths in the Central Provinces of India, when a
man has died a violent death and his body cannot
be found, they construct a small image of him and
burn it with all the ceremonies usually observed at
a regular cremation.[3] In the Himalayan districts
of the North-West Provinces of India, when a father
dies in a strange land and his relatives cannot find

---

[1] H. Oldenberg, *Die Religion des Veda* (Berlin, 1894), p. 581.
[2] W. Crooke, *The Popular Religion and Folklore of Northern India*, ii. 114.
[3] R. V. Russell, *The Tribes and Castes of the Central Provinces of India*, iv. 521.

his body to perform the usual rites, a ceremony called *náráyana-bali* is observed. A figure of the deceased is made of the reed *kans* and placed on a funeral pyre and burned with the dedication that the deceased may not be without funeral rites.[1]

In China the custom of burying an effigy instead of the corpse when the body cannot be found is ancient and apparently universal. " During the reign of the emperor Chan-tuk, in the first century of the Christian era, it was enacted that if the bodies of soldiers who fall in battle, or those of sailors who fall in naval engagements, cannot be recovered, the spirits of such men shall be called back by prayers and incantations, and that figures shall be made either of paper or of wood for their reception, and be buried with all the ordinary rites. It is recorded in the annals of China, that the first persons who conformed to this singular enactment were the sons of an officer named Lee Hoo, who fell in battle and whose body could not be recovered. The custom is now universally observed."[2] " In case the corpse is not brought home to be buried, a letter, or some of the clothing recently worn by the deceased, or his shoes, or part of his baggage, is often sent home instead. The white cock and the mourners go forth to meet the departed just as they would go to

[1] E. T. Atkinson, *The Himalayan Districts of the North-Western Provinces of India* (Allahabad, 1884), ii. 932. For a fuller account of the rite, see E. T. Atkinson, " Notes on the History of Religion in the Himalaya of the N.W. Provinces ", in *Journal of the Asiatic Society of Bengal*, liv. (1885), p. 14.

[2] J. H. Gray, *China*, i. pp. 295 *sq.* On this custom, with the evidence for its antiquity, see J. J. M. De Groot, *The Religious System of China*, vol. iii. Book I, pp. 847 *sqq.*

meet the corpse. On meeting the letter or the relic, the spirit passes as readily into the fowl as it would pass into it were the corpse itself met, and the spirit is conducted home just as surely." [1] Archdeacon Gray witnessed one of these ceremonies of burial in effigy, and he has described it as follows. " On the occasion of a visit which I paid to Tai-laak, the capital of the ninety-six villages, I had the opportunity of seeing so singular a ceremony. An effigy of the missing man, clad in robes of the most costly kind, was placed on the ground, and a number of men and women, dressed in deep mourning, knelt round it. In the centre of the circle a Taouist priest invoked the spirit to come to the body prepared for it, and accompany it to the tomb. Lest the souls of the deceased should be imprisoned in one of the ten kingdoms of the Buddhist hades, miniature representations of the infernal prisons were made by means of small clay flags or tiles. They reminded one of dolls' houses. Prayers in which the kings of the infernal regions were in turn evoked were then offered, and at the conclusion of each invocation the priest with a short magic wand dashed to the ground one of the miniature prisons. The effigy was eventually, with the usual observances, put into a coffin and conveyed to the grave by the sorrowing relatives." [2]

In Japan it is customary to preserve the navel-strings of the family in the old home, and should a

---

[1] Rev. J. Doolittle, *Social Life of the Chinese* (London, 1868), 164.

[2] J. H. Gray, *op. cit.* i. 296.

member of the family die in a foreign land, or be drowned at sea, and his body be not recovered, his navel-string is buried instead of his corpse.[1]

Among the Orotchi, a Tartar tribe of Tungussic origin in north-eastern Asia, if a person has been drowned and his body has not been found within two years, it is customary to carve a wooden image in the likeness of the deceased, and placing it in a coffin to bury it under a small conical hut.[2]

In Madagascar there are cenotaphs for the reception of the souls of persons whose bodies have not been found. These cenotaphs generally consist of a low wall built on three sides of a square. They are intended to be the last resting-place for the souls of those who have died in battle, and whose mortal remains have not been recovered. Their ghosts, it is thought, are allured to repose in the sacred spots thus reared for them by the hands of friends, and thereby find that rest which otherwise they would have sought in vain, while wandering with the owls and animals of ill omen in the forests, or paying unwelcome visits to their former dwellings, and disturbing their surviving friends.[3] On this subject Alfred Grandidier, our great authority on the ethnography of Madagascar, tells us that when the Malagasy cannot recover the body of a deceased relative, they bury his pillow and mat instead of his

---

[1] L. Hearn, *Glimpses of Unfamiliar Japan* (London, 1894), i. 507.

[2] E. H. Fraser, " The Fish Skin Tartars ", in *Journal of the China Branch of the Royal Asiatic Society*, xxvi. (1891–1892), pp. 31 *sq.*

[3] Rev. W. Ellis, *History of Madagascar* (London and Paris, N.D.). i. 255 *sq.*

corpse, and set up a sepulchral monument to his memory.[1]

Among the Tschi-speaking peoples of the Gold Coast in Africa a ceremony called *Toh-fo* is performed when a person has died and his body has been either destroyed or cannot be found, for example, when a man has been burned to death and the body reduced to ashes, or when one has been drowned and the body cannot be recovered. A miniature coffin is made, covered with white cloth, and in the case of the drowned man is carried to the sea-shore. Rum is poured out on the waves, and the name of the deceased is called out three times, the mourners crying at the same time in a plaintive chant, " We have sought for you but cannot find you ". Some sand from the beach is then placed in the coffin, some sea-water poured into it, and, with the usual lamentations, the coffin is buried, commonly on the beach. In the case of a man destroyed by fire, some of the ashes of the body, or of the house in which it was consumed, are placed in the coffin, with similar ceremonies. In this ceremony a fragment of the corpse is always interred if possible, but, if no portion of it can be found, some earth, water, or other substance from the place where the death occurred is buried in the grave. This custom appears to owe its origin to the belief that if respect be not shown to the deceased, by showing him the usual funeral honours, his ghost will come into the dwellings of

---

[1] A. Grandidier, " Des rites funéraires chez les Malgaches ", in *Revue d'Ethnographie*, v. (1886), p. 214.

the neglectful relatives, cause sickness, and disturb them by night. Consequently, no body being forthcoming they perform the funeral rites over a substitute, taking care, however, to announce to the spirit of the deceased that they have sought for the body in vain.[1] Among the Ewe-speaking peoples of the Slave Coast, when a person dies abroad the family try to obtain something that belonged to him, such as locks of his hair or parings of his nails, and over these they perform the funeral ceremonies, for the general belief is that until these rites have been carried out the ghost lingers near the remains, and either cannot or will not depart for Dead-land before this satisfaction has been accorded him.[2] Similarly among the Yoruba-speaking peoples of the Slave Coast, when a man dies abroad his family makes the greatest exertions to obtain something belonging to him, over which the usual funeral rites may be held. Locks of hair or parings of the nails are most sought for this purpose, but if these cannot be obtained a portion of the clothing worn by the deceased suffices. Such relics are called *eta* : they are supposed to bring back the soul of the deceased to the place where the funeral ceremonies are being performed.[3] Among the Ibo-speaking people of Southern Nigeria

---

[1] A. B. Ellis, *The Tschi-Speaking Peoples of the Gold Coast of West Africa* (London, 1887), pp. 222 *sq.*

[2] A. B. Ellis, *The Ewe-Speaking Peoples of the Slave Coast of West Africa* (London, 1890), p. 159.

[3] A. B. Ellis, *The Yoruba-Speaking Peoples of the Slave Coast of West Africa* (London, 1894), p. 163, and Father Baudin, " Le Fétichisme ou la religion des Nègres de la Guinée", in *Les Missions Catholiques*, xvi. (Lyons, 1884), pp. 258 *sq.*

if a man dies far away and his body cannot be recovered they take a palm-leaf and a chicken and go
to the "bad bush." Holding the palm-leaf in the hand,
they kill the chicken, throw it into the "bad bush,"
knock the leaf on the ground, take it on the left arm
and go back, saying, "Dead man follow me home".
If it is a man who has died they put the leaf outside
the yam store, if it is a woman they leave it outside
the door of her house. In the case of a man a goat
and a cock are sacrificed, and blood is put upon the
leaf exactly as it would be upon the dead man's eyes,
the leaf is wrapped in cloth as if for a body; in
the case of a woman the goat's heart is put upon a
spot to represent the chest.[1] Concerning these Ibo
people we are told elsewhere by the same authority
that when the body of a deceased person cannot be
found, as for example in the case of a drowned man,
the leaf of a certain palm (*omu ojuku*) is struck four
times on the bank of the stream where the accident
took place and the dead man's name is called out
four times. The palm-leaf is then covered with a
cloth and laid on a board, and ceremonies are performed for it as for a corpse.[2]

The Giagues are a tribe or nation of conquerors
who, coming from the interior of Africa invaded the
kingdoms of Matamba and Congo about two centuries ago. Among them, as we learn from an old
writer, if anyone dreams of a deceased relation, he
fancies that it is the soul of the dead who suffers for

---

[1] N. W. Thomas, "Some Ibo
Burial Customs", in *Journal of the
Royal Anthropological Institute*,
xlvii. (1917), p. 167.

[2] N. W. Thomas, *op. cit.* pp. 184 *sq.*

lack of food and drink, and therefore appears to demand help, and reproach his kinsman for his neglect. So the man has recourse to the Ganga-ga-Zumbi, the protector or guardian of the dead, or medicine man, as we may call him. It is chiefly with the sick that this guardian of the dead has to do, for they attribute disease to the anger of the neglected dead. The most difficult case with which the protector of the dead has to deal is that of the ghost of a dead person whose body has not been buried, because he has been killed and eaten by his enemies or by wild beasts. In that case the medicine man spreads nets round the house of the sick man and even into the forest, in order that the soul of the dead man may be caught in the net when he comes to annoy the patient. When a bird, rat, lizard, ape, or other animal is caught in the net, it is taken to be the incarnation of the dead man's soul. The medicine man takes it to the sick man and says, " Rejoice : we've got him. He shan't escape." But before he kills the animal he demands a new fee. When this is agreed to, he kills the animal, to the sick man's joy. But to prevent the soul returning the animal must be ground to powder and swallowed by the sick man. For this grinding to powder, the medicine man must be paid again. When the man has swallowed the powder, digested it, and voided it in his excrement, then he is rid of the tormenting spirit finally.[1] In this case the tormenting spirit

---

[1] J. B. Labat, *Relation historique de l'Éthiopie Occidentale* (Paris, 1732), ii. 209 *sqq.*

of the unburied dead is not recalled and propitiated, as in the preceding cases, but is ground to powder and apparently laid to its last rest in the stomach of the person whom he had been persecuting.

Among the Wajagga of Mount Kilimanjaro, if a man has died in a foreign land, and his body has not been recovered, his friends go to the boundary of the land where he died, and from there bring back a skull-shaped stone, over which they perform the usual mourning ceremonies and raise the customary lamentations for the dead, just as if it were the corpse of the deceased.[1] Among the Basoga, a Bantu tribe of Uganda, " a curious custom still remains in connexion with a man who dies at some distance from his home, and whose body therefore cannot be transported back to be buried in his own house. The relatives of the deceased will march for two or three hours into the bush, and come away with a branch or a long reed. The straight branch or reed stem is then thrown on the ground, and one of the relations calls out the dead man's name and says : ' We have come to bring you home for burial '. After this the reed or stick is covered up with bark-cloth, and the relations march back to the dead man's home carrying with them this substitute for burial. As they get near the village one of their number runs on ahead to apprise the neighbours that the dead

[1] B. Gutmann, " Trauer und Begräbnissitten der Wadschagga ", in *Globus*, lxxxiv. (1906), p. 198 ; *id.*, *Dichten und Denken der Dschagga-Neger*, p. 137. Cf. M. Merker, " Rechtsverhältnisse und Sitten der Wadschagga ", in *Petermanns Mitteilungen*, Ergänzungsheft, No. 138 (1902), 18 *sq.*

man's body is being brought to his last home. The women then start wailing for the dead, and continue screaming and shouting until the long stick wrapped up in a bundle of bark-cloth is deposited in the grave. The rest of the ceremony is identical with that which follows the actual deposit of a corpse in its grave under the house."[1]

Among the Bavenda, a Bantu tribe of the Northern Transvaal, if a man has died far from home and his body cannot be recovered, if his spirit becomes troublesome and requires to be propitiated by a sacrifice at the grave, his friends proceed to hold a fictitious burial ceremony. They kill a sheep and use its head to symbolize the corpse of the deceased. A grave is dug and the sheep's head is buried with due reverence in the usual way, together with some of the dead man's clothing or possessions. This grave is afterwards considered to be that of the dead man.[2] Among the Ovaherero, a Bantu tribe of South-West Africa, if a man has died far from home, as in war, and his body has not been brought back, the people of his village select for him at home a place at which they erect for him a monument of stones put together in a peculiar manner, and at these stones they perform the same ceremonies as they would have performed at the grave, if the dead man's body had been brought back and buried.[3]

In America the Eskimo about Bering Strait in

[1] Sir H. Johnstone, *The Uganda Protectorate*, ii. 717 *sq*.
[2] H. A. Stayt, *The Bavenda* (London, 1931), p. 163.
[3] Rev. G. Viehe, " Some Customs of the Ovaherero ", in *South African Folk-lore Journal*, i. (Capetown, 1879), p. 57.

Alaska are wont to erect memorial wooden posts, carved in human shape, for such persons as have died but have remained unburied because their bodies have not been found. At Tununuk village, near Cape Vancouver, Mr. E. W. Nelson saw three such large wooden posts, representing human figures, and several subordinate posts. One of them represented a woman who had been buried in a landslide, while others of them represented men who had been drowned at sea. Mr. Nelson was told " that among the people of this and the neighbouring villages, as well as of the villages about Big Lake, in the interior from this point, it is the custom to erect memorial posts for all people who die in such a manner that their bodies are not recovered. Each year for five years a new fur coat or cloth shirt is put on the figure at the time of invitation to the festival of the dead, and offerings are made to it as though the body were in its grave box there. When the shade comes about the village to attend the festival of the dead, or at other times, these posts are supposed to afford it a resting-place, and it sees that it has not been forgotten or left unhonoured by its relatives." [1] The Tlingit Indians of Alaska used to dispose of their dead by burning them, but towards the close of last century they were persuaded by a missionary to adopt the practice of burying instead of burning. The innovation was followed by a period of storms and bad weather, which the

---

[1] E. W. Nelson, " The Eskimo about Bering Strait ", in the *Eight-* *eenth Report of the Bureau of Ethnology* (Washington, 1899), i. 317 *sq.*

Indians attributed to the wrath of the spirits of their deceased friends at being deprived of the time-honoured ceremony of cremation. So on the beach they kindled great fires, in which they burnt puppets to represent their dead friends, hoping thus to appease their angry spirits. As the ceremony was followed by no improvement in the weather the Indians, not without difficulty, discovered the graves of their dead under the snow, and dug up the bodies, presumably that their spirits might have the satisfaction of witnessing the cremation of the puppets, and so might cease to afflict their surviving kinsfolk with a continuance of bad weather.[1]

Among the Aht Indians of Vancouver Island we read of a bereaved father whose son was drowned at sea and his body not recovered. In default of the corpse the father took two cedar boards, one of which bore the roughly traced representation of a man, while the other supported a small porpoise. These he carried to a resting-place in the forest, where he celebrated funeral rites for the peace of his drowned son's soul. After it he distributed all his own property among the mourners present.[2]

In Ancient Mexico, if a travelling merchant died on a journey or was killed by his enemies and his body had not been brought back, his friends at home used to make an effigy of him of pine-wood, and dressed it in paper garments, such as were usually placed on a corpse. This effigy they carried

[1] A. Krause, *Die Tlinkit-Indianer* (Jena, 1885), p. 231.
[2] G. M. Sproat, *Scenes and Studies* of *Savage Life* (London, 1868), p. 263.

to a temple, where it was left for a whole day, and mourned by the relatives. At midnight it was carried out into the courtyard of the temple and there burned, after which the ashes were buried in the usual fashion.[1]

In modern Greece, when a man dies abroad, a puppet is made in his likeness, and dressed in his clothes ; it is laid on the bed, and mourning is made over it.[2] Mr. T. H. Bent witnessed at Mykonos a formal lamentation for an absent dead man, but where the bier would have stood there was an empty space.[3] A similar custom of mourning over an effigy is observed in some parts of Calabria.[4] In Albania, when a man dies abroad all the usual lamentations are made at home as if the body were present ; the funeral procession goes to the church, but in place of the bier a boy walks carrying a dish on which a cracknel is placed over some boiled wheat. This dish is set in the middle of the church, and the funeral service is held over it ; it is not, however, buried, but the women go and weep at the grave of the relation who died last.[5] Among the Rumanians of Transylvania, when any one dies abroad, his clothes are carried to the churchyard of

[1] B. de Sahagun, *Histoire géné- rale des choses de la Nouvelle- Espagne* (Paris, 1880), p. 264 ; Abbé Clavigero, *The History of Mexico*, trans. by Cullen, i. 387 ; Abbé Bras- seur de Bourbourg, *Histoire des nations civilisées du Mexique* (Paris, 1858), iii. 621 *sq.* ; H. H. Bancroft, *Native Races of the Pacific States of North America*, ii. 616.

[2] C. Wachsmuth, *Das alte Grie- chenland im neuen* (Bonn, 1864), p. 113.

[3] T. H. Bent, *The Cyclades* (Lon- don, 1885), pp. 222 *sq.*

[4] V. Dorsa, *La Tradizione Greco- latina . . . della Calabria* (Cosenza, 1884), p. 93.

[5] J. G. von Hahn, *Albanesische Studien* (Jena, 1854), i. 152.

his home with all the usual formalities of a regular burial. A plain wooden cross is set up to his memory in the churchyard, with his name and the place of his death carved on it.[1]

VIII. *Ghosts of Animals*

The strictly logical character of primitive thought has sometimes been doubted or denied, but in one respect at least primitive man is more consistently logical than his civilized brother, for he commonly extends to the lower animals that theory of the survival of the soul after death which civilized peoples usually restrict to human beings. Hence primitive hunters or fishermen stand in awe of the spirits or ghosts of the animals and fish which they kill and eat, fearing lest their angry ghosts should seek to take vengeance on their killers, or by giving warning to their fellows should prevent them from coming to be caught and killed in like manner, and so diminish or cut off entirely a principal source of the food supply. Accordingly the primitive hunter or fisherman attempts to propitiate the ghosts of the animals which he kills by sacrificing to them or addressing them in complimentary and persuasive language, and certain precautions are taken to guard him against their dangerous attacks. In a work dealing with the fear of the spirits of the human dead in primitive religion we should not omit to

[1] R. Prexl, "Geburts- und Todten- gebräuche bei Rumänen in Sie- benbürgen", in *Globus*, lvii. (1890), p. 30.

notice that parallel fear of the spirits of dead animals which many primitive peoples are reported to entertain. Elsewhere I have discussed this curious side of primitive thought at some length : [1] here I will content myself by illustrating it with some fresh and typical instances.

Thus, for example, with regard to the Bachama, a tribe of Northern Nigeria, we are told that " there are special hunting and head-hunting rites. In every village may be seen a large collection of standing stones surrounded with the heads of the larger game. When a Bachama kills a lion, leopard, rhinoceros, buffalo, elephant, hippopotamus, or wart-hog, the fame of his exploit is soon made known, and on returning he is saluted on the outskirts of the town by everyone who owns a horse. He is escorted to the hunting shrine, before which he sits down. The chief or some senior man takes the tail of the dead animal and, speaking words of congratulation, touches the arm of the hunter with the tail. He then smears some flour over the head and body of the hunter, with the intention, it was stated, of protecting him from pursuit by the ghost of the dead animal." [2] Again with regard to the Bolewa, Ngamo, Ngizim, and Kare-Kare tribes of the Bornu Province of Northern Nigeria, we are told that the leopard seems to be feared by them more than any other animal. " To kill a leopard or even look on its dead body is to expose oneself

---

[1] *The Golden Bough : Spirits of the Corn and of the Wild*, ii. 204 *sqq.*

[2] C. K. Meek, *Tribal Studies in Northern Nigeria* (London, 1931), i. 45.

to the assault of the leopard's ghost, the first sign of which is a violent fit of coughing. The afflicted person is swathed in a white cloth resembling the shroud used for the dead. A hunter attends with his company of fiddlers, playing and singing praises to the leopard : ' If your head is shaven there is no blood (*i.e.* you cannot be scalped by your enemy) ; behold the cloth is becoming covered with spots '. The characteristic spots of the leopard are said to appear on the cloth, and are immediately plucked out by the hunter. In this way the man's life is saved. But if the spots do not appear he is doomed to die. No one would eat leopard's flesh without first providing himself with some protective medicine." [1] Among the Yungur-speaking peoples of Northern Nigeria, after a man has killed a dangerous animal he is treated with the same rites as were formerly accorded to a human being. An official known as Kpana smears the hunter's shoulders with mahogany oil to prevent the dead animal's ghost from pursuing him.[2] The Jen, a small group of people in Northern Nigeria, believe that the hare has a powerful pursuing spirit, and for that reason women and children are not allowed to eat hare's flesh. If a hare is killed by a dog, a small boy is formally charged with the deed, in order to prevent the dog being killed by the pursuing spirit of the hare.[3]

With regard to beliefs and practices of this sort

[1] C. K. Meek, *op. cit.* ii. 274.
[2] C. K. Meek, *op. cit.* ii. 458.
[3] C. K. Meek, *op. cit.* ii. 523.

among the peoples of Northern Nigeria in general, a competent authority well acquainted with the province writes as follows : "Lions, leopards, and all the larger wild animals are universally feared by members of both their own and other clans on account of the supposed powerful spiritual influence which, in the same manner as powerful men, they are held to possess. This fear is in fact at the basis of all hunting and fishing magic, whereby it is sought to propitiate the souls of animals slain, whether members of a totem species or not. The practice of such propitiatory or expiatory rites is as a rule confined to the larger or more important animals, such as, among non-totem animals, hyenas, buffaloes, the larger antelopes and ant-eater. The object is both to protect the individual from future pursuit by the vengeful 'pattern' soul (*ekiti*) of the slain and to purge him from his existing state of 'saturation' with the spiritual influence or 'matter soul' (*kofi*) of his victim.

"I was given the following account by a hunter of the procedure stated to be adopted at the present day where a Kwotto hunter kills a lion at a place within the political jurisdiction of the chief of the lion clan. After slaying the lion, the hunter, before taking any steps to remove it, reports the matter to the chief. At the same time he seeks to obtain the forgiveness of the latter, for having slain his kinsman, by the offer of presents, including a white cock and beer.

"The chief, on his part, rewards the successful

hunter for his valour by gifts, usually including a gown and turban. These, incidentally, are among the traditional items of apparel with which a senior chief invests a junior on appointment, so that the gift may conceivably in origin be connected with the idea of hailing the hunter as ' chiefly ', owing to his having become impregnated with the royal spiritual influence of the lion. The chief then arranges for a bearer party to go and fetch the lion in order that it may be given ceremonial burial. The lion is wrapped round with a red winding-cloth and carried on a bier in procession through the town into the presence of the chief, to the accompaniment of the beating of drums and the joyful shrill cry (' *Kururua* ') of women. The people salute the corpse gravely as it passes, addressing it as ' lion ' and ' grandfather '. Later the animal is flayed, only certain privileged persons of the royal household, such as the Edibo, Shifornu and Audigwa, being allowed to touch the corpse ; and the skin is presented to the chief to adorn his couch. It is in fact a general rule among the Kwottos—not confined to the members of particular clans—that no one but a chief or his relatives may possess, much less wear or sit on, the skins of any of the larger wild beasts, especially those of the lion or leopard. Similar regulations apply also among all the surrounding tribes with which I am acquainted.

" The skull of the dead lion is given to the hunter who killed it, to deposit on the lion-clan chief's grave, where he offers up sacrifices and prays before it.

He beseeches the ghost (*ekiti*) of the lion not to harm him for his presumption in killing it, saying : ' O Lion, I give you refreshment to-day, lest your spiritual power (*kofi*) cause me to die '.

" After burying the lion and before returning to live in his village, the hunter retires to the bush for two days, where he performs certain further propitiatory and purificatory rites. These include the eating of a mixture containing atcha-millet, white beans, rice, seven ears of corn and seven ears of maize. To this is added palm-wine and the whole boiled. Were the hunter to neglect to perform these rites it is believed he would go mad. His fellow-villagers will at any rate refuse to receive him into the village until he has purified himself from the *kofi* of the slain animal, conceived as still attaching to him. They fear that if they do so their houses, food, and all their belongings will become contaminated, and the remaining lions come and avenge their comrades by ' eating up ' the village." [1]

The Ewe peoples of Togoland in West Africa think that leopards are animated by the souls of dead men, and therefore ought not to be killed. Whoever kills a leopard must submit to an elaborate ceremony of expiation and purification. Some of the people believe that a leopard is possessed, not by the spirit of a dead man, but by a son of a God, which naturally deepens the crime of killing a leopard. When the news of the killing of a leopard

---

[1] Capt. J. R. Wilson-Haffenden, *The Red Men of Nigeria* (London, 1930), pp. 167 *sqq.*

reaches a village men who have already killed a leopard go to the spot and bring back the body and the hunter, carrying both on their backs. On arriving at the village they are greeted with cries of joy by the women, and shooting of guns and beating of gongs by the men. At the entrance to the village the body of the leopard is covered with palm-branches, because no one may look on it, for they think that if that rule were not observed a great drought would follow. Then the leopard and its killer are carried to the market-place, followed by the people dancing, singing and drumming. On their arrival at the market-place priests come forward and cover the body of the leopard with palm-branches, and pour libations of water mixed with meal upon the ground, while they express their sympathy with the dead animal by saying, " I pity thee, I pity thee ". If the priests of the leopard-god omitted to perform this ceremony, it is believed that they would die. Afterwards the body of the leopard and the hunter who killed it are taken up and carried by bearers on their shoulders all round the town. Next the leopard's body is carried to a place called *holutime*; there, as we are told, every one can convince himself that a son of God has really been killed. Thither then comes the oldest man or chieftain of the town, carrying a bush-knife and some palm-wine. He offers a prayer, and pours a libation of the palm-wine to the dead god. With a loud lamentation one of the men present unties the cord which fastened the palm-branches round the leopard's body. Then the leopard's body is placed on a new mat and allowed to lie on the spot till next morning. Then begins the process of skinning and cutting up the carcase, which may only be done by men who have themselves killed leopards. They send parts of the flesh first of all to the oldest people of the town. While they are cutting up and dividing the flesh they cry out continually, " So-and-so [naming the leopard killer] and his helpers are dead ". The reason for this cry is not given by our authority, but we may conjecture that its intention is to assure the soul of the dead animal that his death has been avenged by the death of his slayers.

The leopard's skin goes to the king or chief of the town, who may keep or sell it. After this the man who killed the leopard, and any one who helped him at the killing, must undergo a ceremony of expiation and purification for a period of twenty-one days. A special hut is erected for their accommodation during this time. So long as he remains in this hut the killer of the leopard may not speak : he must behave like a leopard, imitating the voice of the animal, sleeping on palm-branches, and has his body painted or smeared with black and white pigments to imitate the skin of a leopard. From time to time a roar like that of a leopard is heard to proceed from the hut, and after that the mock leopard issues forth to seek his prey. While he is on his raid every one avoids him, for they think that if they were to meet him they would die. Since the leopard eats flesh the mock leopard seeks to imitate the real animal by procuring some flesh to devour. For this purpose he goes about armed with a bow and arrows, and shoots any dog that may cross his path. The dog's flesh, when he gets it, may not be laid on a plate, and the water which he drinks may not be quaffed from a vessel, but must be lapped by him from a stream. Thus he imitates his prototype the leopard, both in his eating and drinking. By midday he must return to his hut, because the leopard only prowls for prey at morning and evening. Any one who were to eat or drink of the leopard-killer's food and water would go mad.

The last of the twenty-one days' seclusion is the day of the purification of the leopard-killer. From every side friends flock to him to testify their sympathy and respect, each of them bringing a present of a piece of cloth and a little money. The cloths are fastened to each other and used as a garment with which they clothe the leopard-killer. Women make strings of cowries with which the body of the leopard-killer is decked before he is carried to the place of his purification outside the town. Before he is carried forth some magical medicine is poured into his nose, and the same thing is done to several of the bystanders. After receiving the medicine in his nose the leopard-killer makes a vibratory or trembling motion to right and left, but the meaning of this part of the ceremony was not ascertained by our authority. Thereupon the leopard-killer, stripped of clothing, as he had been during his seclusion, is taken by bearers on their shoulders and carried in great haste to the place of purification, followed by a crowd from the town. While the ceremony of purification is proceeding the people who remain behind gather in an open space of the town, where they dance, brandish knives with wild gesticulations, sing special hunting songs and beat the hunters' drums. Meantime women have cleaned the hut in which the leopard-killer dwelt during his seclusion, throwing away the palm-branches and the rubbish in the forest. After that the hut itself is pulled down. At the place of purification the body of the leopard-killer is washed thoroughly by certain people. Then they all go back dancing, singing and beating drums to the place in the town where the other people are assembled. The procession is headed by men who have themselves slain men, or are the parents of twins, or are famous hunters. The leopard-killer, dressed in a new robe, has now made his peace with the God whose son he has killed, and he may now go about among his fellows as of old.[1]

Among the Kassounas-Bouras, a tribe of the French Sudan, if a man has killed a lion, or a panther, or a buffalo, or an antelope of a special species, or a hyena, a seer will sometimes tell him that evil will befall him. On receiving this warning the killer of the animal will build a miniature house in front of his hut to lodge the spirit of the animal he has killed, and there he sacrifices to the creature's

---

[1] C. Spiess, " Beiträge zur Kenntniss der Religion und der Kultus-formen in Sud-Togo ", in *Baessler Archiv*, ii. (1912) pp. 70 *sqq.*

soul. Another creature, the killing of which requires to be expiated by a sacrifice, is a species of bird called by the natives *kouma* or *koumvava*. It is perhaps the crested crane. If a man has killed a bird of this sort he makes a miniature house for it, and there offers sacrifice to the bird's ghost. The plumage of birds of this sort is used to decorate garments of chiefs and wealthy people. Again, if a man kills a red ape or a boar he will build a miniature house for the animal's soul, and there offer sacrifice to it, should the seer direct him to do so.[1]

Again, among the Gouros, a tribe inhabiting the interior of the Ivory Coast, if a man has killed a deer of a special species he hastens to take the animal's skull, on which he offers a sacrifice to the animal's vengeful ghost in order that it may not pursue him, and he resorts to a similar mode of appeasing the vengeful ghost of an elephant or a leopard which he has killed. Even if he does not consider himself to be related to these animals through his clan, he still sacrifices to them, lest their ghosts should haunt him in his sleep.[2] The Gouros who inhabit the northern part of the Ivory Coast similarly fear the vengeful ghosts of certain animals which they kill. Hunters who are in the habit of killing such animals obtain from old people charms to protect them from these dangerous ghosts. They particularly dread the ghosts of a certain species of deer or antelope, and if they have killed one of them they take the

[1] L. Tauxier, *Le Noir de Soudan* (Paris, 1912), p. 327.

[2] L. Tauxier, *Nègres Gouro et Gagou* (Paris, 1924). p. 204.

animal's skull and on it offer a little sacrifice to the ghost.[1]

The Lango, a Nilotic tribe of Uganda, believe that some species of animals, but not all, possess a shade or soul (*tipo*), which survives the death of its body and may prove dangerous to its slayer. Animals which are credited with the possession of such a soul are the wart-hog, rhinoceros, elephant, roan, giraffe and bushbuck. Some animals, including, curiously enough, the lion and the leopard, are not supposed to possess such dangerous souls. The ghost of the roan is thought to be particularly vengeful and vicious. When a man has killed an animal of that species he must at once return to his village and consult a seer, according to whose advice an offering is made and special rites are observed to pacify the ghost of the animal. The ceremonies vary according to the directions of the seer, but in all cases a black ram must be sacrificed at the door of the slayer's house. The carcase is dragged whole into the bush and left near a river, but the old men of the village may go and eat it there, after which they burn the skin and bones and throw the ashes into the water. Having thus appeased the animal's ghost, the slayer may return and cut up the animal's body, but the horns of the roan may not be brought into the village, on account of the peculiarly vicious and dangerous character of that animal's ghost. For a similar reason it was formerly forbidden to bring into the village the horns of a slain rhinoceros.

<hr />

[1] L. Tauxier, *op. cit.* p. 255.

A like ceremony of expiation has to be performed for the killing of any one of those species of animals which are supposed to possess a vengeful shade or spirit.[1]

Among the Wajagga of Mount Kilimanjaro, boys amuse themselves by shooting birds with a bow and arrows. For every bird that he kills the boy makes a notch in the wood of his bow. When a boy has shot a hundred or a hundred and fifty birds he sacrifices a goat to expiate the bow and himself, and thereafter shoots at no bird, lest he should expose himself to the vengeance of the dead bird's ghost.[2] Among the Wandamba of Tanganyika, when the hunters have killed an elephant, the chief medicine-man, or in his absence the first man who drew the animal's blood, cuts off the tail and the tip of the trunk, burying the latter as ugly and unfit to be seen by women. Then he mounts the carcase and dances, singing, "He is dead, the rumbling one, he is stone dead ". After that the others climb up and dance on the carcase, but a man who has not previously assisted at the killing of an elephant may not do so until he has been invited by the chief medicine-man, who first binds a couple of hairs from the animal's tail round the man's neck and washes him. This necklace of hair the man wears until the morning after the return home, when it is handed back to the head medicine-man, and put by him in his bag. If these precautions were not observed the man

[1] J. H. Driberg, *The Lango* (London, 1923), pp. 229 *sq.*

[2] B. Gutmann, *Dichten und Denken der Dschagganeger*, p. 106.

would be haunted by the spirit of the dead elephant and would be subject to fits of madness in which he would suffer from the illusion that the beast was pursuing him.[1] The Nanzela, a people of Northern Rhodesia, observe a similar ceremony at the killing of an elephant for the purpose of appeasing the animal's ghost. The ceremony has been described as follows, by Messrs. Smith and Dale. "We have never had the opportunity of watching the cutting-up of an elephant, but, sitting once in company with some old Nanzela hunters, we asked and obtained the following description of the process. The motive underlying the rites is to prevent the ghost of the deceased elephant from taking vengeance upon the hunters, and to induce it to assist them in bringing the same fate upon other elephants. When the elephant is dead the hunter runs off and is chased in mock resentment by his companions. Then he comes back and climbs upon the carcase, his companions surrounding the elephant and clapping their hands in greeting and congratulation. They then proceed to cut up the carcase. A beginning is made by cutting out the fat in the hollows of the temples : from its quantity and quality they judge the condition of the animal. They then open the abdomen and remove the intestines. The linings of the cavity are carefully separated and spread out to dry ; they are called *ingubo* (' blankets '), and are intended for presentation to the *bodi*, the ladies

[1] A. G. O. Hodgson, "Some Notes on the Hunting Customs of the Wandamba", in *Journal of the Royal Anthropological Institute*, lvi. (1926) p. 63.

of the community. They then cut through the diaphragm : through the opening the hunter puts his head, seizes the heart in his mouth, and drags it out. He does not eat it, but the biting is to give him strength in future hunting. Having removed the contents of the thorax, they attack the head. There is some special significance attached to the nerve of the tusk, called *kamwale* ('the maiden'). It is carefully abstracted and buried under the site of the camp-fire. It is not to be looked upon by the tiros in hunting—they are called *bana* ('children ') ; all the time it is being handled they must turn away their heads, for were they to see it they would meet with misfortune. Having now completed their work they return to the village, beating their axes together and singing. The people on hearing the noise flock to meet them, and a great feast, with plenty of beer, is made. But first an offering is made to Leza (' the Supreme Being '), to the *mizhimo* (' the ancestral spirits ') and to the ghost (*muzhimo*) of the deceased elephant which has accompanied them to the village. Addressing this last they say : ' O spirit, have you no brothers and fathers who will come to be killed ? Go and fetch them.' The ghost of the elephant then returns and joins the herd as the guardian of the elephant who has ' eaten its name '. Observe that they regard the elephants as acting as men act : one dies and another inherits his position, ' eats his name ', as they say. Before a man can be admitted into the brotherhood of elephant hunters he must undergo a process of being doctored. Gashes are cut in his right arm and ' medicine ' is rubbed in to give him pluck; and other ' medicines ' are administered to enable him to approach his quarry without being seen." [1] With reference to the Ila-speaking peoples generally of Northern Rhodesia the same writers have described for us the parallel ceremony observed by them at the killing of an eland for the purpose of disarming the vengeful ghost of the animal. They say : " We have described the ceremonies following the death of an elephant. When a man kills an eland he must also go through certain rites to avert the retaliating power in the animal. After killing an eland the hunter chews leaves of the Mukono or Munto bush, together with a piece of *kaumbuswa* (ant-heap), holding, meanwhile, a lump of the latter under his foot. Some of the chewed leaves he rubs on his forehead and some on the eland's forehead. Having done this he throws at the eland's head the piece of ant-heap that was under his foot. He also cuts and splits a stick and jumps through the cleft, as the killer of a man does. He then goes off to the village to get people to help him in carrying home the meat. On their arrival at the eland he sits apart while they open the carcase. He must not join them at first, but once it is opened he may help them to skin and cut up the animal. Were these rites omitted, the eland would trouble him— would come at night and horn him, or in any case cause his death. But the power in the eland can be

[1] Rev. E. W. Smith and Capt. A. M. Dale, *The Ila-speaking Peoples* *of Northern Rhodesia* (London, 1920), i. 167 *sq*.

put to use. Medicine put into its horn derives therefrom a more potent efficacy." [1]

Among the Gonds and Korkus in the Central Provinces of India, when a tiger has been killed the hunters singe off the animal's whiskers, because they think that this will prevent the tiger's ghost from haunting them. They often object to touch a man who has been injured or mauled by a tiger, as they believe that to do so would bring down the vengeance of the tiger's ghost upon them. And in some places any Gond or Korku who touches a man mauled by a tiger is put temporarily out of caste and has to be purified and give a feast on being readmitted to the caste. [2] Among the Lushais, a tribe of North-Eastern India, when a man has killed either an enemy or an animal, it is necessary for him to perform a certain ceremony called "Ai" for the purpose of giving him power to control the spirit or ghost of the man or animal. The ceremony consists in the sacrifice of a mithan, goat or pig. After this, before the skull can be placed in the front verandah, a religious ceremony must be performed by a priest or medicine-man. A small white fowl is given to him, and the skull of the animal is placed in front of him. He then takes some rice-beer (*zu*) in his mouth and spits it out over the skull, and, after muttering a charm in so low a tone that no one can hear him, he strikes the skull with the head of the chicken. If some of the feathers stick on the

[1] Smith and Dale, *op. cit.* ii. 88.   *of the Central Provinces of India,*
[2] R. V. Russell, *Tribes and Castes*   iii. 564.

skull it is very lucky. After this the skull can be put up. The reason for the performance of this ceremony (*Ai*) is that if it be omitted the soul of the slain animal or man cannot pass to the spirit land, to be there under the mastery of the slayer ; in other words, the aim of the ceremony is to give the slayer full power over his victim's ghost in the world beyond the grave. No such ceremony has to be performed for tame animals when they are killed, presumably because they are already under the control of their killer. Thus we see that the Lushais treat the souls of killed men and killed animals on exactly parallel lines : they do not substantially distinguish between them. The following is a translation of a native account of the ceremony observed by the Lushai after the killing of a tiger. " When Bengkhawia's village was at Thenzawl, a tiger beset the village and in one day killed a mithan and two goats. The crier called on the people to surround the village, and they did so. Thangbawnga shot it, and performed the Ai ceremony ; the night before he must not sleep. A young man cut off its tail ; he also must keep awake all night. The next day he performed the Ai ceremony, sacrificing a mithan. Thang-bawnga, who was performing the Ai, dressed him-self up as a woman, smoked a woman's pipe, wore a woman's petticoat and cloth, carried a small basket, spun a cotton spindle, wore ivory earrings, let his hair down and wrapped a mottled cloth, which was said to be of an ancient pattern, round his head as a turban. A crowd watched him and yelled with laughter, but it would have been 'thianglo' (unlucky) for him to laugh. Presently he took off his turban and carried it in the basket. Then he took off his woman's disguise and dressed himself as a man, and strapped on a fighting dah (knife or dagger) and carried a gun. He also took 'sailungvar' (white flints) and put them into the tiger's mouth, while he ate eggs. ' You eat the sailungvar ', he said ; ' who will swallow them the quicker ? I have out-swallowed you, you have not swallowed yours ; I have swallowed mine. You will go by the lower road; I will go by the upper. You will be like the lower southern hills; I shall be like the high northern ones. You are the brave man of the south ; I am the brave man of the north ', he said, and cut the tiger's head three times with his dah. Then the men buried the body of the tiger outside the village." If the tiger has killed men, his eyes are gouged out with skewers or needles and thrown away, probably in order to blind the animal's ghost : it is unlucky (*thianglo*) for the performer to laugh, so he holds a porcupine in his arms, and if he laughs by accident they say the porcupine laughed. The idea of the performer disguising himself as a woman is that the spirit of the dead tiger may be humbled, thinking that it has been shot by a woman; and the giving of the flints while the performer eats eggs is to show the power of the performer over the tiger, as he eats the eggs easily, while the tiger is unable to chew the flints.[1]

---

[1] Lt.-Col. J. Shakespear, *The Lushei Kuki Clans* (London, 1912), pp. 78 *sqq.*

Among the Lakhers, another tribe of North-Eastern India, when a hunter has killed any of the larger animals, on his return home he performs a sacrifice called *Salupakia*, the object of which is to give him power in the next world over the spirit of the animal he has killed, to please the dead animal's soul, and so also to help him to kill many more animals in future. Either a fowl or a pig may be sacrificed. If a fowl is used, the sacrifice is performed as soon as the hunter returns home ; if a pig, the sacrifice is postponed till the next morning. When a fowl is killed, the women may not eat any part of it, but if the sacrifice is a pig, women may eat any part of it except the head, which may be eaten only by men. The sacrifice is performed inside the house near a rice-beer (*sahma*) pot, close to which is placed the head of the wild animal for which the sacrifice is being performed. Before performing the sacrifice the hunter sucks a little rice-beer out of each rice-beer pot and spits it out into a gourd. He rubs flour all over the animal's head, takes into his mouth again the rice-beer he has spat into the gourd, and blows it over the animal's head six times. The hunter next intones a hunting-song, and kills the fowl or pig as the case may be. If a fowl is sacrificed, its tongue is pulled out and placed on the animal's head, and some feathers are placed in the nostrils. If the victim is a pig, the animal's head is anointed with the blood, and after the pig has been cooked and eaten its head is placed on the head of the slain animal. The animal's head is then hung up in the verandah, and all the old heads already hanging up there are anointed with flour and beer to make them look beautiful and as though they had been freshly shot. This attention is thought to be pleasing to the souls of the dead animals, who will praise the sacrificer to living animals and so induce them to approach him next time he goes out hunting. For the day and night of the sacrifice the sacrificer and his family are taboo (*pana*), and the women of the house may not weave. That night it is forbidden (*ana*) for the sacrificer to sleep with his wife or any other woman ; he must sleep on the place where the sacrifice was made. The Lakhers believe that on the night of this sacrifice the spirit of the animal shot comes and watches the man who has killed it, and if it saw him sleeping with his wife, would say, "Ah, this man prefers women to me", and would go and inform all the other animals that the man who had shot him was unworthy to be allowed to shoot any more animals, as he was fonder of women than of the chase. A man who broke the prohibition on sexual intercourse on the night of the ceremony would therefore be unable to kill any more animals. The next morning the sacrificer takes his gun and goes outside the village and shoots a bird ; if he cannot shoot a bird he must in any case fire his gun off. Having done this, he returns to the village, the taboo (*pana*) ends, and he may have intercourse with women again. If he has shot a bird it means that the sacrifice has taken effect and that the sacrificer will soon shoot more game.

If a man has wounded an animal and returned home without bagging it and intends to follow it up next day, he must sleep alone that night. It is forbidden (*ana*) for a man in these circumstances to sleep either with his wife or with any other woman, as it is believed that in that case the wounded animal would escape him. Hunters must remain chaste in these circumstances.[1]

Lakhers have a superstitious fear of tigers, as tigers are believed to have a *saw*, that is, a power of causing sickness or misfortune. Leopards also are believed to possess a similar power for mischief (*saw*), and the ceremony performed over a dead tiger or leopard is intended mainly to render the *saw* harmless. So when a tiger has been shot a special ceremony called *Chakei Ia* has to be performed. This ceremony is similar in some respects to that performed over the head of an enemy slain in war. If any one shoots a tiger and leaves it in the jungle no sacrifice is necessary, but if he brings the head into the village he must perform the *Ia* ceremony, because the dead tiger is *saw*—that is to say, has the capacity of causing sickness and harm to any one touching it, and the *Ia* ceremony both makes the tiger's powerful mischief (*saw*) innocuous, and enables the hunter to retain the tiger for his own use in the next world. Most Lakhers dislike tigers, because they fear the *saw* and are not at all keen on shooting them, and if a man who has shot a tiger says he is going to perform the *Ia* ceremony, and asks his

[1] N. E. Parry, *The Lakhers* (London, 1932), pp. 139 *sq.*

friends to come and help him skin the carcase, and then fails to perform the ceremony, he must give each of the skinners a dog and a fowl to sacrifice, to save themselves from the evil effects of the *saw*. The dog and fowl are killed and then thrown away outside the village, and none of their meat is eaten. They believe that the *saw* is thrown out of the village in the same way as the bodies of the dogs and the fowls. Not only the skinners, but any one touching the skin of a dead tiger over which the ceremony (*Ia*) has not been performed must offer this sacrifice. After the tiger has been skinned, the head is brought up and kept outside the village. Two pigs must be killed for the ceremony (*Ia*). In the morning a pig is killed outside the village. The meat of this pig may be eaten only by men. After this pig has been sacrificed, the tiger's head is brought into the village and put down in front of the house of the man who shot it. A tiger's head, like a man's, is never taken inside a house. The second pig is killed near the tiger's head and the *Ia* ceremony is performed. The man who shot the tiger dresses up in woman's clothes, lets down his hair like a woman, and smokes a woman's pipe. He carries a spindle and thread in his hand, and while winding the thread dances round the tiger's head, finally running the spindle through the tiger's nostrils. One of the assistants then picks up the tiger's head and runs through the village with it, pursued by the man who shot it, jabbing at the tiger's nostrils with the spindle. The head is thrown away outside the village. Tigers' heads are never hung up in the verandah like other trophies. In Chapi and Savang tigers' heads are hung outside the village in the same way as human heads, and the head of the animal sacrificed as *Ia* is hung up near by. During the ceremony it is forbidden (*ana*) to laugh. The origin of this ceremony is said to be that once upon a time a woman went to the land cleared for cultivation (*jhums*), and a tiger came to eat her. The tiger knocked her down, but as he did so the spindle she was carrying entered his nostrils and killed him, and so the woman escaped. Ever since then it has been customary for the killer of a tiger to wear woman's clothes when he performs the ceremony of expiation (*Ia*). During the ceremony the dead tiger's brother is said to watch the proceedings from a high hill, and when he sees, as he thinks, a woman dancing round the tiger, he does not get angry, because he imagines it is only a woman who has killed his brother, and if his brother was fool enough to get killed by a woman he had only himself to blame. So, as it is not worth while punishing a woman, he goes away without taking any revenge.[1] The quaint ceremony just described has for its object to lay the ghost of the tiger that has been killed. During the night which follows it the women may neither spin nor weave for fear of the tiger's ghost.[2]

Again, among these same Lakhers, when any one kills a mithan or bullock, the village is taboo (*pana*) on the day the animal is killed. No work may be

---

[1] Parry, *op. cit.* pp. 141 *sqq.*   [2] Parry, *op. cit.* pp. 375 *sq.*

done in the fields, and the women may not weave. The same taboo is observed if a mithan is killed by a tiger and the villagers bring the meat into the village to eat. If the meat is not brought in, there is no taboo. It is believed that if this taboo is not observed the houses will be blown down by a hurricane, and that the rice will be blown down or will dry up. Mithan and cows are the largest and most valuable animals kept by men, and have the loudest voice, and when they breathe their breath is like the wind ; hence, when one of these animals is killed, the wind will punish the village where it has been killed unless a taboo (*pana*) is held to appease the mithan's soul and prevent it from calling the wind.[1]

The Moïs, a primitive people inhabiting the mountains of Indo-China, stand in great fear of tigers which infest the surrounding jungle and carry off many victims. But if they stand in fear of the living tiger, they stand in much greater fear of the tiger's ghost, as will appear from the following account of an incident witnessed by a French official. We read : " Of course it is very unusual to meet this ferocious creature by daylight, even in regions where its ravages are the most frequent. Every traveller will pass by its lair in the bamboo groves, but it is quite exceptional to see the beast itself, except at night-fall, when it comes forth to seek its prey. Once a tiger has tasted human flesh it prefers it to all other food. Accordingly, the natives live in a state of chronic fear of the man-eater, and will willingly

[1] Parry, *op. cit.* pp. 451.

abandon their villages rather than make the least effort to rid themselves of the pest. As I shall show later, they endow their enemy with human qualities and frequently refuse to destroy it when at their mercy for fear of arousing the vengeance of the whole species. One of our party once witnessed the following scene. A tiger had fallen into a pit which had been laid for some deer. It was not wounded, but the space was so cramped that it was quite unable to move. The natives were terrified lest it should die, in which case its spirit would never cease to molest them ; so they decided to set it free. They made a cage without a floor, lowered it into the pit, and then raised it up again by means of ropes passed under the creature. Perched on the neighbouring trees they pulled away the prison and let the captive go, offering their humble apologies for having already detained it so long. Our representative had been compelled to promise his acquiescence, and, lest he should repent and show fight, his rifle was carefully left behind in the village."[1] Thus these primitive people, far from wishing to kill the trapped tiger, took great pains to save its life, because they feared the dead tiger's ghost much more than the living animal. A stronger proof they could hardly have given of their belief in the reality and the danger of a tiger's ghost.

Far from the tiger-infested jungles of Indo-China our next and last scene opens on the ice and snow

---

[1] Commandant Baudesson, *Au pays des superstitions et des rites*, pp. 25 *sq.* ; *id.*, *Indo-China and its Primitive People*, pp. 41 *sq.*

of the Arctic north.   The Eskimo are at great pains not to offend the ghosts of the animals which they kill and eat.   On this subject Mr. Stefansson, who lived among the Eskimo, tells us as follows : " I learned also why it is that animals allow themselves to be killed by men.   The animals are much wiser than men, and know everything in the world—including the thoughts of men ; but there are certain things which the animals need, and which they can only get from men.   The seals and whales live in the salt water, and are therefore continually thirsty.   They have no means of getting fresh water, except to come to men for it.   A seal will therefore allow himself to be killed by a hunter who will give him a drink of water in return ; that is why a dipperful of water is always poured into the mouth of a seal when he is brought ashore.   If a hunter neglects to do this, all the other seals know about it, and no other seal will ever allow himself to be killed by that hunter, because he knows he is not going to get a drink.   Every man who gives a seal a drink of water, and keeps this implied promise, is known by the other seals as a dependable person, and they will prefer to be killed by him.   There are other things which a seal would like to have done for it when it is dead, and some men are so careful to do everything that seals want that seals tumble over themselves in their eagerness to be killed by that particular man.   The polar bear does not suffer from thirst as much as the seal, for he can eat the fresh snow on the top of the ice.   But polar bears are unable to make for themselves certain tools which they need. What the male bears especially value are crooked knives and bow-drills, and the female bears are especially eager to get women's knives, skin-scrapers, and needle cases; consequently when a polar bear has been killed his soul (*tatkok*) accompanies the skin into the man's house and stays with the skin several days (among most tribes, for four days if it is a male bear, and for five days if it is a female). The skin during this time is hung up at the rear end of the house, and with the skin are hung up the tools which the bear desires, according to the sex of the animal killed. At the end of the fourth or fifth day the soul of the bear is by a magic formula driven out of the house; and when it goes away it takes away with it the souls of the tools which have been suspended with it and uses them thereafter. There are certain manners and customs of humanity which are displeasing to polar bears, and for that reason those customs are carefully abjured during the period when the soul of the bear is in the man's house. The bear, in other words, is treated as an honoured guest who must not be offended. If the bear's soul had been properly treated during his stay with the man, and if he has received the souls (*tatkoit*) of implements of good quality, then he will report those things in the land of polar bears to which he returns, and other bears will be anxious to be killed by so reliable a man. If the wives of certain hunters are careless about treating the souls of the bears properly while they are in their houses, this will offend the bears quite as much as if the man who had killed them had done it, and this may cause an excellent hunter to get no bears at all. Certain women are known in their communities for this very undesirable quality, and if a woman becomes a widow, her reputation for carelessness in treating the souls of animals may prevent her from getting a good second husband." [1]

Our survey of the facts, imperfect as it necessarily is, must here end ; but enough perhaps has been said to convince us that fear of the spirits of the dead, whether men or animals, has haunted the mind of primitive man from time immemorial all over the world, from the Equator to the Poles, and we may surmise that the same fear has gone far to shape the moulds into which religious thought has run ever since feeble man began to meditate on the great mysteries by which our little life on earth is encompassed.

[1] V. Stefansson, *My Life with the Eskimo* (London, 1913), pp. 56 *sqq.*

INDEX

THE END

Printed in Great Britain by R. & R. CLARK, LIMITED, *Edinburgh.*

THE LITERATURE OF
DEATH AND DYING

Abrahamsson, Hans. **The Origin of Death:** Studies in African Mythology. 1951

Alden, Timothy. **A Collection of American Epitaphs and Inscriptions with Occasional Notes.** Five vols. in two. 1814

Austin, Mary. **Experiences Facing Death.** 1931

Bacon, Francis. **The Historie of Life and Death with Observations Naturall and Experimentall for the Prolongation of Life.** 1638

Barth, Karl. **The Resurrection of the Dead.** 1933

Bataille, Georges. **Death and Sensuality:** A Study of Eroticism and the Taboo. 1962

Bichat, [Marie François] Xavier. **Physiological Researches on Life and Death.** 1827

Browne, Thomas. **Hydriotaphia.** 1927

Carrington, Hereward. **Death:** Its Causes and Phenomena with Special Reference to Immortality. 1921

Comper, Frances M. M., editor. **The Book of the Craft of Dying and Other Early English Tracts Concerning Death.** 1917

Death and the Visual Arts. 1976

Death as a Speculative Theme in Religious, Scientific, and Social Thought. 1976

Donne, John. **Biathanatos.** 1930

Farber, Maurice L. **Theory of Suicide.** 1968

Fechner, Gustav Theodor. **The Little Book of Life After Death.** 1904

Frazer, James George. **The Fear of the Dead in Primitive Religion.** Three vols. in one. 1933/1934/1936

Fulton, Robert. **A Bibliography on Death, Grief and Bereavement:** 1845-1975. 1976

Gorer, Geoffrey. **Death, Grief, and Mourning.** 1965

Gruman, Gerald J. **A History of Ideas About the Prolongation of Life.** 1966

Henry, Andrew F. and James F. Short, Jr. **Suicide and Homicide.** 1954

Howells, W[illiam] D[ean], et al. **In After Days;** Thoughts on the Future Life. 1910

Irion, Paul E. **The Funeral:** Vestige or Value? 1966

Landsberg, Paul-Louis. **The Experience of Death:** The Moral Problem of Suicide. 1953

Maeterlinck, Maurice. **Before the Great Silence.** 1937

Maeterlinck, Maurice. **Death.** 1912

Metchnikoff, Élie. **The Nature of Man:** Studies in Optimistic Philosophy. 1910

Metchnikoff, Élie. **The Prolongation of Life:** Optimistic Studies. 1908

Munk, William. **Euthanasia.** 1887

Osler, William. **Science and Immortality.** 1904

Return to Life: Two Imaginings of the Lazarus Theme. 1976

Stephens, C[harles] A[sbury]. **Natural Salvation:** The Message of Science. 1905

Sulzberger, Cyrus. **My Brother Death.** 1961

Taylor, Jeremy. **The Rule and Exercises of Holy Dying.** 1819

Walker, G[eorge] A[lfred]. **Gatherings from Graveyards.** 1839

Warthin, Aldred Scott. **The Physician of the Dance of Death.** 1931

Whiter, Walter. **Dissertation on the Disorder of Death.** 1819

Whyte, Florence. **The Dance of Death in Spain and Catalonia.** 1931

Wolfenstein, Martha. **Disaster:** A Psychological Essay. 1957

Worcester, Alfred. **The Care of the Aged, the Dying, and the Dead.** 1950

Zandee, J[an]. **Death as an Enemy According to Ancient Egyptian Conceptions.** 1960